Indoctrination to Hate

Indoctrination to Hate

Recruitment Techniques of Hate Groups and How to Stop Them

Edward W. Dunbar, Editor

PRAEGER™

An Imprint of ABC-CLIO, LLC
Santa Barbara, California • Denver, Colorado

Library of Congress Cataloging-in-Publication Data

Names: Dunbar, Edward, editor.
Title: Indoctrination to hate : recruitment techniques of hate groups and how to stop them / Edward W. Dunbar, editor.
Description: Santa Barbara, California : Praeger, an imprint of ABC-CLIO, LLC, [2022] | Includes bibliographical references and index.
Identifiers: LCCN 2021030099 (print) | LCCN 2021030100 (ebook) | ISBN 9781440857003 (cloth) | ISBN 9781440857010 (ebook)
Subjects: LCSH: Hate crimes—Psychological aspects. | Hate crimes—Prevention. | Hate groups. | Social psychology.
Classification: LCC HV6773.5 .I53 2022 (print) | LCC HV6773.5 (ebook) | DDC 364.15—dc23
LC record available at https://lccn.loc.gov/2021030099
LC ebook record available at https://lccn.loc.gov/2021030100

ISBN: 978-1-4408-5700-3 (print)
978-1-4408-5701-0 (ebook)

26 25 24 23 22 1 2 3 4 5

This book is also available as an eBook.

Praeger
An Imprint of ABC-CLIO, LLC

ABC-CLIO, LLC
147 Castilian Drive
Santa Barbara, California 93117
www.abc-clio.com

This book is printed on acid-free paper ∞

Manufactured in the United States of America

"My idea of good company . . . is the company of clever, well-informed people, who have a great deal of conversation; that is what I call good company. 'You are mistaken,' said he gently, 'that is not good company, that is the best."

Jane Austen

With the greatest respect and memory of wonderful colleagues, Megan Elizabeth Sullaway, Carl Compton Bell, and Raphael Ezekiel; they were the best company.

EWD

I would like to thank Sneha Gupta and Jitendra Kumar for their cooperation and enthusiasm in the execution of the final edits of the manuscripts.

Contents

CHAPTER ONE

Three Cataclysms and Two Ways to Do Good Work: The Mash-up of Hate Crimes in the Twenty-First Century

Edward W. Dunbar

Since the start of this century, the United States has experienced three cataclysmic events: the societal body blow of the 9/11 terror attacks, the hate unleashed with the 2016 presidential election, and the viral and racial pandemics of 2020, which have heightened intergroup hostility and violence across the country. These cultural cataclysms have transformed the country and our social conventions. These events call out for individuals and organizations to understand the psychological vicissitudes of hate in struggling to reestablish a civil society.

The psychological study of hate crimes requires our understanding of the motives of the individual offender as well as the cultural context in which the infraction occurs. The roles of policy makers, law enforcement, and the general populace—including the willing followers of hate extremists—need to be understood as well. We would do well to follow the advice of Carl Bell and ask the "hard questions" of behavioral science. This means examining not only who perpetrates crimes of hate, but also who and what motivates these individuals to act, and how our stakeholders respond, in times of social upheaval.

The societal problem of intergroup violence obviously far exceeds the scope of our hate crime statutes. However, in focusing on the brief history of these laws, two distinctly different problems are encountered: controlling aberrant hatred and normalizing hatred as an instrument of political change. These are summarized below.

Controlling Aberrant Hatred

The advent of hate crime laws sought to address problems of aggression occurring concurrently with the increase in cultural diversity in North America and Europe. The passage of the Hate Crimes Statistics Act of 1990 and signed into law by President George Walker Bush sought to establish a methodology to measure and respond to intergroup violence. The promulgation of these federal laws also created a means for the standing government to intervene in communities where protection of targeted minority groups was inadequate in terms of law enforcement response or absent sufficient state-based statutes. Moreover, the original intention of these laws was consistent in part with the efforts to support liberal democracy and the principles of the civil society movement. As such, hate crime laws serve to control intergroup violence that is in defiance of social norms and the ruling government. The documentation and analysis of hate crimes provides a method of maintaining the stasis of a multicultural society. Their enforcement serves to suppress socially aberrant—and potentially deviant—acts of hate violence.

Normalizing Hatred as an Instrument of Political Change

The alternative narrative of hate ideology considers how conflict between social groups can be employed as a method of political control by a standing government. The scholarship on intergroup and political violence is substantial and vast (Krugler, 2015; Paxton, 2004; Shirer, 1960). This literature stresses how political movements that are driven by authoritarian, ultranationalistic, and xenophobic (AUX) ideologies prescribe the perpetration of hate-based behavior. These AUX ideologies (Dunbar, 2018) stand in opposition to the principles of liberal democracies: AUX ideologies seek to overturn gender equity, secularism, freedom of expression, and the rights of religious, racial, and sexual minorities.

Hate crime laws, which were promulgated in societies that support the practices of democratic representation and inclusion, stand in contrast to ascending AUX-type political movements. Consequently, the enforcement of these laws conflicts with the social animus fomented by an AUX-type movement or ascending government. In this circumstance, enforcing hate crime laws is in conflict with the political will of the ruling government that endorses the oppression of culturally diverse groups.

Cataclysmic Cultural Change and Hate Violence

A concern of human relations practitioners, law enforcement, and policy makers is how major social events can fuel violence between social groups. Sudden and often unanticipated events (e.g., cultural cataclysms) can fundamentally change political norms and activate deep cultural presumptions of entitlement and out-group hostility. This redefining of the social stasis often results in conflict for power between social groups and heightened intergroup hostility. "In the long view of history, these events become narratives that legitimize the social norms and beliefs of a society. Events which are particularly traumatic, while personally destabilizing, serve to create a collective narrative which defines a group and their age" (Dunbar, 2018).

Cultural cataclysms are collectively experienced. At the end of the twentieth century, a Gallup poll (Newport, Moore, & Saad, 1999) reported that Americans felt that World War II was the most significant event of the twentieth century (71%). This was followed by the Holocaust (65%), dropping the atomic bomb on Japan (66%), the right to vote for women in 1920 (66%), and the passage of the Civil Rights Act of 1964 (58%). These events all explicitly invoked intergroup conflict and violence. Cultural cataclysms are characterized by three "signal" phenomena. These are: (1) the enmeshment of dramatic social change with the scapegoating of a cultural out-group, (2) the habitual introjection of hate speech into social discourse, and (3) reframing economic and political conflict between groups into a winner–loser narrative. Figurehead leaders who stress ideological intolerance often invoke these assumptions.

The cataclysmic social changes seen in the past 20 years have shaped how we respond to hate violence. The question of how dramatic social change has affected our attitudes about hate crimes as socially deviant infractions or as a centerpiece of changing political norms will be considered below.

The First Cataclysm: The 9/11 Terror Attack

The September 11, 2001, terror attack in New York and Washington, D.C., delivered the United States to the realities of international terrorism. The impact on the cultural consciousness of the country led to a merging of concerns about domestic hate with global intergroup violence. As Carl Bell stated, 9/11 was a wake-up call to white Americans, a "Welcome to the world" of the chronic reality of victimization experienced by racial and sexual minority groups for centuries (Bell, personal communication, September 13, 2001).

The psychological sequelae of 9/11 were felt proximally and distally from ground zero in Manhattan. Persons living close to the 9/11 site in New York evidenced symptoms consistent with post-traumatic stress disorder (PTSD). While those closest to ground zero revealed the highest levels of PTSD six months after the attack, a substantial number not situated nearby also met the criteria for PTSD (Galea et al., 2003). Among those with the highest levels of exposure and highest probable PTSD, the proportion was as high as 66% (Bonanno et al., 2006). Farach et al. (2008) reported another aspect of the impact of the 9/11 cataclysm in their study of premorbid cases of generalized anxiety disorder (GAD) for individuals subsequently exposed to the 9/11 attacks. They reported that GAD was associated with greater social and work disability, loss of psychosocial resources, anxiety and mood symptoms, and worry assessed one year after the attack. In their review of the consequences of the 9/11 cataclysm on mental health consumers, Franz et al. (2009) noted that the terrorist attacks had a well-documented psychological effect, irrespective of whether or not individuals were proximally nearby the target sites.

The Deadly Other: Middle Easterners as Terrorists

Another form of psychological injury was, of course, the impact of the attack on American principles of inclusion—as reflected in the rise after 9/11 in anti-Muslim attitudes and hate violence. With the 9/11 attack, the populace experienced the first foreign combatant that had struck the country since Japan bombed Pearl Harbor in 1941—the most significant cultural cataclysm for the United States in the twentieth century. Importantly, too, in 1941 the United States was galvanized against a standing government in Japan. With the 9/11 attack, hostility was directed not at a political entity but at a cultural and religious population that spanned the globe and did not reflect a singular geographic location or political ideology.

After 9/11, there was both an initial increase of anti-Islamic attitudes after 9/11 and enduring hostile attitudes after the terror attacks in Western countries (Sheridan, 2006). The anti-Muslim rhetoric, frequently tied to 9/11, has become part of the talking points of the second cataclysm, the 2016 presidential election of Donald Trump. As Kahn (2017) comments, "Islamophobia has become a campaign tool used to galvanize voters." During their presidential campaigns, now-President Trump famously said, "I think Islam hates us"; while the future secretary of Housing and Urban Development, Ben Carson, said, "Muslims shouldn't be allowed to become president;" and U.S. senator Ted Cruz talked about patrolling Muslim neighborhoods.

The creation of a "deadly other"—a signal of a cultural cataclysm—was one of the first consequences of 9/11. The heightened anxiety of Muslims as a threat to the United States activated stereotypes and engaged cultural, religious, and political ideology as being in opposition to everything Middle Eastern, including the secular government of Iraq under the control of Saddam Hussain. The 9/11 terror attacks importantly heightened our hostility toward a class of people—Muslims and persons of Middle Eastern heritage—who constitute about 1 percent of the U.S. population and constituted the third-largest religious group in the country. Following September 11, 2001, the Federal Bureau of Investigation (FBI) reported a 1,700% increase in hate crimes against Muslim Americans between 2000 and 2001 (Anderson, 2002). The number of assaults against persons of Middle Eastern heritage increased more than seven-fold from 2000 to the end of 2001; this level of physical violence was not seen again until the second cultural cataclysm of the 2016 presidential election (Pew Research, 2017). Hate-based violence toward Muslim/Middle Eastern persons spiked after both the cataclysm of 9/11 and the 2016 presidential election (Dunbar, 2018).

The post-9/11 rise in anti-Muslim aggression reflects the tenets of terror management theory (TMT). Research on TMT notes that an individual's enhanced awareness of their mortality results in adopting strategies to enhance collective self-esteem—as a protective belief—and potentially to control perceived harmful others (Heen, Lieberman, & Arndt, 2016). TMT has also been shown to increase out-group prejudice in part as a function of an increased motivation to identify with cultural ingroups (Solomon, Greenberg, & Pyszczynski, 2015). The consequences of the cataclysm of 9/11 included retribution-fueled hate activity against Muslims, Middle Easterners, and others and supporting shifting political policies concerning domestic law enforcement, the role of state-sponsored torture, and retrenching of the civil rights of the civilian populace.

A significant consequence of the 9/11 cataclysm was the degradation of the human rights practices of the government through the systematic detention and torture of Middle Eastern suspects thought to be affiliated with terrorist groups. Many of these individuals had been caught in security sweeps in areas of conflict with U.S. military troops in the Middle East. The detention and torture of suspects was vividly portrayed in the 2003 photographs of prisoners held in Abu Ghraib prison in Iraq. The images represented prisoners being subjected to cruel and dehumanizing treatment at the hands of U.S. military forces. Additionally, accounts of torture at the U.S. detention facility at Guantanamo Bay—as well as elsewhere—were reported. This was made most famous by the use of waterboarding (e.g., drowning) as a technique of interrogation.

The legal question of the use of torture was debated by the Bush administration. The government argued that the human rights provisions of the Geneva Convention did not apply to interrogation of "unlawful combatants" (Center for Constitutional Rights, 2007). Additionally, the practice and exposure of torture shifted attitudes about punishment of socially malevolent actors. The ruling government in this case put aside cultural and legal traditions in the service of meeting political goals.

The impact on the victims of our state-sponsored torture was, of course, substantial. However, more relevant in terms of hate violence is the impact that the perpetration of torture had on the stakeholders and the general population. The utilization of torture as a form of social control changed the practice of peacekeeping and security for the country. Lifton (1986) provides an early examination of how torture was viewed by the (medical) perpetrators in his interviews with Nazi doctors who participated in human experimentation and killings. He found them to be "normal professionals" who provided medical justifications for the killings. This is interesting and largely consistent with the experiences of German military recruits of World War II who had been assigned to the eastern front for the execution of ethnic groups—most frequently Jews—as documented by Christopher Browning (1992). This normalization of state-sponsored atrocities for political ends was also noted recently by Davies-Rubio and Mirón in the experiences of young death squad members in Colombia (2022). The author has spoken at length with medical staff at the "Gitmo" interrogation site. The commentary of being expected to comply with the torture practices was strongly enforced. It was also noted that grooming of interrogation staff was itself disturbing and traumatic. This orientation to violence of the interrogation staff was compared to the indoctrination scenes in the film *A Clockwork Orange*, directed by Stanley Kubrick.

The use of torture to respond to cultural conflict is consistent with the practices of AUX-style regimes. The work of Altemeyer (1988) has noted that authoritarianism placed importance on punishment as a practice in controlling social deviance (Duckitt, 2004). The interrogation/torture practice conducted in our response to the 9/11 cataclysm brought a greater tolerance for inhuman forms of control of suspected opponents to our society. In accomplishing this, our cultures of armed forces and medicine became willing executioners of these psychologically terrifying and lethal practices. This also led to changes in our police culture.

The Militarization of Law Enforcement

Since 9/11, there has been a proliferation of combat-based enforcement tactics used by U.S. law enforcement. During the past 20 years, it become routine for combat-ready units and police SWAT ("special weapons and tactics") teams to enforce routine law enforcement functions across the country (Rizer & Hartman, 2011). Municipal law enforcement agencies have been provided significant funding to acquire military combat equipment—specialized weapons, body armor, and attack helicopters. The introduction of armed forces–based officer training for fighting terrorism has shaped an organizational culture of a warrior class of officers—in sharp contrast to the community policing objectives found across the country a decade earlier.

While initially thought of as a means of preparing local law enforcement for a war against terror on U.S. soil, these officers and special police units have frequently engaged in more brutal and confrontational responses to routine domestic police work. Fortunately, the need for local police departments to fight 9/11-type terrorism (terror from afar) has not occurred. However, the militarization of our police has failed on several broad fronts. Mummolo (2018) noted that the deployment of militarized special ops units was unrelated to a measurable reduction in either violent crime or the improvement of officer safety. Additionally, as he points out, survey research has found that our militarized police forces are related to a decline in public opinion about law enforcement. Finally, as exemplified in the pandemic of racial violence by law enforcement, militarized SWAT teams were most frequently employed in communities of color. This merging of government initiatives and explicit forms of aggression against (within-country) visible minority groups has been seen as a harbinger of ascending authoritarian regimes (Paxton, 2004). This will be discussed elsewhere in more detail.

The Second Cataclysm: Hate Unleashed, the 2016 U.S. Presidential Election

The election of Donald Trump and the political right-shift in the United States and elsewhere have dramatically galvanized white and nationalist groups. As this writer has argued, "The cultural cataclysm of the 2016 election made concrete the habitual introjection of intolerance into our political discourse and the normalizing of intergroup conflict as a means of solving social problems" (Dunbar, 2018). Politically, the Trump victory ushered in a shift in economic and civil rights realities. The election results were seen as a rejection of the standing federal government, multiculturalism, and the instruments of control that were part and parcel of the liberal democratic tradition. This implicitly made the objectives of hate crime laws inconsistent with the practices of the standing government.

The three signals of a cultural cataclysm—making political choice a function of intergroup conflict, the chronic use of hate speech in political discourse, and the punishment or oppression of cultural out-groups—were manifested by President Trump and his comments about the "fine people" who perpetrated violence at the 2017 "Unite the Right" Charlottesville riot. Trump became the most recent illustration of a figurehead leader who legitimized the use of hate as a political instrument of influence.

The use of key phrases and images that signify the white hegemony have become endemic of the Trump presidency. Toward the end of his first term, the Trump reelection campaign used an inverted red triangle—a symbol used in Nazi Germany for political prisoners. The social media platform Facebook stated that this violated its anti-hate content guidelines. Facebook had been criticized for failing to police those in and outside of the administration that had employed hate terms as part of the political rhetoric. “We don’t allow symbols that represent hateful organizations or hateful ideologies unless they are put up with context or condemnation,” Facebook head of security policy Nathaniel Gleicher said at a House of Representatives committee hearing. “That’s what we saw in this case with this ad and anywhere that that symbol is used we would take the same actions.”

Civil Unrest of the Trump Years

The Hate Unleashed argument proposes that the 2016 election activated a deep cultural assumption of the hegemony of white Americans in North America. From this perspective, the 2016 election and the rhetoric of president Trump revived Eurocentric entitlement as a norm of society. Almost the moment Trump was elected, hate activity spiked nationally. The first week after the election saw a surge in the number of hate events (SPLC, 2016); 437 cases of verbal threats and intimidation were reported, primarily related to anti-immigrant bias (136), anti-Black (89) and LGBT bias (43). Forty-one of the reported cases (approximately 10%) included pro-Trump references made by the perpetrators. At one month after the election, the SPLC reported 1,094 hate incidents (Dunbar, 2018). After one month, the SPLC noted that 37% of the reported incidents referenced Trump, his campaign slogans, or his remarks (SPLC, 2016). In the first year after the Trump election, the number of reported hate crimes (n=7,175) increased about 17% from 2016, according to the Uniform Crime Reporting (UCR) Program’s annual Hate Crime Statistics report (FBI, 2018).

Importantly, in 2017 the FBI and the Department of Homeland Security reported that white supremacist groups had carried out more terrorist attacks than any other domestic extremist group over the past 16 years. The FBI noted, “White extremists were likely to carry out more attacks over the next year” (Winter, 2017). The following year (2018) the FBI noted a rise in the number of “crimes against persons,” such as intimidation, assault, and homicide (NPR, 2019).

Some of the anti-Muslim hate activity *preceded* the November election. In 2016, there were 307 incidents of anti-Muslim hate crimes in 2016, a 19% increase from the previous year (Kishi, 2017). In this sense, the rise in hate violence targeting Muslims and persons of Middle Eastern heritage signaled the voter sentiment for a more white-oriented federal voice than was found under the Obama administration. Eric Lichtblau of the *New York Times* commented that “Hate crimes against American Muslims have soared to their highest levels since the aftermath of the Sept. 11, 2001 attacks, according to data compiled by researchers" (Lichtblau, 2016). He attributed these concerns as being about international terrorist attacks and the divisive language of candidate Trump on the campaign trail.

The spate of hate violence was characteristic of instrumental—that is, planned—trigger activity. That is, hate activity was a behavioral consequence of hate-based social commentary and political pronouncements that support white hegemony and intergroup conflict. These public announcements were frequently found coming from the right-wing media as well as the White House on Twitter and Fox News. These instrumental triggers would often activate cultural stereotypes, call political attitudes inconsistent with an ultranationalist narrative, and make intergroup hostility a form of political discourse. The code term of "good people" as used by President Trump was frequently employed to indicate the support for alt-right and related social movements consistent with the standing government.

Berger (2018) conducted an analysis of the relationship between right-wing ideologues and their affiliation with President Trump. He examined 30,000 Twitter accounts to map the linkage of content areas for extremists. Berger noted that support for Trump was the underlying bond that held the disparate political ideologies of the extremists together. As he stated, the convergence on support for President Trump "was the glue that held the alt-right social network together. Support for Trump was shared by virtually all parts of the network and was reflected in nearly every metric, including tabulations of the most followed, most retweeted, and most influential accounts; the most used words in Twitter profiles; and in the top two hashtags (#maga, which outperformed all other hashtags by a wide margin, and #trump)."

Children in Cages: The Winner–Loser Landscape of 2016

The change in cultural norms after the 2016 election was reinforced in the distinction between the winners and losers of the culture wars of the election. For AUX-style leaders this is central to their political worldview. As Fromm (1941) said of authoritarians, the world consists of persons with power and those without it. Those without power, characteristically, were marginalized, based on their race, gender, sexual orientation, and age. The winner–loser dichotomy influenced both the supporters of AUX-style regimes and those oppressed by such as a society.

The experience of social powerlessness has been influential for hate crime victims reporting incidents to law enforcement (Dunbar, 2006). In this study of LGBT hate crime victims, both the gender and racial status of the victim dramatically influenced the likelihood of reporting the event to the police. In the post-2016 society, the composite vulnerable individual could, for example, be a childbearing-aged woman of color, facing a reduction in her reproductive health choices, employment rights, and restriction of her right to vote. For some ethnic groups—most notably Muslims and Latinx—the rhetoric of intolerance additionally suggested a heightened level of hostility; one that was instituted by the leadership in Washington (Dunbar, 2018).

Another gripping body blow to the traditions of the civil society involved the issue of migration by Central Americans to the United States. In 2018, the U.S. Immigration and Customs Enforcement (ICE) detention centers had in custody approximately 54,000 refugees, asylum-seekers, and migrants. An additional 20,000 were held in the custody by Customs and Border Protection personnel; 11,000 more children were held by the Department of Health and Human Services (Sukin, 2019). There have been multiple reports of immigrant children being held in substandard conditions once they had been separated from their guardians (Helmore, 2019). Since U.S. president Donald Trump took office in early 2017, approximately 26 people have died in the centers—seven of whom were children (Sukin, 2019). The United States has received more than 4,500 complaints concerning the sexual abuse of immigrant children who were being held at government-funded facilities (*Washington Post,* 2019). The American Academy of Pediatrics warned of long-term trauma faced by these children (Earls et al., 2010).

This process of dominating the defenseless is tragic on its face and is irreconcilable with the principles of a civil society. It also brings the world of authoritarianism closer to that of raw sadism (Manson, 1988). Unlike many domestic hate crimes, which are impulsive, symbolic, and carried out by singular perpetrators, this form of privation is systemic and maintained in accord with a political ideology of a ruling government. Fromm (1941), decades ago, commented on the fascination with authoritarianism with such sheer force. Once again, the influence of AUX-style policies shapes how stakeholders view those they interact with and are responsible for. In the case of child detention at the U.S. border, this is reflected by a social media account created by Customs and Border Protection officers who mocked the circumstances of migrant children (Silverstein, 2019). It is worth considering that since the federal statutes for hate crimes include infractions perpetrated due to the victims' national origin, the victimization experiences of Central American migrants would seemingly correspond to the intentions of those statutes. In addition, unlike the Abu Ghraib torture incidents, the federal government is not detaining nor interrogating combatants of the United States. Acts of violence against migrant families and children seem to fall outside of both international and federal legal guidelines, yet nothing has been done to protect these individuals.

Helplessness in the winner–loser outcome of the 2016 election was felt right away. The impact of helplessness was felt particularly hard by the non-Trump citizen. In the first weeks after his election, survey data revealed the significant interpersonal conflicts occurring within families and communities. For young adults, these interpersonal conflicts were more emotive and contentious. Likewise, women who did not support Trump reported being particularly likely to encounter conflicts about the direction that the country was headed (Dunbar, 2018). At one-month post-election, survey findings indicated that experiences of interpersonal conflict had increased. Interestingly, numerous associations were drawn between the 2016 election and the 9/11 terror attacks. The sense was that the country was under attack. Acute stress symptoms were correlated to arguments and fights among coworkers and intimate partners. Even at this early point in the cataclysm, the divide in the country was experienced interpersonally (Dunbar, 2018).

The hard-right swing toward xenophobia and hate violence was not solely an American phenomenon. The recent ascent of ultranationalist leaders in traditionally democratic societies underscores the globally felt deep cultural insecurity. This social anxiety of ecological, cultural, and economic change occurred in the context of an increasingly globally interdependent world. The xenophobia of the Brexit referendum in the United Kingdom, for example, served to provide a legal form of national hegemony (Golec de Zavala, Guerra, & Simao, 2017) even if the cost to the economy might linger for years to come (Begg & Mushövel, 2016).

An important motivator in the support of ultranationalist leaders was the racial hegemony of the populace. The presence of racial anxiety in the citizens of these countries might have been more persuasive than arguments of economic privation. The thesis of economic threat has, of course, been a critical part of the discussion of both the erosion of the civil society and the perpetration of hate crimes. The conventional argument centered on the financial vulnerability of working-class and rural individuals, as well as the undereducated young men of urban America. The displacement of manufacturing jobs to offshore countries, the loss of unskilled living-wage jobs, and the failure of social democratic institutions have been proposed to support hostility toward non-U.S.-born persons as well as women, sexual minorities, and educated "elites" (Hasan, 2018). This has been referred to as the "left behind thesis" (Mutz, 2018). More importantly, reanalysis of survey data suggests that anti-immigrant attitudes and hostility toward visible racial minorities played a greater role in the outcome of 2016. Several of these studies pointed toward the role of racial anxiety more so than economic threats as supporting the ultranationalism of Trump and AUX-style leaders. Schaffner, Macwilliams, and Nteta (2018) reported that racism and sexism attitudes were strongly associated with voter choice in 2016. The sophisticated neuroscience research examining voter opposition to candidate Clinton found that the resistance was emotive and inherently nonlinguistic; fMRI research showed a lack of linguistic processing and rather emotional processing of fear and anxiety. These latent Trump voters were ambivalent about their support of the male candidate and the female candidate. Anxiety, *gendered anxiety*, tipped these ambivalent voters toward the anti-diversity candidate. This voter ambivalence was characterized by an inability to express a language-based argument (Dunbar, 2018). As such, anxiety, based on race, gender, and nationality, led members of the populace to support an overtly hostile cultural ideology.

Cultural anxiety has been studied for decades and seen as a consequence of intercultural interaction (Stephan & Stephan, 1996). As a mental health problem, race-based anxiety may influence the level of individual functioning (Bell, 1978, 1980; Cotharin & Milkulas, 1975) as well as behavior in settings of nonviolent intergroup contact (Dunbar, 1997; Sullaway & Dunbar, 1996). The experience of political intolerance was to become more pathological and disease based in the pandemics of 2020.

The Third Cataclysm: COVID-19

The phenomena of ethnic and racial diversity became a focal issue in the third cataclysm of the century, namely the coronavirus COVID-19 pandemic of 2020. The coronavirus is a viral illness transmitted from person to person. COVID-19 was first reported in Hunan Province of China toward the end of 2019. It rapidly spread across the globe, hitting the United States in the spring of 2020.

Political differences initially were seen internationally in how governments responded to COVID-19, with some countries imposing significant social control over the behaviors of their populace while others adopted a more laissez-faire strategy. As COVID-19 spread across the United States, the federal government deferral to local states and municipalities and impressed many as a playing-out of a political philosophy of noninvolvement. The illness as political metaphor consequently resulted in the spiking of mortality figures of the vulnerable elderly. More importantly, the higher incidence rates of infection and death for persons of color were acknowledged by government epidemiologists, but were ignored by policy makers within the White House (Lipton et al., 2020). As Milton Bennett noted, the Trump administration's denial of the prevalence of COVID-19 had an "outsize effect on exactly the groups" the administration has suppressed and targeted. "Bluntly, they are letting the pandemic perform the genocide they actually support" (Milton Bennett, personal communication, July 8, 2020). An analog between the tolerable level of intergroup animus and an equivalent issue of the tolerable level of a disease base rate for COVID-19 became implicitly a point of debate across the political spectrum. This public health problem came to reflect interlinked political attitudes.

The Deadly Other: Asians as Disease Carriers

The out-group scapegoat associated with COVID-19 by the standing government in the United States was China. Senior leadership from President Trump downward recast the disease as the "Chinese flu." Federal leadership echoed some of this anti-China rhetoric, with Republicans in Congress scapegoating China for the spread of the pandemic. This ongoing rhetoric, picked up by mainstream media, shaped how Americans viewed Chinese people and Asian Americans.

From early March 2020 with the spread of the pandemic in the United States, numerous media sources reported on the COVID-Asian hate phenomenon. The *New York Times*, as well as other online social media news sites, noted interpersonal provocation of Asian-Pacific Islanders in Jezebel, the impact of conservative rhetoric on the Asian-Pacific Islander community by MSNBC, and a review of anti–Asian-Pacific Islanders hate victimization. As the Asian American scholar Russell Jeung stated, "The incidents reflect a disturbing trend, that Americans are blaming Asian Americans for a biological virus. Instead, we need to hold our American government accountable to controlling the disease and to safeguarding our public health. Both the virus and racism are dangerous threats to the Asian American community" (Jeung, Kulkani, & Choi, 2020).

In response to the spiking of Anti-Asian COVID-19 rhetoric, community groups worked to document hate incidents in the United States. The Asian Pacific Planning and Policy Council (A3PCON), Chinese for Affirmative Action (CAA), and the Asian American Studies Department of San Francisco State University initiated a program to gather data about anti-Asian American and Pacific Islander hate violence and harassment. In the first two months of their data collection, this network recorded "over 1700 reports of coronavirus discrimination from Asian Americans across the country" (CAA, 2020; Jeung, Kulkarni, & Choi, 2020). These incidents of hostility toward Asian-Pacific Islanders included verbal threats, nonphysical harassment, and physical attacks. This is similar to the anti-Muslim hate activity that was documented post-9/11. To understand this spike, the 2018 FBI hate crime annual report numbered only 375 hate crime offenses and hate incidents targeting Asian and Pacific Islander persons. This pandemic of Asian hate victimization was also reported in the United Kingdom. Hate crimes against South and East Asian communities increased 21% during the first month of the coronavirus crisis in Britain (Grierson, 2020).

The pandemic was in many ways intertwined with hostility toward visible racial minorities, as well as with the public demonstrations of right-wing pseudo militia groups. Additionally, impacted urban communities with higher levels of racial and linguistic diversity were seen as less worthy targets for public health intervention and support during the most dramatic stages of the COVID-19 pandemic. The country's public health crisis became a crisis of racial violence and nationwide hostility toward minority groups. How one aligned on COVID-19 pretty clearly said where you stood on anti-Black violence by the cops.

The anti-science pushback against prescribed public health guidelines of the COVID-19 pandemic became entwined with the right-wing ideology of the country and the (para) militarized conservative movement. This latter issue was writ large by the storming of the Michigan state house in May 2020 by armed white men garbed in camouflage uniforms. Their protest concerned the establishment of safety guidelines for social distancing and the required use of face masks. This had been criticized by right-wing media during the pandemic as a means of taking away civil rights and harming the operation of business. The presence of weaponry was significant in the protests across the country. The commentary ranging over this outburst of white hegemony—"protesting to eat in a (Fuddruckers) restaurant"—occurred at the same time that police violence against Black men and women was making the national headlines. Similarly, the adoptive rights of LGBT adults were being restricted, as were the rights of transgender student athletes to compete in secondary school. This political mash-up underscored the question of whose rights were the protests in the service of, anyway.

During the initial wave of the pandemic in America, ideological clusters of white anti-science, pro-militia groups were contrasted with younger, nonwhite, and pro-science clusters. Shortly after the zenith of these ideological protests had crossed the media horizon, a much more dramatic and culturally enmeshed series of events occurred. The social protests against public health guidelines were starkly contrasted with a sudden nationwide protest against racial violence.

Racism as Pandemic: I Can't Breathe

A dramatic plot turn occurred in May 2020 as the country was coming to grips with the 100,000+ deaths from COVID-19. In the midst of this period of social distancing, a series of homicides perpetrated by whites against Black individuals gripped the nation. The first of these involved the shooting death of 25-year-old Ahmaud Arbery, a Black man who had been pursued by armed white men in a coastal South Georgia neighborhood. Arbery was shot on February 23, 2020, while jogging near his home. Importantly, prior to any suspects being brought in by law enforcement, a video was posted online that went viral in which a struggle between Mr. Arbery and one of his pursuers is shown. This, along with an article in the *New York Times*, brought public attention to his murder—prior to the outcry, local law enforcement refused to bring charges against the men who shot and murdered Mr. Arbery.

The Arbery case is illustrative of both explicit racial violence—his homicide—and the systemic nature of animus in our criminal justice system. Specifically, a delay in bringing suspects in after his death had been attributed to the assailants as acting within Georgia's citizen arrest and self-defense statutes (Fausset, 2020), indicating that charges were not warranted under this statute. Under Georgia law the assailant was "allowed to use deadly force to protect himself" while trying to make a citizen's arrest of the victim. Notably, one of the two assailants, Gregory McMichael, was a recently retired police officer in the county. Two prosecutors had recused themselves from the case due to their prior work with him.

A second case involved the officer-based murder of a young woman in her home. On March 13, 2020, shortly after midnight, three Louisville police officers entered the apartment of Breonna Taylor, a 26-year-old African American emergency medical technician. Employing a "no-knock search warrant," the officers used a battering ram to break into her residence. As reported by the *New York Times*, "After a brief confrontation, they fired several shots, striking her at least eight times." According to the *Louisville Courier Journal*, the police were investigating two men who they believed were selling drugs out of a house that was far from Ms. Taylor's home. However, a judge had also signed a warrant allowing the police to search Ms. Taylor's residence because they believed that one of the men had used her apartment to receive packages (Oppel et al., 2021). Gunfire was exchanged between Taylor's boyfriend, Kenneth Walker, and the officers. Walker stated that he thought the officers were intruders. The "no-knock" search warrant permitted the police to enter without warning and without identifying themselves. As of this writing three months after the homicide, the officers involved in the shooting were on administrative reassignment; there have been no charges brought against them.

The case that blew the top off of America was the police homicide of George Floyd. On May 25, 2020, Minneapolis police officers responded to a call from a convenience store employee who reported that Mr. Floyd had bought cigarettes with a counterfeit $20 bill. Mr. Floyd, a 46-year-old Black man, was dead 17 minutes after police had arrived. As reported in the *New York Times*, "By combining videos from bystanders and security cameras, reviewing official documents and consulting experts, the *New York Times* reconstructed in detail the minutes leading to Mr. Floyd's death. Our video shows officers taking a series of actions that violated the policies of the Minneapolis Police Department and turned fatal, leaving Mr. Floyd unable to breathe, even as he and onlookers called out for help" (Hill et al., 2020).

Importantly, as reported by the local newspaper, "On the morning of May 26, Minneapolis police spokesman John Elder sent a brief statement to reporters under the subject line: 'Man Dies After Medical Incident During Police Interaction.' According to Elder, a suspected money forger had 'physically resisted' arrest. After police managed to get him into handcuffs, the officers 'noted he appeared to be suffering medical distress'" (Mannix, 2020). Just hours after the statement was released, the first bystander video of the encounter went viral on social media. The day after Mr. Floyd's death, the Police Department fired all four of the officers involved in the episode, and as of the writing of this chapter all four officers have been arrested, charged, and are awaiting trial. It is quite doubtful there would have been such a response if the police had been allowed to police themselves.

Law enforcement played a critical role in all three of these homicides. The words of a dying Floyd, "I can't breathe," became a rallying cry against the violence perpetrated by whites against Blacks. How these deaths were viewed became a political litmus test. For liberals, the deaths of Ahmaud Arbery, Breonna Taylor, and George Floyd were the most significant hate crimes of the year, if not the decade. In two of these homicides, the officers themselves had become the hate offenders. For right-leaning supporters of the president, their deaths were seen as protecting law and order and the white hegemony.

A highly relevant area of behavioral theory to the police-as-offender problem is found in the study of stereotype activation. Wheeler and Petty (2001) discuss how self-stereotype and other-stereotype activation results in individuals performing in a manner consistent with the stereotype (e.g., elderly persons walking more slowly if an age-related stereotype is activated). Frequently the behavioral correlates of self-stereotype activation involve perceived stereotype threat. In contrast, the frequent behavioral effects of other-stereotype activation yield a more logic-based explanation, something referred to as an "ideomotor process"—that is, a matching of the perception of the other person with a habituated action.

The police-as-offender problem is in part explained by the process of stereotype threat. The study of stereotype threat has been considered in such conditions as anxiety (Spencer, Steele, & Quinn, 1999), stereotype activation (Davies-Rubio et al., 2002), self-doubt (Steele & Aronson, 1995), working memory (Schmader & Johns, 2003), and arousal (Ben-Zeev, Fein, & Inzlicht, 2005). Schmader, Johns, and Forbes (2008) have articulated specific facets of stereotype threat activation. The authors argue that stereotype threat disrupts performance via three interrelated processes: (1) a physiological stress response that directly impairs prefrontal central nervous system processing, (2) capacity to self-monitor performance, and (3) the suppression of negative thoughts and emotions. Prior research on police shootings of Black men describes a "shooter bias" in which the other stereotype facilitates homicidal police behavior against unarmed Black individuals (Kahn & McMahon, 2015).

These studies are consistent with the classic work of Steele (1997) that found that stereotype threat resulted in impaired skilled performance. The rapid escalation in aggression between police and Black individuals underscores the failure of officers to employ de-escalation tactics or effective self-monitoring of risk. Stereotype activation constitutes an empathic failure in the interaction between the office and the Black citizen. Similarly, the recurrent harassment of Black persons can heighten a self-stereotype of vulnerability and "healthy paranoia." Chronic experiences of such aversive intergroup contact only strengthen the stereotype network, leading in many instances to unnecessary escalation of brutality and violence.

The problem of violent other-stereotype activation starts long before officer–Black interactions happen on the street. Taslitz (2006) has argued that negative representations of African Americans in entertainment media contribute to the aversive perceptions and mistreatment of Blacks. He further notes that these aversive socializing processes contribute to not only police brutality but all aspects of the criminal justice system, resulting in disproportionate and wrongful convictions of Blacks in America. Experimentally, video representation of ethnic stereotypes exacerbated negative reactions to stereotypes, by whites. This activated in-group stereotypes and predicted greater enjoyment of stereotypical film material (Schmader, Block, & Lickel, 2015).

Importantly, the socialization via officer training in applying use of force policies establishes how and when an officer can employ lethal tactics. These vary by municipality—meaning the local culture shapes what is considered an appropriate tactic about police force of restraint. For example, the neck restraint or chokehold that killed George Floyd had been banned in New York City since 1993. Some cities require officers to report use of force incidents or to intervene if an officer violates these standards. These guidelines are typically fought by the police unions when they are proposed. In contrast, professional training of law enforcement includes skill-based programs in lethal officer response. One popular program is entitled "killology," which has been provided nationally. "These classes on policing and the use of force have become hugely popular in the law enforcement community" (Balko, 2017). The local culture of the community can influence the promulgation and enforcement of use of force standards—as well as the enforcement of bias crime laws. As this author has noted previously, hate crimes are chronically underreported nationally based on two criteria: (1) if the state was a member of the Confederacy during the Civil War and (2) the state-based prevalence of Black lynching deaths during the 100 years prior to the enactment of federal hate crime laws in 1990 (Dunbar, 2017).

The actions of individual citizens, in recording the awful images of these hate-based murders, and by speaking out, underscored the terrible fact that the officers charged with enforcing crimes against hate were arguably their perpetrators. The turning of peace officers into warriors and the use of hate rhetoric by our political leadership were not lost on the thousands of citizens who poured into the streets to fight against hate. Again, we face a bifurcation of a hate unleashed as a deep cultural norm of America that is in combat with the promise of a liberal and inclusive democracy. During the 2020 cataclysms, Americans found themselves concurrently turning to their public health experts to "smooth the curve" of a deadly pandemic while their community and civil leadership—acting outside of the federal government—tried to smooth the curve of hate-based violence.

Choosing How to Deal with Hate Crimes in America

A consequence of the cultural cataclysms of the past 20 years has been the enactment of hate-based hostility and violence. From the 9/11 cataclysm, Americans were presented with an entire cultural group—Muslims and Middle Easterners—to denigrate in a manner unknown since Pearl Harbor; our habituation to the use of torture to deal with culture-based conflict was another consequence of 9/11. With the Trump election of 2016, the second cataclysm normalized hate rhetoric as part of policy discourse; it also established intergroup aggression as a plausible political instrument. The winner–loser status of political differences was made clear through the chronic hostility toward social out-groups and the permission giving to aggressive actors of the white hegemony. Our country also was asked to view migration by Central Americans as necessitating the separation of families and putting children in cages. The third cataclysm of the COVID-19/police violence pandemic further emphasized the cultural and political divide between the white hegemony and an increasingly culturally diverse, evidence-based populace. This cataclysm of pandemics established the rejection of science as a tenet of far-right white ideology; it also stereotyped Asians as a scapegoated out-group responsible for the COVID-19 pandemic.

An escalation in hate "crimes" and intergroup animus became a consequence of these cataclysmic events. Additionally, the role of the standing government in shaping the response of federal agencies and municipal police departments to social protest amplified the experiences of racial anxiety. This sanctioned racial hostility became a valuable and predictable instrument in wielding political power by the time of the third cataclysm.

So how does cataclysmic cultural change influence individuals to engage in hate violence? The larger social forces of the past 20 years have clearly changed intercultural and intergroup attitudes. From our review of these cataclysmic changes in our country, it is possible to identify some of the factors that fueled hate violence—and which meet the criteria of state and federal hate crime statutes. Motivations for aggression can be tied to events such as the 9/11 terror attacks, as well as the labeling of a migrant threat and "Chinese flu" that have been endorsed by the standing government since 2016. The motives of retribution-fueled aggression, typified by a tit-for-tat strategy or a "righteous anger" of whites, are observed in some of the rhetoric that has incited violence in our country. In addition, however, the social changes our society has experienced have surfaced deeper cultural assumptions of privilege and power. This hate-unleashed argument proposes that the marked social change of the past 20 years has mobilized individuals to engage in harassment and violence to maintain a Eurocentric white hegemony, one that is now inconsistent in many ways with the demographic realities of contemporary society. This line of thought sees hate crimes as a more radical form of social protest against the cultural diversity of the country and presents a more real representation of the conservative culture wars thesis of the past decades.

It is not unimportant to ask if the perpetrators of hate violence hold radically atypical attitudes about social problems compared to the larger society. Attitudes about the use of torture, for example, have been found to be opposed by many, though not necessarily a majority of citizens in the country. A Pew survey conducted in late 2016 found that 48% of a national survey sample supported torture under circumstances of threat to national security, with 49% stating there were no circumstances under which the use of torture is acceptable (Tyson, 2017). Similarly, there are clear divisions in how U.S. citizens view the policies to respond to illegal immigration, with liberal voters taking a more inclusive approach to the issue than Republicans do. Still, overall, most Americans support a pathway toward citizenship of illegal immigrants. Two-thirds of Americans (67%) say it is very or somewhat important to establish a way for most immigrants in the country illegally to remain here legally (Daniller, 2019). What these and other studies illustrate is that attitudes about aggression and privation of social out-groups are not rare in the general population. At the same time, racial attitudes have progressively become more supportive of equity and inclusion over the course of several decades (Bobo et al., 2012). Even so, many Americans still note a preference for racial and in-group contact. Therefore, the preference for in-group engagement is also, in and of itself, not a unique feature of perpetrators of intergroup violence.

The Washington Riot: A National Cataclysm

As of this writing, the United States is in the process of trying to comprehend the January 6, 2021, capitol riot, in which several thousand followers of former President Trump stormed the Capitol at a time that lawmakers were preparing to vote on the ratification of the 2020 election results. This monumental event in the history of the United States will be discussed by historians for years to come. As of now the events then and thereafter serve as a marker of a heightened level of the intergroup problems of our time.

Other than to say the insurrectionists were overwhelmingly white, it is unclear as of now what the sociographic characteristics of the group actually were. Their motivational intention, however, is fairly obvious, the refutation of a popularly elected leadership that ran contrary to the ultranationalist rhetoric of the Trump administration. In terms of the typology that Dunbar (2022) has proposed, the insurrections included both premediated and ideologically motivated offenders as well as many followers. Members of white nationalist groups such as the Three Percenters, the Oath Keepers, and Proud Boys were prepared for a violent confrontation with Capital police. Other insurrectionists—indeed the vast majority of them—as with many mobs, were nonviolent and more likely to follow the sequence of events as they unfolded.

If we consider the notion of what a hate crime is—as has and will be discussed by others—then the insurrection is not a bias-motivated crime. The form of aggression was political and societal. The targeted victims were also not members of a cultural group but rather a political body. So the motivation was not to target a cultural group—for example, race or religion, or sexual identity. This is legally accurate but psychologically naive. Specifically, the insurrectionists were almost exclusively white and affiliated with networks that endorse white nationalism. Equally, the targeted group constituted a political movement that was ushering in a president more amenable to racial equity and diversity that the recently defeated Trump administration.

Pape and Ruby (2021) reviewed the backgrounds of insurrectionists arrested after January 6th. They argue that the insurrectionists constituted a broad range of the American populace. In their review of court filings—inclusive of arrest records, criminal complaints, affidavits, and the search of the media coverage of the individual—they found that the large majority of insurrectionists were not affiliated with a right-wing movement; they found 1 in 10 of the arrested insurrectionists were members of militias or right-wing groups. The average age of the insurrectionists was 40, with two-thirds over the age of 35. Pape and Ruby also noted that 40% of the arrested insurrectionists had professional jobs or were business owners. Interestingly, research conducted by this author with hate crime offenders similarly reveals many of the individuals are over the age of 30 (Dunbar, 2016), so the current findings in that regard appear comparable to other ideologically motivated offenders. Likewise, the numerous non-militia members are comparable to many hate crime offenders, who also do not belong to organized hate groups. Perhaps the most significant difference is the representation of middle-income and professional persons at the insurrection. This stands in contrast to the frequently marginalized perpetrators of hate offenses. This author would speculate that may of the insurrections at the capital were there out of a political and economic motivation rather than an ideological one. As with the Nazis and the Soviets, many individuals may join movements when it is good for their careers.

The social upheaval in the United States—and elsewhere—over the past 20 years has resulted in a rise in reported hate crimes. The increase in hate violence is seen as a consequence of the racialization of white nationalism as a social movement. The cultural wars rhetoric espoused by white nationalist leaders has served as a behavioral priming of their followers' intergroup hostility. What will be considered is how physiological aspects of bias—as found in the neuroscience literature—and behavioral disinhibition—as noted in the forensic and psychological literature—moderate the choice for violence as a means of dealing with perceived social inequities and in-group threat. This choice for violence in turn shapes the offender's social group identity. Through understanding the interplay of social forces as agents of influence on the lone wolf (Gallagher, 2022) and collective perpetrator(s) (Sullaway, 2022), we may understand how hate violence becomes a choice for social change—and just possibly, therefore provide a means of avoiding its more destructive objectives.

There are two ways to do good work in fighting hate crimes. One approach is to view bias-motivated acts of violence as inherently deviant and in contrast to the traditions of a liberal democracy. In this scenario, advocacy groups work to promote effective policing of hate and the application of the rule of law by the criminal justice system. The principles of a civil society are advocated for in the media and via educational initiatives, to reduce animus and the risk of future hate violence. The other approach is to work against a far more sinister dynamic of a ruling government that foments violence among its own people to attain a desired political stasis. In this case, the agencies of policing and law enforcement are provocateurs and actors in the perpetration of hate. "Good people" promote racial hate and undermine public safety, even during a global pandemic. Under these conditions, the citizenry, with nongovernment agencies, must oppose a governance of hate via collective action to halt erosion of social norms and civil rights. As the Argentine poet Luisa Pasamanik (1973) wrote, "Choose, choose now."

References

Altemeyer, B. (1988). *Enemies of freedom: Understanding right-wing authoritarianism.* San Francisco, CA: Jossey-Bass.

Anderson, C. (2002, November 25). FBI reports jump in violence against Muslims. Associated Press.

Balko, R. (2017, February 14). A day with "killology" police trainer Dave Grossman. *Washington Post.* https://www.lse.ac.uk/europeanInstitute/LSE-Commission https://www.washingtonpost.com/news/the-watch/wp/2017/02/14/a-day-with-killology-police-trainer-dave-grossman/

Begg, I., & Mushövel, F. (2016). The economic impact of Brexit: Jobs, growth and the public finances (No. 67008). London, UK: London School of Economics and Political Science, LSE Library.

Bell, C. C. (1980). Racism: A symptom of the narcissistic personality. *Journal of the National Medical Association*, 72(7), 661–665.

Bell, C. C. (1978). Racism, narcissism, and integrity. *Journal of the National Medical Association*, 70(2), 89–92.

Ben-Zeev, T., Fein, S., & Inzlicht, M. (2005). Arousal and stereotype threat. *Journal of Experimental Social Psychology*, 41(2), 174–181.

Berger, J. M. (2018, October 29). Trump is the glue that binds the far right. *The Atlantic.* https://www.theatlantic.com/ideas/archive/2018/10/trump-alt-right-twitter/574219/

Bobo, L. D., Charles, C. Z., Krysan, M., & Simmons, A. D. (2012). The real record on racial attitudes. In P. V. Marsden (Ed.), *Social trends in American life: Findings from the General Social Survey since 1972* (pp. 38–83). Princeton, NJ, and Oxford, UK: Princeton University Press.

Bonanno, G. A., Galea, S., Bucciarelli, A., & Vlahov, D. (2006). Psychological resilience after disaster: New York City in the aftermath of the September 11th terrorist attacks. *Psychological Science*, 17(3), 181–186.

Browning, C. R. (1992). *Ordinary men: Reserve Police Battalion 101 and the final solution in Poland.* New York. NY: Harper Perennial.

Center for Constitutional Rights. (2007). Factsheet: The Violent Radicalization and Homegrown Terrorism Prevention Act of 2007. https://ccrjustice.org/home/get-involved/tools-resources/fact-sheets-and-faqs/factsheet-violent-radicalization-and

Chinese for Affirmative Action (CAA). (2020). In six weeks, STOP AAPI HATE receives over 1700 incident reports of verbal harassment, shunning and physical assaults. https://caasf.org/press-release/in-six-weeks-stop-aapi-hate-receives-over-1700-incident-reports-of-verbal-harassment-shunning-and-physical-assaults/

Cotharin, R. L., & Milkulas, W. L. (1975). Systematic desensitization of racial emotional responses. *Journal of Behavior Therapy and Experimental Psychology*, 6, 347–358.

Daniller, A. (2019). Americans' immigration policy priorities: Divisions between—and within—the two parties. https://www.pewresearch.org/fact-tank/2019/11/12/americans-immigration-policy-priorities-divisions-between-and-within-the-two-parties/

Davies-Rubio, A., & Mirón, L. (2022). Joining Colombian illegal armed groups and the role of ideology. In E. W. Dunbar (Ed.), *Indoctrination to hate: Recruitment techniques of hate groups and how to stop them.* Santa Barbara, CA: Praeger.

Davies, P. G., Spencer, S. J., Quinn, D. M., & Gerhardstein, R. (2002). Consuming images: How television commercials that elicit stereotype threat can restrain women academically and professionally. *Personality and Social Psychology Bulletin*, 28(12), 1615–1628.

Duckitt, J. (2004). The cultural bases of ethnocentrism and prejudice. In Y.-T. Lee, C. McCauley, F. Moghaddam, & S. Worchel (Eds.), *The psychology of ethnic and cultural conflict: Looking through American and global chaos or harmony* (pp. 155–174). Westport, CT: Praeger.

Dunbar, E. (1997). The relationship of DSM Diagnostic Criteria and Gough's Prejudice Scale: Exploring the clinical manifestations of the prejudiced personality. *Cultural Diversity and Mental Health*, 3(4), 247–257. https://doi.org/10.1037/1099-9809.3.4.247

Dunbar, E. (2006). Race, gender, and sexual orientation in hate crime victimization: Identity politics or identity risk? *Violence & Victims*, 21(3), 323–337.

Dunbar, E. (2016). Cultural and psychological characteristics in the evolution of hate crime initiatives. In E. Dunbar, A. Blanco, & D. Crèvecoeur-MacPhail, (Eds.), *The Psychology of Hate Crimes as Domestic Terrorism: US and Global Issues* (pp. 1–42). Santa Barbara, CA: Praeger.

Dunbar, E. (2018). *Hate unleashed: America's cataclysmic change*. Santa Barbara, CA: Praeger.

Earls, M. F., Yogman, M. W., Mattson, G., Rafferty, J., & Committee on Psychosocial Aspects of Child and Family Health. (2019). Incorporating recognition and management of perinatal depression into pediatric practice. *Pediatrics*, 126(5), 1032–1039.

Farach, F. J., Mennin, D. S., Smith, R. L., & Mandelbaum, M. (2008). The impact of pretrauma analogue GAD and posttraumatic emotional reactivity following exposure to the September 11 terrorist attacks: A longitudinal study. *Behavior Therapy*, 39(3), 262–276. https://doi.org/10.1016/j.beth.2007.08.005

Fausset, R. (2020, February 28). What we know about the shooting death of Ahmaud Arbery. *New York Times*. https://www.nytimes.com/article/ahmaud-arbery-shooting-georgia.html

FBI. (2018). 2017 Hate crime statistics released. https://www.fbi.gov/news/stories/2017-hate-crime-statistics-released-111318

FBI. (2019). 2018 Hate crime statistics released: Report shows slight decline in incidents from 2017 to 2018. https://www.fbi.gov/news/stories/2018-hate-crime-statistics-released-111219

Franz, V. A., Glass, C. R., Arnkoff, D. B., & Dutton, M. A. (2009). The impact of the September 11th terrorist attacks on psychiatric patients: A review. *Clinical Psychology Review*, 29(4), 339–347. https://doi.org/10.1016/j.cpr.2009.02.002

Fromm, E. (1941). *Escape from freedom*. New York, NY: Farrar & Rinehart.

Galea, S., Vlahov, D., Resnick, H., Ahern, J., Susser, E., Gold, J., Bucuvalas, M., & Kilpatrick, D. (2003). Trends of probable post-traumatic stress disorder in New York City after the September 11 terrorist attacks. *American Journal of Epidemiology*, 58(6), 514–524.

Gallagher, M. (2022). Lone wolf terrorists. In E. W. Dunbar (Ed.), *Indoctrination to hate: Recruitment techniques of hate groups and how to stop them*. Santa Barbara, CA: Praeger.

Golec de Zavala, A., Guerra, R., & Simao, C. (2017). The relationship between the Brexit vote and individual predictors of prejudice: Collective narcissism, right wing authoritarianism, social dominance orientation. *Frontiers in Psychology*, 27. https://doi.org/10.3389/fpsyg.2017.02023

Grierson, J. (2020, May 13). Anti-Asian hate crimes up 21% in UK during coronavirus crisis. *The Guardian*. https://www.theguardian.com/world/2020/may/13/anti-asian-hate-crimes-up-21-in-uk-during-coronavirus-crisis

Hasan, M. (2018, September 18). Time to kill the zombie argument: Another study shows Trump won because of racial anxieties—not economic distress. *The Intercept.* https://theintercept.com/2018/09/18/2016-election-race-class-trump/

Heen, M., Lieberman, J. D., & Arndt, J. (2016). Terror management, crime, and law. In L. A. Harvell & G. S. Nisbett (Eds.), *Denying death: An interdisciplinary approach to terror management theory* (pp. 62–78). Oxfordshire, UK: Routledge/Taylor & Francis Group.

Helmore, E. (2019, July 3). Migrant children's drawings depict "horrific" conditions in cages. *The Guardian.* https://www.theguardian.com/us-news/2019/jul/03/migrant-children-drawings-horrific-conditions-cages

Hill, E., Tiefenthäler, A., Triebert, C., Jordan, D., Willis H., & Stein, R. (2020, May 31). 8 minutes and 46 seconds: How George Floyd was killed in police custody. *New York Times.* https://www.nytimes.com/2020/05/31/us/george-floyd-investigation.html

Jeung, R., Kulkarni M. P., & Choi, C. (2020, April 1). Op-Ed: Trump's racist comments are fueling hate crimes against Asian Americans. Time for state leaders to step in. *Los Angeles Times.* https://www.latimes.com/opinion/story/2020-04-01/coronavirus-anti-asian-discrimination-threats

Kahn, A. (2017, September 11). Seventeen years after 9/11, Muslims are still "presumed guilty." *National Catholic Reporter.* https://www.ncronline.org/news/people/seventeen-years-after-911-muslims-are-still-presumed-guilty

Kahn, K. B., & McMahon, J. M. (2015). Shooting deaths of unarmed racial minorities: Understanding the role of racial stereotypes on decisions to shoot. *Translational Issues in Psychological Science*, 1(4), 310–320.

Kishi, K. (2017, November 15). Assaults against Muslims in U.S. surpass 2001 level. https://www.pewresearch.org/fact-tank/2017/11/15/assaults-against-muslims-in-u-s-surpass-2001-level/

Krugler, D. F. (2015). *1919, the year of racial violence: How African Americans fought back.* New York, NY: Cambridge University Press.

Lichtblau, E. (2016, September 16). Hate crimes against American Muslims most since post-9/11 era. *New York Times.* https://www.nytimes.com/2016/09/18/us/politics/hate-crimes-american-muslims-rise.html

Lifton, J. R. (1986). *The Nazi doctors: Medical killing and the psychology of genocide.* New York, NY: Basic Books.

Lipton, E., Sanger, D. E., Haberman, M., Shear, M. D., Mazzetti, M., & Barnes, J. E. (2020, April 11). He could have seen what was coming: Behind Trump's failure on the virus. *New York Times.* https://www.nytimes.com/2020/04/11/us/politics/coronavirus-trump-response.html

Mannix, A. (2020, June 3). Minneapolis police cite "fluid" situation for troubling misinformation released after George Floyd death. *Star Tribune.* https://www.startribune.com/mpls-police-still-haven-t-explained-misinformation-after-floyd-s-death/570970152/

Manson, W. (1988). *The psychodynamics of culture: Abram Kardiner and neo-Freudian anthropology*. Westport, CT: Praeger.

Mummolo, J. (2018, September 11). Militarization fails to enhance police safety or reduce crime but may harm police reputation. *Proceedings of the National Academy of Sciences*, 115(37), 9181–9186. https://doi.org/10.1073/pnas.1805161115

Mutz, D. C. (2018, May). Status threat, not economic hardship, explains the 2016 presidential vote. *Proceedings of the National Academy of Sciences*, 115(19), E4330–E4339. https://doi.org/10.1073/pnas.1718155115

Newport, F., Moore, D., & Saad, L. (1999). Long-term Gallup Poll trends: A portrait of American public opinion through the century. *Poll Releases*. https://news.gallup.com/poll/3400/longterm-gallup-poll-trends-portrait-american-public-opinion.aspx

NPR. (2019, November 12). FBI reports dip in hate crimes, but rise in violence. https://www.npr.org/2019/11/12/778542614/fbi-reports-dip-in-hate-crimes-but-rise-in-violence

Oppel, R. A., Taylor, D. B., & Bogel-Burroughs, N. (2021, January 6). What you need to know about Breonna Taylor's death. *Equal Justice Now*. https://equaljusticenow.org/what-to-know-about-breonna-taylors-death/

Pape, R. A., & Ruby, K. (2021, February 2). The Capitol rioters aren't like other extremists. *The Atlantic*. https://www.theatlantic.com/ideas/archive/2021/02/the-capitol-rioters-arent-like-other-extremists/617895/

Pasamanik, L. (1973). *The exiled angel*. E. Hirshman (Trans.). Fairfax, CA: The Red Hill Press. (Original work published 1962)

Paxton, R. O. (2004). *The anatomy of fascism*. New York, NY: Alfred A. Knopf.

Pew Research. (2017). Anti-Muslim assaults exceed 2001 total. https://www.pewresearch.org/fact-tank/2017/11/15/assaults-against-muslims-in-u-s-surpass-2001-level/ft_17-11-14_muslimhatecrimes/

Rizer, A., & Hartman, J. (2011, November 7). How the war on terror has militarized the police. *The Atlantic*. https://www.theatlantic.com/national/archive/2011/11/how-the-war-on-terror-has-militarized-the-police/248047/

Schaffner, B. F., Macwilliams, M., & Nteta, T. (2018), Understanding white polarization in the 2016 vote for president: The sobering role of racism and sexism. *Political Science Quarterly*, 133(1), 9–34. https://doi.org/10.1002/polq.12737

Schmader, T., Block, K., & Lickel, B. (2015). Social identity threat in response to stereotypic film portrayals: Effects on self-conscious emotion and implicit ingroup attitudes. *Journal of Social Issues*, 71(1), 54–72. https://doi.org/10.1111/josi.12096

Schmader, T., & Johns, M. (2003). Converging evidence that stereotype threat reduces working memory capacity. *Journal of Personality and Social Psychology*, 85(3), 440–452.

Schmader, T., Johns, M., & Forbes, C. (2008). An integrated process model of stereotype threat effects on performance. *Psychological Review*, 115(2), 336–356. https://doi.org/10.1037/0033-295X.115.2.336

Sheridan, L. P. (2006). Islamophobia pre-and post-September 11th, 2001. *Journal of Interpersonal Violence*, 21(3), 317–336.

Shirer, W. L. (1960). *The rise and fall of the Third Reich*. New York, NY: Simon & Schuster.

Silverstein, J. (2019). Customs and Border Protection investigating secret Facebook page where agents allegedly mocked migrant deaths. CBS News. https://www.cbsnews.com/news/customs-and-border-protection-investigating-secret-facebook-page-where-agents-allegedly-mock-migrant-deaths/

Solomon, S., Greenberg, J., & Pyszczynski, T. (2015). *The worm at the core*. New York, NY: Random House.

Southern Poverty Law Center (SPLC). (2016). Ten Days After: Harassment and Intimidation in the Aftermath of the Election. https://www.splcenter.org/20161129/ten-days-after-harassment-and-intimidation-aftermath-election

Spencer, S. J., Steele, C. M., & Quinn, D. M. (1999). Stereotype threat and women's math performance. *Journal of Experimental Social Psychology*, 35(1), 4–28.

Steele, C. M. (1997). A threat in the air: How stereotypes shape intellectual identity and performance. *American Psychologist*, 52(6), 613–629.

Steele, C. M., & Aronson, J. (1995). Stereotype threat and intellectual test performance of African Americans. *Journal of Personality and Social Psychology*, 69(5), 797–811.

Stephan, W., & Stephan, C. (1996). *Intergroup relations*. New York, NY: Avalon Publishers.

Sukin, L. (2019, July 26). The United States treats migrants worse than prisoners of war. *Foreign Policy*. https://foreignpolicy.com/2019/07/26/the-united-states-treats-migrants-worse-than-prisoners-of-war/

Sullaway, M. E. (2022). Lone wolves and wolf packs: Revenge porn, cyber mobs, and creepshots. In E. W. Dunbar (Ed.), *Indoctrination to hate: Recruitment techniques of hate groups and how to stop them*. Santa Barbara, CA: Praeger.

Sullaway, M. E., & Dunbar, E. (1996). Clinical manifestations of prejudice in psychotherapy: Toward a strategy of assessment and treatment. *Clinical Psychology: Science and Practice*, 3(4), 296–309. https://doi.org/10.1111/j.1468-2850.1996.tb00084

Taslitz, A. E. (2006). Wrongly accused: Is race a factor in convicting the innocent? *Ohio State Journal of Criminal Law*, 4(1), 121–133.

Tyson, A. (2017, January 26). Americans divided in views of use of torture in U.S. anti-terror efforts. https://www.pewresearch.org/fact-tank/2017/01/26/americans-divided-in-views-of-use-of-torture-in-u-s-anti-terror-efforts/

Washington Post. (2019, September 15). A report documents the systematic abuse inflicted on migrant children. https://www.washingtonpost.com/opinions/a-report-documents-the-systematic-abuse-inflicted-on-migrant-children/2019/09/15/29f6e388-d0f3-11e9-8c1c-7c8ee785b855_story.html

Wheeler, S. C., & Petty, R. E. (2001). The effects of stereotype activation on behavior: A review of possible mechanisms. *Psychological Bulletin*, 127(6), 797–826.

Winter, J. (2017, August 14). FBI and DHS warned of growing threat from white supremacists months ago. *Foreign Policy*. https://foreignpolicy.com/2017/08/14/fbi-and-dhs-warned-of-growing-threat-from-white-supremacists-months-ago/

CHAPTER TWO

Hate, Ideology, and Intergroup Violence: Bias Motivation and Membership in a Multicultural World

Edward W. Dunbar

Risk Factors of the New Terrorism

Historians tell us how, somewhere during the eleventh century, Western civilization essentially created our notion of romantic love (Paden & Paden, 2014). Love as it came to be articulated in both literature and the song lyrics of the Occitanian troubadours was both the ideal attachment to an individual and the creation of a bond between peoples. The troubadour Jarufe Rudel (1125–1175) extended this idea of an idyllic love to include romantic devotion of a princess in Tripoli who lived across the sea in another land and culture. The popular story told of Rudel (in his *Razo*) is that he traveled by sea to reach her, fell ill on the journey, and died in her arms. The medieval ideal of love transcended generations and was even passed down in legal documents—in the sharing of love between families (Kehew, Pound, & Snodgrass, 2005). This idea of idealized love brought with it the ascription to courtly behaviors. The violation of the established manners of love and respect further led to review in the courts of love of Eleanor of Aquitaine

(1124–1204), a charismatic political leader who sought to establish expectations of romance and could assign sanctions for the violation of these standards of love. The troubadour Macabru (born circa 1130) railed against the deterioration of the romantic ideal as early as the twelfth century.

Romantic love would in our current day be thought of as a strong emotion. Yet the origins of romantic love in Western society incorporated social norms, and proscribed behaviors for the differing actors/actresses in the pursuit of "fin amour" and a popular culture of literature and music to promote it. This notion of love incorporated politics—with the love of country being used to promote by the aristocratic poet Bertran de Born. In his lyrics honoring chivalry and warfare, de Born exhorted his fellow aristocrats to overthrow the liberal monarchy of Occitania. Bertran intertwined his love lyrics with allegorical references to potential battle sites. Love became intertwined with hate in the service of politics. King Richard Coeur de Lion penned his famous "Ja nus hons pris" while being held for ransom at Durnstein Castle in the Wacchau Valley. Richard lamented the failings of his subjects to find the needed money to free him to return home and resume his rule of the Plantagenet Empire. Furthermore, society established standards within which expression of love was acceptable and where it crossed the line. Pier Vidal, a famous troubadour crossed this line by being too attached to the lady of court and was banished. He had to write a canso to beg his forgiveness to return to the region where the lord and lady lived. In another case, when the troubadour was too amorous, the lord had his heart cut out and served to his wife as a reminder of where power resided in the kingdom (Paden & Paden, 2014). Most importantly, however, was the court of love, in which Eleanor resided over claimed offenses to fin amour and, in concert with her peers, provided redress to the offended.

In Western society, our polar experience to feelings of love is hate. Hate, by comparison, particularly when accompanied by violence, extends back in human society to before recorded history. As Stanley Kubrick envisions it in his masterpiece film *2001*, the organization of the group and the use of tools are intimately linked to violence, as he depicts in the battle of the apes over a water hole at the beginning of his film. As asserted elsewhere (Dunbar & Blanco, 2013), violence and hate are defining characteristics of the human experience. Violence, they posit, meets a variety of psychological needs. Research on aggression has sought to distinguish between goal-oriented and reactive forms of violence (Berkowitz & Macaulay, 1971), which opens us to the question of differences in motivation, vulnerability toward, and desire to perpetrate acts of violence. This area of study has considered aggression as a motivator of crimes related to the pursuit of material reward and the creation of a sense of personal power for the offender, vis-à-vis a spontaneous reaction to interpersonal provocation. The study of intergroup violence further distinguishes between premeditated and reactive aggression in terms of collective identity, efforts to enhance in-group status, and forms of symbolic aggression to maintain in-group–out-group inequities (Dunbar, 2017). These acts may be planned and organized or be in response to situational determinants of random contact, perceived provocation by the victim group, or be in reaction to recently occurring events of intergroup conflict.

We will consider the cultural, psychological, and individual forces that result in individuals adopting a hate-based lifestyle. Additionally, how these factors shape an individual's identity and lead them into a lifestyle centered in out-group animus will be examined. We will also consider how our social contexts and traditions make sense of and sanction the choice of violence as a means of addressing intergroup problems. From a public safety standpoint, the critical issue to address is not how people enter hate groups but rather how their risk for expression of hate violence is realized. The problem of hate violence needs to be considered broadly and not simply how people come to belong to intolerant gang groups. Rather, we need to acknowledge the risk of individuals to engage in hate violence. It is also essential to consider how otherwise socially conforming individuals ascribe to social assumptions that normalize oppression and violence of denigrated out-groups. The motivational factors that lead an individual to perpetrate hate violence can be determined through the analysis of the nature of aggression evidenced in the criminal infraction. These psychological processes will allow us to examine the dynamics of entry, membership, and (the potential for) desistance from a hate-based lifestyle.

Societal Distinctions between Hate and Terror-Based Violence

Understanding the relationship of hate crimes and domestic terrorism—two substantial social problems—requires that we acknowledge the legal, social, and governmental presumptions of whether violence is motivated by hate, or ideology, or both (Dunbar, 2017). To do so necessitates that we consider the antecedent conditions that have brought these issues—which are often highly intertwined—to the foreground of social consciousness. The distinction between these two forms of violence reflects the societal and institutional assumptions about civil liberties and the liberal democratic tradition of the West.

In the United States, hate crime statutes were first enacted federally in the early 1990s. Domestic terrorism by comparison has been addressed under various federal and state laws since the beginning of the twentieth century and has been more fully defined subsequent to the 9/11 terrorist attacks under laws referred to as the Patriot Act. The basic definition of a hate crime is found in the 1990 Hate Crime Statistics Act, or HCSA (which has been modified since its original passage). In this legislation, it was established that the U.S. attorney general will annually gather data on crimes of prejudice related to race, gender and gender identity, religion, disability, sexual orientation, or ethnicity (FBI, 2010). Subsequent legislation federally and at the state level defined these offenses as being a penalty enhancement due to the bias motivation found as a motivation in the perpetration of the offense. As with other penalty enhancements, these laws allow for more severe punishment and a greater range of prosecutorial options. As noted by Benjamin Wagner, a U.S. Department of Justice prosecutor, "Hate crimes also have a much broader impact within communities than many other types of violent crimes or property crimes. Because they are motivated by bias, hate crimes are often intended to, and do, send a broader message of violent intolerance toward a broad class of persons. Like terrorist incidents, the 'message' aspect of the offender's motive can be profoundly threatening to people far removed from the actual scene of the crime" (Focus on Essentials, 2013). Under the Patriot Act of 2001, domestic terrorism was defined as infractions that: "(A) involve acts dangerous to human life that are a violation of the criminal laws of the United States or of any State; (B) appear to be intended—(i) to intimidate or coerce a civilian population; (ii) to influence the policy of a government by intimidation or coercion; or (iii) to affect the conduct of a government by mass destruction, assassination, or kidnapping; and (C) occur primarily within the territorial jurisdiction of the United States" (U.S. Government Printing Office, 2001).

The legal commonalities in how hate crimes and domestic terrorism are defined are striking in terms of motivation and the presumed psychological impact on the communities in which the infractions occur. As has been suggested elsewhere (Dunbar, 2017) it is plausible to understand these acts as being highly interrelated. Two particularly significant examples of these conceptual dilemmas are found in the Charleston, South Carolina, and San Bernardino, California, mass killings in 2016. The motivation of Dylann Roof and Syed Rizwan Farook/Tashfeen Malik—the perpetrators in these incidents—reveal differences in our perception of the legal implications of bias-motivated violence. In the United States, there is a presumed difference between hate crimes, homegrown domestic terror, and global terrorism. The debate as to what is hate motivated and what is terror motivated is practically and conceptually challenging.

Hate crimes and domestic terrorism may be distinguished by differences in the political attitudes of the supporters of these initiatives (Dunbar, 2017). Additionally, hate crimes and domestic terrorism are, in part, distinguishable by the governmental agencies that monitor and respond to these events. There is substantial difference in U.S. government funding to eradicate terror versus hate crimes. The financial resources directed to terror-driven initiatives dwarf those devoted to fighting hate crimes (Dunbar, 2017).

How important are the problems of intergroup conflict to contemporary society? In the United States, a recent CNN survey asserted that respondents felt that inter-race/ethnic problems had increased over the past decade (CNN, 2015). In Europe, issues of intergroup concerns have been amplified by the refugee crisis from the Middle East war, the rise of nationalism, and the occurrence of several high-profile terror attacks related to Western–Middle Eastern conflict. Survey work on attitudes in the new EU are, however, hampered by regional differences in survey research as well as differing areas of study of ethnicity (Zick, Pettigrew, & Wagner, 2008). As Zick and colleagues note, the heterogeneity of the ethnic populations and the varying governmental structures found throughout Europe make region-wide studies difficult to execute. In total, intergroup conflict itself remains a concern to the populace. By extension, then, violent intergroup conflict is likely to be of similar if not greater concern.

What happens when we refocus the question to that of in-country or "homegrown" terrorism? A 2009 Pew survey research study conducted in the United States with Muslim Americans found little support for such terror groups as al-Qaeda (5% of respondents reporting a favorable opinion). The majority of (68%) Muslim Americans expressed an unfavorable rating of al-Qaeda—including 58% who describe their view as very unfavorable. Interestingly Muslim American respondents under the age of 30 were more than twice as likely as over-30 respondents to believe that suicide bombings in the defense of Islam can often or sometimes be justified (15% vs. 6%). Importantly, at the same time, political rhetoric in the United States has sought to link Islam per se with ideological violence; this was most clearly displayed in the run-up to the 2016 presidential election in the United States, in which then-candidate Trump repeatedly invoked images of Islamic terrorists crossing the southern border and entering the country (Dunbar, 2018).

Attitudes about right-wing extremism have also been an area of concern. Eidelson and McCauley (2010) note increasing public hostility toward the federal government and its policies that may lead to greater support for right-wing violence. Extremist right-wing ideology is at once anti-government and racist. We again run into the conceptual dilemma of what the distinction is between hate crimes and homegrown terrorism. Domestic terror has been seen to include the 1995 Oklahoma City bombing as well as violence at abortion clinics and attacks at gay bars (Chermak, Freilich, & Shemtob, 2009). Additionally, it is unclear whether general support of right-wing extremism has a direct relationship to the perpetration of ideological violence. We again run into the conceptual dilemma in distinguishing between hate crimes and homegrown terrorism.

Survey research conducted in Europe reveals that there is consensus concerning the risk of ideological violence that is more likely viewed as happening throughout the EU as a region rather than in the survey respondent's immediate community. A recent article in *The Guardian* (2015) in the United Kingdom observed that while many Europeans saw terror as a global threat, perceptions of personal vulnerability in their community placed common crime victimization as being of greater concern than political or intergroup violence.

The interested reader will have noticed that these opinion surveys reflect respondent attitudes drawn from the general population. A significantly more elusive question arises when we consider if ideological bias is increasing within a specific national or regional context, as well as whether the number of persons who sanction intergroup hatred has changed over time. To answer these questions our findings are significantly more inferential, as there is no direct sampling of these behaviors in mainstream opinion research. Perhaps the most common approach to this question is via the monitoring of the prevalence of organized hate and extremist groups in a society. Human rights watchdog groups will, with some regularity, note the rise or fall of membership in these groups year over year. Similarly, crime statistics might be thought to portray if there has been a reported rise in hate violence (IRR, 2015). As will be elaborated on below, a criminological body count of bias-motivated violence does not address the same issue, which is inherently more psychological than legal. Due to a variety of methodological problems, there are significant challenges in gauging how biased and potentially violent are a subset of members of a given society. It may well be that knowing how many members of a nation-state or region endorse a violent bias ideology cannot be determined.

The Cultural Coherence of Intergroup Violence

Violence that is attributable to hate and ideology occurs in a cultural, historical, and social context. This context establishes when violence is bias motivated. The identification of hate and ideology constitutes the "cultural coherence" of intergroup violence. The coherence of the act is achieved when the norms and traditions of the in-group explain—that is, normalize—the habitual practice of violence that targets members of a specific out-group. This means that the infraction, while a violation of the standards of a civil society, assigns meaning to acts of violence and is salient to the cultural worldview of the offenders' in-group.

The meaning—for example, coherence—of intergroup aggression is communicated to the in-group via an informative net that incorporates a historical narrative, shared symbols, stereotypes of the out-group, and a continuous reexperiencing of intergroup conflict. Violence between the two groups is comprehended through a shared history of contention, presumptive adverse stereotyping of out-group individuals, and the collective memory of problematic intergroup contact. Bar-Tal (2013), in his analysis of intractable intergroup conflicts, identifies three core functions of culturally coherent intergroup violence: (1) satisfying in-group needs, (2) providing a means of coping with the stress of conflict, and (3) withstanding and habituating experiences of intergroup conflict. As described by Dunbar and Blanco (2013), culture makes normal (coherent) the abnormal (violence). The coherence of intergroup violence is further normalized when it is framed in terms of cultural norms, orientations, and worldviews.

The coherence of intergroup hostility is a consequence of what has been called the "cultural anchoring" of animus deeply within the history and ideology of the social in-group. As proposed by Huang, Liu, and Chang (2004), high levels of political consensus are related to deep cultural reference points. This anchoring of culture-specific symbols, values, and events can activate social identity—that is, identification with a specific social group—and influence attitudes and actions about social issues. Liu, Sibley and Huang (2014) have commented that "History is an important symbolic resource in mobilizing support for public policies regarding intergroup relations, because temporal continuity is central to claims of legitimacy for peoples . . ." (p. 2). Historical events, embedded in specific cultural traditions, shape member attitudes, and solidify their in-group identity.

In the United States, the cultural anchoring of racial violence has been found in terms of the predictive power of the lynching of black Americans in the 100 years after the Civil War with both lower reportage of hate crimes by law enforcement, on the one hand (Dunbar, 2016), and the state-by-state success of Donald Trump in winning the presidency in 2016 (Dunbar, 2017). The deeply embedded nature—that is, anchoring—of racial violence is revealed in resistance to enforcement of anti-hate laws and the endorsement of xenophobic political ideologies, based in part on the manifestation of race-based violence from over a century before.

The deep cultural anchoring of racial bias was also seen in the 2016 U.S. presidential election. The success of candidate Trump was based substantially along the alignment of states during the Civil War (Dunbar, 2017). As I have stated elsewhere, "This Civil War analysis of voting patterns found that the Confederate Jim Crow Southern states—with the exception of Virginia—were all carried by Mr. Trump (92%), whereas Trump won thirty-five percent of the states of the Civil War Union and seventy-five percent of the unaligned states. So Trump's percentage of the popular vote was a function—in part—of the allegiance of the states during the Civil War" (Dunbar, 2017).

So our traditions of bias, racial violence, and ideology run across generations and fuel experiences of intergroup conflict today. At the same time, the expression of racial hostility is also found in very contemporary references as well. For example, in the first month after the highly publicized violent confrontation in Charlottesville, Virginia, between right-wing extremists and social activists, a national poll found notable levels of support for several alt-right beliefs. In a Thomson Reuters and the University of Virginia Center for Politics poll conducted in the early autumn of 2017, it was found that while the majority of Americans say they oppose racism and white nationalism, a significant minority endorsed extremist alt-right ideology (HuffPost, 2017). Online polling results found that as many as one-third (31%) felt that "America must protect and preserve its White European heritage" and that 57% felt that "Confederate monuments should remain in all public spaces (i.e., parks, public squares, court houses)." So while less than 10% of the respondents supported the white nationalist movement, many shared some of the attitudes of the alt-right, with 39% agreeing that "white people are currently under attack in this country."

It is important to consider not only the cultural but also the inherently political nature of hate violence. The cultural anchoring of intergroup prejudice—as articulated by Allport (1954) as a continuum of animus—and violence have been and continue to be influential forces in cataclysmic societal change. Periods of relatively benign intergroup relationships have been found in European history from the multiculturalism of high Andalusian (*al-Andalus*) Umayyad culture, as exemplified by the libraries and mosques with interwoven Islamic, Christian, and Judaic images; to the multiculturalism of fin de siècle Budapest and its intermingling of Croats, Jews, Serbs, and Bosnians for over the better part of two centuries. In these and many other situations, the activation of ethnic, religious, and racial ideologies resulted in a violent shift away from tolerance and into ultranationalist regimes of oppression and persecution. In the recent case of the former Yugoslav Republic, the genocide of the Serbo-Croatian conflict was a consequence of the extreme-right Ustase movement to create an ethnically pure Croat state through the extermination of minority Serbian and Muslim residents of Croatia.

This cataclysmic societal shift was evidenced in the presidential campaign of Donald Trump, who ran on a platform of a nationalism of nostalgia and anti-immigration. As has been suggested, the 2016 election signaled a shift away from a liberal democratic tradition of cultural inclusion and toward an ultranationalistic—and potentially autocratic—political system. This transition from a liberal democratic form of government was fueled by voters who supported an anti-immigration, anti-taxation, pro-gun ownership, and American-first nationalism—one that included hostility toward both sexual minorities and the legitimacy of women in positions of ultimate power. For a sizable number—if still a statistical minority—of persons in the United States, the social attitudes they report in numerous polling studies are not significantly different from the perpetrators of racial and religious violence.

Cross-national research in social psychology and anthropology provides several frameworks by which to conceptualize differences of intergroup attitudes. While the area of cultural study is extensive, none of the major contributions set out to examine culture norms as predictors of intergroup violence. That being said, the work of scholars such as Triandis (1995) has considered cultural value differentials as a basis for out-group bias. Triandis (1995) proposed that individuals in highly collectivistic cultures are more likely to express out-group bias, but cautions that any such relationship is extremely complex and that persons of individualistic and collectivistic cultures may be motivated to hold out-group bias for different reasons. Highly individualistic cultural orientations emphasize an autonomous social identity, a fluid entry into and exit from social roles, and a relativistic perception of the rights of others. Social attitudes are more apt to engage in rational choice decisions that weigh out equality, equity, and the opportunity for personal achievement. Prototypically collectivist cultural orientations emphasize group well-being over individual interests, yielding an interrelationship of proscribed roles—which are assigned by family and community traditions, and situated in particular roles or status—that are then assessed by the individual. Traditional and often paternal institutions govern personal choice and behavior, which is comprehended by members of the in-group as a set of collective moral codes.

There has been some effort to examine the relationship of individualism–collectivism to out-group bias (e.g., Lee & Ward, 1998; Mullen, Brown, & Smith, 1992; Verkuyten & Kwa, 1996). Dimensions of cultural worldviews and orientations have also been proposed by Kluckhohn and Strodtbeck (1961) and Hofstede (1984). These influential models employed field and qualitative methodologies as well as questionnaire methods. The anthropological work of Kluckhohn and Strodtbeck (1961) proposed that there were universally encountered issues of social group functioning, in which the orientation of the cultural group was reflected in perceptions on the core nature of the individual, the perception of time, the balance of the individual to nature, the notion of personal development, and the interrelationship of the individual to the group. They asserted distinct patterns of how these worldview dimensions could be discerned to distinguish between cultural groups. The survey research of Geert Hofstede (1984) provides a useful empirical model to think about cultural factors and intergroup attitudes. Hofstede's research on cultural dimensions revealed empirically derived constructs—power distance (PDI), uncertainty avoidance (UAI), masculinity/femininity (MAS), and individualism/collectivism (IDV). Subsequent research has identified two additional dimensions of culture, long-term orientation vs. short-term orientation (LTO) and indulgence vs. restraint (IND).

The Hofstede cultural dimensions have been seen as supporting, in some instances, intergroup inequity; specifically high-power distance cultures may treat inequity as a means of maintaining the social order (Hofstede, Hofstede, & Minkov, 2010). Hofstede's model of cultural orientations is not correlated to the occurrence of terrorism (Kluch & Vaux, 2015) but was instead related to the frequency of more violent terrorist acts.

From a cultural perspective, the collective narrative of bias may be imposed on the individual as part of their socialization to the in-group. The individual comprehends the culturally mediated rationale of the act, irrespective of their personal acceptance or rejection of the validity of the underlying narrative. For example, the generations-old conflict between Israelis and Palestinians is (culturally) comprehended by both social groups. Indeed, even if an individual in Israel personally rejects violence against Palestinians, the action itself is coherent to the in-group in which the dissenting individual resides. Similarly in Northern Ireland, conflict between Catholics and Protestants has been the social norm for generations. In situations of ideological violence, the majority of the in-group by definition comprehends acts of aggression against members of a specific out-group. Again, we may not agree with the use of violence, but we understand the thoughts and feelings of those of our in-group who committed the act.

Offenses marked by hate may reveal idiosyncratic motives and targets of violence that are not endorsed by—that is, are culturally coherent to—significant numbers of the perpetrators in-group. These hate offenses may represent the overextension of frequently endorsed social biases against an out-group. For example, a male perpetrator may engage in acts of sexual violence against women in a society that practices de facto economic discrimination against women or in which the ideals of traditional male machismo are condoned. The perpetrator may express a rationale—if pressed for one—for the series of assaults, which is incongruent or potentially incoherent in terms of the proscribed behaviors of the majority of the offenders' in-group. The manifested bias may, however, exceed the tolerable norms of behavior for the majority of the in-group. In the United States, for example, violence targeting immigrants is likely to be frowned on by many citizens, even those who oppose providing other civil rights to undocumented persons. We may say anti-immigrant violence is comprehended but not sanctioned. Many male-dominant cultures witness significant violence against women (Kalra & Bhugra, 2013), even when many men in the cultural in-group may oppose such violence or when cultural attributes for gendered violence differ (Kersten, 1996).

The bias-based worldview of the hate-motivated offender is frequently personalized and in conflict with the social norms of liberal democratic systems. Core psychological processes include social dominance orientation, aggression–frustration and self-aggrandizement. The behavioral manifestation is frequently reactive and in some cases spontaneous. For example, violent assaults against gay men may be a function of a socially conservative or dogmatic faith orientation concerning issues related to sexuality and gender. Motives of male dominance (Franklin, 2004) and heterosexism (Herek, 2000) may additionally serve as motivators in the perpetration of a hate crime. Conversely, while many—if not even now in many settings a numerical majority—members of the perpetrators' in-group would share these biases, the behavioral manifestation may not rise above that of endorsing stereotypes about LGBTQ persons or employing avoidance strategies to minimize intergroup contact. The active engagement, provocation, and violent perpetration targeting an LGBTQ person would therefore not be consistent with the proscribed behaviors of the majority of the perpetrators in-group. Additionally, as many hate crimes are perpetrated when there is no financial motive, these (hate) offenses are inconsistent with the motivations of many career criminals. To many offenders, hate crimes "don't make sense." So the hate-motivated offender is often engaging in violence that is not sanctioned by their in-group and is rather characteristic of personally held attitudes and experienced affects. For example, a gay-bashing offender may be acting out their anger due to conflicts with their own gender attitudes, as a function of a need for revenge for experiences of personal sexual trauma, or an idiosyncratic revulsion to gender-atypical/gender-bending behaviors of their victim. The "thinking error" is less an extreme extension of a shared social bias than it is the distortion of the underlying social attitude of the in-group concerning out-groups persons.

Sanctioning of Intergroup Violence

Experiences of intergroup violence extend beyond recognition of in-group history and the group's attendant narrative. Importantly, members of the in-group must personally sanction the use of violence to respond to intergroup problems. The sanctioning of violence constitutes a decision-making process that is inherently driven by a narrative that is congruent with the dominant biases and postulates of the group. As Allport (1954) has observed, such a bias-based narrative is inherently reductionist and therefore economical in its adherence to the social norms of the in-group. Indeed, a biased worldview often involves an anti-intellectual presentation. This declaration may include the recitation of historical facts concerning the in-group; the expression of commonly shared out-group stereotypes, the identification of recent incidents that signal conflict between the groups, or the expression of moral values that align the member with their in-group. If the in-group defines the meaningfulness of the violence—that is, the cultural coherence of the act—the member of the in-group must determine if they sanction the perpetration of violence against a specific target group. To understand this fully, it must be stressed that if the violence is incoherent to the group—that is, if the target group of violence is not explained by a shared narrative of conflict—then the violence is never sanctioned or credible. Such incoherent targets may reflect a unique motivation of the offender or constitute a crime concerned with opportunistic and material motives that have nothing to do with the victim's social in-group.

A study that looked at the role of community political activity observed this permission giving for bias during the 2016 presidential campaign. As has been argued, the candidacy of Donald Trump drew significantly on themes of anti-immigrant and anti-women ideologies (Dunbar, 2017). One indicator of the consequence of this biased rhetoric was the occurrence of physical violence at his rallies and in the communities in which he appeared. Investigative journalists noted that there were 20 violent incidents between October 2015 and June 2016 at Trump events during his campaign (Mathis-Lilley, 2016). Review of the incidents found that anti-Trump protesters instigated three of the assaults, while Trump supporters perpetrated 14 of the attacks. A link between candidate Trump's comments and this activity was not hard to establish; as in Iowa in 2016, he stated in front of his rally audience to "knock the crap out of" protesters, he additionally said he would "pay for legal fees" for any assailants (Sputniknews, 2018).

In addition to aggression perpetrated at his events, the cities where Trump rallies were held revealed a 24-hour bump in violent crimes as well. University of Pennsylvania researchers examined 31 Trump campaign rallies and 38 held by his opponent, Hillary Clinton, during the general election. They computed the number of reported assaults reported on the day of the rally and compared it to assaults reported on the corresponding day of the week, for each of the four weeks before and after the event. Findings indicated that there were 2.3 more assaults in cities where Trump rallies were held; there was no increase for the cities where Clinton rallies were held. Nationally, in 2016, U.S. cities noted an average of 19.4 violent incidents. On days when the Trump rallies were held, an average of 21.7 assaults were reported. The finding was not affected by population size of the city or day of the week in which the rallies were held (New York Times, 2018).

The literature on the motivation to perpetrate political violence has identified a number of factors that may result in the sanctioning of violence and in some cases the intention to commit ideologically motivated violence. For example, economic poverty within the social context and expressed group-based options to alleviate economic hardship have been considered as factors in collective choice for intergroup violence (CITE). What, however, explains individual decisions—a rational choice—to perpetrate intergroup violence? It has been suggested that individual choice is fueled by the perception that the in-group will provide personal rewards for violent engagement. The perpetrator, serving as an actor for the group in the commission of the violence, anticipates future rewards for their actions (MacCulloch, 2004). Personal standing in the group, influence power, and material gain may serve to motivate the individual to action in committing intergroup violence versus electing for nonparticipation.

This self-interest motivation in the commission of intergroup violence allows for the inclusion of both extrinsic and intrinsic rewards as motivators in the decision to act. However, such a rational choice theory that would lead to the commission of violence has been disputed. Ginges and Atran (2009) in a community study in Gaza found that social attitudes toward suicide bombing were more effectively explained by a commitment to a moral basis for the commission of violence, one that took preeminence over commitment to one's own family. As they explain, "these types of conflicts are more akin to intuitive moral decision making ('is this mandated or prohibited?') than to utility maximization" (p. 115). They further link the idea of a moral imperative to a sacred or religious presumption that necessitates violent engagement. This finding may also underscore the power of a collectivist society to view commitment to the group as more important than to individual relationships.

Individualism as a cultural orientation by comparison assigns personal motivation and interpretation of social relations as of greatest salience. This individualistic perspective also allows for questioning of group norms, as reflected in the famous E. M. Forster quote, "If I had to choose between betraying my country and betraying my friend, I hope I should have the guts to betray my country."

The Ginges and Atran study is compelling in its juxtaposing of a commitment to a collective moral presumption over that of a relationship to the individual's immediate family. This is instructive in terms of the cultural norms found in some societies that sanction intergroup violence. As a point of contrast, classical developmental theory in the work of Kohlberg (1984) has proposed that commitment to the family and the individual vis-à-vis that of the social collective is of greatest importance. Kohlberg's work, resulting in a model of moral development, was mostly interested in how individuals reasoned about moral issues. In Kohlberg's famous moral reasoning task of Heinz and his dilemma, the subject must reason about the legitimacy of stealing medicine for the aid it would provide to a family member. From such a Kohlbergian perspective, pre-advanced moral reasoning pitted the in-group/social norms against protecting one's family. For Kohlberg, mature complex moral reasoning esteemed personal relationships over that of obedience to the social group. In this regard, the moral perspective of Western culture esteems the challenging of doctrinal norms validated by the in-group.

Turiel (1983) has further examined the reasoning about moral questions as framed in a Western cultural tradition. He has proposed that moral reasoning involves coordinating (1) moral universals, (2) cultural traditions, and (3) social norms with questions of personal choice. The motivation to promote the well-being of the group has, of course, been observed in a variety of social psychological studies. Other forms of social action that are nonviolent similarly support the proposition that the individual participates in collective actions across cultures to increase power of the in-group, rather than as a function of personal reward (Tropp & Brown, 2004). Ginges and Atran

(2009) refer to this as a "collective commitment hypothesis" in the commission of intergroup violence. What is important to consider is that in-group identity in and of itself does not motivate an individual to perpetrate violence against out-group persons. Indeed, identity may be a component of a collective commitment. Similarly, there is a question as to whether personal status gain as a choice is sufficient to perpetrate intergroup violence. Rather, these factors may be thought of as predictors—albeit modest—of a commitment to an ideological imperative that leads to violence against an out-group target. Finally, it is plausible that it is when a cultural norm of collectivism is emphasized—particularly for individual with high-in-group identity—the probability of out-group bias is greatest (Gouveia et al., 2011). To summarize, if the act of violence is coherent to the in-group, the individual views their perpetration of violence against an out-group as sanctioned. Broadly, we can consider the status of individual sanctioning of intergroup violence as (1) endorsed, (2) ambivalent, or (3) rejected. This will be discussed elsewhere in terms of both offender identity and attitudes about violence.

Distal and Proximal Physicality of Hate Violence

A very discernible issue in studying hate crimes includes the differences between immediate up-close forms of aggression and the symbolic and interpersonally removed forms of hate. These differences in hate violence will be referred to as proximal and distal aggression. The interested reader needs to distinguish how the terms are used here from the literature in domestic violence and substance abuse, which describe factors associated with the occurrence of these phenomena (Johnson et al., 2015). In our discussion we will consider the *physicality of the aggression* as found in hate crimes in which the infraction may be verbal, symbolic, or lethal. These forms of aggression will be considered in terms of the anticipated characteristics of the perpetrators of intergroup violence.

Distal offenses represent actions where the offender and the target individual or group are interpersonally removed. The symbolic and "message" element of hate is an essential element to distal offenses. A frequent example are the graffiti crimes that target places of worship. Distal crimes also reveal the deindividuation of the target group and designated victim as a thing or a "less-than" entity. As Harry Lime, the anti-hero of the classic film *The Third Man*, says to an old friend as they look far below on to a public scene:

> Victims? Don't be melodramatic. Look down there. Tell me. Would you really feel any pity if one of those dots stopped moving forever? If I offered you twenty thousand pounds for every dot that stopped, would you really, old man, tell me to keep my money. . . ."

Proximal offenses in contrast are hands-on forms of interpersonal violence. The immediacy or proximal nature of the offense may be quite intimate. These offenses are characterized by assaults, crimes involving weapons, and altercations in which the victim tries to defend themselves. As some forensic scientists note, such violence can serve as a yardstick of the level of pathology of the offender. These offenses reflect the capacity of the offender to act (in some instances) in a highly impulsive manner; frequently alcohol and drug use may disinhibit the individual to escalate toward extreme violence. There is also ample evidence that neurobiological differences can also make some antisocial individuals prone to violent activity (Dunbar, 2017). Proximal offenses are therefore immediate in their experience and interpersonally intimate. In some cases, perpetrators of hands-on violence may even suffer from trauma symptoms due to their actions.

It may appear that, at a first impression, we think of distal crimes as less severe than proximal offenses. This is in many cases entirely untrue. Acts of arson, for example, not only may include significant damage to property but also may reveal a highly threatening message to a collective—such as members of a synagogue or mosque. The infamous racially motivated 1963 bombing of the 16th Street Baptist Church in Birmingham, Alabama, that resulted in the deaths of four young African American girls (Addie Mae Collins, Cynthia Wesley, Carole Robertson, and Carol Denise McNair) is one such instance that has haunted the memory of U.S. race relations for half a century. Another famous instance of distal ideological violence is found in the 1995 Oklahoma City bombing of a federal building in which 168 lives were lost. Similarly, drive-by shootings reflect a form of lethal violence where there is minimal proximal engagement of the offender with their victim. As violent individuals have noted, pulling a trigger and seeing someone at some distance fall is virtually unreal.

The symbolic and value-expressive nature of distal crimes—as community psychologists emphasize—communicates a threat to the collective. These offenses, which may involve graffiti or other forms of messaging inclusive of hate or gang-related crimes—may create significant disturbance and fear for a collective. The advent of social media has also led to both online terrorism and harassment of individuals (Sullaway, 2017). An issue that these threats pose includes the promise of future (and potentially proximal) forms of violence. In this sense, hate crimes, which include explicit threats—such as threats to target perceived illegal immigrants of visible ethnic minorities—are a form of the "broken windows hypothesis," in which community characteristics are indicators of an increase in subsequent criminal activity.

As we examine factors that bring individuals to perpetrate hate violence, we will also examine the nature of the crimes they commit. By looking more closely at the "who and what" of hate violence, stakeholders may be able to intervene and respond to the investigative and case management challenges these offenders pose.

Hate and Bias Ideology

Our discussion of intergroup violence is frequently complicated by concepts that are treated as being interchangeable. For example, the escalation of terrorism in this decade has led to the proposition of a "hate ideology" (Yanay, 2012); this would suggest in part that out-group attitudes have become inherently more strident and ultimately more hateful. More fundamentally, such a hate ideology hypothesis proposes that political violence is now explicitly moderated by a hatred of the targeted group. From this perspective it would be expected that the constructs of prejudice, hate behavior, and bias are significantly interrelated. Indeed, much of our contemporary discourse on hate is based on research concerning social norms of bias and stereotyping. It might therefore be difficult to consider "hate violence" as occurring without the ascription to negative stereotypes of the target victim. Similarly, it might be assumed that the acts of mass homicides that we witness in the more extraordinary forms of domestic terrorism constitute the sine qua non of hatred. The differences between hate as an emotional status and ideological signs of bias as factors in the commission of intergroup violence will be considered below.

Intergroup violence constitutes a unique challenge for keeping the peace in a civil society. The commission of bias-motivated violence is frequently a function of either a bias ideology or a state of hate, or both. These two factors may be highly intercorrelated in some situations and largely independent in others. Examining the interrelationship of beliefs (i.e., ideology) and hate can potentially inform us about the motivations to perpetrate violence. Additionally, insight into hate and ideology can help identify how individuals enter into extremist groups or, conversely, take it on themselves to function as independent actors in the commission of bias-motivated violence. If stakeholders can think clearly about the role of hate and ideology in the commission of violence, it can aid in developing strategies to intercede in the process of radicalization, as well as in the management and rehabilitation of perpetrators of these special-case offenses.

There have been prior efforts to identify within-group differences among the perpetrators of hate violence. The work of Levin and McDevitt (1993) has been widely cited in the criminal justice arena. Their typology was derived from interviews with police officials, victims, and hate crime offenders. They described three primary motivations: for excitement ("thrill"), defending of neighborhood turf, and a true believer ideology. Their subsequent work led to an expanded four-factor model (McDevitt, Levin, & Bennett, 2002). They described a typology of hate offenders inclusive of "mission type," "thrill seeking," defensive," and "retaliatory" infractions, based on review of law enforcement reports.

This author has also examined the motivational dimensions of hate offenders found in crime reports (Dunbar, 2002, 2017) and has related these differences to instrumentality and severity of the offense. Neither of these methodologies has been applied to the questions of entry, membership, and desistance from a hate-based lifestyle.

What is needed is the examination of the characteristics that may be related to, or potentially predictive of, involvement in a hate-based lifestyle, particularly in terms of the choice to perpetrate hate-based violence. Any such model may additionally be useful in terms of conceptualizing the factors of hate membership in establishing strategies for rehabilitation.

Hate as Affect Dysregulation

So what is the "hate element" of bias-motivated violence? Psychological science would suggest that it is best to consider hate as a complex interaction among socialization, language, and affect (Roginsky & Tsesis, 2015); a condition that is both transient and responsive to external stimuli—for example, provocation. As with other emotional states, hate is mediated by environmental stressors that impact the metabolic and neurological status of the individual (Dunbar, 2018). As discussed elsewhere (Dunbar, 2022), hostile intergroup attitudes reflect the activation of sensory, motor, and emotional systems in the brain. This implies that the expression of hate is itself malleable to linguistic, situational—such as intergroup contact—and shifting psycho-physiological factors—such as alcohol consumption. This hate element of the individual offender is also influenced by relatively chronic pathological states such as attention deficit hyperactive disorder, substance use, neurological insult, and the consequences of distal post-traumatic stress. These factors can be expected to affect (the level of) the perpetrator's emotional reactance, which in turn mediates the risk for commission of intergroup violence. Arguably, therefore, it is plausible to consider hate crimes as crimes of passion.

For the volatile hate offender, behavioral dysregulation can be expressed in situations of benign intergroup contact. This is in contrast to the behaviors found typically involving out-group bias; most individuals who hold prejudicial attitudes about a specific social group are inclined to avoid contact with members of the perceived out-group (Sullaway & Dunbar, 1996). This position was taken by the Pennsylvania Superior Court, in response to a defense argument involving feelings of disgust of gay individuals in the homicide of a lesbian victim: "A reasonable person would simply have discontinued his observation and left the scene" (Commonwealth v. Carr, 1990). For the labile hate offender, displays of aggression may evidence classic fight–flight behavior. Fight–flight activation has been linked to vagal nerve dysregulation, implying a more global, mind-body response to experiences of hatred. The specific neuro-pathways and brain-behavior mechanisms of bias can moderate the nature of aggression and the level of violence found in the hate offense (Dunbar, 2018).

The affect dysregulated offender plays a role in many hate-based social networks and gangs. At the same time, highly volatile members of hate gangs may prove disruptive to the in-group norming and forming needed in any group or organization. The author has examined situations in which the highly volatile offender was excluded from hate-based groups, due substantially to the erratic nature of their behavior.

At times, our conceptualization of hate violence diverges from psychological fact. For example, violence targeting sexual minorities is often attributed to "homophobia" that literally connotes a fear or "phobic" state of homosexual experience. The psychological study of anti-LGBTQ bias reveals that emotions of anger (Commonwealth v. Carr, 1990), disgust (Kahan, 1998; Olatunji & McKay, 2009), and negative affect (Olatunji, 2008) more accurately describe prejudice toward sexual minorities. As Sullaway (2004) comments, "The inference could be made that attacks in response to homosexual advances are based, not in panic and fear, but rather in feelings of disgust and a desire to punish perceived deviance." The proposition of a fear element in LGBTQ violence has been most famously debated in terms of the panic defense found in some legal defenses of hate crime offenders (Dunbar, 1999; Sullaway, 2004). This contentious issue when removed from the courtroom and applied to the review of actual LGBTQ hate crimes suggests that panic and sexual self-defense arguments are infrequently observed. In a review of 273 hate crimes targeting sexual minorities reported to a law enforcement agency, identification of the panic and sexual self-defense elements were reported in less than 2% of the incidents, whereas punishment of "sexual deviancy"—which is more aligned with the classic notion of authoritarianism—was found in 15% of the cases (Dunbar, 2017). Kahan (1998) and others (Olatunji, Lohr, & Meunier, 2002) have proposed that disgust is a function of viewing homosexuality as a threat to the social stasis and maintenance of social norms.

Viewing affect dysregulation as a precursor to intergroup violence is, however, far from complete. Many criminologists would argue that carefully planned acts of intergroup violence are more than the expression of an agitated affect state. Therefore, by comparison we need to understand how socially learned attitudes can guide individuals and groups to target specific victim groups based on race, nationality, sexual orientation, or gender.

It is also evident that intergroup violence constitutes more than simply being angered and that holding a hostile belief in and of itself may be only weakly related to a discernible ideology or worldview—particularly one that holds any coherence to the victims or the members of the perpetrator's in-group.

Hate as Ideology

For psychological investigation, it is important to consider how an emotion-based experience such as social bias can result in an act of aggression. Ideological violence includes acts of aggression committed against an out-group that is a function of the collective bias of the perpetrator's in-group. The violent act is based on the cultural coherence of animus between the in-group and the out-group. This involves the acquisition of a shared narrative of the in-group and the activation of stereotypes and biases concerning the target out-group. The components of an ideological motivation to commit bias-motivated violence includes: (a) in-group identification, (b) articulation of shared in-group biases, and (c) a collective tolerance for aggression toward social out-groups. As we have suggested, ideologically driven acts of violence are coherent—for example, meaningful—to members of the perpetrator's in-group as well as that of the target victim.

The bias ideology can be found in the targeting of numerous individuals and communities. The belief-based violence of race and anti-immigration may also reveal itself in terms of anti-LGBTQ violence. Additionally, hate violence as ideology may also show itself in terms of culturally embedded notions of entitlement by whiteness and hostility toward women, as has recently been observed in the incel groups of North America. These belief-based targets of hate may be framed in terms of punishment of deviancy, in-group revenge, or community/national efforts of protection of the in-group.

In his analysis of the origins of fascism, Paxton (2004) has noted how the ideological basis of this political movement was quintessentially vague. From a historical analysis of authoritarianism, Paxton argues that fascism only marginally reflects an epistemological inquiry. Rather, fascism constitutes a collective, emotion-driven presumption of social grievances driven by a (inherently) worldview. As he noted, fascism is an amorphous political system; the role of deep cultural assumptions would therefore be expected to influence the rise of inherently xenophobic and hostile social norms. Paxton notes that fascism is manifested by behaviors more than by beliefs. As such, fascism is more a psychological than an intellectual experience for its members. Further, deep culture norms may facilitate the advent of fascism and as an alternative to traditional political postulates of democratic liberties (Payne, 1996).

For Paxton and others, ultranationalism becomes an alternative to intergroup inclusion. He argues that the enactment of universal suffrage, giving the right to vote to all citizens, is an example of the triggering phenomena, which the fascism reacts against. More recently, legislated hate crime initiatives, which are the product of democratic political systems (Dunbar, 2017), have similarly been criticized by right-wing pundits. Fascists were preoccupied with community decline and collective humiliation. In-group victimhood was resolved via adopting ultranationalist ideology. What is important for the study of hate violence is how ultranationalist, fascist attitudes are predicated on core cultural norms, sanctioned intergroup aggression, and the rejection of the inclusive politics of liberal democracy.

Such a hate-based ideology, from the author's clinical experience, is not based on a rigorous dialectic inquiry or process of experimentation; rather, the core function of a hate ideology is to provide an explanation for social problems encountered by the individual and understood in terms of the experiences of his or her in-group. This owes a lot more to Allport's application of the law of least effort in prejudice (1954) than to some carefully wrought Hegelian means of inquiry. This is more aligned with Paxton's understanding of fascism. As such, hate violence reflects how the individual expends a minimum of cognitive energy in choosing to engage in an act of violence, which again is consistent with Paxton's observation it is action and not complex ideation that constitutes the experience of fascism. The offender's hate ideology does not adhere to a set of ethical presumptions. As proposed by Paxton, it is the absence of a clear set of rules or actions that characterizes extremist ideology. This intellectual, and ultimately moral, ambiguity therefore allows individuals to act out their hostility toward social out-groups based on social cues, on the one hand, and internal psychobiological forces on another. The ideological motivation of many hate offenders is essentially ideational, that is, ruminative and perseverative. It is not unlike homicidal ideation (Thienhaus & Piasecki, 1998); the individual experiences a range of stereotypes or biased attitudes that incorporate a range of beliefs that may be vague and inarticulate or fixed and rigid. This "ideation as ideology" may incorporate the classic psychological drivers of revenge, social dominance, or punishment of deviancy. This motivational network of biased beliefs can be articulated—if often superficially—by the perpetrator.

It is central to our line of inquiry to consider how identity and ideology are dynamic experiences of the individual that are forever changing. Therefore, contextual and institutional forces may profoundly shape and reshape a hate-based worldview. For example, law enforcement professionals frequently comment on the tit-for-tat nature of many community hate crimes between race/ethnic groups. Symbolic message-type offenses often escalate actions of retributional violence in gang-on-gang violence. Similarly, incarceration of offenders of many forms of intergroup violence results in the strengthening of their in-group identity and out-group animus. Incarceration can amplify ideology at a juncture where many antisocial individuals are vulnerable and isolated from community supports. We also see how punishing an individual's biased beliefs may only enhance their resistance to a more balanced perspective on in-group and out-group relationships.

The ideological motive that the perpetrator experiences as legitimizing the commission of hate violence can be declared and described in a manner that is culturally coherent. Typical forms of ideological violence include weaponized conflict between members of independent nation-states or tribes, conflict between varying religious sects, and domestic terrorism between social groups within the nation-state. Of course, no social movement is all of one thing or another. Likewise, individuals who are actors of cultural and political violence vary among themselves as well. The distinctions between such prototypical ideological and affect-disturbed hate offenders are summarized in what follows.

The Interplay of Emotion and Ideology in Intergroup Violence

As has been discussed, there are important distinctions between ideology and emotionality in the commission of intergroup violence. We can consider an act of hate aggression in terms of two motivating factors, bias ideology and affect dysregulation. Table 2-4 below details the prototypical characteristics of varying forms of intergroup violence. The interrelationship between bias ideology and impulsive forms of hate has both theoretical and practical importance.

Distinctions we can draw in terms of how hate and ideology shape issues of intergroup violence. When considered in terms of relative presence and absence as these factors, we can anticipate differences in individual and group actions in the carrying out of the bias-motivated offense. In Table 2-1 below, four prototypical motivational types are considered, based on the ideology by arousal characteristics of the individual offender.

A brief summary of these offender patterns is provided below.

Table 2-1 Four Status Conditions of Arousal and Ideology in Commission of Hate Violence

		Ideology	
		Low	High
Arousal	Low	Context-mediated Spontaneous	Premeditated soldier Mission-style lone wolf Suicide bomber
	High	Impulsive/reactive Spontaneous lone wolf	True believer Revenge terrorism

Willing Followers

The first cluster of offenders we will consider are individuals who evidence minimal ideology or hateful emotions. These willing followers subscribe to the ideology of the group and value membership as potentially identity-affirming. At the same time, they are less reactive to intergroup contact and not as engaged in a hate-based lifestyle as others subscribing to the group or ideology. Ezekiel (1995) describes these individuals in the hate groups he interviewed in his field research in the mid-1990s. He describes the need for belonging of the young men from fatherless homes who viewed their lives as marginalized. As with other forms of criminal gangs, the group became a primary place for membership and identity. Kimmel (2018) has likewise discussed the anger and frustration he encountered in talking with members of right-wing extremist groups in the United States. What needs to be considered is that men, specifically white men, in the United States today may enter into a hate-based lifestyle simply to find a place for community and shared grievances.

What is important to consider is that acts of aggression are committed against members of social out-groups continuously in which the perpetrating party does not express nor evidence a strong emotional reaction against the target person, nor does the individual articulate a belief system that is organized in terms of denigration of the out-group. Nonviolent forms of discrimination are commonly found in situations involving competition for material reward—the work of Muzafer Sherif (Sherif, 1958; Sherif et al., 1961) provides but one such example—or in the enforcing of institutional forms of discrimination. This latter case may be found in terms of legal professionals who work for organizations that engage in racial minority voter suppression or airline employees who remove Middle Eastern customers from commercial flights. These individuals are simply carrying out the proscribed functions their employing organizations require. Similarly, there is extensive research on implicit attitudes that details how individuals readily and (arguably) unconsciously engage in the utilization of negative stereotypes of out-group persons. Such "prejudiced" individuals typically deny holding such aversive beliefs against minority populations. So there is ample evidence from psychological science that has found discriminatory attitudes and behaviors occur in which the actor denies any discernible animus toward the target out-group person.

The above arguments of how bias is observed in seemingly non-biased persons are, however, not explicitly related to intergroup violence. We need to consider, then, how and when low-bias participants engage in interpersonal violence. Such instances can be found in crimes committed by criminal gangs that are formed along race/ethnic lines. Gang behavior may include the commission of hate crimes, due principally to the intention to control illicit markets—for example, the drug trade—or to control neighborhoods in which they strive to maintain dominance. Gang-on-gang violence may indeed be racialized, but the ascription to a specific racial/ethnic out-group ideology may be minimal.

For the willing followers, hate aggression is frequently group based and distal, the targets are often institutions—inclusive of mosques and synagogues—or targeting of anonymous and vulnerable individuals. Physiological reactions may be more situation-contingent, that is, the individual may become aroused through the incident but is not otherwise agitated or aggressive in their exposure to out-group stimuli. These group members are likely compliant with the directives of more influential members of the group. What has been referred to as an "oxytocin hypothesis" would explain the sense of bonding found for the low-labile and low-ideology willing follower. This is summarized in Table 2-2.

More extraordinary forms of intergroup violence may also involve persons who do not per se manifest hatred of a social group nor who may express a discernible ideological motive. The author once talked with an individual who had been at a public lynching; he said he "thought it was like being at a football rally." A well-documented example of group-based hate violence is found in the World War II solders of German Reserve Police Battalion 101 (Browning, 1992). This unit of policemen from Hamburg was responsible for the massacre of Polish Jews in 1942. While a war crime, the critical issue in this case of genocide was the absence of any political or xenophobic orientation of the perpetrators of violence. This phenomenon has been seen in many death squads, where members are socialized to perform mass killings as a prerequisite to group membership (Davies-Rubio, Abarca, & Redondo, 2017).

Table 2-2 Characteristics of Prototypical Offenders: Willing Followers

(low ideology and low arousal)

1. Group Orientation
   Socially bonded and adherent to group norms
2. Nature of Aggression
   Opportunistic target
   Distal aggression
   Response to perceived provocation
   Identity-affirming role of aggression
3. Neurobiological Status
   Oxytocin hypothesis motivation

Calculated Believers

A second form of hate aggression is marked by a strong ideological motive where there is an absence of reactive aggression—that is, when the aggression is controlled rather than impulsive. We can describe these individuals as calculated believers, where violence is driven by ideology and where arousal is largely absent.

I must comment that any pundit of hate crime laws who says "all crimes are hateful" has met my definition of idiocy. The author has evaluated and treated far too many offenders who demonstrate no particular animus toward their victims. Career criminals, while perhaps highly antisocial, do not view their victims with animus but rather engage in aggression to meet material needs. This is true of many crimes involving burglary, robbery, and white-collar money crimes, for example, as well as drug-related offenses. It can be argued that a hate crime may be substantially absent any sign of true hatred. How do we explain such a seeming disconnect? Let us consider what some of our reported hate crimes include.

The planned high-ideology offenses have a significant symbolic component to them with intent to terrorize communities and specific cultural groups. As such, the messaging of the ideology is the primary goal of these offenders. The actual victims become secondary to the harm intended to the larger social context. The politically motivated domestic terrorists may engage in planned forms of violence, where messaging of the ideology may include verbal statements at the time of commission of the offense, or published manifestos on social media, which links the act to a specific cultural or political goal. The characteristics of this class of offenders—the calculated believers—are summarized in Table 2-3.

Table 2-3 Characteristics of Prototypical Offenders: Calculated Believers (High-Ideology and Low-Affect Dysregulation)

1. Group Orientation
   Frequent lone wolf actor
2. Forms of Aggression
   Clear goal and target—instrumental aggression
   Rehearsed aggression
   Message offense
   Predatory target approach
3. Neurobiological Features
   Minimal arousal
   Frontal CNS-moderated aggression

The issue of arousal is, for this class of offender, tempered by the dominating role of belief and execution of the offense to maximize threat to the target group. Higher cortical structures in the central nervous system regulate excitatory pathways. The psychophysiology is more predatory and stalker-like than aroused and impulsive. The psychological goal is realized via the execution and communication of the ideology rather than in the action of invoking harm to the unique target victim. This self-regulation is in service of attaining a greater impact on the larger social context.

Another single-offender assault is found in the widely publicized Charleston murder of African American church members by Dylann Roof, a young white man. As in the San Bernardino case, the June 2015 homicides in Charleston were committed by an offender with an articulated bias ideology, a close-at-hand nature of the killings (Roof had spent a few hours in a prayer meeting with his victims prior to shooting them), as well as the premeditated nature of the homicides. Roof reportedly targeted the Mother Emanuel Church, due to the historical significance of the church within the African-American community. What is interesting is how the head of the FBI, James Comey, viewed this offense as a hate crime and not an act of terror. The U.S. Department of Justice did not charge Roof with domestic terrorism, or include terrorism in the indictment, even though U.S. attorney general Loretta Lynch stated the Charleston shootings were "racially motivated violence" that constituted "the original type of domestic terrorism." In contrast, former attorney general Eric Holder told an online news source that Charleston was clearly an act of terrorism (NewsOne, 2015). The spate of violent, ideological offenses witnessed in the United States has furthered speculation as to the distinction of hate and ideologically motivated offenses (CNN, 2017).

A highly publicized incident concerned the San Bernardino, California, terror attack in 2015. This well-known case of mass killings received national attention at the time. The incident involved the shooting of government coworkers of one of the two perpetrators, Syed Rizwan, who, along with his wife Tashfeen Malik, murdered 14 individuals in December 2015. The incident has been attributed to the offender's adoption of a radical anti-Western ideology. The ideological element of this offense is quite evident; the level of arousal (the *hatefulness* of the offenders) was tempered by the premeditated nature of the homicides.

The premeditated motivation of this offense was discussed by the couple online in 2013 before they were married. Malik had declared her allegiance to the Islamic State on social media shortly before the homicides. Their motivation for conducting jihad was, as such, more salient than Rizwan's relationship with his coworkers at a county health department—which supposedly in some cases was contentious (New York Times, 2015). In this case the head of the FBI, James Comey, described the homicides as an act of terrorism and acknowledged the entrenched element of bias ideology—"ISIL inspiration may well have been part of this, but these two killers were starting to radicalize towards martyrdom and jihad as early as 2013" (New York Times, 2015). This offense incorporates a discernible bias ideology, as well as a history of animosity between one of the offenders and (some) of the victims. It is also premeditated and involved proximal (e.g., close-at-hand) violence perpetrated by the killer.

Another well-publicized incident involved the homicide of an international student from Ethiopia in Portland, Oregon. In this case, a prominent ideologue promoted the idea of racial violence to his followers. Thomas Linton Metzger had been a notorious representative for white racists in North America for decades. Through his cable television programming and as leader of the White Aryan Resistance (WAR) group, Metzger promoted racial violence as a means of creating a white United States. His solicitation of violence led in 1988 to white skinheads targeting and murdering a black man of Ethiopian nationality in Portland. This case incorporates the aspects of hate solicitation, the explicit messaging, the linkage of violence as a solution to racial problems, and his sanctioning of action as consistent with the ideological cause that WAR supported.

Labile Bigots

In contrast to the planned and belief-driven offenders, the affect-dysregulated perpetrator of hate violence may commit an offense where there is little to no premeditation. It is also found that for some of these offenders—whom we will label as "labile bigots"—a chronic pattern of impulse disturbance and antisocial behavior will include a hate motivation in some but not all of the potentially multiple infractions these highly stress-reactive individuals evince. These individuals engage in a particularly violent form of stereotype activation where the hostility leads to spontaneous aggression in situations that are frequently unprovoked by the victim. These individuals experience significant psychophysiological arousal and a highly excitatory and impulsive response to aversive stimuli. There is minimal higher cortical regulation of these aggressive impulses to attack (perceived) out-group persons. Violence driven by affect disturbance with minimal ideology is summarized in Table 2-4.

Violent Extremists

Hate violence is, of course, also perpetrated by individuals who evidence both marked emotionality and a discernible ideology. Membership for these individuals may include a process of socialization in which the ideological motive may evolve over time. High-ideological offenders may constitute the

Table 2-4 Characteristics of Prototypical Offenders: Labile Bigot (Low Ideology and High Arousal)

1. Group Orientation
   Violent member of group, may function independently
2. Nature of Aggression
   Highly stress-reactive
   Spontaneous targeting
   Opportunistic target
   Attributed to perceived provocation or self-defense
3. Neurobiological Status
   Impulsive and aroused
   Limbic/amygdala activation
   Fight reaction

true believer hate member. What this can be seen in developmentally is how offenders in the middle thirties (and older) may evidence a range of behavioral traces of a hate orientation (Dunbar, 2017). This may include prior arrests for hate violence, an explicit endorsement of a hate belief system, involvement with other hate group members, or the presence of hate symbols—including tattoos—at the time of commission of a hate crime. For the highly socialized hate extremist, their role in a group may be influential on other members, and they may play a highly instrumental role in motivating others to perpetrate bias-motivated violence.

There are cases where there is both an ideological and high-emotion element. One well-documented example is found with James Fields, who drove his automobile into a crowd protesting at an alt-right ("Unite the Right") rally in Charlottesville, Virginia, in 2017, killing Heather Heyer, one of the counterprotesters. Fields, who evidenced many of the features of a labile and hate-identified offender, had been involved with the alt-right movement for several years prior to Charlottesville. A fatherless child, he was socially isolated when young and by high school showed a preoccupation with the history of the Nazis. Not quite two years prior to the homicide at Charlottesville, Fields had briefly been enlisted in the U.S. Army and associated with symbols of Vanguard America, an anti-government group opposed to social equality. Fields, who pled guilty to federal hate crime charges, had a long-standing behavioral pattern of extreme bias. A former classmate describes Fields as being happy while visiting Dachau concentration camp in Germany. "On a trip to Europe, the defendant came alive when they visited a Nazi concentration camp where Jews were exterminated by the thousands, claiming, 'this is where the magic happened' and acting 'like a kid at Disney World. Like he was loving it.'" The prosecution in this case noted that "The crowd angered him. They stood for everything that he had grown to hate, and he viewed them as the enemy. . . ." Motivated by his hatred of African Americans, Jewish people and anyone he considered non-white, he pressed the gas pedal and accelerated down the hill (Hammell & Knott, 2019).

Another example of the high-ideology and high-emotionality offender is found in the lone wolf terror attack by white supremacist Buford Furrow. Furrow was an underling in the White Aryan Resistance organization. In the summer of 1999, he traveled from the state of Washington to the metropolitan Los Angeles area, intent on attacking a Jewish cultural center. He subsequently targeted a Jewish daycare center in the San Fernando Valley region of Los Angeles. When he attacked the center, there were 250 children in attendance. Using a submachine gun, he sprayed from right to left, getting off more than 70 rounds. He injured three children, a program counselor, and the center receptionist. At this point he left the center grounds and carjacked a vehicle; and, using a Glock handgun, he shot to death Joseph Ileto, a Filipino-American and U.S. Postal employee who was delivering the mail. In his abandoned van, he had ammunition, rifle magazines, and explosive devices. He also had copies of *The Story of the Phineas Priesthood*, Christian identity books, and other ideology-based writings. Furrow surrendered to the FBI in Las Vegas, Nevada, and stated he had sought to promote the murder of Jews. He was sentenced to life in prison; his legal defense team argued that Furrow suffered from serious psychiatric problems. Furrow's motivation was articulated both in his words and literature and via his association with a hate organization. His crime was carried out independently of other cohorts and was absent direction from any third party. His ideological motivation is clear. The offense itself, while directed at a secondary target—the initial sites were too well protected—was clearly premeditated. At the same time, his assault evidenced a high level of (offender) arousal and confusion. There were countless defenseless targets at the daycare center that he did not pursue. It is therefore likely that his hate state was elevated at the time of the attack. Table 2-5 summarizes the dynamics of this offender type.

On a case-by-case basis it is possible to see the presence and absence of both emotionality and bias ideology that fuel out-group violence. What we will now consider is how these factors are related to hate crimes in terms of the perpetrator and victims they targeted, and the nature of the types of offenses recorded by law enforcement.

Evidence-Based Examination of Affect and Hate Ideology

To examine the role of affect dysregulation and hate ideology, a reanalysis of data collected to study bias motivation (Dunbar, 2017) was conducted. The study included 555 hate crimes cases reported to a metropolitan law

Table 2-5 Characteristics of Prototypical Offenders: Violent Extremist (high Ideological and high affect dysregulation)

1.	Group Orientation
	Instrumental and influential within group, advocate of or actor of violence
2.	Forms of Aggression
	Clear goal and target—instrumental aggression
	Message offense
	Gratuitous violence
	Predatory target approach
3.	Neurobiological features
	Frontal CNS activation
	In situ arousal

enforcement agency. Analyses were conducted by a research team; ratings were assigned for the criminal charges, the instrumentality, and the bias element of the index offense. The infractions were classified by law enforcement personnel for primary hate motivation, with 53% (n =2 94) attributed to race/ethnicity 17% to religion (n = 96), 23% to sexual orientation (n = 130), and 6% to other infractions—such as gender and disability. Criminal infractions recorded in the crime reports included 32% for violence against the person—including assault (12%), assault with a weapon (11%), and attempted murder/homicide (2%). Vandalism to property was reported for 16% of the cases; the use of verbal threats was noted for 45% of the cases.

Level of Offender Arousal: this was based on review of the crime report and supporting documents. Analyses of the infractions employed the Cornell rating system (Cornell et al., 1996) of instrument and reactive aggression. The four-point scale for offender arousal was included in our analyses. Ratings on this scale were assigned for offender arousal as "calm" (29% of the cases), "excited" (48% of the cases), "angry" (17% of the cases), and "enraged/out of control" (less than 1% of the cases). For suspects who were apprehended (n = 401), there was a significant age-by-arousal relationship (F (398,3) = 5.63, $p <$ .001) with adolescents and offenders under 25 years having lower arousal than those over the age of 25—the age band of 25- to 35-year-old offenders were the most aroused of the offender groups. Level of arousal in perpetrating the offense did not vary for infractions based on race/ethnic, sexual orientation, and religious hatred.

Level of Offender Hate Ideology: this was also determined via report review. Analyses were based on ratings using the Bias Motivation Profile-Revised (BMP-R) for (1) expressed racial ideology, (2) expressed religious ideology, and (3) expressed ideology against sexual minorities. Among all of the offenses (n = 555), 39.8 percent of the cases (n = 221) met one or more of these BMP-R criteria. Race/ethnic bias ideology was found for roughly one-half of the infractions (31.6% clearly present and 19.1% implied/possible), for religious bias in 20% of the infractions (15.1% clearly present and 5.4% implied/possible), and for bias toward sexual minorities roughly a quarter of the infractions (19.4% clearly present and 4.6% implied/possible).

Offender Typology and Hate Aggression: Based on the ratings, a two-by-two classification was computed for the identified offenders. The cases were classified into low-arousal (calm and excited) and high-arousal (angered and enraged) categories along with the BMP-R criteria for one or more of hate ideology criteria (high versus low) as described above. These four categories placed 149 offenders in the willing follower group, 159 as calculated believers, 65 as labile bigots, and 29 as (violent) hate extremists. The average age of these offender categories was 28.5 for willing followers, 26.8 for calculating believers, and 29.46 for hate extremists. Interestingly, the labile bigots tended to be older than the others with a mean age of 35.2. This information is summarized in Table 2-6.

In examining the presence of the three indicators employed to define hate ideology, Chi-square computations found that evidence of religious hate

Table 2-6 Offender Typology by Law Enforcement Hate Crime Classification

Ideology by arousal:	**Willing follower (low/low)**	**Calculated offender (high/low)**	**Labile bigot (low/high)**	**Hate extremist (high/high)**
Percent of sample:	**48.8%**	**34.2%**	**7.7%**	**9.2**
Age	29	27	35	30
Male gender	80%	88%	90%	90%
Single offender	22%	27%	85%	61%
Violent infraction	15%	41%	42%	67%
Material reward	18%	5%	20%	6%
Distance from home[a]	1.8	3.5	>.75	9.1
Instrumental aggression	77%	81%	44%	76%
Group/gang member	44%	66%	3%	50%
Anonymous victim	65%	76%	70%	86%

Sample 555 hate crimes.

[a] distance of infraction from the offender's home

ideology was greatest for the two of the four groups ($X^2 = 39.01$, $p < .001$). The presence of race/ethnic hate ideology was "clearly present" for nearly one-half of the calculated offenders (44.6%) and extremist offenders (43.9%) versus less than one-fifth of the willing follower (21.5%) and labile bigot groups (10.8%). This underscores the relationship of premeditation and race-based hate ideology in the commission of hate crimes. Infractions related to religious hate identity were almost exclusively committed by offenders who evidenced low level of arousal. Slightly less than 20% of the willing followers (18.5%) and the calculated believers (17.5%) evidenced a clear religious hate ideology. The presence of a clear hate ideology targeting sexual minorities was found for one-quarter of the calculated offenders (25.3%), and nearly one-half of the hate extremists (45.1%) evidenced a stated hatred for sexual minorities.

The rating of the severity of hate offense—using the Cornell rating scale—indicated the hate extremists perpetrated more violent hate crimes than the other three groups (F (3,398) = 6.95, $p < .01$). The primary inferences of the data would suggest the willing follower is involved in less violent hate infractions; they were nearly as likely to target victims due to religious and sexual orientation bias as race/ethnic bias. Roughly a tenth of these offenders were considered to have engaged in prior hate violence. These individuals made up about one–half (48.8%) of the offenders identified in this sample.

The calculated offender—similarly to the willing follower—frequently perpetrated crimes against victims due to religious and sexual orientation bias. They were the most likely to evidence prior hate criminality and most typically engaged in crimes where there was no material—for example, extrinsic—motive. In contrast to the willing follower, these offenders very frequently engaged in violent crimes against the person—for example, assault or use of a weapon. These offenders were the most likely to be affiliated with a hate group or criminalized gang. Approximately a third (34.2%) of the sample were characterized by this low-arousal/high-ideology type.

The least frequent of the offender types was the labile bigot. These high arousal, lower-ideology offenders perpetrated offenses that were classically "lone wolf" infractions. They very infrequently showed a group/gang affiliation and almost always engaged in a violent offense. These offenders tended to be relatively older than other offender groups—having a mean age of 35. The majority of these offenders were identified by law enforcement as having targeted their victims based on race or ethnic group membership. These offenders often engaged in crimes that were less than a mile from their identified residence. The offenders made up roughly 8% of the current sample.

The highly aroused and highly bias-motivated offenders—the violent extremist—in our sample made up a small number of the cases, roughly 9%. These offenders would commit hate crimes typically outside of their immediate neighborhoods—traveling on average 10 miles from where they were

Table 2-7 Offender Typology by Law Enforcement Hate Crime Classification

Ideology by arousal:	Willing follower (low/low)	Calculated offender (high/low)	Labile bigot (low/high)	Hate extremist (high/high)
Percent of sample:	**48.8%**	**34.2%**	**7.7%**	**9.2**
Hate speech	87%	92%	89%	98%
Hate symbols	24%	20%	0%	21%
Defended neighborhood	23%	52%	22%	53%
Prior hate activity	11%	21%	2%	4%
Bias Motivation				
Race/ethnicity	53.32%	59.1%	70.7%	56.4%
Religion	26.6%	14%	4.9%	18.4%
Sexual orientation	19.7%	26.9%	24.4%	25%

Sample 555 hate crimes.

living at the time of the index offense. More than one-half of these offenders engaged in offenses by themselves, though they were often affiliated with a hate group or criminalized gang. Virtually all of these offenders committed a hate crime that was violent. There was very infrequently evidence of a prior relationship between the victim and the offender.

In the crime report and case review, additional information was coded and is presented in Table 2-7.

Hate, Ideology, and Belonging: Motives for Engagement in Violent Groups

This author has his own reservations as to the utility of the hate-versus-ideology distinction as being comprehensive enough to examine the motivations and actions of any individual hate crime offender. There are always numerous other factors not accounted for in this or any other typology to assign risk for future violence. Any such classification method can aid in how we think about the perpetrators of hate violence. A psychological approach to hate perpetration needs to critically consider the factors that contribute to the prevention, interdiction, and management of offenders of hate crimes/domestic terror.

It is particularly important to draw a further distinction, psychologically, between what I will call the solicitation into a hate lifestyle versus recruitment into a violent ideology group. There are practical distinctions to consider. Solicitation involves the communication of an explicitly biased belief system, the promotion of violence as a solution to the problems as defined by the biased belief system, and the sanctioning of violence by individuals to engage the problems defined by the belief system. The solicitation to hate and violence is viable on an individual basis and may occur without direct contact with other hate-identified individuals. The FBI and the Department of Homeland Security reviewed right-wing violence perpetrated in the United States from 2000 to 2016. It was reported that singular offenders ("lone actors") and "small cells" perpetrated a significant number of the acts of domestic terrorism during this period (DocumentCloud, 2017). The report commented that white supremacist extremists (WSE) will pose a threat of spontaneous and opportunistic violence for the future.

While some of the perpetrators of hate violence are members of extremist groups, the FBI report underscores that many offenders operate outside of the context of an organized network. More recently, FBI director Christopher Wray stated that the bureau documented "about the same number" of domestic terrorism incidents as offenses attributable to international terrorism. He stated that the majority of domestic terror incidents were perpetrated by white supremacists. Wray noted that he considered "homegrown violent extremists" to be the greatest threat to the United States (Newsweek, 2019).

It is interesting that the concept of ideological radicalization has been largely ignored in the literature on hate crimes. It seems—superficially—that radicalization happens *elsewhere*. The plethora of books and writings on jihadism in the West has captured—and arguably fetishized—the collective attention of Western society. This is a function, no doubt, of the events of 9/11, the ongoing ideological wars in the Middle East, and the wave of Islamic terrorism in Europe. What this has accomplished, in some degree, is the collective distancing of bias and violence as being an external threat imposed on civil societies *from elsewhere* that are carried out by *the other*. Our social order and we, ourselves, are not per se the issue. This externalization of the problem—we can say the offshoring of hate—creates its share of practical problems. As one international affairs professional said to me, it is hard to promote a civil society agenda—or that of a liberal democratic tradition—when persons in other societies observe how poorly it is being run in our own countries. Yet how do we describe the evolution of an individual born and raised in a country becoming violently opposed to their fellow citizens?

Conclusion

Violence itself constitutes a core experience of the species and the cultural traditions of our social groups, and intergroup violence is nothing new under the sun. However, in our current society, the commission of intergroup violence serves as a bellwether of cultural change. Hate violence threatens the dominant model of governance but not per se the deeper cultural traditions of the group. As such, hate violence is in opposition to both conventional liberal and conservative models of governance.

Our study of individual psychological factors of ideology and arousal underscores differences in the perpetration of bias-motivated violence. We have tried to consider the differences in highly hateful acts of impulse from those of planned and rehearsed forms of bias-motivated violence. Investigating the how and what of hate violence can be useful in the detection of and intervention with potential hate perpetrators. Furthermore, this process involves the sequencing of specific brain-behavior processes that need to mobilize aggressive urges and the directing of these impulses against specific individuals or institutions. This two-factor model may also provide insight into the perpetrator's choice to commit hate crimes and their capacity for rehabilitation.

References

Allport, G. W. (1954). *The nature of prejudice*. Cambridge, MA: Addison-Wesley.

Bar-Tal, D. (2013). *Intractable conflicts: Socio-psychological foundations and dynamics*. Cambridge, UK: Cambridge University Press.

Berkowitz, L., & Macaulay, J. (1971). The contagion of criminal violence. *Sociometry*, 34(2), 238–260. https://doi.org/10.2307/2786414

Browning, C. (1992). *Ordinary men: Reserve Police Battalion 101 and the final solution in Poland*. New York, NY: HarperCollins.

Chermak, S. M., Freilich, J. D., & Shemtob, Z. (2009). Law enforcement training and the domestic far right. *Criminal Justice and Behavior*, 36(12), 1305–1322.

CNN. (2015). Race and reality in America: Five key findings. https://www.cnn.com/2015/11/24/us/race-reality-key-findings/

CNN. (2017). When is a crime a hate crime and when is it terrorism? https://www.cnn.com/2017/04/19/us/hate-crime-or-terrorism-definition-trnd/index.html

Commonwealth v. Carr, 580 A.2d 1362,1363 (Pa. Super. Ct. 1990).

Cornell, D. G., Warren, J., Hawk, G., Stafford, E., Oram, G., & Pine, D. (1996). Psychopathy in instrumental and reactive violent offenders. *Journal of Consulting and Clinical Psychology*, 64(4), 783–790.

Davies-Rubio, A., Abarca, A.B., & Redondo, L.M. (2017). Hate and revenge in the life of a repented killer. In E. Dunbar, A. Blanco, D. A. Crèvecoeur-MacPhail, C. Munthe, M. Fingerle, & D. Brax (Eds.), *The psychology of hate crimes as domestic terrorism: US and global issues* (pp. 263-278). Santa Barbara, CA: Praeger.

DocumentCloud. (2017, May 10). White supremist extremism poses persistent threat of lethal violence. https://www.documentcloud.org/documents/3924852-White-Supremacist-Extremism-JIB.html

Dunbar, E. (1999). Defending the indefensible: A critique and analysis of psycholegal defense arguments of hate crime perpetrators. *Journal of Contemporary Criminal Justice,* 15(1), 64–77.

Dunbar E. (2017). Employing a criterion-based strategy to assess the bias component of hate crime perpetration: Its utility for offender risk assessment and intervention. In E. Dunbar, A. Blanco, D. A. Crèvecoeur-MacPhail, C. Munthe, M. Fingerle, & D. Brax (Eds.), *The psychology of hate crimes as domestic terrorism: U.S. and global issues.* Santa Barbara, CA: Praeger.

Dunbar, E. (2018). *Hate unleashed: America's cataclysmic change.* Santa Barbara, CA: Praeger.

Dunbar, E. (2022). The neuroscience of hate and bias ideology: A brain-behavior perspective on bias aggression. In E. Dunbar (Ed.), *Indoctrination to hate: Recruitment techniques of hate groups and how to stop them.* Santa Barbara, CA: Praeger.

Dunbar, E., & Blanco, A. (2013). Psychological perspectives on culture, violence, and intergroup animus: Evolving traditions in the bonds that tie and hate. In F. Leong (Ed.), *APA Handbook of Multicultural Psychology* (pp. 378–399). Washington, DC: APA.

Eidelson, R., & McCauley, C. (2010). U.S. polls: Public opinion and right-wing extremism. https://www.dhs.gov/sites/default/files/publications/OPSR_TP_START_Research-US-Public-Opinion-Right-Wing-Extremism-Report_Apr2010-508.pdf

Ezekiel, R. (1995). *The racist mind: Portraits of American neo-Nazis and Klansmen.* New York: Viking Penguin.

FBI. (2010). Hate crime statistics 2010. https://www.fbi.gov/about-us/cjis/ucr/hate-crime/2010/resources/hate-crime-2010-hate-crime-statistics-act

Focus on Essential Issues. (2013, February 3). Lombard victims of heinous hate crimes: Unique approaches for a unique type of crime—prosecuting hate crimes. https://focusonessentialissues.blogspot.com/2013/02/

Franklin, K. (2004). Enacting masculinity: Antigay violence and group rape as participatory theater. *Sexuality Research and Social Policy,* 1(2), 25–35.

Ginges, J., & Atran, S. (2009). What motivates participation in violent political action: Selective incentives or parochial altruism? *Annals of the New York Academy of Sciences,* 1167(1), 115–123.

Gouveia, V. V., Milfont, T. L., Martínez, M. C., & Paterna, C. (2011). Individualism-collectivism as predictors of prejudice toward Gypsies in Spain. *Revista interamericana de psicología/Interamerican Journal of Psychology,* 45(2), 223–233.

The Guardian. (2015). What are Europeans afraid of most? http://www.theguardian.com/world/2015/feb/05/europe-europeans-fears-terrorism-unemployment-pandemics

Hammel, T., & Knott, K. (2019, June 19). Memorandum: Fields showed pattern of hateful behavior. https://dailyprogress.com/news/memorandum-fields-showed-pattern-of-hateful-behavior/article_594bb29c-9478-11e9-bac4-53df1637a9e9.html

Herek, G. M. (2000). The psychology of sexual prejudice. *Current Directions in Psychological Science*, 9(1), 19–22.

Hofstede, G. (1984). *Culture's consequences: International differences in work-related values* (2nd ed.). Beverly Hills, CA: SAGE Publications.

Hofstede, G. H., Hofstede, Gert J., & Minkov, M. (2010). *Cultures and organizations: Software of the mind* (3rd ed.). New York, NY: McGraw-Hill.

Huang, L. L., Liu, J. H., & Chang, M. (2004). "The double identity" of Taiwanese Chinese: A dilemma of politics and culture rooted in history. *Asian Journal of Social Psychology*, 7(2), 149–168.

HuffPost. (2017, September 16). Most Americans oppose white supremacists, but many share their views: Poll. https://www.huffpost.com/entry/reuters-poll-white-supremacist-views_n_59bc155fe4b02da0e141b3c8

Institute on Race Relations (IRR). (2015). Racial violence statistics. https://www.irr.org.uk /research/statistics/racial-violence

Johnson, K. L., Desmarais, S. L., Grimm, K. J., Tueller, S. J., Swartz, M. S., & Van Dorn, R. A. (2016). Proximal risk factors for short-term community violence among adults with mental illnesses. *Psychiatric Services*, 67(7), 771–778.

Kahan, D. M. (1998). The anatomy of disgust in criminal law. *Michigan Law Review*, 96(6), 1621–1657.

Kalra, G., & Bhugra, D. (2013). Sexual violence against women: Understanding cross-cultural intersections. *Indian Journal of Psychiatry*, 55(3), 244–249.

Kehew, R., Pound, E., & Snodgrass, W. D. (2005). *Lark in the morning: The verses of the troubadours, a bilingual edition* (English and French Edition). Chicago, IL: University of Chicago Press.

Kersten, J. (1996). Culture, masculinities, and violence against women. *British Journal of Criminology*, 36(3), 381–395.

Kimmel, M. (2018). *Healing from hate: How young men get into—and out of—violent extremism*. Oakland, CA: University of California Press.

Kluch, S. P., & Vaux, A. (2015). Culture and terrorism: The role of cultural factors in worldwide terrorism (1970–2013). *Terrorism and Political Violence*, 29(2), 323–341.

Kluckhohn, F. R., & Strodtbeck, F. L. (1961). *Variations in value orientations*. Evanston, IL: Row, Peterson.

Kohlberg, L. (1984). *The psychology of moral development: The nature and validity of moral stages*. New York, NY: Harper & Row.

Lee, L., & Ward, C. (1998). Ethnicity, idiocentrism–allocentrism, and intergroup attitudes 1. *Journal of Applied Social Psychology*, 28(2), 109–123.

Levin, J., & McDevitt, J. (1993). *Hate crimes: The rising tide of bigotry and bloodshed*. New York, NY: Plenum.

Liu, J. H., Sibley, C. G., & Huang, L. L. (2014). History matters: Effects of culture-specific symbols on political attitudes and intergroup relations. *Political Psychology*, 35(1), 57–79. https://doi.org/10.1111/pops.12027

MacCulloch, R. (2004). The impact of income on the taste for revolt. *American Journal of Political Science*, 48(4), 830–849.

Mathis-Lilley, B. (2016, April 25). A continually growing list of violent incidents at Trump events. *Slate Magazine.* http://www.slate.com/blogs/the_slatest/2016/03/02/a_list_of_violent_incidents_at_donald_trump_rallies_and_events.html

McDevitt, J., Levin, J., & Bennett, S. (2002). Hate crime offenders: An expanded typology. *Journal of Social Issues,* 58(2), 303–317.

Mullen, B., Brown, R., & Smith, C. (1992). Ingroup bias as a function of salience, relevance, and status: An integration. *European Journal of Social Psychology,* 22(2), 103–122. https://doi.org/10.1002/ejsp.2420220202

NewsOne. (2015, July 10). FBI director unsure if Dylann Roof's Charleston attack was act of terrorism. https://newsone.com/3149745/fbi-dylann-roof-charleston-attack-act-of-terrorism/

Newsweek. (2019, July 23). FBI director Christopher Wray says a majority of domestic terrorism cases are motivated by white supremacist violence. https://www.newsweek.com/domestic-terrorism-white-supremacy-violence-fbi-director-1450748

New York Times. (2015, December 3). Couple kept tight lid on plans for San Bernadino shooting. https://www.nytimes.com/2015/12/04/us/san-bernardino-shooting-syed-rizwan-farook.html

New York Times. (2018, March 16). Assaults increased when cities hosted Trump rallies, study finds. https://www.nytimes.com/2018/03/16/us/trump-rally-violence.html

Olatunji, B. O. (2008). Disgust, scrupulosity and conservative attitudes about sex: Evidence for a mediational model of homophobia. *Journal of Research in Personality,* 42(5), 1364–1369. http://www.sciencedirect.com/science/article/pii/S0092656608000524

Olatunji, B. O., Lohr, J. M., & Meunier, S. A. (2002, June). *Emotional mediators of homophobia: Implications for construct and psychometric validity.* Paper presented at the meeting of the American Psychological Society, New Orleans, LA.

Olatunji, B. O., & McKay, D. (2009). *Disorders of disgust: Assessment, theory, and treatment.* Washington, DC: American Psychological Association.

Paden, W., & Paden, F. (2014). *Troubadour poems from the South of France.* Suffolk, UK: D. S. Brewer.

Paxton, R. O. (2004). *The anatomy of fascism.* New York, NY: Knopf.

Payne, S. G. (1996). *A history of fascism, 1914–1945.* Boca Raton, FL: Routledge.

Pew Corporation. (2009). Little support for terrorism among Muslim Americans. http://www.pewforum.org/2009/12/17/little-support-for-terrorism-among-muslim-americans/

Roginsky, A. B., & Tsesis, A. (2015). Hate speech, volition, and neurology. *Journal of Law and the Biosciences,* 3(1), 174–177. https://doi.org/10.1093/jlb/lsv058

Sherif, M. (1958). Superordinate goals in the reduction of intergroup conflict. *American Journal of Sociology,* 63(4), 349–356.

Sherif, M., Harvey, O. J., White, B. J., Hood, W. R., & Sherif, C. W. (1961). *Intergroup conflict and cooperation: The Robbers Cave experiment* (Vol. 10). Norman, OK: University Book Exchange.

SputnikNews. (2018). Surprise: New study documents violence increase in US cities where Trump speaks. https://sputniknews.com/us/201803181062670546-new-study-documents-violence-increase-in-US-cities-where-trump-speaks/

Sullaway, M. (2004). Psychological perspectives on hate crime laws. *Psychology, Public Policy, and Law*, 10(3), 250–292.

Sullaway, M. (2017). Hate crime, violent extremism, domestic terrorism—Distinctions with difference? In E. Dunbar, A. Blanco, D. A. Crèvecoeur-MacPhail, C. Munthe, M. Fingerle, & D. Brax (Eds.), *The psychology of hate crimes as domestic terrorism* (Vol. 1, pp. 89–121). Santa Barbara, CA: Praeger.

Sullaway, M., & Dunbar, E. (1996). Clinical manifestations of prejudice in psychotherapy: Toward a strategy of assessment and treatment. *Clinical Psychology*, 3(4), 296–309.

Thienhaus, O. J., & Piasecki, M. (1998). Assessment of psychiatric patients' risk of violence toward others. *Psychiatric Services*, 49(9), 1129–1147.

Triandis, H. C. (1995). *Individualism and collectivism*. Boulder, CO: Westview Press.

Tropp, P. R., & A. C. Brown. (2004). What benefits the group can also benefit the individual: Group enhancing and individual enhancing motives for collective action. *Group Processes Intergroup Relations,* 7(3), 267–282.

Turiel, E. (1983). *The development of social knowledge: Morality and convention.* Cambridge, UK: Cambridge University Press.

Uniting and strengthening America by providing appropriate tools required to intercept and obstruct terrorism (USA Patriot) Act, 18 U.S.C. § 1 (2001).

Verkuyten, M., & Kwa, G. A. (1996). Ethnic self-identification, ethnic involvement, and group differentiation among Chinese youth in the Netherlands. *Journal of Social Psychology*, 136(1), 35–48.

Yanay, N. (2012). *The ideology of hatred*. New York, NY: Fordham University Press.

Zick, A., Pettigrew, T. F., & Wagner, U. (2008). Ethnic prejudice and discrimination in Europe. *Journal of Social Issues*, 64(2), 233–251.

CHAPTER THREE

A Discussion of Entry and Membership in Hate Groups

Silvina Ituarte

While research on bias-motivated crimes has predominantly focused on data collection, First Amendment challenges to legislation, and penalty enhancement sanctions, little research has examined the offenders engaged in actions across the hate crime continuum. Bias-motivated offenses are considered a category of crimes rather than a specific crime (Gavrielides, 2012) and consist of behaviors ranging from incidents involving noncriminal acts such as verbal slurs to criminal actions including murder. Also known as hate crimes, acts of bias are defined as "offenses motivated by hatred against a victim based on his [or her] race, religion, sexual orientation, handicap, ethnicity, or national origin" (Bureau of Justice Assistance, 1997). While most of the attention has focused on high-profile homicides, the majority of the acts of bias occur at the lower to middle range of the hate crime continuum and often include assault and acts of property damage.

Nationally in 2016, 4,720 bias-motivated offenses committed against persons included acts of intimidation (44.7%), simple assault (35.7%), and aggravated assault (18.5%). Additionally, nine homicides and 24 rapes were also reported (FBI, 2017), yet it is essential to recognize that Uniform Crime Report data only account for the reported offenses and do not take into account bias-motivated actions not coming to the attention of law enforcement. In addition, three-quarters of the 2,519 bias-motivated crimes committed against property included acts of destruction, damage, and vandalism, with the remaining 25 percent consisting of robbery, burglary, theft, arson, and any other bias-motivated acts (FBI, 2017).

Bias crime offenders typically comprise young men in their late teens and early twenties (Finn, 1988; Spillane, 1994; Steinberg, Brooks, & Remtulla, 2003; Woods, 2009), even though some women have participated in acts of bias (Castle, 2009). For many of these young offenders, acts of bias offer a means for establishing solidarity with a group of peers; a feeling of camaraderie, excitement, or risk-taking; and a sense of strength and empowerment (Bjorgo, 1998; McDevitt, Levin, & Bennett, 2002). Levin and McDevitt's (1993) seminal work on bias-motivated offenders led to the creation of a bias-motivated offender typology that was later expanded in 2002 to include a fourth offender group including the following categories: 1) *thrill-seekers* who represent youthful offenders acting in groups and pursuing a quick thrill, 2) *reactionists* who feel they are protecting their resources (i.e., neighborhoods and workplaces), 3) *mission offenders* who believe they are appealing to a higher loyalty by eradicating an inferior group, and 4) *retaliatory offenders* who seek to avenge a past negative interaction with members of an identifiable marginalized group (McDevitt, Levin, & Bennett, 2002).

Beyond motivation typologies, one must examine how personal experiences with trauma and mental health concerns can influence participation of bias-motivated offenders in their actions. Experiences with family divorce, abuse, bullies, anger, pain, and loneliness shape the thoughts and behaviors of all young people. According to Earls and Reiss (1994), "complex interactions among an individual's health, stressful life experiences, and social environment keep individuals away from antisocial behavior or push them toward it" (29). A large majority of juveniles living in residential programs have experienced traumatic experiences such as abuse, abandonment, or loss (Gray, 2015). Mental health concerns can be a barrier in an offender's progress toward ending their criminal behaviors. When these concerns are taken into consideration in planning the treatment strategy, offenders are more successful in their progress and recovery. Gray (2015) argues that institutionalizing those who continue to struggle with unresolved traumas intensifies a sense of powerlessness and aggravates their harmful behaviors.

Mass shooters, for example, have been characteristically shown to suffer from a sense of marginalization in their families, place of work, school, or social arena (Capellan & Gomez, 2018; Lankford, 2013) and their criminal behaviors often offer them, what they perceive as, a resolution. Research on mass shooters reveals offenders routinely experienced troubled personal backgrounds afflicted with depression, isolation, social incompetence, lack of significant connections, or suicidal propensities (Capellan & Gomez, 2018). It is worth exploring whether offenders of bias-motivated offenses also identify their behaviors as a "solution" to a problem they may have been experiencing.

Individuals with unstable families are much more likely to gravitate toward disruptive or harmful behaviors as a result of diminished protective factors that cannot counteract the influence of numerous risk factors (Kirby & Fraser, 1997). Negative experiences and trauma can leave a lasting impact in the lives of anyone suffering a trauma, yet with the proper assistance and resources, individuals are able to develop new coping skills through the process of post-traumatic growth (Tedeschi & Calhoun, 2004). Resiliency is developed through a robust support system and resources that facilitate emotional endurance in coping with stressful or traumatic circumstances (Agaibi & Wilson, 2005). When family environments are unable to provide the support needed to foster resiliency, school environments provide the next logical source of support. Unfortunately, without the appropriate resources, schools customarily respond to misbehavior by isolating students even further through the use of suspension or expulsion. According to the National Council on Disability (2015), 85% of young offenders housed in detention facilities struggle with mental health issues or learning disabilities that make them eligible for specialized services, yet only a small fraction of them ever received the needed services while attending school. In school, young people struggling with mental health issues are also likely to have their academic performance affected. If no intervention is offered to the students, they often become disengaged and find disruptive coping strategies (i.e., truancy, fights, or other destructive behaviors) for dealing with their problems (Emmons & Belangee, 2018).

Young people who experience depression are more likely to become involved with excessive substance use and experience higher rates of recidivism (van der Put, Creemers, & Hoeve, 2014). Additionally, the emotional and psychological underdevelopment of younger individuals makes them susceptible to hate group recruiters (Godinet & Stotzer, 2016) who seek those who are suffering to offer a "big brother figure" for support and understanding (Blazak, 2009). In essence, hate group recruiters have excelled in identifying and managing "outreach" to those in greatest need of help and attention while many of those cries for help continue to be overlooked by mainstream culture. As vulnerable youth continue to be susceptible to negative influences, approximately 40% of youth offenders engage in their criminal involvements with codefendants (NIJ, 2005). If these codefendants already have an established history of using violence, then the likelihood of using violence increases (NIJ, 2005). Despite the fact that organized hate groups commit only a fraction of the bias-motivated offenses, members of organized hate groups often possess lengthier criminal histories, and their bias-motivated actions typically involve more severe levels of violence (Dunbar, Quinones, & Crevecoeur, 2005).

Table 3-1 Participants Interviewed across the Continuum of Bias Crimes

Verbal Slur	Graffiti/ Vandalism	Aggravated Assaults	Homicide (accessory)	Homicide (primary role)
Jeffrey	Paulie	Fender	Dirk	Derek
Jacqueline	Tannen	Buck	Chadlie	Harley
				Damian
				Walden

This study explores the lives and characteristics of offenders committing acts of bias across the entire hate crime continuum from name-calling to murder. By using interviews with offenders, the study explores similarities and difference among offenders including their family and school backgrounds; their experiences with anger, depression, and loneliness; their ideologies; their experiences with victimization; and their membership or nonmembership in hate organizations. Table 3-1 shows the continuum of bias-motivated behaviors from least to most serious. Despite the fact that several of the participants were engaged in numerous activities, the participants were placed along the continuum according to their most serious bias crime. Fender is the exception to this since he was typically involved in assaults, yet one of those assaults resulted in a mother's miscarriage.

Methodology

The single most challenging element of conducting research on bias-motivated offenders entails identifying a pool of possible and willing participants across a range of bias-motivated behaviors. Several approaches were involved in attaining this sample of participants. The greatest success resulted from gathering bias-motivated offenders' names from LexisNexis searches of bias crimes from newspapers and newsletters. The next most successful method came from the New York City Anti-Defamation League's (ADL) Bias Crime Diversion Program, which ran a program for nonviolent bias crime offenders at the time of the research but has since closed. The ADL in Philadelphia also acted as a liaison between the researcher and a young man who had been a leader in the skinhead movement, and the last of the participants was recruited through a referral from a correctional institution in New Jersey.

Because seven of the 12 research participants resided at correctional facilities, the researcher completed the correctional departments' institutional review forms, as well as the university's form, to request permission for conducting the interviews. If the institutions approved the request, a date and time with the specific offender was scheduled for a two-hour interview. The interviews with ADL participants were handled differently. The assistant director of the ADL distributed both an explanatory letter and consent forms to be taken home and signed by the participant's guardian. In this manner, anonymity was maintained until the participants voluntarily chose to take part in the study. Those choosing to participate had their names stricken from any notes immediately and replaced by pseudonyms.

The interview data were gathered using a semi-structured questionnaire with open-ended questions that focused on the personal characteristics of participants as well as the bias-motivated event. The questionnaire was divided into sections, which asked the participant to describe themselves, family, activities, and aspirations. Next, the participant was asked to describe their residence, family life, education, marital status, military status, and employment history. The third portion of the questionnaire asked the more sensitive and revealing questions regarding the participant's substance use, mental health history, and criminal involvement. Additionally, letters were used as a means of establishing a rapport prior to the interview.

Participants

The interview participants included those affiliated, and not affiliated, with organized hate groups and ranged in involvement across the hate crime continuum. Jeffrey yelled at a young boy of Indian descent while one of his friends jumped out of the vehicle and attacked him. Jacqueline, a 15-year-old Latina, called out a racial slur during a physical altercation with another girl. Paulie reacted to an argument with a friend by writing "Jews suck" on wet cement outside the friend's home. Tannen placed explicit sexual diagrams, pentagrams, swastikas, and other offensive words and diagrams on school walls. Buck and Fender were both former skinheads who participated in bias assaults either as part of a group activity or as a means of releasing built-up anger and hostility. Dirk and Chadlie were both involved in hate-motivated homicides, yet their roles in these homicides were more as accessories. Meanwhile, Walden, Harley, Derek, and Damian acted as primary offenders in the hate-motivated homicides for which they were currently incarcerated (see Table 3-2). Although this study provides only 12 interviews, the number of self-reported bias-motivated offenses committed by these participants is much larger and will be revealed later in the chapter.

Biographies

The participant biographies are listed according to the level of severity from least violent to most violent, and the level of detail of the biographies varies according to the participant's level of maturity, complexity of the crime, and participant cooperation.

Table 3-2 Interview Participants' Age, Affiliation, and Offense

Name	Age at Offense	ADL/ Referral/ Incarcerated	Hate Group Affiliated	Offense
Jeffrey	16	ADL	none	Riding in a vehicle with friends, one of the friends says "Get out of here" while his friend exits the vehicle and attacks a juvenile of Indian descent.
Jacqueline	15	ADL	none	Called another girl a "monkey" during the course of a physical fight.
Paulie	16	ADL	none	Wrote "Jews suck" on wet cement after having an argument with a friend/neighbor.
Tannen	17	ADL	none	Placed pentagrams, swastikas, upside-down crosses, and sexually explicit drawings on the side of the school walls.
Buck	15	referral	yes	Joined a local skinhead group in order to engage in assault sprees.
Fender	15	referral	yes	Committed approximately 15 bias-motivated attacks on individuals from different victim groups as part of skinheads.
Dirk	17	Correctional Facility	none	He and two codefendants robbed a gay man of his money and vehicle, but the encounter resulted in a homicide.
Harley	19	Correctional Facility	none	Co-defendants (Dirk, Harley, & Derek)

(continued)

Table 3-2 (*continued*)

Name	Age at Offense	ADL/ Referral/ Incarcerated	Hate Group Affiliated	Offense
Derek	29	Correctional Facility	none	Co-defendants (Dirk, Harley, & Derek)
Chadlie	16	Correctional Facility	yes	Went out with two friends to drink beer, but this resulted in the murder of an African American male.
Walden	16	Correctional Facility	yes	Co-defendants (Chadlie & Walden)
Damian	19	Correctional Facility	yes	After a while of playing pool with his brother, he stabbed a gay man.

Jeffrey—Verbal Slur

At the time of the interview, Jeffrey was a 16-year-old enrolled in the Anti-Defamation League's (ADL) Bias Crime Diversion Program in Manhattan. He lived with his mother, and despite doing well in school, Jeffrey felt like an outcast and was involved in school fights until the age of 13. He and four of his friends were driving when one of them stopped the car and punched a juvenile walking along the street. Only two of the juveniles participated in the fight, but as a result of Jeffrey standing outside of the car and telling the victim to "get out of here," he was also charged with an attempted bias-motivated assault. Of the five juveniles, Jeffrey received the ADL program, probation, and community service. Jeffrey believes the fight was over a girl and not attributed to the victim being Indian, but he blames himself for spending time with the wrong people, and he no longer associates with those friends. In Table 3-1, Jeffrey is listed under the category of "verbal slur" since he admitted to yelling at the other juvenile and the ADL director also believed that Jeffrey was not directly involved in a physical act.

Jacqueline (15)—Verbal Slur

Jacqueline was a 15-year-old ADL participant who was busy with schoolwork and her duties with the Student Activities Council. At the age of 12, Jacqueline was involved in fights with girls, and in the eighth grade, she was transferred to another school. In the bias-motivated incident, Jacqueline was in class when a young girl threw figurines at her. The next day, Jacqueline went into a deli near the school and the same girl attacked her. She fought back and called the young girl a "monkey" during the course of their fight. Jacqueline claims to not have understood the racist connotation of her comment, but both of her parents pled guilty in court and spent one night in jail. Jacqueline received probation, community service, and the ADL diversion program. Her parents were sentenced to a two-year probation term, and her father was ordered to view a video on tolerance. Since Jacqueline was already involved in a physical fight before making the racist comment, she was listed on Table 3-1 under the category of "verbal slur."

Paulie—Vandalism

Paulie was a 17-year-old ADL participant who was assigned to the program after writing "Jews suck" on wet cement outside the house after his friend insulted Paulie's father. Although Paulie was the one who wrote the statement in the cement, a friend who was with Paulie drew a swastika next to Paulie's words. He claimed to only want to retaliate against the young girl for hurting him, yet his involvement deeply wounded the family since members of the family were survivors of the Holocaust. While in school, Paulie was never involved in any school fights, but he was sent to the principal's office for not paying attention, talking back, and arguing. He regrets hurting the family and damaging a friendship with someone with whom he used to spend time playing pool, ping-pong, and watching movies. Although he had no prior convictions, Paulie spent six weeks detained, was sentenced to probation until the age of 18, and mandated to attend the Anti-Defamation League's Diversion Program. This incident caused Paulie to miss three months of school, forcing him to take the GED and not finish high school with his friends.

Tannen—Graffiti

Tannen was interviewed in the conference room of the New York City Anti-Defamation League when he was 18 years old. When he was born, his C-5 nerve was damaged during the delivery, permanently stunting the development of his right arm. The doctor was sued and Tannen began receiving a $20,000 yearly malpractice settlement since the age of 18. He endured several major muscle transplants and was unable to look at himself in the mirror until the age of 14. His parents were divorced and his mother left Tannen when he was almost three years old. For some time, Tannen lived with his aunt until his father removed Tannen and placed him with his grandmother, when it was discovered that Tannen was being physically abused. Tannen grew up thinking his grandmother was his mother, but when his mother returned while he was 7½ years old, the courts made Tannen chose between living with his mother or his grandmother. Tannen chose to live with his mother despite having to "sit by her side at 11 years old to make sure she would not suffocate on her own vomit."

Tannen had been in psychological counseling since the age of five, and in the sixth grade, he began acts of self-mutilation, proclaiming that "the more I bleed, the better I feel." He attempted suicide and made many cries for help, including claims that he "popped bottles of pills when [he] felt like a failure, used cocaine, was addicted to heroin, and almost overdosed." Although he attended a rehabilitation program for alcohol and marijuana at the age of 16, he was kicked out of school and transferred to an alternative high school.

While intoxicated one night, he and a friend used a black marker to draw genitalia, pentagrams, swastikas, and upside-down crosses on the walls of a local elementary school. A press release from the prosecutor's office also stated that the two wrote "Hitler is God" on the walls. When asked why he did this, Tannen exclaimed that he just wrote the things he knew would "piss everyone off." Although Tannen did not believe he deserved to be placed in the Anti-Defamation League's program, one of the speakers during the 10-week program had a tremendous impact on him. When a Holocaust survivor had presented her experiences and explained the symbolic meaning of the swastika to her and her family, Tannen was profoundly moved. Until then, Tannen had not realized the meaning and impact of the swastikas he placed on the school walls. He felt deeply remorseful for the significance of his actions, which he did not completely comprehend previously.

Buck—Assault

Buck was 18 years old when he was interviewed in a cottage at a juvenile detention facility. When he was six months old, his mother abandoned the family, resulting in Buck feeling anger, rejection, and abandonment throughout his life. He lived in a neighborhood filled with criminal opportunities, and his older brother, father, and cousins had all been incarcerated.

Buck was incarcerated since the age of 11 and was placed in a program between six and seven times. At the age of nine years old, he began breaking into homes and stealing vehicles. Eventually, at the age of 13, he led police on a high-speed pursuit. Despite being the son of an interracial couple, Buck joined a neighborhood skinhead organization; not because he agreed with their ideology, but rather because he was looking for an excuse to fight. His official file contained 65 charges, 54 dismissals, three adjudications, and six active charges ranging from theft/burglary, violations of parole, criminal mischief, and conspiracy. Buck confesses to his involvement in well over a hundred aggravated assaults, including bias-motivated attacks, and claims that fighting provided him with an opportunity to release his rage over his mother's departure. Buck's psychological reports showed he was classified as emotionally disturbed after he combined the use of pills and alcohol during multiple suicide attempts. He was described as having a learning disability and inconsistent behavior, which led to numerous hospitalizations for suicidal tendencies. He did attain his high school diploma and has a one-year-old daughter.

Fender—Kidnapping and Assaults

Fender was interviewed at the age of 23 after having left the skinhead movement and began collaborating with the Anti-Defamation League. He admitted to having participated in many hate crimes during which the victims were chosen because they were perceived to be different, weak, or simply outnumbered. He was a recovering alcoholic who regularly attended Alcoholics Anonymous (AA) meetings, and his goals included completing his degree and owning his own youth sports program. Fender witnessed his parents using drugs and alcohol, so he first began drinking alcohol on weekends at the age of 12 years old. By the age of 18, he had experimented with drugs and was using them daily.

Throughout his childhood, Fender suffered from depression, attempted suicide, and endured mental abuse from his stepfather. He was the target of violence from his stepfather, and when he was 12 years old, his head was put through a desk by his stepfather. He began jumping on trains and stealing from them at the age of 10. He frequented the principal's office for fighting from elementary school through high school and had no supervision after school. He joined the skinheads at the age of 13 after being introduced into the culture by his cousins and was not apprehended for his misdeeds until at the age of 15 years old. At the ages of 16 and 17, Fender escaped from a mental institution where he was being treated for his suicide attempts and still continues taking Zoloft for depression.

Fender admitted to attacking people in attempts to earn his "web," and participated in bias-motivated incidents to cure boredom; demonstrate courage and strength; express anger or revenge; impress others; make friends; and earn respect/honor. He described the skinhead culture of music, magazines, and racist television shows as addictive. Fender became the leader of the local White Aryan Resistance (WAR) group as well as the group's primary recruiter. He admits "it was easy finding troubled kids with low self-esteem to recruit." He claimed to have participated in approximately 50 to 75 bias-motivated aggravated assaults and about 300 acts of vandalism. At the time, killing was not a problem for him.

He and his friends described themselves as the "Terminator Squad" or "TS." At the age of 15, after having several drinks, Fender and a few skinheads went on a bashing spree where they committed approximately

15 bias-motivated assaults in one evening. The group was finally apprehended during one of their attacks against two gay men. Fender was waived to the adult criminal justice system, where he received a 2½-year prison sentence. After his release, he was placed on parole but was rearrested for first-degree murder in an attack on a pregnant Ethiopian woman who miscarried.

Since these incidents, Fender's life has changed radically. While incarcerated, Fender found himself with little in common with the older inmates associated with the Aryan Brotherhood and was more drawn to younger, athletic inmates who were typically members of oppressed groups. While participating in prison sports and work assignments, Fender developed friendships with diverse inmates and began questioning his beliefs. His girlfriend, the leader of the Aryan Women's League (AWL), delivered his first child, and viewing his baby for the first time forced him to think about his role in the death of a "non-white" baby. Fender has three children, is currently involved in coaching young people in sports, and continues to work with the ADL in the fight against hate crimes.

Dirk—Homicide

The next three offenders, Dirk, Harley, and Derek, all participated in the same bias-motivated crime. Dirk was 22 years old when he was interviewed at a correctional facility. He appeared much younger and lacked the vocabulary to express himself well. He appeared as someone who could easily be persuaded due to his eager need for acceptance. He was 17 years old when he committed his crime and spent three years in a county jail before being transferred to prison at the age of 20. Although Dirk did not have any prior convictions, he admitted to underage drinking and toilet-papering neighbors' homes. Dirk never experimented with drug use, but he began drinking beer on the weekends at the age of 14. He and his friends would drink to fill a need in what he perceived to be a "dreary life." He described himself as one of "a bunch of stupid youngsters listening to someone older telling them what to do" and admits the highest grade he completed prior to his incarceration was the 10th grade. Despite always being bullied, Dirk was never the victim of violence before he entered prison, and he explains that "In prison, friendliness is considered a weakness."

Prior to his incarceration, Dirk had been involved in four or five prior antigay robberies for which he was not apprehended. He explained that gay men represented easy targets, since they "were hidden way out there trying not to be found." Initially, Dirk was charged with aggravated robbery and kidnapping, but the charge was ultimately changed to capital murder. He received two life sentences for which he must serve at least 30 years in prison. Dirk was the driver in the bias-motivated incident, but admitted to shooting at the victim to scare him. According to Dirk, Derek baited the victim and Harley was the one who shot him. Once they "picked up" the victim, they drove to a remote location "in the middle of nowhere where the car could be burned." Dirk confessed to participating in the antigay attacks due to peer pressure, to assert strength, to show courage, to release bitterness for being bullied, to impress others, to make friends, and to avenge having been teased for being poor. He also admitted he had a tendency to suppress his emotions, creating a "time bomb that had to go off."

Harley—Homicide

Harley, Dirk's codefendant, was an African American male incarcerated for the capital murder of a gay man. He was interviewed at the age of 24 while on death row, and his responses were typically either "yes," "no," or "I don't know."

Harley's parents were divorced, and no one in his family was ever abusive toward him, yet he stated that on various occasions, strangers were violent toward him during his teen years. The first time Harley was involved in an illegal activity was for stealing at the age of 13, but he had not been convicted previously. He did admit to prior criminal behaviors including burglaries, shooting at someone, assaults, underage drinking, drug use, and minor possession. Harley began drinking alcohol at the age of 13, and was introduced to marijuana through friends at the age of 15. Although he had not received any medical treatment, he complained of migraine headaches since the age of 15 or 16 years old. Prior to his incarceration, he spent most of his time with friends, many of whom belonged to the Crips gang. He completed the 10th grade and earned "good money for [his] age" working as a cook, maintenance worker, and machine operator.

On the night of the bias crime, Harley was 19 years old. He went to the park to take the victim's truck and his money, but when the victim did not give up his money, the three men began shooting to scare him. Harley claims to have engaged in this type of criminal activity with Derek on two other occasions. The researcher later learned that Harley had been executed a few years after the interview.

Derek—Homicide and Robbery

At the time of the interview, Derek was a 33-year-old divorced father of four teenage boys who had earned his General Equivalency Diploma (GED). Throughout his teen and adult years, Derek was hit, punched, kicked, pushed, or bitten by acquaintances ranging from his neighbors, coworkers, teachers, parents, siblings, his children, and friends. In 1994, Derek suffered a head injury, and doctors found blood clots between his skull and brain.

Since the age of five or six, he had been sexually abused by family members, and his first sexual experience was with his neighbor. He claims he spent most of his life as a bisexual man, since much of his early experiences were with men. He became involved with alcohol and drugs by the age of nine after being introduced to illegal substances by his cousins. At the time of the bias attack, Derek claimed to have been under the influence of both marijuana and cocaine. His philosophy was that gay men had money and jewelry and were less likely to report their victimizations. Typically, once the victim was taken to a desolate location, the three men would steal the money and proceed to humiliate the victim by requesting that he take off his clothing.

Derek pled not guilty to charges of capital murder at his trial but was given the death penalty. He had previously been sentenced to 4 to 10 years for burglary and 12 years for breaking into refrigerators and stealing power tools from garages. Derek believes he probably participated in almost 100 burglaries and robberies. In terms of hate crimes, Derek participated in about eight other hate crimes, with about three to seven codefendants each time.

Chadlie—Homicide and Organized Crime

The next two offenders, Chadlie and Walden, are both skinheads who were codefendants in a bias-motivated homicide of an African American man. Chadlie was 24 years old at the time of the interview and had already served the first seven years of a 40-year sentence. This was Chadlie's first time in prison, and his only prior criminal charges included jaywalking, underage drinking, and truancy. Chadlie was affiliated with the Confederate White Vikings as well as Strike Force, and he expressed pride in his knowledge of the mythology of the Viking and Norse gods as well as Odinism.

His parents were divorced and his father participated in Chadlie's life financially until his death. From a very young age, Chadlie had been in therapy for depression. He explained that he struggled with the pain of dealing with unresolved feelings from childhood and claimed to be diligently working at moving forward. He believed that sobriety has changed his life and described his prior alcohol consumption as representative of using self-medicating methods.

Chadlie completed the ninth grade but disliked his teachers and was bored in class. He frequently avoided attending school and was sent to an alternative school, where he met Walden and other juveniles who introduced him to the skinhead subculture. For Chadlie, his membership with the skinheads provided him with a sense of belonging and afforded him a sense of cultural pride. He claimed not to be interested in hurting anyone unprovoked, but admitted to having participated in several gay bashings.

According to Chadlie, on the night of the bias-motivated homicide, he and his two friends went out driving looking for "chicks and beer." Chadlie was lying in the back of the car when Walden shot and killed an African American man. Chadlie recalled the shooter (Walden) saying he wanted to scare someone. He admitted to being involved in other illegal activities for which he was not apprehended since the age of 13 years old including "car hopping," assaults, underage drinking, and gay bashings. Chadlie was released a few years ago and has continued experiencing difficulties but remained committed to his ideological beliefs.

Walden—Homicide

Walden's parents were divorced and he lived with his father until the age of 11. Walden's first encounter with drugs came from hanging out at the movie theaters or skateboarding ramp with friends who were two or three years older than him. At the age of 13 years old, Walden became a member of the Confederate Hammerskins and a founding member of the Strike Force. He experimented with drugs and alcohol at 13, and by the time he reached the age of 15, his alcohol consumption was daily. Up until the sixth grade, Walden attained A's and B's in his classes, but after the sixth grade, he stopped attending classes. From the time he was enrolled in elementary school until the time he was in high school, Walden was involved in fights and sent to the principal's office, resulting in a transfer to an alternative school during the ninth grade.

Walden described himself as someone who was involved in many fights because of an inability to debate well, which led him to react without thinking. Prior to his incarceration, Walden used violence for fun. He explained, "It feels good to beat on someone once in a while." He quit school and moved out of his home at the age of 15 to attain his goal of "making lots of money."

Prior to the bias-motivated murder for which he is serving his prison sentence, Walden was charged at the age of 14 years old with criminal mischief for another bias act when he "knocked a telephone pole into the house of another black guy." Walden admitted he was not apprehended in the bias acts he perpetrated every weekend including shooting at several people on numerous occasions. He participated in approximately 100 antigay and anti-Black attacks and recalls occasions when he would go out every night and commit several attacks in one evening. Usually, he acted with two other codefendants, but at concerts or small shows, almost 20 skinheads would act out at one time. He admitted to only having shot at African Americans, but acknowledges that attacking "gays was for fun, not because I was mad at them."

Walden was charged with murder for the death of an African American male but accepted a plea bargain in which he testified against Chadlie in exchange for a 40-year sentence on the charge of first-degree murder. Walden admitted that he acted as the shooter and explained that he had already been irritated earlier in the day and was seeking someone to harm. Walden said to the driver, "Turn this car around. I'm going to kill this ni—." Prior to the incident, Walden was mad at the world, but during the incident, he felt a release of tension "like a balloon that popped."

Damian—Homicide

During the interview, Damian, who was 21 years old, exhibited a distant and unfeeling demeanor while utilizing menacing terminology such as having to "chop up" the victim. When questioned about newspaper clippings that described him as a skinhead, he simply said, "If that's what they say." He later denied his affiliation in a letter, although he did not deny it when asked during the interview. Moreover, he described his tattoos as "peckerwood art," but his words were contradictory (skinheads are often referred to as "peckers").

> No I am not, was not and never will be part of the "skin heads," their philosophies Do not and never have fit into my life style. This was not a "hate crime," but now that I look, it should have been. I HATE people that deliberately distribute drugs to the multitudes, knowing its effects! I HATE someone who carries a life style that is harmful and pushes it on to others! . . . (Letter from Damian)

Damian participated in school fights and was sent to the principal's office from elementary school through high school. According to him, he only attended school to "flirt and fight," and believes that his teachers hated him. Damian witnessed violence between family members, but he chose not to elaborate. When he was 11 years old, Damian was introduced to marijuana by his friends and began drinking small quantities of alcohol at the age of 13. At the age of 11 or 12, Damian was involved in a bicycle accident that he believes "screwed up [his] head" and was hospitalized when his mother perceived him to be "crazy and out of control." He also attended alcohol and drug treatment after experimenting with cocaine, inhalants, and hallucinogens.

Damian had prior convictions for aggravated assault and served a short sentence in juvenile hall. He was charged with a bias-motivated murder and sentenced to 20 years to life for stabbing a gay man when he was 19 years old. Damian had been playing pool in a bar and listening to Black Sabbath with his stepbrother when he received a sexual advance by an older gentleman in the restroom of a bar. He claimed the intoxicated man "peeked at him" and offered cocaine for Damian to "suck dick." Although Damian exclaimed his disinterest in accepting the man's sexual proposition, he agreed to use the drugs. Later that evening, Damian, his stepbrother, the victim's partner, and the victim all drove to the victim's home, where the man could supply more drugs. Enraged by the man's persistence, Damian lost his patience and "kicked him in the head and chopped him up" by stabbing the victim 35 times.

Although in the interview Damian blamed himself for the incident, in a later letter, Damian rationalized his behaviors by claiming that gay men perpetrate harm to society by spreading AIDS and molesting innocent young children. When asked if he could go back in time and change anything, Damian said "no."

At the time of the interview, Damian resided in the administrative segregation unit of the correctional facility due to a new murder for which he had not yet been tried. This was the only interview which was conducted across a glass divider and through the use of the phones located next to the windows.

Analysis

Hirschi (1969) explained that law-abiding individuals avoid involvement in criminal behaviors due to their strong social bonds, exemplified in their intimate attachments (i.e., family), belief in formal institutions, commitment to goals, and involvement in multiple activities. For many of the participants interviewed in this study, these bonds were often nonexistent. The participants involved in the lower-level offenses experienced stronger family environments and felt less alienated from mainstream culture than offenders involved in the more serious crimes who lacked stability or supervision from a caring adult. All the participants in this study experienced some form of difficulty at school whether as fights, truancy, disengagement, or transfer to alternative schools.

Family, Substance Use, and Mental Health

The family lives of 12 twelve interview participants could be divided into the four categories: "abusive," "substance-dependent," "neglectful," or "stable." Participants who had a stable family environment possessed a meaningful bond with at least one parent, yet often lacked supervision. Of the participants who witnessed their family's substance abuse (Tannen, Fender, and Buck), all three resorted to using a wide assortment of drugs and alcohol. For them, observing their family members abuse drugs or alcohol was a fact of life. Tannen and Buck engaged in illegitimate activities partly as a result of their stored-up resentment about being abandoned by family members. Three participants (Tannen, Fender, and Derek) endured or witnessed physical, sexual, or emotional abuse from friends, family, and strangers, and one

Table 3-3 Interview Participant Background Influences

	Continuum (low to high)	Family	School Issues	Substance Abuse	Depression	Prior	Hate Affiliated
Jeffrey	low violence	stable	✓				
Jacqueline	↓	stable	✓				
Paulie	↓	stable	✓				
Tannen	↓	unstable	✓	✓	✓		
Buck	↓	unstable	✓	✓	✓	✓	✓
Fender	↓	unstable	✓	✓	✓	✓	✓
Dirk	↓	stable	✓	✓	✓	✓	
Chadlie	↓	stable	✓	✓	✓	✓	✓
Walden	↓	unstable	✓	✓	✓	✓	✓
Harley	↓	stable	✓	✓	✓	✓	
Derek	↓	unstable	✓	✓	✓	✓	
Damian	high violence	unstable	✓	✓	✓	✓	✓

participant (Damian) would not expand on the abuse his mother endured from her boyfriends, or whether he had been involved in any altercations with these men.

All of the participants, with the exception of the three young people involved in the least serious acts of bias, used alcohol primarily as a bonding tool. Alcohol not only disinhibited the participants to commit their crimes but also provided a social pastime through which to bond with peers and establish relationships. Dirk described that much of his free time was spent drinking with friends, and every single participant affiliated with the skinheads described that a significant portion of the skinhead subculture involved mass consumptions of alcohol and listening to music. By providing a social activity, the consumption of alcohol allowed participants to escape their troubles, experience temporary pleasure, and connect with others. Additionally, Chadlie described alcohol as a means of self-medicating (Friedman, 1998) his problems from childhood. Several of the participants in this study discussed involvement in multiple substance abuse treatment programs, but for those who were successful in their sobriety (e.g., Chadlie, Fender, and Tannen), their recovery process often began with reaching a low point in their lives (i.e., incarceration) or the birth of a child (Maruna & LeBel, 2003) as in the case of Fender.

Five out of 12 participants admitted to having had medication prescribed for depression, registering at a mental health facility, or attempting suicide. Additionally, two other respondents admitted to periods of depression or anger but did not indicate having attended a program or receiving medication to address these issues. Tannen, who was still struggling with depression at the time of the interview, attempted suicide multiple times and frequently engaged in acts of self-mutilation. Buck, who attempted suicide by combining pills with alcohol, was diagnosed as needing serious therapy for depression as well as anger management. Fender was prescribed Zoloft for depression and was hospitalized after his suicide attempt. Chadlie was also prescribed medication for depression, and Damian was hospitalized for being "out of control." Neither Derek, who disclosed feelings of being depressed about his childhood victimization, nor Dirk, who expressed feelings of depression and loneliness, mentioned receiving any mental health treatment, medication, or a formal clinical diagnosis.

Many of the participants discussed arguing, a loss of temper, or an overall involvement in fights as a means of releasing their feelings. Two participants in particular claimed to experience difficulty in expressing themselves, and both described a physical need to release emotions. Dirk, who acted as an accessory in a homicide, and Walden, who shot and killed an African American man, referred to the sense of "release" or "relief" experienced during the commission of the crime. Walden explained it best when he placed his hands over his chest and made the motions of an explosion when comparing the feeling of shooting the victim to that of a "balloon popping" to release all the tension constrained inside. Similarly, Dirk discussed how his suppressed emotions were bottled up in a manner that felt like a "bomb that needed to go off." Moreover, Tannen discussed how the words and drawings he placed on the school wall were intended to "piss people off" and have others experience and understand the pain that he felt on a regular basis. While the actions are inexcusable, these three men were unable to express their emotions in socially acceptable ways and acted in a manner that drew fear rather than understanding.

Schools and Peers

All of the participants experienced challenges in school whether through the form of fights, truancy, disengagement, or poor academic performance. According to Woods (2009), the U.S. Department of Justice and the U.S. Department of Education both agree that schools provide an important intervention opportunity for preventing bias crimes. School may be a student's sole "safe place" even when the cries for help present themselves as disruptive behaviors. Dirk was the target of school bullies, Jacqueline had to change schools as a result of physical altercations with other female students, and

Jeffrey did not like many of the students at school. Paulie attended classes regularly, but he was often sent to the principal's office for either not paying attention or talking back. While in school, the participants either experienced difficulty relating to other students, or they did not excel as a result of skipping class and not paying attention. Walden exemplified this point when he stated that he was not a skilled debater and therefore turned to fighting to express his points. When these juveniles lacked the skills to express themselves in conventional ways, they often used acts of bias to express their pain from personal dilemmas. Researchers have speculated that youth involvement in bias-motivated behaviors may result from unsuccessful completion of the appropriate developmental stages (Godinet & Stotzer, 2017; Roxell, 2016), resulting in a lapse of the essential decision-making skills or an inability to effectively articulate feelings.

When school did not provide the type of environment in which these participants could succeed, they were often labeled as troublemakers or separated from the rest of the class. The impact on students transferred to alternative schools can have lasting repercussions including earning less credits toward graduation and higher rates of truancy (Wilkerson et. al., 2016). For participants who were transferred to alternative schools (i.e., Walden, Chadlie, and Tannen), their exclusion from traditional activities limited their legitimate opportunities.

Many of the participants who endured various forms of adversity turned to peers who shared in their adversity, accepted their shortcomings, or provided them with a source of support and understanding that was missing elsewhere. Of the participants interviewed, Dirk represented an excellent example of a conventional adolescent who became involved with a delinquent group in order to make friends, overcome his loneliness, and counteract the fact that he was regularly bullied. Spending time drinking and engaging in delinquent activities provided Dirk with a peer group with whom to establish a sense of belonging, acceptance, and strength. In many cases, this led to delinquent acquaintances, and in the most extreme cases, it led to membership in organized hate groups. Two of the 12 participants regard themselves as ex-skinheads (Fender and Buck), two still consider themselves skinheads (Chadlie and Walden), and one later repudiated his involvement with the skinheads in a letter (Damian). One participant was initially attracted to the Nazi regalia worn by skinheads, and the other participant was drawn into the skinhead subculture through skateboarding acquaintances. Slowly, through participating in the skinhead subculture of "oi" music and drinking, they became indoctrinated with, and adopted, the racialist ideology.

According to Bjorgo (1998), "the most common way youths get in direct contact with racist groups is probably by being introduced through friends or older siblings [or other family members] who are already members themselves" (7). The two ex-skinheads in this study both joined the skinheads partially as a result of their unstable family environment and partially as a means of releasing their anger and frustration through violence. Fender and Buck are the only two participants in this study who terminated their skinhead affiliation. Bjorgo (1998) found various factors involved in deciding to end one's involvement with racist organizations, including a feeling of "getting too old" to engage in unlawful behaviors and a desire to establish a family life with a spouse and children. For others, they may become disillusioned with the group's activities, lose faith in the group's ideology, burn out from the pressures of being a part of the group, grow tired of negative social sanctions, or choose to leave the groups in search of a "normal" life. Fender and Buck both left their hate organizations primarily after reevaluating their beliefs during their incarceration as well as due to their renewed interest in spending time with their children. Traditionally, aging out and factors such as establishing a family or employment responsibilities have led to decreased participation in criminal activity (Sampson & Laub, 2003).

Prior Criminal Involvement and Violence

All 12 participants were involved in their illegal behavior at an early age. Three of the lower-level offenders had only participated in school fights or truancy and did not have other criminal behaviors beside their bias-motivated act. The rest of the participants had participated in illegal activities for which they were not apprehended including theft, robbery, and "car hopping." Seven participants had a previous arrest record. Derek had been incarcerated previously for burglary and robbery, while Buck was arrested 65 times for crimes such as theft and drug possession. Fender, Buck, and Walden, all skinheads, were also arrested for assaults, while the remaining participants avoided justice officials or were apprehended for minor offenses such as underage drinking or criminal mischief. The collective self-reported acts of bias committed by all the participants, many of which did not come to the attention of law enforcement, totaled well over 500 bias-motivated acts of vandalism, harassment, and assault. Although the estimated number of bias acts seems unusually high, an analysis of the participants' actions provides a context for these estimates. Three participants admitted to participating in over 75 bias-motivated assaults by committing numerous bias acts per outing. If these participants committed between five and 10 acts of bias per weekend, then each month they could each potentially commit approximately 40 or more bias-motivated offenses.

Seven of the 12 interview participants admitted to participating in several bias crimes prior to their apprehension, and all seven committed multiple bias crimes per outing. Those individuals who were affiliated with organized hate groups experienced more encounters with the criminal justice system, but when compared to the three non-hate-affiliated offenders convicted of serious crimes, both sets of participants exhibited similar illegal behaviors for which they were not apprehended. All of the affiliated offenders had participated in bias-motivated sprees with the exception of Damian, who would not discuss whether he had been involved in prior bias-motivated behaviors.

The participants involved in the more serious acts of bias had varying motivations, ranging from wanting to experience a sense of power, releasing frustration over personal issues, or engaging in an activity with a group of peers. Of the serious offenders, the skinheads were more likely to engage in bias-motivated sprees that involved minimal planning, while nonaffiliated offenders committed a smaller number of bias acts. Those participants who were involved in lower-level bias offenses attempted to resolve their conflict in a manner that would elicit a reaction. In this study, Jacqueline and Paulie responded to insults to themselves or their families by committing acts of vandalism or engaging in derogatory name-calling. Tannen also attempted to communicate the pain he felt by drawing a swastika on the school premises even though he did not fully understand the meaning of the swastika. The participants involved in the least serious acts of bias inadvertently learned from society that certain statements would cause a strong reaction in people, yet none of them completely understood the meaning of their actions or the reasons for the strong reaction from others. In each of their cases, the juveniles (Jaqueline, Paulie, and Tannen) committed their acts to evoke a strong reaction from others, but they did not completely comprehend why their actions would elicit such a strong reaction or understand the harm that their words and actions could cause.

For those committing acts of bias along the lower and middle range of the hate crime continuum, these participants appear to validate Woods's (2008) assertion that matching the offender to the appropriate program may deliver a better outcome than solely implementing penalty enhancements that do little to address the participant's needs and stop the behavior. Woods (2009) asserts that the prejudice within correctional facilities does little to challenge a hateful ideology. From this sample, Chadlie, Walden, and Damian continued their racialized beliefs even after serving several years at the correctional facility. For Fender, on the other hand, his incarceration led him to question his beliefs upon realizing how little he had in common with the older members of the Aryan Brotherhood who were incarcerated with him.

Damian, Derek, and Harley, on the other hand, may be beyond the scope of reintegrative efforts for altering their behaviors. All three participants demonstrated either indifference or hostility for the harm caused by their actions. While it remains unclear whether their attitudes or behaviors might have changed after receiving the appropriate services for dealing with their ordeals, it was evident that the passage of time and incarceration made little change in their attitudes. Although each had been incarcerated for several years, few aspects of compassion or empathy came across in their communication. Years after the attack, Damian's rationalization of stabbing of a man, his word choice in describing "chopping up" the victim, and his bursts of anger during the interview suggested that he still did not feel regret for the loss of a human life. During the interview, Derek exposed a sense of pride in his criminal accomplishments and raised several contradictions regarding his feelings toward homosexuality. Harley expressed indifference toward the incident, life, and his incarceration on death row. Walden's amenability to change remains a mystery. Throughout the interview, he demonstrated more sentiment and concern for human life than the last three offenders mentioned, yet he did not express a sincere regret for the harm caused by his actions. Chadlie remained committed to his ideological beliefs, yet he was not committed to the use of violence and showed signs of working on improving himself.

Conclusion

The goal of the research was to examine offenders, both affiliated and nonaffiliated with organized hate groups, across a continuum of bias-motivated behaviors. All of the interview participants, with the exception of three, experienced difficulty in coping with problematic circumstances in their lives. In several cases, the participants experienced family instability in the form of abandonment, abuse, or substance abuse problems. Four out of five offenders affiliated with hate groups admitted to receiving prescription medication for depression, having been placed in a mental health facility, or attempting suicide. Of the nonaffiliated participants involved in serious acts of bias, one disclosed his repeated suicide attempts and acts of self-mutilation while two other participants stated they suffered from bouts of depression. Some of the interview participants handled their unresolved personal family conflicts through their involvement with violence, while for others, the activity of committing a bias act provided a peer group set of responsibilities, and a collection of activities.

Nothing excuses bias-motived behavior, yet these acts may represent signs of reaching out for assistance in dealing with obstacles the participants are not equipped to handle on their own. Possibly, they may be outcasts at school, the victims of bullies, or acting out against problems within their families. At the less serious end of the continuum, participants were more likely to engage in a bias-motivated act as a means of expressing their pain through drastic measures that would attract attention and convey a message. In examining how the participants are distributed across the continuum of bias-motivated behavior, the researcher is optimistic about the possibility of preventing bias-motivated behaviors.

Restorative practices, in combination with an appropriate array of wraparound services, offer a noteworthy prospect for confronting bias-motivated behaviors. Restorative justice provides a framework that emphasizes acknowledging the harm committed by the offense, finding ways for the wrongdoer to repair the harm, and prioritizing healing for the victim and community (Zehr, 2002). Bias crimes harm not only the intended victim, but also members of the victim's group, who are often overlooked. Additionally, restorative justice focuses on all parties equally and acknowledges that victim healing can happen concurrently with the offender receiving the appropriate treatment. This framework recognizes that victims and communities are safer when offenders receive the assistance needed to stop their wrongful behaviors (Zehr, 2002). From a restorative justice perspective, in many situations, bias crimes lend themselves well to rehabilitating the offender with the community's assistance while also better serving the needs of the victim.

Efforts to implement restorative practices with hate crimes have been utilized globally, yet two cases taking place in the United States are most appropriate when discussing our participants. One example utilized restorative conferences to address racial tensions at a school in Minnesota (Coates, Umbreit, & Vos, 2006). The other example involved a face-to-face dialogue between the leaders of a mosque with a man who made phone threats after watching the events of September 11 unfold (Coates, Umbreit, & Vos, 2006). In these situations, the restorative processes required a bit of planning and effort, yet the outcomes in both circumstances eventually yielded healing and restorative results for both those who had been hurt and those who had caused the harm. Restorative justice holds offenders accountable while also providing them with the tools needed to address the misbehaviors.

The interview participants involved in the lower-level offenses could benefit from understanding the harm and impact resulting from their actions. The participants who required help in coping with their depression, alienation, or frustration would benefit from wraparound services that include coping skills and problem-solving as part of the overall rehabilitative approach (Wormith et al., 2007). Focusing on suitable social services and programs that address the underlying causes of the participant's behavior (Grisso, 2008) is the best approach to combat acts of hate. Problem-solving courts, such as mental health courts and drug courts, offer a holistic approach for addressing some of the needs of the youth while also holding them accountable for their misbehaviors. According to Kang et. al. (2015), young offenders who suffer from depression experience higher rates of aggression, substance use, and suicide. For these offenders, holistic approaches serve as a good starting point for confronting underlying troubles (Burriss et al., 2011) prior to them being ready to concentrate on their bias-motivated behaviors. For individuals experiencing mental health complications, every part of their life including their physical and emotional well-being, social interactions, and academic achievement is impacted by their struggles. By focusing on addressing their personal struggles first, the participants might be in a better place to understand the impact of their actions and more receptive to other rehabilitate efforts that focus on the bias crime.

Close examination of the participants demonstrates that many offenders are much like the rest of mainstream society (Levin & McDevitt, 1993): individuals struggling to cope with personal dilemmas or fulfilling a void through the use of destructive behaviors. Fortunately, those who were truly motivated by pure bias were far fewer than those who had the potential for change.

As society grows more complex and individuals face intense and complicated issues at earlier ages, young people will require assistance in processing, interpreting, and deciphering information. Social media and the expanding exposure to incivility, hate, and negativity will require an even more multifaceted set of coping skills to navigate life successfully. For young people who are "lacking in diverse personal experiences, [and] . . . are generally unprepared to reject prejudiced claims" (Levin & McDevitt, 1993, 43), the guidance of caring adults will become even more critical. While some individuals innately possess poor coping skills that can be magnified when placed in adverse environments, others with better coping skills find strength in adversity. The goal is to foster resiliency.

Societal stigmas against groups such as members of the lesbian, gay, bisexual, transgender, and queer (LGBTQ) community, immigrants, and other marginalized groups, communicates a message of "accepted aversion." A discriminatory climate laden with social norms that exclude members of LGBTQ community suggests that antigay persecution and harassment is practically regarded as conventional behavior (Dunbar, Quinones, & Crevecoeur, 2005; Franklin, 2000; Herek, 2000). In 2018, the U.S. Supreme Court ruled in favor of a business being able to refuse service to customers based on religious beliefs in the case *Masterpiece Cakeshop v. Colorado Civil Rights Commission* regarding the refusal of a cake shop owner to bake a wedding cake for a same-sex couple (Masterpiece Cake Shop, 2018). While refusal to bake a cake does not constitute a hate crime, one must examine how the participants in this study would know that acts of bias against the LGBTQ community are wrong when the messaging in society communicates that it is acceptable to view members of this community as inferior. Additionally, social discrimination against marginalized groups provides an advantage for offenders by stigmatizing the victim, lessening the victim's willingness to report a crime, and providing a lower risk of apprehension; as in the case of Dirk, Harley, and Derek who specifically targeted gay men to reduce the likelihood of the attacks being reported.

Also in 2018, the Southern Poverty Law Center filed a lawsuit against the U.S. Department of Homeland Security (DHS) for violating the U.S. Constitution by hampering detained immigrants from attaining legal assistance (Southern Poverty Law Center v. Homeland Security et. al., 2018). The U.S. Supreme Court's finding against the rights of immigrants in *Homeland Security v. Thuraissigiam* raises the question, what are the appropriate ways to address acts of hate when our own socially "acceptable" actions communicate that discrimination and unequal treatment represent conventional viewpoints (Southern Poverty Law Center v. Homeland Security et al., 2018)?

In order to seriously address bias-motivated offenses, mainstream culture needs to explore the messages conveyed by "legitimized" forms of discrimination and understand that individuals struggling with personal ordeals often target those who are already marginalized. These 12 interview participants illustrated that their behaviors were not solely driven by a hate ideology, but also by an inability to cope with alienation, family problems, substance use, and mental health concerns. Restorative practices and a variety of problem-solving strategies offer promising options for addressing the needs of many bias-motivated offenders, yet additional research regarding offenders involved across the entire hate crime continuum is essential.

References

Agaibi, C., & Wilson, J. (2005). Trauma, PTSD, and resilience: A review of the literature. *Trauma, Violence, & Abuse*, 6(3), 195–216.

Bjorgo, T. (1998, June 21–24). *Recruitment and disengagement from extreme groups: The case of racist youth subcultures.* Paper presented at 7th International Seminar on Environmental Criminology and Crime Analysis, Barcelona, Spain.

Blazak, R. (2009). Interview with a hate offender. In B. Perry (Ed.), *Hate crimes* (pp. 189–205). Westport, CT: Praeger.

Bureau of Justice Assistance. (1997). *A policymaker's guide to hate crimes.* Washington, DC: U.S. Department of Justice.

Burriss, F. A., Breland-Noble, A. M., Webster, J. L., & Soto, J. A. (2011). Juvenile mental health courts for adjudicated youth: Role implications for child and adolescent psychiatric mental health nurses. *Journal of Child and Adolescent Psychiatric Nursing*, 24(2), 114–121.

Capellan, J. A., & Gomez, S. (2018). Change and stability in offender, behaviours, and incident-level characteristics of mass public shootings in the United States, 1984–2015. *Journal of Investigative Psychology & Offender Profiling*, 15(1), 51–72.

Castle, T. L. (2009). Female-perpetrated hate: A content analysis of hate incidents. In B. Perry (Ed.), *Hate crimes* (pp. 85–101). Westport, CT: Praeger.

Coates, R. B., Umbreit, M. S., & Vos, B. (2006). Responding to hate crimes through restorative justice dialogue. *Contemporary Justice Review*, 9(1), 7–21. https://doi.org/10.1080/10282580600564784

Dunbar, E., Quinones, J., & Crevecoeur, D. A. (2005). Assessment of hate crime offenders: The role of bias intent in examining violence risk. *Journal of Forensic Psychology Practice*, 5(1), 1–19.

Earls, F. J., & Reiss, A. J. (1994). *Breaking the cycle: Predicting and preventing crime.* Washington, DC: National Institute of Justice.

Emmons, J. M., & Belangee, S. E. (2018). Understanding the discouraged child within the school system: An Adlerian view of the school-to-prison pipeline. *Journal of Individual Psychology*, 74(1), 134–153.

Federal Bureau of Investigation (FBI). (2017). *Hate crime statistics 2016: Characteristics of hate crimes in 2016—Summary of hate crime data collection.* Washington, DC: U.S. Department of Justice.

Finn, P. (1988). Bias crime: A special target for prosecutors. *Prosecutor*, 21(4), 9–15.

Franklin, K. (2000). Antigay behaviors among young adults: Prevalence, patterns, and motivators in a noncriminal population. *Journal of Interpersonal Violence*, 15(4), 338–362.

Friedman, A. S. (1998). Substance use/abuse as a predictor to illegal and violent behavior: A review of the relevant literature. *Aggression and Violent Behavior*, 3(4), 339–355.

Gavrielides, T. (2012). Contextualizing restorative justice for hate crime. *Journal of Interpersonal Violence*, 27(18), 3624–3643. https://doi.org/10.1177/0886260512447575

Godinet, M. T., & Stotzer, R. (2016). Juvenile perpetrators of race/ethnicity-based bias crimes. *Journal of Ethnicity in Criminal Justice*, 15(1), 21–35.

Gray, P. (2015). "I hate talking about it": Identifying and supporting traumatized young people in custody. *Howard Journal of Criminal Justice*, 54(5), 434–450. https://doi.org/10.1111/hojo.12143

Grisso, T. (2008). Adolescent offenders with mental disorders. *Future Child*, 18(2), 143–164.

Herek, G. M. (2000). The psychology of sexual prejudice. *Current Directions in Psychological Science*, 9(1), 19–22.

Hirschi, T. (1969). *Causes of delinquency.* Berkeley, CA: University of California Press.

Kang, T., Eno Louden, J., Ricks, E. P., & Jones, R. L. (2015). Aggression, substance use disorder, and presence of a prior suicide attempt among juvenile offenders with subclinical depression. *Law and Human Behavior*, 39(6), 593–601. http://dx.doi.org/10.1037/lhb0000145

Kirby, L. D., & Fraser, M. W. (1997). Risk and resiliency in childhood. In M. W. Fraser (Ed.), *Risk and resiliency* (pp. 10–33). Washington, DC: NASW Press.

Lankford, A. (2013). *The myth of martyrdom: What really drives suicide bombers, rampage shooters, and other self-destructive killers?* New York, NY: St. Martin's Press.

Levin, J., & McDevitt, J. (1993). *Hate crimes: The rising tide of bigotry and bloodshed.* New York, NY: Plenum.

Levin, J., & McDevitt, J. (2002). *Hate crimes revisited: America's war against those who are different.* Boulder, CO: Cambridge.

Maruna, S., & LeBel, T. (2003). Welcome home? Examining the "re-entry court" concept from a strengths-based perspective. *Western Criminology Review,* 4(2), 91–107.

Masterpiece Cakeshop Ltd. et al., Petitioner v. Colorado Civil Rights Commission, et al. (2018). https://www.supremecourt.gov/opinions/17pdf/16-111_new2_22p3.pdf

McDevitt, J., Levin., J., & Bennett, S. (2002). Hate crime offenders: An expanded typology. *Journal of Social Issues*, 58(2), 303–317.

National Council on Disability. (2015). Breaking the school-to-prison pipeline for students with disabilities. Washington, DC: National Council on Disability.

National Institute of Justice (NIJ). (2005). Annual report: U.S. Department of Justice Office of Justice Programs. https://www.ojp.gov/pdffiles1/nij/213267.pdf

Perzigian, A. B., Afacan, K., Justin, W., & Wilkerson, K. L. (2017). Characteristics of students in traditional versus alternative high schools: A cross-sectional analysis of enrollment in one urban district. *Education and Urban Society,* 49(7), 676–700.

Roxell, L. (2016). Imprisonment and co-offending: Results from a 10-year follow-up study. *Journal of Scandinavian Studies in Criminology and Crime Prevention*, 17(2), 203–219. https://doi.org/10.1080/14043858.2016.1260327

Sampson, R. J., & Laub, J. H. (2003). Desistance from crime over the life course. In J. T. Mortimer & M. Shanahan (Eds.), *Handbook of life course* (pp. 295–310). New York, NY: Kluwer Academic/Plenum.

Southern Poverty Law Center. (2020). SPLC statement on U.S. Supreme Court's decisions in DHS V. Thuraissigiam. https://www.splcenter.org/presscenter/splc-statement-us-supreme-courts-decision-dhs-v-thuraissigiam

Southern Poverty Law Center v. U.S. Department of Homeland Security, et al. (2018). https://www.splcenter.org/seeking-justice/case-docket/southern-poverty-law-center-v-us-department-homeland-security-et-al

Spillane, L. A. (1994). Hate crimes: A legal perspective. In J. E. Hendrichs & B. Byers (Eds.), *Multicultural perspectives in criminal justice and criminology* (pp. 233–257). Springfield, IL: Charles C. Thomas.

Steinberg, A., Brooks, J., & Remtulla, T. (2003). Youth hate crimes: Identification, prevention, and intervention. *American Journal of Psychiatry*, 160(5), 979–989.

Tedeschi, R. G., & Calhoun, L. G. (2004). Target article: "Posttraumatic growth: Conceptual foundations and empirical evidence." *Psychological Inquiry*, 15(1), 1–18.

U.S. Department of Justice. (1990). *Hate crime data collection guidelines*. Washington, DC: Federal Bureau of Investigation.

van der Put, C. E., Creemers, H. E., & Hoeve, M. (2014). Differences between juvenile offenders with and without substance use problems in the prevalence and impact of risk and protective factors for criminal recidivism. *Drug Alcohol Dependence*, 134, 267–274.

Wilkerson, K. L., Afacan, K., Perzigian, A. B., Justin, W., & Lequia, J. L. (2016). Behavior-focused alternative schools: Impact on student outcomes. *Behavioral Disorders*, 41(2), 81–94.

Woods, J. B. (2008). Taking the "hate" out of hate crimes: Applying unfair advantage theory to justify the enhanced punishment of opportunistic bias crimes. *UCLA Law Review*, 56(2), 489–541.

Woods, J. B. (2009). Addressing youth bias crime. *UCLA Law Review*, 56(6), 1899–1934.

Wormith, J. S., Althouse, R., Simpson, M., Reitzel, L. R., Fagan, T. J., & Morgan, R. D. (2007). The rehabilitation and reintegration of offenders: The current landscape and some future directions for correctional psychology. *Criminal Justice and Behavior*, 34(7), 879–892.

Zehr, H. (2002). *The little book of restorative justice*. Intercourse, PA: Good Books.

CHAPTER FOUR

Devoted Actors and Devoted Fraternity: The Necessary Role of Ideology in Intergroup Violence

Amalio Blanco, Rubén Blanco, and Luis de la Corte

A couple of years ago, an international group of archaeologists and anthropologists (Mirazón-Lahr et al., 2016) documented a case of intergroup violence (supposedly the first found to date in a fossil record) that occurred around the Holocene period (approximately 12,000 years ago) whose victims (12) were a group of hunter–gatherers from Nataruk (Kenya). The authors noted that this massacre was motivated by the struggle for food and to conquer a territory rich in resources. This event would support the realistic theory of conflict (Sherif & Sherif, 1953): the origin of many violent conflicts staged by human beings is the dispute over limited resources, the interference in the achievement of goals, and the rivalry of interests. The "opportunity hoarding", together with exploitation, have historically played a decisive role in collective violence. Privileged access to valuable and renewable resources subject to monopoly by a certain group leads to inequalities and frustrations that could be developed through violent actions (Tilly, 2003, 10).

At the Kataruk massacre, Henri Tajfel would have guessed that the victims would have been deprived of these goods, resulting in their very negative attitude towards the "powerful" group (ideology) accumulating with it frustration, anger, resentment (hate), which would have fed into the conflict. Certainly, these processes are not at the origin of scarce resources or goal incompatibility, but once they come into play, they acquire a functional autonomy independent of the objective situation itself, becoming one of the causal factors of intergroup relationships, including violent conflict (Tajfel, 1981, 225). That is to say, competition over tangible resources is not the only pathway to conflict; add to that the incompatibility of values, the protection of certain beliefs or the attempt to forcefully impose these beliefs.

A motive that has reached powerful functional autonomy as a trigger for violent conflicts is religion. Neuberg, et al. (2011) examined the role of competition over tangible resources, the incompatibility of values, and the infusion of religion into intergroup conflicts, which are, as Tajfel (1981, 31) rightly observed, one of the fundamental problems of our time. To do this, Neuberg, et al. (2011) use the information provided by 471 experts (political scientists, anthropologists, historians, sociologists, or economists) around the world by completing an internet survey about current and well-known intergroup conflicts in countries such as Algeria, Cyprus, India, Rwanda, Sri Lanka, etc., and other sites randomly sampled. Beyond the potential that, independently, each of these three predictors has on the presence of conflict (unique item regarding negative prejudice against members of other groups), the main conclusion is that religious infusion improve the extent to which incompatible values predict intergroup conflict, and when religious infusion interacts with incompatible values and resource-power differential, we are facing the most dangerous and disruptive conflicts.

In one way or another, cognitive–emotional processes have always been present in the history of violence; they have been, and continue to be, a force to be reckoned. Certainly, "nothing happens in an ideological vacuum, and everything happens through its discursive density" (Del Águila, 2008, 16), which does not necessarily coincide with its rich plot. Now, when we think of collective violence protagonists, three nuances cannot go unnoticed: ideological discourse is not born out of nothing nor in the solitude of the human mind; this discourse does not have the same intensity in all of them; and, finally, it does not appear at the same moment. Sometimes the discourse acts as an instigator of violent action; in other cases, it does so as a post hoc justification of actions caused by circumstances beyond beliefs and values (beyond ideology). In the end, the circle of violence opens and closes with the same clasp: either we start with internal processes (ideology or hate) that mark the beginning of the path, or we justify our actions based on our acceptance of the reality. The key is that we look for legitimacy in its roots or we try to justify the results. Attaching a subjective meaning to the behavior, defined by Max Weber as social action (1978), is not always necessary to precede its realization, but it is always necessary to validate its results, justify its rationality a posteriori, when it comes to actions that undermine dignity, integrity, and life of people: "Violence always requires a justification against the reality to which it applies; and that is where the rationality of violence converges with the legitimacy of its results or with the legitimacy on the part of those who dispose of power" (Martín-Baró, 1983, 375).

In *Soldiers of the Third Reich*, Sönke Neitzel and Harald Welzer analyze the conversations of WWII German prisoners recorded by the British in the Combined Services Detailed Interrogation Center (CSDIC). Firsthand testimony of these soldiers gives special value to this study as outlined in the prologue: "most soldiers are hardly interested in issues of ideology, politics, world order and the like; they do not wage war out of conviction, but because they are soldiers and their job is to fight" (Neitzel & Welzer, 2012, 13).[1] The argument that unfolds throughout the book: it is time "to end the overvaluation of the ideological," because in war people do things "that in other circumstances they would not do" (Neitzel & Welzer, 327). In the case of radicalization, the implicit or explicit tendency to see involvement in terrorism as stemming from the adoption of radical beliefs contrasts with "the vast majority of radicals who never become involved in terrorism and are not all terrorists primarily motivated by their beliefs" (Schuurman & Taylor, 2018, 3), not even suicide terrorists (Sheehan, 2014, 83).

Specific circumstances is one of the keys, because under their (oppressor's) influence, people act by simply following the demands of the role with which they have been entrusted, following the orders of an authority figure(s), or they give in to group pressure to inflict harm on innocent people, even going so far as to take lives. But after participating in these barbaric events under these specified circumstances, the journey back is devastating: "after a certain amount of time soldiers become brutal when exposed to immense brutality" (Neitzel & Welzer, 2012, 71), they are accustomed to violence, desensitized to the others' pain, and turn the victim into an enemy by way of moral disengagement (Bandura, 1999), and so on. In his well-known research on Battalion 101, Christopher Browning describes it crudely: the soldiers became increasingly brutalized, the atrocities became routine, and killing turned out to be easier and easier. "In this sense, brutalization was not the cause but the effect of these men's behavior" (Browning, 2001, 161). All this is related to a simple and elementary ideology of hatred, but of a secondary hatred, almost involuntary; however, in its independent functioning as an originally triggering motive, it ends up having the same power as instigating hatred.

The journey back (the need to give meaning and justification to collective violence that is not motivated by incompatibility of values or by the defense of religion or religious beliefs) will be the first objective of this chapter. The perpetrators of collective violence usually travel this path in groups because that is where they find the primary support to reduce the dissonance that results from acting against their own convictions. It is also in a group, or as a consequence of group influence, when they usually make the decision to join violent activities, against either infidels or the members of rival gangs,

Some Lessons to Be Learned (or Remembered)

The first author of this chapter was surrounded, during his childhood and adolescence, by people who had fought in the Spanish Civil War, all of them belonging to the losing side, among them his own father. He heard them tell, over and over again, stories of battles, victories, defeats, punishments, threats, deaths (many deaths), and so on, but never heard a story full of hate, resentment, or desire for revenge against the victors. They told their stories without the drama that is usually associated with a war, which was also fought between people from the same country, from the same city, from the same community, and even from the same family. And when they talked about those killed from the opposing side, they did it with more resignation than dejection, assuming that in war people kill each other, and can do it "sine ira et studio" (without anger or passion)[2] They narrated the events with notable psychological distance, peaceful peasants whose historical circumstances (living in an area dominated by the legitimate government of the Republic) forced them to be on one side of the trench shooting against those who, due to similar circumstances (living in an area dominated by the forces that gave rise to the coup against the legitimate government) were on the opposite side, many of them, also, peaceful peasants. In both cases, they were reluctant warriors, since their involvement in the war front depended much more on geography than on ideology (Matthews, 2012). In fact, the soldiers were much more concerned with their materials and security at the front (food, cold weather, permits, news about their families, health, etc.) than with the ideals for which the war was supposedly fought.[3] In fact,

> In July 1936 only a small minority of militants had internalized one of the ideologies and was willing to fight and kill to impose their views on the other Spain. . . . Recruits from both sides resorted to creative and often desperate measures to elude service. Many others reluctantly served and tried not to be noticed while the hostilities lasted, and others easily changed sides when it was convenient or when it was possible. (Matthews, 2012, 318)[4]

The aforementioned study by Sönke Neitzel and Harald Welzer offers a very similar image:

> War forms a context of actions and events in which human beings do things that, in other circumstances, they would never do. Within this context, soldiers kill Jews even when they are not anti-Semitic, and defend their country with fanaticism even when they are not nationalists. The time has come to end the overvaluation of the ideological; ideology might lead to war, but it does not explain why soldiers kill or perpetrate war crimes. (Neitzel & Welzer, 2012, 327)

The same seems to have occurred among American soldiers in World War II, Korea, and Vietnam; "among American military historians, psychologists, and sociologists, the conventional wisdom on why soldiers fight is that ideology is relatively unimportant" (Atran et al., 2014, 42). This is not, then, a surprising fact; rather the opposite, in the innumerable wars that have taken place in human history, many (in some cases, the majority) of the participants have not acted under the influence of their attitudes.

Counter-attitudinal behavior has been studied and was derived from empirical evidence outlined in Richard LaPiere's research. The actual admission of a Chinese couple in several hotels in the United States was examined (behavior); and only two months later, a follow-up of negative responses (attitude) came from the employees of those same hotels. When asked "if they would accommodate an important Chinese gentleman," their reply was, "No" at 91 percent (LaPiere, 1934, 231). There is no doubt that attitude is an important trigger for behavior, but it would be a mistake to think that it is the only one, that it is the most decisive, or that it is always present. Jack Brehm thought that counter-attitudinal behavior was an isolated event; only "sometimes an individual engages in behavior inconsistent with his beliefs and feelings" (Brehm, 1960, 164). Festinger (1957), however, considered it an everyday condition, and in a wide variety of situations nearly unavoidable, especially when certain circumstances defined by forced compliance are involved.

Anyone familiar with psychosocial research involving counter-attitudinal behavior can immediately recall three emblematic investigations in which forced compliance reaches its most lethal level: those of Solomon Asch on peer pressure, those of Stanley Milgram on obedience to authority figures, and the Stanford Prison Experiment (SPE). Milgram (1975) pointed directly to the Holocaust, Zimbardo to the climate of violence and violation of the most elementary rights in United States prisons. The results of Asch's (1952) investigations leave the question about whether group pressure could lead to actions that endanger the integrity and even the lives of third parties.

Christopher Browning wonders if the massacre at Józefów was a radicalized Milgram experiment, with real killers as participants. Although it is not easy to draw a parallel between the environments in which the experiments were carried out and the forest where the Józefów massacre took place, "many of Milgram's insights find graphic confirmation in the behavior and testimony of the men of Reserve Police Battalion 101" (Browning, 2001, 174). That was what explicitly, accompanied by a modest realism,[5] the author himself had intended when he conducted his 18 experiments (620 participants) on obedience to authority figures: "these inhumane policies [Gas chambers, death camps, etc.] may have originated in the mind of a single person, but they could only have been carried out on a massive scale if a very large number of people obeyed orders" (Milgram, 1975, 1).

Milgram clearly establishes the historical framework in which his work takes place. As is well known, the concrete trigger were the chronicles of Hannah Arendt on the trial against Adolf Eichmann held in Jerusalem in the early sixties, later bounded in a book (Arendt, 1963). It is not our purpose to enter into the debate on the banality of evil, but to remember that banality is not a quality of the action or its consequences, but of the person who performs it ("ordinary men doing extraordinary tasks," says Raul Hilberg [1985]). Milgram understood it, and that was the antecedent for his experiments, "After witnessing hundreds of ordinary people submit to authority in our own experiments, I must conclude that Arendt's conception of the banality of evil comes closer to the truth than one might dare imagine" (Milgram, 1975, 5). What comes as a surprise to Mark Juergensmeyer and many others is "why are things done by people who otherwise appear to be good—in the case of religious terrorism by pious people dedicated to moral vision of the world" (Juergensmeyer, 2003, 7). In any case, it should be added that this banality begins to falter on the back end and calls for an additional effort of justification to avoid psychological collapse.

Reducing the complex machinery of the Nazi regime to obedience to authority figures (not Milgram's intention[6]) is as inappropriate as denying its role in the events that gave rise to this regime, especially in the development of the Final Solution. At that point, says Arthur Miller, the author who has vastly studied Milgram's legacy, the relationship between Milgram's experiments and the Holocaust (M-H thesis) "is thus convincing" (Miller, 2004, 234). This thesis, adds Miller, would be complete if the importance of dehumanization is introduced. Certainly, Milgram did not address it directly, but commented on "the catalog of inhuman actions performed by ordinary Americans in the Vietnamese conflict" (Milgram, 1975, 181). This catalog would lay the foundations of the rationality of outcomes, and would therefore be part of the path, which seeks the legitimization of the results through very simple but efficient cognitive–emotional strategies (see Table 4-1).

Table 4-1 Steps to Dehumanization (Milgram, 1975, 181–183)

- Radical change of social setting: the adolescent travels from a civilian context to that dominated by military authority in which, "an oath of allegiance is employed to further strengthen the recruit's commitment to his new role" (181).
- The military training is aimed not only to get technical skills, but "to break down any residues of individuality and selfhood" (181).
- Total institution: immersion of the young recruits into a total institution in which the obedience to authority has to be learned and accepted as his main characteristic.
- Indoctrination: construction of enemy image: "those he confronts in battle are enemies of his nation" who want it to see destroyed. The death and any inhumane action seen justified (181): "he kills others in a just cause" (182).
- Bureaucratic structure: each one must comply with his duty, and carry out in the most adequate way the task entrusted to him. For this, discipline must be maintained, and the best way to it is obedience.
- Agentic state through which "the soldier experiences no individual constraints against killing, wounding, or maiming others, whether soldiers or civilians" (182).
- Rebellion: the possibility of disobeying is very remote. First, because of the punishment that this implies ("the defector must be isolated, or severely punished to discourage imitation," 182), and then, because "the soldier does not wish to appear as coward, disloyal, or un-American," but as patriotic, courageous (182).
- Technology: the physical distancing of the victim through technology "helps reduce strain by providing needed buffers" (183).

This highlights the difference in behavior of the young soldiers in Vietnam, which "makes the behavior of our experimental subjects appear as angels' play" (Milgram, 1975, 183). That is probably the primary key: what deserves the most concern and criticism from any social scientist are not only the possible methodological errors of Milgram's experiments or the supposed violation of ethical codes that should govern the research,[7] but the critique of those circumstances that have caused, and continue to cause, the greatest personal damage and social destruction that human beings have known throughout history through political and religious wars, terrorist actions, genocides, ethnic cleansings, and so on. From all points of view it is necessary to review the political and religious structures that are presided over by blind obedience to authority figures. That none of these events have happened in an ideological vacuum, revisiting Rafael Del Águila (2008), is as unquestionable as that many of the people who participated in them did so under powerful circumstances. Milgram himself, as we have just covered, establishes a clear difference between the policies originated in the mind of a single or several persons (ideology), and those who implement these guidelines for no other reason and without any obligation other than to obey the orders of an authority figure and fulfill their duty; that is, without the need to share those ideological policies, and even openly oppose them. These are the "ordinary men" that have been alluded to in both psychological and historiographical research. Whether or not Adolf Eichmann is one of them is a marginal issue to the central issue: what occurred in the laboratory at Yale University is an angelic anecdote compared to the violence displayed by that very large number of reluctant warriors (unwilling executioners) who "simply doing their jobs, and *without any particular hostility on their part*, can become agents in a terrible destructive process" (Milgram, 1975, 6. Italics added).

Commenting on Milgram's experiments, Zygmunt Bauman aptly picks up the generalized feeling that lurks within it—when we are able to strip ourselves of the illusive belief in our moral superiority over that of those Germans who participated in carrying out the tasks of the Holocaust or of the subjects who participated in the obedience to authority experiments: the most worrisome data "was not the likelihood that 'this' could be done to us, but the idea that we could do it" (Bauman, 1989, 152). The retort that Jerry Burger makes of Milgram's experiments puts us once again in the face of harsh reality, the "average Americans react to this laboratory situation today much the way they did 45 years ago" (Burger, 2009, 9). Most frightening is the close resemblance of the perpetrators to any of the people we meet and interact with in our daily lives, "ordinary men were to perform extraordinary tasks" (Hilberg, 1985, 263). This was the strange and bitter surprise of the Jews of Jedwabne: what they saw before their eyes were not anonymous faces in uniform, but, to a greater horror and bewilderment, their own neighbors willing to kill them (Gross, 2001, 211). They are the same "exemplary neighbors" of whom the people of Madrid knew were the terrorists who perpetrated the 11-M attacks. Of them, from Jamal Zougan, Mohamed Chaoui, and Mohamed Bakkali, only good words were heard in the Lavapiés (Madrid) neighborhood where they lived (see Blanco, 2005, 153–158; see also Del Águila, 2005, 15–18). Many of us, like Elie Wiesel, are also annoyed to think that Eichmann is human. We would have preferred him to be a monster with three ears and four eyes, like Picasso (Wiesel, 1996, 416).

When thinking about Eichmann, Milgram allocates obedience as a piece of the social system, of a system of hierarchical coordination, and as a prerequisite of the social organization, and asks himself what happens when "the autonomously acting individual is embedded in a social structure where he functions as a component of a system rather than on his own" (Milgram, 1975, 126). The answer is immediate; when that happens, the person "comes to see himself as an agent for executing the wishes of another person" (133), renouncing to act according to his own ideas, his own desires, his way of perceiving and assessing the situation from his own accord. Here is a powerful circumstance in which the person will behave in a manner counter to his convictions (Festinger, 1957, 84). The agentic state, the keystone of Milgram's analysis, is a state of mind that renders the person completely "open to regulation by a person of higher status" and with that, ceasing to be considered responsible for his own actions.

This is the point; the person dispenses with their attitudes, momentarily puts aside their convictions, engaging in behavior inconsistent with their beliefs and feelings all while under the pressure of an authority figure. The ideological justification invoked by the participants in the experiments is part of the circumstances; scientific research as a legitimate social enterprise is accepted (Milgram, 1975, 142). We are therefore faced with actions whose path does not need ideological support and reasoning. If we analyze some of the results of Milgram in light of the banality of evil hypothesis, it could be said that the agentic state is a state of mind characterized by the absence of thought (thoughtlessness), an evil devoid of reason occupied by the majority of perpetrators. The strange thing is that among them was a person who held a high position within the Nazi system, as was Adolf Eichmann. But the image that Arendt renders from him is unmistakable: "I have never realized what he was doing. . . . It was sheer thoughtlessness that predisposed him to become one of the greatest criminals of that period" (Arendt, 1964, 291).

Crimes of obedience are, then, a paradigmatic example of counter-attitudinal behavior in which, as we have just seen, the figure of authority becomes the primordial ingredient of the context. Assuming that "the occurrence of sanctioned massacres cannot be adequately explained by the existence of psychological forces," Kelman and Hamilton (1989) add two important conditions to the authority figure, bureaucracy and dehumanization, under whose influence a decisive part of our ideology (moral codes) becomes weakened, paving the way to becoming agents in a destructive process (15–16; see Table 4-2).

That said, it cannot go unnoticed that in the experiment designed by Milgram, obedience to the authority figure is an optional fact whose violation has no consequences. However, in certain organizational contexts (the military, terrorist groups, gangs, etc.), obedience to authority is part of the structure and is inherent to normal functioning. This can convert obedience into ideology, as is the case of Islamic groups such as Hamas and Islamic Jihad (Post, 2005b): "the introduction to authority and unquestioning obedience to Allah and authority is instilled at a young age and continue to be evident in the individual members' subservience to the larger organization" (626). This is new proof of how the processes involving

Table 4-2 Processes That Create the Conditions for Authorized Massacres (Source: Kelman & Hamilton, 1989)

Authority	Bureaucracy	Dehumanization
It is based on the submission process.	It is based on identification.	The victim is readily identified as belonging to a category stigmatized, discriminated and excluded.
The law and the norm are instruments of orientation for the subjects.	The role, mechanism by which the subjects are oriented.	Definition of the victim according to the social category to which he belongs.
Obedience as a priority response.	Careful division of tasks between the actors.	Construction of the enemy image.
There is no possibility to choose.	Role execution: regularized and mechanized behaviors.	Denying the victim two qualities essential to be considered a human being: identity and community.
It requires answers in terms of obligation and not personal preferences.	The different parts (roles) reinforce each other in order to project the image that what happens is perfectly normal, correct, and legitimate.	
The actors are not responsible for the consequences of their actions.	It is more concerned with the proper and correct execution of the action than with its consequences.	
The supreme value is loyalty.	Reduction of the need to make decisions.	
	Minimization possibility of raising moral issues.	

group-organizational structure and ideological structure end up giving feedback.

Browning believes, however, that in the criminal history of Battalion 101 compliance plays a more important role than obedience. If that were the case, and we have no reason to think otherwise, it is necessary to do something Browning does not do: turn to Solomon Asch and his universally known experiments on group pressure. We are interested in three considerations, which can help us unravel some of the secrets of extreme violence without having to rely on cognitive–emotional processes as triggers of violence.

The first affects an important psychological process: group pressure undermines confidence in our way of seeing and interpreting the events that surround us. Given the unusual response from some of the participants regarding a simple task of comparing the length of two lines, several of the experimental subjects, in a perverse and damaging strategy, turned to the use of self-blame, which exempts the group (within the context) of responsibility. The general tone of the argument is exemplified in the following testimony: "To me it seems I'm right, but my reason tells me I'm wrong, because I doubt that so many people could be wrong and I alone right" (Asch, 1952, 464).

The second consideration is part of a keystone of group theory: the group never goes unnoticed for those who are in it and for those who belong to it. Much less, a group has tasks entrusted to test the psychic strength of its members and whose realization requires the commitment and collaboration of all of them to carry them out effectively and with integrity. In this case, in a particularly significant way, the group becomes a shared living space, a common field of activity and experiences that in part has formed each and every one of the phenomena that has accounted for more than a century of group theory: pressure, groupthink, polarization, conflict, decision making, cohesion, social climate, leadership, identity fusion, which already has an important presence in research on jihadist radicalization (e.g., Atran et al., 2014; Gómez et al., 2017; Pape, 2005; Post, 2005b). In short, "as soon as a person is in the midst of a group he is no longer indifferent to it. He may stand in a wholly unequivocal relation to an object when alone; but as soon as a group and its direction are present he ceases to be determined solely by his own coordinates" (Asch, 1952, 483). All this acquires maximum expression in a fact, which is theoretically significant, to which Kurt Lewin paid special attention: the group is the living space par excellence in the life of any person (Lewin, 1948),[8] so that the danger of being deprived of its protection and support is a risk for which a high price is paid: rejection, exclusion, isolation. "Those who did not shoot risked isolation, rejection, and ostracism," says Christopher Browning of the members of Battalion 101, a psychosocially ill-advised perspective in a group that lived a year and a half doing unusual and psychologically destructive tasks in a strange and hostile environment. Those same terms are those employed by the Islamist terrorists from Hamas: "anyone who did not enter that period (intifada) would have been ostracized" (Post, 2005b, 627). Things are not very different in the case of gangs: the group imposes its logic, its rationality, its vision of reality:

> Although of some occasions the aggressions could be considered illegitimate or without much basis, there comes a time when the group logic becomes the person's own logic, in situations where the freedom to act differently is reduced. As the group logic imposes itself, at an experiential level, the women begin adopting and assuming it as a way of functioning that is regular, standardized, and legitimated, which in turn deepens the emotional distance between them and their victims. (IUDOP, 2010, 254)

This occurs because the group is also, and above all, an environment of support, protection, identity, belonging, and so on. That is why "the comrade not only voluntarily or involuntarily relinquishes autonomy to integrate into a community, but also gets something in return: the community preserves, gives security, support, recognition" (Neitzel & Welzer, 2012, 35), and as this happens successfully, it will be more difficult to face pressure. The perverse circumstances of Battalion 101 demanded companionship, mutual support, and commitment to solidarity in the fulfillment of an extremely uncomfortable, disgusting, and depraved task. Loyalties to intimate cohorts of peers become "the critical factor determining suicide terrorism behavior. In this particular case, loyalty is based on religious communion (Atran, 2003, 1537), showing, once again, that in many cases, the group and friendship pathway is not an alternative process or an excluding variable of ideology; however, it is complementary. In the end, and regardless of the instigating mechanisms of violence and the content that define the way, "nothing binds people to each other stronger than shared responsibility for an act they admit is criminal" (Bauman, 1989, 158).

Through a simple experimental design, Solomon Asch provides compelling evidence against methodological individualism and alerts against the danger of being within a group whose view is distorted, and defends ideas contrary to the most basic human rights. The group transforms these ideas and normalizes racism, xenophobia, discrimination, machismo, homophobia, or the extermination of people because of their ethnicity, their religious beliefs, their nationality, and so on.

> When individuals abrogate their capacity to think and judge in their own way, when they cease to relate themselves independently to things and persons, when they surrender initiative and delegate it to others, they are

> altering the social process and introducing into it a radical arbitrariness. The act of independence is productive from the social point of view, since it is the only way to correct errors and to steer the social process in accordance with felt requirements. On the other hand, the act of yielding is antisocial, because it spreads error and confusion. (Asch, 1952, 495)

From our point of view, this is the most decisive conclusion and the most important lesson of Asch's studies on group pressure. Overshadowed by the foolish responses of the participants to a simple task and the recalcitrant individualism that dominates American psychology, the social dimension of conformity and fallacy that sometimes hides behind unanimity has gone unnoticed.

Victor Klemperer, a Jewish intellectual, wrote a document of great historical and psychological value (an extensive diary covering the 12 years of the Nazi regime, 1933–1945) in which there is convincing evidence regarding radical arbitrariness and social confusion that Solomon Asch attributed to conformity. Those of us who have lived far from these realities have been able to turn the unusual into normal, which we then find it difficult to understand how it was possible to reach such extremes and allow ourselves to think that we would not have reached such excesses. With this we again give rise to the fundamental attribution error believing, incidentally, that we are immune to the contextual influence. Klemperer takes us off this dreaming naively.

We live surrounded by circumstances and conditions (the subject of the action is a situated subject) that sometimes allows, advises, pressures, forces, or in some cases reinforces in us an attitude-discrepant behavior in the following terms (Blanco, 2011, 67):

1. The uncritical dependence that characterizes the climate defined by a figure that exercises unqualified authority and without restraint (agentic state) leads us to abdicate the most elemental moral convictions and feelings.
2. The diffusion of responsibility limits our actions, practically in the same terms as the agentic state, to the mere fulfillment of duty (instrumental rationality) without paying attention to the consequences that could derive from it (ethical rationality).
3. Group pressure leads us on the path of conformity, undermines our confidence in ourselves, and makes us faithful acolytes of the majority.
4. Unanimity as a norm in social functioning forces us to renounce the richness of diversity, independence, and autonomy.
5. Anonymity (the possibility of hiding behind a mask without showing the face) lowers the threshold of the restrictions of conduct and opens the doors to actions in which the personal face of the other disappears.

There are behaviors that, in their origin, do not require the support of the cognitive and effective component of attitudes. There are social actions that need neither preferences nor inferences. For decades (e.g., Cohen, 1962; Festinger, 1957; Festinger & Carlsmith, 1959) we have known that the situation of discrepancy between attitude and behavior is very frequent in everyday life. However, we should not consider the image of a man seeking for consistency, consonance, or balance among his thoughts, feelings, and actions or among his actions, feelings, and thoughts. There is always a way back. William McGuire, a member of that extraordinary group of investigators (Milton Rosenberg, Irving Janis, Harold Kelley, among others) commanded by Carl Hovland, defined it with meridian clarity: "a person's need to maintain harmony between his feelings, thoughts, and actions is a powerful determinant of his belief systems and of his gross behavior "(McGuire, 1960, 65). The evidence accumulated over the years allows us to affirm: a) that cognitive consistency is a core motive "that is indeed as fundamental as claimed by Festinger" (Gawronski, 2012, 653); b) that when there is an inconsistency between thought and action, the implied inconsistency requires a reassessment of beliefs, a reorganization of meanings, a reinterpretation of the circumstances, and c) that people are often more concerned with what makes them feel good than what is accurate (659). Suffice it to recall the testimonies of the soldiers in the Spanish War, in the Vietnam War, or in World War II, which we alluded to at the beginning of the chapter.

Together with the rationality of the motives that instigate violent action, the search for the legitimacy of the results comes into play. The first seeks, protects, and reinforces the second, but this does not necessarily suppose, nor does it need, any motivating reason. "The rationality of outcomes" is a situated, local rationality, circumscribed to a concrete action at a precise moment. This is the core assumption of the relativity theory of rationality: "all human judgments and behavioral choices are coherent in the restricted, local, sense of the term" (Kruglanski & Oerhek, 2009, 665). From the local perspective, from the psychology of the moment, "all our choices and judgments are locally rational." This is probably the framework used by the unwilling executors for a world that makes sense in which facts and ideas are consistent. Leon Festinger gives us some clues:

1. To some degree, dissonance (strain, frustration, disequilibrium, psychological discomfort) is "an inevitable consequence of forced compliance," but with a particularity of special relevance: "the greater the importance of the situation, the greater will be the magnitude of the dissonance" (Festinger, 1957, 92). In the cases that concern us the importance of the situation is beyond doubt: it is about applying extreme violence against innocent people, the strain and psychological discomfort is especially high and the need to reduce it especially intense.

2. Forced compliance (being forced to perform an action either for fear of punishment or for the search for reinforcement) ends up having an influence on cognition. When, for any reason, we are forced to act outside of our convictions, we tend to put in line what we do with what we think, above all, should be added if that action is continued or it is a behavior that violates the most basic moral principles. "If a person is induced to say something which is contrary to his private opinion, there will be a tendency for him to change his opinion so to bring it into correspondence with what he has done or said" (Festinger & Carlsmith, 1959, 209).
3. The dissonance may be reduced by three ways: a) by decreasing the number of dissonant relations; b) by increasing the number of consonant relations; and c) by getting the social support from other people, something that is "easy to obtain when a rather large number of persons are together in the same situation" (Festinger, 1957, 192). In that case, "the dissonance will be materially reduced and perhaps even eliminated" (191).

The most important challenge faced by the Nazi regime to carry out its genocidal policy was not administrative, but psychological: "the ability of the perpetrators to cope with weighty psychological obstacles and impediments," to avoid the psychological disintegration; prevent the breakdown of men and their conversion into "either 'savages' or 'neurotics'" (Hilberg, 1985, 274). The strategies to overcome the moral inhibitions of those "ordinary men" performing "extraordinary tasks" were two: a mechanism of repressions and a system of rationalizations.

The latter were numerous. In the case of the bureaucrats, Hilberg (1985) distinguishes the following: a) the Jews dominated the world: "the Germans drew a picture of an international Jewry ruling the world and plotting the destruction of Germany and German life" (Hilberg, 1985, 284); b) the "Jewish conspiracy": they were spies, enemy agents, inciters of revolt, saboteurs, and assassins who were plotting the destruction of Germany; c) Jewry is a lower form of life. Regarding the perpetrators, the rationalizations and excuses were: a) the doctrine of superior orders. This was "the oldest, the simplest, and the most effective rationalization": first and foremost there was the discipline (Hilberg, 1985, 288). The presumption of legitimacy, trustworthiness, and expertise are common characteristics to the authorities in charge (Kelman & Hamilton, 1989, 152); b) it is not the personal vindictiveness nor hate that was behind the actions against the Jews; c) the need to collaborate, to be supportive in the task; d) life is struggle, and whoever does not fight perishes.

Despite these strategies of rationalization, it was not always possible to avoid the psychological breakdown. The psychic suffering of the victimizers was important and quite generalized, so that "sometimes, the shell cracks.

The executioners confess to being traumatized by what they have done, what they have seen, what they have heard and what they have felt" (Ingrao, 2017, 406). The need for searching for the meaning after the commission of the extreme violent action (e.g., kill an innocent English soldier in the name of the independence of Israel, a value-rational action, according to Max Weber) exemplifies the following story.

The Social Cycles of Group Membership and the Need of Belonging

Apparently, neither the soldiers of the Third Reich (Neitzel & Welzer, 2012) nor those who participated in the Spanish Civil War (Matthews, 2012) nor those who were part of the North American army in the Vietnam War were interested in issues of ideology. For them, loyalty to the group, the defense of comrades, the moral group, the "devoted fraternity" among the soldiers in the front line, and for all the survival for one's self were much more important. The reluctant soldiers should not be presumed, then, that ideology is the instigator of their joining ranks. Edward Shils and Moritz Janowitz were part of the Intelligence Section of the Psychology Division of the "Supreme Headquarters Allied Expeditionary Force" (SHAEF) during World War II. The tenacity, the willpower, and the fighting spirit of the German Army did not reside in the political conviction of its soldiers, but in "the steady satisfaction of certain primary personality demands" by the social organization of the army "(Shils & Janowitz, 1948, 281): affection, esteem, support, protection, sense of power, and so on. From the psychosocial point of view, this can become a truism; from the field of political science, this would be a surprising hypothesis. But it is even more so if we suspect it in those who voluntarily join groups or organizations whose main objective is to attempt against the lives of "enemies" or against those who impede the achievement of their objectives, as, for example, with the people who join the gangs ("maras") in the Central American countries or the jihadist groups (Berg & Carranza, 2018).

In recent years, hypotheses and empirical data have come to question—or at least moderate—the importance of ideology, frequently by combining it with the presence of other motivational forces in the genesis of terrorist groups (e.g., Abrahms et al. 2018; Atran et al., 2014; Cottee & Hayward, 2011; De la Corte, 2015; Post, 2005a, 2005b; Sageman, 2008; Schuurman & Taylor, 2018; Sheehan, 2014). These authors note that social networks and personal ties between people play a significant role in the entering into and belonging to jihadist groups. Besides a "sacred values" pathway, there is also a "sacred fraternity" as an incentive for joining jihadist groups. The working group on culture in the International Summit on Democracy, Terrorism and Security held in Madrid came to the conclusion, regarding the sources of recruitment, that "young people attracted to the global jihad may not be particularly religious when they join: they are recruited through social networks,[9] and radicalization takes place within the group" (Stern, 2005, 36). Schuurman & Taylor (2018) define this position in the following terms: "by raising beliefs as the key element to understanding terrorism, what we might call 'mainstream' radicalization not only incorrectly inflates beliefs with behavior, but overstates the explanatory potential of this variable while leaving others under-emphasized" (15). Those other forgotten variables come from group and organizational processes known to those we have referred to in the previous section (norms, pressure, obedience, fulfillment of duty, polarization, group thinking, etc.). Among them, we have seen that some authors emphasize the importance of collective identity and the fusion of individual identity with group identity.

Through a complex analysis of the terrorist attacks from 1998 to 2005 using the Global Terrorism Database (GTD), Abrahms et al. (2018) differentiate between outputs, held by "parent group" (viz. principal terrorist group), and process goals independently hold by the affiliates (viz. agents). The hypothesis that they put to the test is that the affiliates are groups especially prone to cruel and indiscriminate violence against civilians no matter the political costs or even the achievement of outcomes goals. They do so to expand their audience and to ensure their survival by associating with other terrorist groups, that is, not for ideological convictions but for organizational imperatives, "to sustain the group by attracting attention, gaining media coverage, and that boosting membership through recruitment" (Abrahms et al., 2018, 24). The core finding of the analysis is that "ideology continues to fail to explain why affiliates are prone to civilian targeting," even after controlling for the official ideologies of the groups (35).

Schuurman & Taylor (2018, 5) take the starting point of the case study of the Dutch homegrown jihadist Hofstadgroup (to this group belonged Mohammed Bouyeri, the confessed assassin of Theo Van Gogh, the Dutch filmmaker, in November 2004) to show through the Dutch police files on the group and semi-structured interviews with former participants why and how only some of those who hold radical views will act on them. As a paradigmatic example, the authors describe the process of radicalization of one of the young people belonging to the group. The process (involvement in the Hofstadgroup) began when this young man determined that not being able to obtain the internship needed to complete his studies was an act of discrimination due to his Moroccan origin. An older Syrian man pursuaded him that his failure to get an internship is related to "being a Muslim in a land of unbelievers." This is the way that he is in touch with the Hofstadgroup, a youth gang.

"At least initially, it was not the radical and extremist discussions being held at Hofstadgroup gatherings that bound this individual to the group. Instead, he simply enjoyed spending time with people who he got along well with. Only gradually did he adopt the Salafi-Jihadist convictions brandished by the group's inner-circle. Group-level factors were thus critical to binding him to the Hofstadgroup and bringing about his internalization of an extremist ideology. His ultimate arrest on terrorism-related charges was similarly influenced by more than convictions alone" (Schuurman & Taylor, 2018, 12).

Often terror groups start from a "bunch of guys" that got together for some other reason (to play soccer, to go eating, to join a student association, etc.). Then they all became radicalized together. Nobody is radicalized alone. The decision to join a terrorist organization is very often a collective one, not an individual one: "the decisions that promote and support terrorist campaigns respond to collective ideological motives" (De la Corte et al., 2007, 370). Friendship and kinship are the main reasons for joining the global Islamist terrorism social movement. The investigations carried out by Marc Sageman offered surprising results: over 84% of the people in the sample were in the diaspora: terror is a diaspora phenomenon; about two-thirds were friends with other people joined together or having some connection to terrorism; about a fifth were close relatives—sons, brothers, first cousins—of people already belonging to a Islamist terrorism social movement; 68% knew each other before they became terrorists, and 10% were family members (see Sageman, 2008, 71–88).

The experiences of self-radicalization or radicalization without social interaction constitute a strangeness or, depending on how one looks at it, an impossibility because even the few examples of subjects apparently radicalized in solitude are powerfully influenced by other individuals with whom they interact via the Internet. When investigating a radicalization dynamic in the previous or initial phases, there is usually a trace of a relationship with one or more people who already frequent a radical environment or who are active members of a terrorist group or organization (De la Corte, 2015, 6).

In many cases, it is a relationship of friendship that is forming processes close to those that occur within the primary groups. Five of the seven Madrid bombers—the ones that committed collective suicide on April 3, 2004, in Leganés—were born in Tetouan (Morocco) and were childhood friends. Of the seven people involved in the London bombings, six were friends. The backbone of the Hofstadgroup in Amsterdam came from the port of al-Hoceima (Rif region of Morocco) (Sageman, 2008, 84). Ultimately, "the attributes of terrorists are shaped by processes of social interaction" (De la Corte et al., 2007, 368) typical of the dynamics that develop within small groups, practically in the same terms that make an appearance in the gangs: pressure, obedience to the leader, fulfillment of the tasks that have been entrusted, polarization, group thinking, development of in-group love and out-group hate. There is no doubt that "the process of becoming a terrorist [as well as a member of a mara] involves a cumulative, incrementally focused commitment to the group" (Post, 2005a, 9). The numerous data collected through online and field studies by Gómez et al. (2017) reveal that the sacred values are not only religious but also secular, and that such values are always learned and shared inside a group. The devoted actors ready to make costly sacrifices are always members of groups: "all combatants were fused with at least one group whose members were perceived to be sharing at least one sacred value" (Gómez et al., 2017, 674). There is no combatant without group. The power of group dynamics is a key to understanding the "fighting spirit" that characterizes the members of groups that define their raison d'etre not only in comparison but in violent opposition with other groups, whether these groups pertain to jihadist terrorism or Central American gangs.

Life in the gang generates a common history, a constant exchange of knowledge, and a strengthening of friendship ties. Although the criminal aspect is the one that stands out for the external observer, the fundamental motivation for its members is to access a more immediate space of socialization and source of identity (Sosa & Rocha, 2001, 373).

Similar to the jihadist groups, the maras are also a "bunch of guys" spending time with people with whom they get along well. They are, above all else, an extremely violent group, becoming "one of the greatest challenges for the development and well-being of the inhabitants of the region, especially for the youth" (ERIC, IDESO, IDIES, & IUDOP, 2004, 17). In fact, "crime and violence are now a key development issue for Central American countries. In three nations—El Salvador, Guatemala and Honduras—crime rates are among the top five in Latin America" (World Bank, 2011, ii), which is like saying that they are among the three highest in the world for reasons not due to war or civil conflicts.

In 1998, José Miguel Cruz and Nelson Portillo carried out the first systematic investigation on gangs in El Salvador. It involved 1,025 young gang members of both sexes (78% men and 22% women). The participants answered a questionnaire of 50 questions divided into four sections: a) sociodemographic data; b) entry into the gang; c) life in the gang, and d) personal history. The answers to the question about what the individual likes best about their gang membership is as follows: the "hesitant" (42%), well-being (17.9%), the understanding you have found in the group (6.5%), and "hainas" (girls) (5.9%). Although they may seem naive, these answers are far from insignificant. The first three reasons for satisfaction that the Salvadoran street corner boys see in the gang should not go unnoticed. The "vacil" is a term that accommodates a wide range of activities, ranging from "take a walk, drink, go to parties, have sex, meet in a park, to consume drugs or perform criminal actions" (Cruz & Portillo, 1998, 59). The young people are in the billiard halls, on the street corners, or in the parks. They first get involved in criminal activities that are the prelude to their incorporation into the mara where their friends, their brothers, their neighbors are. Also here, with as much or more reason than in the jihadist scenarios, the personal ties, the social networks created around the neighborhood, play a preponderant role in the recruitment. In the study by Santacruz and Eastman (2001), the influence of friends was the main reason to join the group for 20% of gang members. One of the participants in the study in Nicaragua describes it in the following way: "Friendships take you to the group. You integrate because there are your brokers" "(Sosa & Rocha, 2001, 372). The vacil is, therefore, at the base of sociality and responds with maximum precision to the four reasons why people seek the company of others (the affiliation motive): to seek positive stimulation, for emotional support, to gain social comparison information, and to get attention from other people (Leary, 2010, 865).

For this, the following data is sufficient: in 2016, the homicide rate per 100,000 populations in these three countries was as follows: 81.2 in El Salvador, 27.3 in Guatemala, and 59.1 in Honduras. The percentage of these homicides perpetrated by gangs is uncertain. The Report of the Institute of Reflection, Research and Communication (ERIC) of Honduras, the Institute of Surveys and Opinion Polls (IDESO) of Nicaragua, the Institute of Economic and Social Research (IDIES) of Guatemala, and the University Institute of Opinion Public (IUDOP) of El Salvador estimate that it would approach 20% in Guatemala, 40% in El Salvador, "a majority" in Honduras, and a minority (1%) in Nicaragua (ERIC, IDESO, IDIES, & IUDOP, 2004, 16).

That need for positive stimulation, for emotional support, and attention are at the origin of the entrance to the maras of many young Central Americans. In Cruz and Portillo's (1998) research, for example, questions about the reasons for entering the gang, and for the benefits or advantages of belonging to the gang, result in the following (see Table 4-3).

It is not necessary to conduct a sophisticated analysis to find a clear correspondence in the answers, which could be summarized in the following terms: the gang members like the vacil because they seek protection, respect,

Table 4-3 Reasons for Entry into a Gang and the Benefits of Membership (Source: Cruz & Portillo, 1998, 64, 66)

Reasons to Enter the Gang	Benefits or Advantages of Belonging to the Gang
For the "vacil": 46%	None: 19.1%
Problems with parents: 12.3%	Respect: 16.3%
For friends: 10.3%	Friendship: 15.6%
Lack of understanding: 9.3%	Support: 13.4%
For protection: 5.8%	Money: 7.9%

support, understanding, and a relationship they have not enjoyed in the family and community environment. All these are basic emotional needs, which congregate around the need to belong (Baumeister & Leary, 1995) whose main way of satisfaction is the primary groups. The mara fully covers all these needs, thus becoming the group of belonging and of primary reference for its members. The mara becomes, in this way, a psychological group in the full sense of the term, that is, a group that has a special psychological meaning for its members because it acts as its main frame of social comparison, as normative and evaluative guideline, and, therefore, as the main agent of influence on the members' attitudes and behaviors (Turner, 1987). But the vacil also has a point of connection with the search for adventure, excitement, "thrills" or "kicks," one of the subterranean values that characterized the delinquent street gangs in the United States (Matza & Sykes, 1961). It would be an "existential choice," which in the case of some of the members of the terrorist groups would result in a desire for excitement (the pleasures of violent combat, the excitement of taking a guerrilla identity, etc.), for ultimate meanings (to defend the sacred, to fight out of fidelity to the primary group, to sacrifice the life for the causes of the comrades, etc.), and for glory (for pride, for personal self-affirmation, and to view themselves as heroic figures) (Cottee & Hayward, 2011).

There is a correspondence between the reasons for recruitment and membership and the advantages of belonging to a group in which violence is part of their reason for being. Where there are problems with parents, there is respect; where friends are sought, friendship is found; where there is a lack of protection, there is support. This is a game of complementarities that is almost perfect: the mara offers what is sought, in the mara you will find satisfaction of emotional needs; the mara becomes the real family: "the main function of the gang is to provide the young people who constitute it all those elements of which they have been deprived or have received a certain deficit during their life "(Cruz & Portillo, 1998, 70). This substitute function is again evident when gang members are asked, "What have you gained and lost in the gang?" The answers point in the same direction. The gains affect the need for relationship: friends (86.6% in the case of boys and 74.3% on the part of girls), union (68.5% in boys and 55.8% in girls), power (80% boys and 68.6% girls), respect (87.2% boys and 73.9% girls), protection (73.3% boys and 64.6% girls), and self-confidence (64.2% boys and 56.6% girls). The losses are reflected in confidence in society (91.7% boys and 94.7% girls), education opportunities (80% boys and 87.6% girls), tranquility (65, 3% boys and 74.8% girls), and job opportunities (82% boys and 87.6% girls) (Cruz & Portillo, 1998, 213–221).

Family disintegration, abandonment, or neglect; lack of affection; abuse or mistreatment of children within the home; poor parental authority, and so on, are repeated very consistently throughout the investigations in various countries of Central America (e.g., Castro & Carranza, 2001; Cruz & Santa Cruz, 2001; Merino, 2001; Sosa & Rocha, 2001). By the way, in his analysis of the youth violence in the United States, Ervin Staub comes to the same conclusion: "Gang membership is at least partly the outcome of a course of development. Neglectful, hostile, and permissive parenting—combined with the observation of violence in the home, in surrounding communities, and on television—lead to a negative orientation toward people, to the belief that aggression is normal, acceptable and unavoidable or even good, and to poor social skills" (Staub, 1996, 126).

All these shortcomings are especially evident in a novel investigation carried out with 15 women gang members who are serving prison for crimes of homicide. In their stories, three reasons for admission are present: a) dysfunctional interfamilial dynamics; b) desires for revenge towards an aggressor (family member or not); and c) interest, curiosity, or pleasure for this type of group (sensation seeking). Among the three, this research highlighted the harmful experience that all of them, had in the family environment, practically for the same reasons: lack of affection, interfamily violence, sexual harassment, abuse, negligence, and so on.

The gang comes to fill the gaps left by other instances. It becomes a family, because it provides the affection that the disintegrated family did not give. It replaces the school, because the street becomes the primary stage of socialization and learning. It even acquires a certain religious connotation, because "it offers a vision of the world and a framework of values and demands an unconditional adhesion" (Rocha, 2001, 436). There is, then, a "cycle of family expulsion" (abandonment, discrimination, and violence, which in the case of girls is completed with sexual violence), which sets the basis for entry into gangs. Added to this is a feeling of social exclusion in terms of low family income, lack of job opportunities, poor educational and health infrastructure, adverse material conditions of life, and so on, which remind us of the difficult life conditions that Ervin Staub refers to. Staub also makes this point in his studies on genocide and youth violence (Staub, 1989, 1996).

In the narrative of gang members, the cycle of family expulsion and social expulsion go hand in hand; both are experienced as negative emotional experiences in terms of rejection, discrimination, exclusion, and constant humiliation, which leave a deep and bitter mark on their self-esteem and their identity. It is not surprising, then, that the testimonies describe the moment of admission "in addictive terms, like the rapid charm of a hallucinogenic drug" (Castro & Mendoza, 2001, 277).

In the case of jihadist radicalization, there is also a cycle (feeling) of social expulsion. De la Corte (2017) points out to experiences and personal circumstances that may induce feelings of radicalization: a) punctual or repeated episodes of discrimination, mistreatment, or abuse because of national, ethnic, or religious identity; b) experiences of marginalization and social exclusion; c) traumatic experiences of sociopolitical origin (repression and persecution, armed conflict) and family crisis (loss of relatives) or personal crisis (fall in crime, sentimental disappointments); d) familiarization with foreign cases of discrimination, marginalization, injustice, and trauma (140–141). For Marc Sageman, those feelings are part of the "moral outrage" that characterizes the terrorists of the diaspora by hearing and watching the suffering, the humiliation, of fellow Muslims from around the world (Sageman, 2008). And the group of experts convened to mark the first anniversary of the terrorist attacks in Madrid (2004) also refers to the cycle of social expulsion we are talking about: "although most Muslim immigrants and refugees are not 'stateless,' many suffer from an existential sense of loss, deprivation and alienation from the countries in which they live" (Post, 2005a, 9).

These gang members see violence as "a form of defense and/or reaction to the offenses or mistreatment of others" (Santacruz & Cruz, 2001, 65) and that coming from the institutions. For them, the use of violence is a way to defend the territory, to intimidate the enemy, to gain prestige for the in-group, to take the first step in the voracious chain of death that surrounds the gang members: to kill before being killed, be the victimizer before becoming a victim. Violence against the police is part of this argument: "the police agents are the people who make the marero feel the exclusion that society feels towards them" (Merino, 2004, 135). Those who condemn must be condemned: that seems to be the logic, and that is one of the rationalization techniques used by gangsters in Nicaragua (Rocha & Bellanger, 2004, 348). Elliot Aronson explains the massacre perpetrated by Eric Harris and Dylan Klebold at the Columbine High School in the same way: in the eyes of both adolescents the rejection, the continuous insults, and humiliations to which they were subjected by their companions (those who condemn) deserved a response (they must be condemned). The desire to avenge the humiliations could have been at the origin of that massacre (Aronson, 2000).

The violence acquires, then, an instrumental value: through it, the gang member "is noticed and asserted," acquires status (power), wins and instills respect, tries to have a visible place, gains prominence (Sosa & Rocha, 2001, 401) and acceptance: "as family disintegration has left a vacuum in self-esteem and as young people seek identity, street fights are the best device to gain fame, respect, and show who they are" (Rocha, 2001, 437). Those were precisely the "profits" to which the Salvadoran gangs alluded to: friendship, union, power, respect, protection, and self-confidence (Cruz & Portillo, 1998). Valga describes the response of one gang member as feeling "calm." In the focus groups conducted with members of these gangs (Santacruz & Cruz, 2001), one participant stated that "when you enter the gang you are like a rebel without a cause, and sometimes with attitudes or with the actions that you want to make known one's capabilities, and many times to survive, one has to exert violence, as a demonstration that I am also worthy, that they listen to me, that they look at me" (Santacruz & Cruz, 2001, 91).

The same event happens in the case of jihadist terrorism. Belonging to these groups and being willing to make costly sacrifices is "the true path to glory and fame with respect to their friends," family, leaders, neighbors, etc. The terrorists know "their friends would respect them, watch their videos for inspiration and celebrate their sacrifice" (Sageman, 2008, 87). The testimonies collected by Jerrold Post are very revealing (see also Atran, 2003, 1537): "After recruitment, my social status was greatly enhanced. I got a lot of respect from my acquaintances, and from the young people in the village." This is the testimony of a Palestinian terrorist (Post, 2008b, 623). "Perpetrators of armed attacks were seen as heroes, their families got a great deal of material assistance, including the construction of new homes to replace those destroyed by the Israeli authorities as punishment for terrorist attacks" (Post, 2008b, 626). "Recruits were treated with great respect. A youngster who belonged to Hamas or Fatah was considered more highly than one who did not belong to a group and got better treatment than the unaffiliated kids" (Post, 2008b, 627).

One of the gang members who participated in the study of Juan José Sosa and José Luis Rocha in Nicaragua offers the following testimony:

> In 1992 it was the first time I killed. . . . It was to rob a couple of men in Don Bosco. But they were puyas and robbed two young people who were with us and one cut off an ear. Then we went and found them sitting on a bench, careless. One of them was able to flee. But the one we grabbed we stabbed. The others dropped a stone quarry on the testicles and another on the head. That's how we retaliate. And so I was implanting respect. Before nobody respected me because I was poor. But I made myself respected, and it is very important to gain respect. (Sosa & Rocha, 2004, 423)

Respect (status, power), honor, fame, identity, even economic solvency are achieved thanks to belonging to the group. This becomes, then, the center of the affections, attentions, and favors on the part of its members (Tajfel et al., 1971): in-group love. The other side of the coin is the out-group hate. The relationship between these two processes so central in intergroup relations is not always direct or reciprocal. Marilyn Brewer considers them "separable phenomena," but that there are certain conditions in which "maintaining in-group integrity and loyalty for the way to outgroup hate and hostility" (Brewer, 1999, 435). Three of the four conditions that Brewer points out (sense of moral superiority, perceived threat, search for positive distinctiveness, and transformation of the group in a political entity) are present in many of the terrorist groups, among them, in the Islamic terrorists groups.

For very similar reasons, especially perceived threat and search for a positive distinctiveness, so are they in gangs. In both cases, then, it is easy to identify a direct relationship between in-group love and out-group hate. However, the decision to join the jihad has a frame of reference and a more collective moral commitment. The humiliation of friends, the humiliation of Muslims in general, the defense of a worldview shared by millions of people, the desire for revenge, the fight for a collective future (Atran et al., 2014) play a decisive role. In fact, the willingness to get involved in costly sacrifices is the most convincing expression of in-group love: "Many acts of suicide terrorism are a murderous form of what Durkheim called altruistic suicide. . . . The homicidal dimension of the act should not cause us to overlook an important cause leading to it: that many suicide terrorists are killing themselves to advance what they see as the common good" (Pape, 2005, 181).

Marilyn Brewer considers the search for positive distinctiveness as a condition that paves the way to out-group hate and hostility. In the balance of the studies carried out in four Central American countries on gangs, Juan Luis Rocha concludes: "Because, as family disintegration has left a gap in self-esteem and as young people seek identity, street fights are the best device to gain fame, respect. Hunger joined with the desire to eat, and fights come to raise self-esteem and provide identity" (Rocha, 2001, 437).

Distinctiveness, self-esteem, identity, all these psychological processes have as a frame of reference the group belonging and, more particularly, the emotional and value significance for the person of this group membership (Tajfel, 1981, 255). Both the emotional and value significance not born in a vacuum, but rather are the result of the processed intergroup comparison in which the members of the groups are much damaged. Repairing that damage and looking for a positive social identity are not only always an expected response, but also an individual and collective need (Tajfel, 1974, 1981; Turner, 1975). In some cases, the need to repair the battered social identity can lead to violent conflict. This hypothesis has been widely considered by practically all of the jihadist terrorism investigators cited in this chapter. There are "murderous identities" (Maalouf, 2004; Sen, 2006) "that reduce identity to one thing, install people in a partial, sectarian, intolerant, domineering, sometimes suicidal attitude, and often transform them into people who kill or [are] in favor of those who do it" (Maalouf, 2004, 38). In fact, many of the conflicts and barbarities in the world are a result of choiceless identity. The art of constructing hatred takes the form of invoking the omnipresent power of some allegedly predominant ideology that drowns out other affiliations, and in a bellicose form can also overpower any human sympathy or natural kindness that we may normally have. The result can be homespun elemental violence, or globally artful violence and terrorism (Sen, 2006, xv).

Conclusions

If we go back to the Kataruk massacre with which we opened the chapter, the positions of Sherif and Tajfel are clearly outlined. For the first, it is the self and/or group interest that is at the origin of the conflict. The ideas and/or negative representations about the other are a consequence of conflict of interests, and none of it is related to self-esteem or self-concept. For Tajfel (as for Lewin or for Asch), the group is the psychological scenario par excellence, our main emotional support; it is not only the custodian of our interests as the custodian of our personal image, and when it is perceived in danger as a consequence of the deprivation of certain goods or services that we consider fair, of discrimination, rejection, and so on, violence has its doors open. It is not always necessary to be convinced that this is the only way out of a personal or collective situation. In many contexts marked by violence (war is one of them), people do things that in other circumstances they would not do; they do them even against their own will and regardless of their convictions. Let us recall again Festinger (1957): "there are circumstances in which persons will behave counter their convictions" (84).

In the case of the Holocaust, Milgram gave the clue: it is necessary to differentiate between those who design evil following the dictates of their ideology and those who implement obeying the orders of the authority, folding to the pressure of group or faithfully fulfilling their duty, and so on, all this "without any particular hostility" against the victims. "Ideology is not the only essential causal condition for the emergence of terrorism." In addition, it is necessary to have a set of people willing to mobilize (De la Corte, 2006, 268) or to be mobilized, capable of organizing or being organized.

To dispense with these and other circumstances when analyzing any of the many manifestations of human behavior again gives wings to the fundamental error of attribution (Ross, 1977): the belief of being immune from the influences of the environment, the world; and carries out an ontological rupture between levels of reality (the person and society, the person and the group, the self and the world, etc.) that contravenes the principles of the most elementary epistemology. It is not, therefore, individual psychology that can help us to clarify the issues that are at the origin of terrorist violence or that perpetrated by gang members, but a psychology that looks at and takes into account the main circumstance that surrounds a person's life: the group.

The conclusions of one of the groups of experts that participated in the International Summit on Democracy, Terrorism and Security held in Madrid in 2005, a year after the terrorist attacks on March, 11, 2004, concluded that, in spite of the many controversies, debates, and doubts about terrorism, there is a clear consensus: "that is not individual psychology, but group, organizational and social psychology, that provides the greatest analytical power in understanding this complex phenomenon." There is a group and friendship pathway in the roots of evil. In some cases, this pathway works independently of the ideology as a driving force behind the action; in others, both processes are fed back under the shared assumption that "ideologies have an existence independent of any individual single; and those which exist at a particular time are both of historical processes and of contemporary social events" (Adorno et al., 1950, 2). There are "no men in general who think, or even isolated individuals who do the thinking, but men in certain groups who have developed a particular style of thought in an endless series of responses to certain typical situations characterizing their common position." The main thesis of the sociology of knowledge (Mannheim, 1936, 3) summarizes perfectly the internal process that is lived in the bosom of many of the groups whose raison d'etre is the exercise of violence against them by enemies, whether infidels, the soldiers of the opposing enemy army, or the members of a rival gang.

The fact that nothing happens in the ideological vacuum (Del Águila, 2008), that the action has a meaning attached (Weber, 1978), and that social psychology, which is the frame of reference for the analysis of collective violence, is conceived as the study of action as ideological (Martín-Baró, 1983), does not imply the moment when ideology comes into play. The widespread belief that it must be in the original moment of the action contrasts with numerous data from both psychological and historiographical research, some of which seriously challenge the hypothesis that participants in the Holocaust (Goldhagen, 1996) or in any other war have been able to act protected in their ideology, thus becoming willing accomplices. The possibility that cognitive–emotional processes are part of the rationality of outcomes (Kruglanski & Oerhek, 2009) is indicated by the most solid psychosocial theory, the need to seek consistency and consistency between what we do and what we think or between what we think and what we do (Festinger, 1957; Festinger & Carlsmith, 1959; Gawronski, 2012; McGuire, 1960).

If we start from the assumption that the making of meaning is experienced via the sense of "me" (e.g., Greenwald et al., 2002; Markus, 1977), then the salience of the experience is based on the emotional and value significance for the person. Concerning group membership (Tajfel, 1981), it should not be surprising that people struggle to place the self in the most privileged situation possible and to rebel against those who ignore it, reject it, and despise it. "We are not only gregarious animals, but we have an innate propensity to get ourselves noticed, and noticed favorably, by our kind" (James, 1890, 293). And when that is denied as a consequence of our group or categorical belonging, the doors to the conflict are opened wide. This has a high probability of becoming violent when the main and/or only source of support, respect, consideration, prestige, and so on, comes from our group membership.

Notes

1. In a detailed study, Christian Ingrao argues that the ideological background of Nazism was elaborated by a group of about 80 people—"graduates, economists, jurists, linguists, philosophers, historians, geographers, some of whose university careers paralleled the activity of dogmatic construction, political surveillance and internal or external information in the workings of repression of the Third Reich, and especially in the Security Service (SD) of the SS, and that were mostly involved as of June 1941 in the attempt to exterminate the Jews of Eastern Europe, within the mobile commandos called Einsatzgruppen" (2017, 9). They build their ideology around two axes: utopian (the re-foundation German identity turned into a "promise of kingdom") and defensive (vigilance and war against the named enemies of the world portrayed primarily by the Jews). These axes appear, practically in the same terms, in Islamist terrorist rhetoric.

2. Weber alludes to the types of domination that characterize bureaucratic administration. This has often been considered a root cause of the Holocaust. Zygmunt Bauman's work "Modernity and the Holocaust." Kelman and Hamilton (1989) also refer to the bureaucratic administration when analyzing crimes of obedience. The bureaucratic administration carries with it "the domination of a formalistic impersonality: *sine ira et studio*, without hatred or passion, and hence without affection or enthusiasm. The dominant norms are concepts of straightforward duty without regard to personal considerations" (Weber, 1978, 225).

3. The same happened to the soldiers of Vietnam. Once they assumed the agentic state and parked their own convictions (agentic state as opposed to the state of autonomy) for the recruitment, "simply getting through the day and staying alive is chore enough; there is no time to worry about morality" (Milgram, 1975, 182).

4. However, the Spanish Civil War also featured willing fighters. John Dollard, a well-known psychologist, interviewed members of the Abraham Lincoln Brigade who fought together with the Republican soldiers against Franco. He posed the question: "What would you say are the most important things that help a man overcome fear in battle?" The answers were the aims of the war (fight against fascism) (77%); leadership (49%); esprit de corps (28%), hatred of enemy (21%), and distraction and keeping busy (17%) (as cited in Atran et al., 2014, 44).

5. Despite the differences between the laboratory and the reality of historical events, "I thought it worthwhile to start careful observation of obedience even in this modest situation, in the hope that it would stimulate insights and yield general propositions applicable to a variety of circumstances" (Milgram, 1975, 4).

6. The author himself is perfectly aware of this: "there are, of course, enormous differences between carrying out the orders of a commanding officer

during times of war and carrying out the orders of an experimenter." And he immediately adds what can be considered the key question: "How does a man behave when he is told by a legitimate authority figure to act against a third individual?" (Milgram, 1975, 4).

7. Zygmunt Bauman is surprised at the severe criticism Milgram received: "Milgram's techniques were put under the microscope, pulled apart, proclaimed faulty and even disgraceful, and reproved" (Bauman, 1989, 152). These criticisms, Milgram would say, are due to unexpected and very unassuming results (I could also have been, and could be at any moment, a necessary link in a chain of destruction). Bauman does not doubt that this is the reason for the criticism: "Milgram was right, of course. And he still is."

8. In the construction and acquisition of the normal and the abnormal, Lewin suggests that the process by which (an) individual becomes a criminal is the same as the process by which the individual avoids a criminal lifestyle. "What counts is the effect upon the individual of the circumstances of his life, the influence of the group in which he has grown up" (Lewin, 1948, 57).

9. The importance of social networks in the recruitment has been highlighted by practically all of the specialists. The mosques, the places of leisure, the prisons, the "halal" butcher shops, the radical Muslim student associations, and so on are propitious scenarios to start the path of radicalization, and even to join the suicide bomber production line, especially among the young people of the diaspora. Marc Sageman describes it precisely: the radicalization "could begin with low-risk participation—a soccer team, a youth gang, a student association." Even when they assist at a mosque, most of them go in search of companionship (Sageman, 2008, 86). In many cases, it's about spending time with people with whom they get along well. Christian Ingrao also grants a special role to the "networks of affinities and solidarity formed throughout studies and careers" in the process of radicalization of Nazi intellectuals (Ingrao, 2017, 198ff.).

References

Abrahms, M., Ward, M., & Kennedy, R. (2018). Explaining civilian attacks: Terrorist networks, principal-agent problems and target selection. *Perspective on Terrorism,* 12(1), 23–45.

Adorno, T., Frenkel-Brunswik, E., Levinson, D. J., & Sanford, R. N. (1950). *The authoritarian personality.* New York, NY: Harper & Row.

Arendt, H. (1963). *Eichmann in Jerusalem: A report on the banality of evil.* New York, NY: Viking Press.

Aronson, E. (2000). *Nobody left to hate: Teaching compassion after Columbine.* New York, NY: Henry Holt & Co.

Asch, S. E. (1952). *Social psychology.* Englewood Cliffs, NJ: Prentice-Hall.

Atran, S. (2003). Genesis of suicide terrorism. *Science,* 299(5612), 1534–1539.

Atran, S., Sheikh, H., & Gómez, A. (2014). For cause and comrade: Devoted actors and willingness to fight. *Cliodynamics, 5*(1), 41–57.

Bandura, A. (1999). Moral disengagement in the perpetration of inhumanities. *Personality and Social Psychology Review, 3*(3), 193–209.

Bauman, Z. (1989). *Modernity and the Holocaust.* Cambridge, UK: Polity Press.

Baumeister, R. F., & Leary, M. R. (1995). The need to belong: Desire for interpersonal attachments as a fundamental human motivation. *Psychological Bulletin, 117*(3), 497–529.

Berg, L. A., & Carranza, M. (2018). Organized criminal violence and territorial control: Evidence from northern Honduras. *Journal of Peace Research, 55*(5), 566–581. https://doi.org/10.1177/0022343317752796

Blanco, A. (2005). Obediencia, desindividuación e ideología: El drama de la libertad. In A. Blanco, R. del Águila, & J. M. Sabucedo (Eds.), *Madrid 11-M: Un análisis del mal y sus consecuencias* (pp. 153–187). Madrid, Spain: Trotta.

Blanco, A. (2011). *Psicología social.* Madrid, Spain: Ediciones CEF.

Brehm, J. W. (1960). A dissonance analysis of attitude-discrepant behavior. In M. J. Rosenberg, C. I. Hovland, W. J. McGuire, R. P. Abelson, & J. W. Brehm, *Attitude organization and change: An analysis of consistency among attitudes components* (pp. 164–197). New Haven, CT: Yale University Press.

Brewer, M. B. (1999). The psychology of prejudice: Ingroup love or outgroup hate? *Journal of Social Issues, 55*(3), 429–444.

Browning, C. R. (2001). *Ordinary men: Reserve Police Battalion 101 and the Final Solution in Poland.* London, UK: Penguin Books.

Burger, J. M. (2009). Replicating Milgram: Would people still obey today? *American Psychologist, 64*(1), 1–11.

Castro, M., & Mendoza, M. (2001). Las maras en Honduras. In ERIC, IDESO, IDIES, & IUDOP (Eds.), *Maras y pandillas en Centroamérica, Vol. I* (pp. 219–332). Managua, Nicaragua: UCA Publicaciones.

Cohen, A. R. (1962). An experiment on small rewards for discrepant compliance and attitude change. In J. W. Brehm & A. R. Cohen (Eds.), *Explorations in cognitive dissonance* (pp. 73–78). New York, NY: Wiley.

Cottee, S., & Hayward, K. (2011). Terrorist (e)motives: The existential attractions of terrorism. *Studies in Conflict & Terrorism, 34*(12), 963–986.

Cruz, J. M., & Portillo, N. (1998). *Solidaridad y violencia en las pandillas del gran San Salvador: Más allá de la vida loca.* San Salvador, El Salvador: UCA Ediciones.

Cruz, M. L., & Santacruz, J. M. (2001). Las maras en El Salvador. In ERIC, IDESO, IDIES e IUDOP (Eds.), *Maras y pandillas en Centroamérica, Vol. I* (pp. 17–107). Managua, Nicaragua: UCA Publicaciones.

De la Corte, L. (2006). *La lógica del terrorismo.* Madrid, Spain: Alianza.

De la Corte, L. (2015). ¿Por qué se radicalizan? Apuntes sobre la implicación en el terrorismo yihadista y su abordaje desde la psicología social. *Boletín de la Sociedad Científica Española de Psicología Social. Mayo-Agosto, 2015.*

De la Corte, L. (2017). The jihadi path to hate and terrorism: Questions and answers for risk management. In E. Dunbar, A. Blanco, A., & D. Crèvecoeur-MacPhail (Eds.), *The psychology of hate crimes as domestic terrorism, Vol. III: Interventions, treatment, and management* (pp. 133–159). Santa Barbara, CA: Praeger.

De la Corte, L., Kruglanski, A., de Miguel, J., & Sabucedo, J. M. (2007). Siete principios psicosociales para explicar el terrorismo. *Psicothema,* 19(3), 366–374.

Del Águila, R. (2005). Políticas perfectas: Ideales, moralidad y juicio. In A. Blanco, R. del Águila, & J. M. Sabucedo (Eds.), *Madrid 11-M. Un análisis del mal y sus consecuencias* (pp. 15–42). Madrid. Spain: Trotta.

Del Águila, R. (2008). *Crítica de las ideologías. El peligro de los ideales.* Madrid, Spain: Taurus.

Equipo de Reflexión, Investigación y Comunicación (ERIC), Instituto de Encuestas y Sondeo de Opinión (IDESO), Instituto de Investigaciones Económicas y Sociales (IDIES), e Instituto Universitario de la Opinión Pública (IUDOP). (2001). *Maras y pandillas en Centroamérica, Vol. I.* Managua, Nicaragua: UCA Publicaciones.

ERIC, IDESO, IDIES, & IUDOP (2004). *Maras y pandillas en Centroamérica, Vol. II.* San Salvador, El Salvador: UCA Ediciones.

Festinger, L. (1957). *A theory of cognitive dissonance.* Stanford, CA: Stanford University Press.

Festinger, L., & Carlsmith, J. (1959). Cognitive consequences of forced compliance. *Journal of Abnormal and Social Psychology,* 58(2), 203–210.

Gawronski, B. (2012). Back to the future of dissonance theory: Cognitive consistency as a core motive. *Social Cognition,* 30(6), 652–668.

Goldhagen, D. J. (1996). *Hitler's willing executioners: Ordinary Germans and the Holocaust.* New York, NY: Alfred Knopf.

Gómez, A., López-Rodríguez, L., Sheikh, H., Ginges, J., Wilson, L., Wazari, H., Vázquez, A., Davis, R., & Atran, S. (2017). The devoted actor's will to fight and the spiritual dimension of human conflict. *Nature Human Behaviour,* 1(9), 673–679.

Greenwald, A., Banaji, M., Rudman, L. Farnham, S., Nosek, B., & Mellott, D. (2002). A unified theory of implicit attitudes, stereotypes, self-esteem, and self-concept. *Psychological Review,* 109(1), 3–25.

Gross, J. T. (2001). Neighbors. *The destruction of the Jewish community in Jedwabne, Poland.* Princeton, NJ: Princeton University Press.

Hilberg, R. (1985). *The destruction of the European Jews.* New York, NY: Homes & Meier.

Ingrao, C. (2017). *Creer y destruir: Los intelectuales en la máquina de guerra de las SS.* Barcelona, Spain: Acantilado.

Instituto Universitario de Opinión Pública (IUDOP). (2010). *Seconds in the air: Women gang-members and their prisons.* San Salvador, El Salvador: UCA Editores.

James, W. (1890). *The principles of psychology, Vol. I*. New York, NY: Henry Holt & Company.
Juergensmeyer, M. (2003). *Terror in the mind of God: The global rise of religious violence*. Berkeley, CA: University of California Press.
Kelman, H. C., & Hamilton, V. L. (1989). *Crimes of obedience: Toward a social psychology of authority and responsibility*. New Haven, CT: Yale University Press.
Klemperer, V. (2001a). *I will bear witness: Diary of the Nazi years (1933–1941)*. New York, NY: Modern Library.
Klemperer, V. (2001b). *I will bear witness: Diary of the Nazi years (1942–1945)*. New York, NY: Modern Library.
Kruglanski, A. W., & Orehek, E. (2009). Toward a relativity theory of rationality. *Social Cognition, 27*, 639–660.
LaPiere, R. T. (1934). Attitudes vs. actions. *Social Forces*, 13(2), 230–237.
Leary, M. K. (2010). Affiliation, acceptance, and belonging. In S. T. Fiske, D. T. Gilbert, & G. Lindzey (Eds.), *Handbook of social psychology* (pp. 864–897). Hoboken, NJ: John Wiley & Sons.
Lewin, K. (1948). *Resolving social conflicts: Selected papers on group dynamics*. New York, NY: Harper & Row.
Maalouf, A. (2004). *Identidades asesinas*. Madrid, Spain: Alianza.
Mannheim, K. (1936). *Ideology and utopia*. New York, NY: Routledge & Kegan Paul.
Markus, H. (1977). Self-schemata and processing information about the self. *Journal of Personality and Social Psychology*, 35(2), 63–78.
Martín-Baró, I. (1983). *Acción e ideología: Psicología social desde Centroamérica*. San Salvador, El Salvador: UCA Editores.
Matthews, J. (2012). *Reluctant warriors: Republican Popular Army and Nationalist Army conscripts in the Spanish Civil War, 1936–1939*. Oxford, UK: Oxford University Press.
Matza, D., & Sykes, G. (1961). Juvenile delinquency and subterranean values. *American Sociological Review*, 26(5), 712–719.
McGuire, W. J. (1960). A syllogistic analysis of cognitive relationships. In M. J. Rosenberg, C. I. Hovland, W. J. McGuire, R. P. Abelson, & J. W. Brehm, *Attitude organization and change: An analysis of consistency among attitude components* (pp. 65–111). New Haven, CT. Yale University Press.
Merino, J. (2001). Las maras en Guatemala. In ERIC, IDESO, IDIES e IUDOP (Eds.), *Maras y pandillas en Centroamérica, Vol. I* (pp. 109–218). Managua, Nicaragua: UCA Publicaciones.
Merino, J. (2004). Políticas juveniles y rehabilitación de mareros en Guatemala. In ERIC, IDESO, IDIES, & IUDOP (Eds.), *Maras y pandillas en Centroamérica, Vol. III* (pp. 89–186). Managua, Nicaragua: UCA Publicaciones.
Milgram, S. (1975). *Obedience to authority*. New York, NY: Harper & Row.
Miller, A. G. (2004). What can the Milgram obedience experiments tell us about the Holocaust? In A. G. Miller (Ed.), *The social psychology of good and evil* (pp. 193–239). New York, NY: Guilford Press.

Mirazón-Lahr, M., Rivera, F., Power, R. K., Mounier, A., Copsey, B., Crivellaro, F., Edung, J. E., Maillo Fernandez, J. M., Kiarie, C., Lawrence, J., Leakey, A., Mbua, E., Miller, H., Muigai, A., Mukhongo, D. M., Van Baelen, A., Wood, R., Schwenninger, J.-L., Grün, R., … Foley, R. A. (2016). Intergroup violence among early Holocene hunter-gatherers of West Turkana, Kenya. *Nature,* 529(7586), 394–398.

Neitzel, S., & Welzer, H. (2012). *Soldados del Tercer Reich: Testimonios de lucha, muerte, y crimen.* Barcelona, Spain: Crítica.

Neuberg, S. L., Warner, C. M., Mistler, S. A., Berlin, A., Hill, E., Johnson, J. D., Filip-Crawford, G., Millsap, R. E., Thomas, G., Winkelman, M., Broome, B. J., Taylor, T. J., & Schober, J. (2011). Religion and intergroup conflict: Findings from the Global Group Relations Project. *Psychological Science,* 25(1), 198–206.

Pape, R. A. (2005). *Dying to win: The strategic logic of suicide terrorism.* New York, NY: Random House.

Post, J. M. (2005a). Psychology. In P. R. Neumann (Ed.), *The Club de Madrid Series on democracy and terrorism, Vol. I: Addressing the causes of terrorism* (pp. 7–12). Madrid, Spain: Club de Madrid.

Post, J. M. (2005b). When hatred is bred in the bone: Psycho-cultural foundations of contemporary terrorism. *Political Psychology,* 26(4), 615–636.

Rocha, J. L. (2001). Balance de los estudios en los cuatro países. In ERIC, IDESO, IDIES, & IUDOP (Eds.), *Maras y pandillas en Centroamérica, Vol. I* (pp. 431–444). Managua, Nicaragua: UCA Publicaciones.

Rocha, J. L., & Bellanger, W. (2004). Políticas juveniles y rehabilitación de pandilleros en Nicaragua. In ERIC, IDESO, IDIES, & IUDOP (Eds.), *Maras y pandillas en Centroamérica, Vol. III* (pp. 293–399). Managua, Nicaragua: UCA Publicaciones.

Ross, L. (1977). The intuitive psychologist and its shortcomings. In L. Berkowitz (Ed.), *Advances in experimental social psychology* (pp. 174–220). New York, NY: Academic Press.

Sageman, M. (2004). *Understanding terrorist networks.* Philadelphia, PA: University of Pennsylvania Press.

Sageman, M. (2008). *Learderless jihad: Terror networks in the twenty-first century.* Philadelphia, PA: University of Pennsylvania Press.

Santacruz, M. L., & Eastman, A. C. (2001). *Barrio adentro: La solidaridad violenta de las pandillas.* San Salvador, El Salvador: UCA Editores.

Schuurman, B., & Taylor, M. (2018). Reconsidering radicalization: Fanaticism and the link between ideas and violence. *Perspective on Terrorism,* 12(1), 3–22.

Sen, A. (2006). *Identity and violence: The illusion of destiny.* New York, NY: Norton & Co.

Sheehan, I. S. (2014). Are suicide terrorists suicidal? A critical assessment of the evidence. *Innovations in Clinical Neuroscience,* 11(9–10), 81–92.

Sherif, M., & Sherif, C. (1953). *Groups in harmony and tension.* New York, NY: Harper.

Shils, E. A., & Janowitz, M. (1948). Cohesion and disintegration in the Wehrmacht in World War II. *Public Opinion Quarterly,* 12(2), 280–315.
Sosa, J. J., & Rocha, J. L. (2001). Las pandillas en Nicaragua. In ERIC, IDESO, IDIES, & IUDOP (Eds.), *Maras y pandillas en Centroamérica, Vol. I* (pp. 333–421). Managua, Nicaragua: UCA Publicaciones.
Staub, E. (1989). *The roots of evil: The origins of genocide and other group violence.* New York, NY: Cambridge University Press.
Staub, E. (1996). Cultural-societal roots of violence: The examples of genocidal violence and of contemporary youth violence in the United States. *American Psychologist,* 51(2), 117–132.
Stern, J. (2005). Culture. In P. R. Neumann (Ed.), *The Club de Madrid Series on democracy and terrorism, Vol. I: Addressing the causes of terrorism* (pp. 35–39). Madrid, Spain: Club de Madrid.
Tajfel, H. (1974). Social identity and intergroup behaviour. *Social Science Information,* 13(2), 65–93.
Tajfel, H. (1981). *Human groups and social categories.* Cambridge, UK: Cambridge University Press.
Tajfel, H., Billig, M., Bundy, R., & Flament, C. (1971). Social categorization and intergroup behaviour. *European Journal of Social Psychology,* 1(2), 149–178.
Tilly, C. (2003). *The politics of collective violence.* Cambridge, UK: Cambridge University Press.
Turner, J. C. (1975). Social comparison and social identity: Some prospects for intergroup behaviour. *European Journal of Social Psychology,* 5(1), 5–34.
Turner, J. C. (1987). *Rediscovering the social group: A self-categorization theory.* Oxford, UK: Basic Blackwell.
Weber, M. (1978). *Economy and society. An outline of interpretative sociology.* Los Angeles, CA: University of California Press.
Wiesel, E. (1986). *La noche, el alba, el día.* Barcelona, Spain: Muchnik Editores.
Wiesel, E. (1996). *Todos los torrentes van a la mar.* Barcelona, Spain: Anaya & Mario Muchnik.
World Bank. (2011). *Crime and violence in Central America: A development challenge.* Washington, DC: World Bank.

CHAPTER FIVE

Lone Wolf Terrorists: Examining Motives and Methods of Stand-Alone Terrorists

Martin J. Gallagher

Introduction

This chapter considers the concept of "individualized terrorism," arguing for greater attention to be paid to individuals undertaking terrorist attacks rather than solely concentrating on terrorist groups. Using the anarchists for comparison purposes, the chapter highlights the resonance of current "lone wolf" activity with the disparate and very loosely linked collective that constituted their historical counterparts.

The chapter draws attention to the geographical spread of recent attacks, the disparate causes of participants, and identifies factors contributing to the ongoing changes to terrorism dynamics, including the role of the internet and the mental health of the lone wolf terrorist.

The chapter concludes by suggesting the increased incidence of lone wolf terrorism is likely to continue, and recommends greater alignment among police, psychiatry, and social work in an effort to identify the triggers that can evidence the likelihood of highly individualized "terrorist-inspired" activity.

Individualized Terrorism

There is a great deal of consternation presently around acts of terrorism, mental health, and mass casualty events. Identifying what constitutes an act of terrorism can be difficult, and controversial. This is not helped by the lack of an agreed definition of a terrorist act.[1] The most comprehensive definition appears to be that of the 2004 United Nations Security Council Resolution 1566[2] (United Nations, 2004). The definition clearly does not exclude the actions of an individual as being regarded as those of a terrorist. It is the men's rea, the perpetrator's intent in carrying out their actions, which is of the most significant import. Nowhere is this truer than when we consider lone wolf terrorism, a phenomenon whose definition has been debated at length. That provided by Becker appears the most persuasive, defining it as "ideologically driven violence, or attempted violence, perpetrated by an individual who plans and executes an attack in the absence of *collaboration* (*italics mine*) with other individuals or groups"[3] (Becker, 2014, 964).

Orla Lynch (2017) has recently perfectly captured the nub of the problem that exists for many when we look at lone wolf terrorism (and terrorism per se) in noting that

> In an effort to understand terrorism, particularly for those individuals who work with the perpetrators of political violence, it is vital that we separate the notion of terrorism from the terrorist. Terrorism is a highly politicized term, a pejorative label applied unevenly across groups . . . the terrorist actor must be understood and considered in his/her local context in conjunction with the entirety of their social network, personal background, ideological affiliations and offending history. In effect, practitioners must deal with what is in front of them, and not be seduced by the hysteria (understandably so) that so often accompanies terrorism and terrorist events. (Lynch, 2017, 79–80)

Significant conceptual issues within the study of terrorism have contributed to these difficulties. Corner and Gill (2015) consider these in some detail, identifying a false dichotomy that has emerged in academia and beyond between seeing terrorists (in the 1970s) as harboring significant psychological flaws and their being regarded as quite psychologically normal individuals, but also being persons participating instead in complicated (and extreme) group and social dynamics. They found that in 40 years of research "the literature has jumped from one extreme position ('they are all mentally ill') to the exact opposite ('by definition, a terrorist cannot be mentally ill')". This chapter supports their research finding that those with mental health difficulties can certainly be involved in terrorist behavior, but not perhaps within the rigid concepts that are currently applied. Such concepts need to be challenged.

Presidents and Anarchists

There have been lone individuals throughout history who have carried out acts of politically inspired violence. One of the most notable is Leon Czolgosz, the assassin of U.S. president William McKinley in 1901. The unfortunate President McKinley was not alone in being a targeted U.S. president, either before or since. Lee Harvey Oswald is perhaps the most controversial "lone wolf" actor of the last 70 years. Speculation on Oswald's status as a sole actor continues to rage today, with many documents relating to the investigation of his assassination of President John F. Kennedy only recently being released, and some still withheld (Harnden, 2017). In 1981, an attempt on the life of another U.S. president, Ronald Reagan, was perpetrated by John Hinckley Jr. President Reagan was wounded, but survived.

What differs about these three ultra-high-profile assailants beyond anything else is their *motive*. It is interesting to contrast these three instances to begin to question when lone actions step into lone wolf terrorism.

Czolgosz is widely accepted by academics and historians as being part of a very loose anarchist wave of terrorism that lasted between the 1880s and the 1910s (Rapoport, 2003). A crumpled newspaper found in the assassin's pocket covering the story of Italy's King Umberto's murder in 1900 by another "anarchist terrorist" is utilized as an indicator for his wider politically fueled anarchist-inspired motivation (Burleigh, 2008).

The inability of cobbler Leon Leuathier to make a functioning bomb and instead sitting down in restaurant and then stabbing a fellow diner (who turned out to be the Serbian ambassador), and the assassination of Elizabeth, Empress of Austria, are seen, with the murder of King Umberto and President McKinley, as examples of anarchist terrorism, but with accepted weak ties between the perpetrators, and their apparent shared "anarchist cause" being the link between them (Bell, 1987).

Each of these anarchist actions did, though, have one element in common. They are all reasonably construed as extreme acts to drive forward a political goal. How widely understood, or agreed, that goal was among the perpetrators is highly debatable. The perpetrators had virtually no interaction. Additionally, although in wider society they were perceived to be acting to achieve a common goal, it is extremely questionable as to whether the perpetrators had a shared understanding of a common purpose.

It may have been the case that for the general public, "improved telegraphy and successive newspaper editions updating the cycle of atrocity, arrest, trial, speeches from the dock, imprisonment or execution meant (they) could quite justifiably conclude that the activities of the bomb-throwing maniacs were being coordinated on behalf of sinister objectives across Europe or North America" (Burleigh, 2008, 21). But Burleigh (2008) cautions that evidence suggesting any real degree of coordination was limited.[4]

Jensen shares Burleigh's caution around any significant degree of anarchist cooperation. He also notes that despite the anarchists' actions' notoriety, casualties from their actions were relatively light (Jensen, 2009). During the period between 1880 and 1914, they killed 160 and injured 500. These largely uncoordinated actions had succeeded, though, in the objective of sowing terror. The new means of publicity meant that those among their number, such as Czolgosz, knew of the likely level of international coverage their actions would bring.

Oswald, best described as a "misfit and sociopath," would have been in no doubt as to the significance of the actions he was undertaking, and the worldwide implications. His time as a very odd Marxist in the U.S. Marines, and thereafter in the Soviet Union, have given rise to all form of conspiracy theories as to his direction and orders. However, recent coverage suggests it was far more likely that any agency such as the KGB that may have been attempting to utilize his services for wider goals would have eventually realized his fragile mental state meant he could not have been controlled (Harnden, 2017). Oswald's actions occurred against the backdrop of a worldwide leftist-inspired wave of terrorism, which David Rapoport (2003), in his seminal work on terrorism's waves, has illustrated as taking place between the 1960s and 1980s.

The shooting of President Reagan differs greatly from the actions undertaken by Czolgosz and Oswald. With both Czolgosz and Oswald, their motivations have been examined, and with historical inquiry and hindsight, placed within a conceptualization of the wider political struggles of their time, with terrorist acts at the razor's edge of extreme anarchist and new left political activity respectively. What is fundamentally different with Hinckley Jr. from the other two presidential attackers is that his motivation, which has been examined at length, stemmed from an obsession with the actress Jodie Foster, and his intent was to in some perverse way draw her attention to him. Hinckley Jr. had suffered significant mental health issues prior to carrying out the shooting (Associated Press, 2016).

Discussion often turns to failing mental health as an explanation for a significant amount of lone wolf activity, with consequent attempts to bracket Czolgosz, Oswald, Hinckley Jr., and individuals such as Stephen Paddock, of recent infamy for the shooting in Las Vegas that killed 58 and injured 500, together (Levenson, 2017). The author believes this is fundamentally wrong, and fails to grasp the central concepts at work in respect to terrorist-inspired lone wolf activity. Czolgosz's and Oswald's actions have been determined to have fallen within the sphere of influence of the wider political struggles of their times, with motive intimated from these. Paddock has been found to have no discernible motive whatsoever, although plenty of issues.

A reset of how we conceptualize lone wolf terrorist activity and the role of mental health is necessary. Paddock may have had difficulties in this area; however, his actions had no apparent political meaning or inspiration. Sageman (2017) has recently contended that the same applies to lone wolf suffering from mental disorders, and that their actions have no further group meaning. In this chapter, the author seeks to challenge this view, demonstrating clearly the differences between individuals such as Paddock and those engaged in lone wolf terrorist activity, which certainly does influence terrorist group behaviors. To address this a paradigm shift will be necessary in the concept of terrorism (including, particularly, terrorism-inspired acts) and mental health, but one far removed from the stereotyped "sadistic madman" theme favored in the 1970s that Corner and Gill allude to. Reality is far more nuanced. Without this change in outlook and understanding, we are likely doomed to see ever-increasing numbers of terrorist-inspired outrages committed by those acting alone.

Understanding Where We Are Now

Between 1968 and 2007, there were 72 acts of what we now consider to be "lone wolf" terrorism.[5] The vast majority of terrorist attacks during this period were committed by groups whose members largely acted in concert, with identifiable aims. These ranged from the extreme left politics of Baader-Meinhof to the startling atrocities of al-Qaeda and its call to jihad, most obviously evidenced by the 9/11 hijackers.

However, toward the end of the period, the FBI (2014) had already foreseen significant likely changes in modus operandi of those involved in political violence. As early as 2004, its Strategic Plan contained the observation that "the most significant domestic terrorism threat over the next five years will be the lone actor or lone wolf terrorist" (FBI, 2014).[6]

As the FBI predicted, there were many instances of lone wolf terrorism in the years that followed, both in the United States and in other Western Nations. The most infamous atrocity until 2016 remained the actions of Anders Behring Breivik, who on July 22, 2011, detonated a car bomb in Oslo, Norway, and then undertook a shooting spree at a Labor Youth summer camp, killing 77 in total.

Breivik was inspired by anti-Islamic far-right rhetoric, citing much of this in a self-published manifesto immediately prior to his actions (Berntzen & Sandberg, 2014). Breivik's actions heralded an unprecedented rise in lone wolf activity, which rose to a recent crescendo in 2016 when more than 20 attacks resulted in 168 people killed and 663 injured in lone wolf incidents

(Gallagher, 2017). Accepting the availability today of automatic weapons, the sheer volume of attacks and lethality is still startling. The variety of causes apparently driving the attacks has been unprecedented, from the Reichsburgers in Germany (individuals who refuse to acknowledge the legitimacy of the state and drive vehicles into traffic police officers, set fire to the homes of asylum seekers, and shoot police officers carrying out evictions and confiscations)[7] to the agent of carnage claiming Islamic State (IS) allegiance who drove his stolen truck into tourists in Nice (BBC, August 19, 2016).

The year 2017 has been just as grim for the West, with some examples of terrorist-related lone wolf activity perpetrated being:

- French policeman Xavier Jugele was shot dead and two colleagues injured on the famous Champs Elysees in Paris by a Kalashnikov-wielding Frenchman of Muslim descent, although he had never been seen at his local mosque and had numerous convictions for violence. A note defending Islamic State was found near his body (Henley, 2017).
- A Polish-born "Britain First" supporter giving Nazi salutes, stating he wanted to "Kill Muslims," shouting "white power," and driving his motor vehicle over an Asian restaurateur. When arrested he was found in possession of "Britain First" flyers and Nazi memorabilia. He suffers from depression (Roberts, 2017).
- A Bangladeshi-born resident of New York attempted to carry out a suicide bombing on the underground trains in Manhattan. He pledged allegiance to Islamic State, posting on Facebook "Trump you failed to protect your nation" (Baker & Weiser, 2017).
- Adrian Russell Ajao, a Muslim convert also known as Khalid Masood, hired a car in Birmingham and drove to Westminster Bridge, mowing down members of the public; after crashing his vehicle, he ran from it armed with knives and murdered police officer Keith Palmer, who was guarding the UK parliament, before Ajao was fatally shot by police. He killed five and injured 50. Ajao had an extensive record of petty criminality (BBC, April 7, 2017).
- A Palestinian asylum seeker ran amok in a Hamburg supermarket, shouting "Allahu Akbar" as he stabbed people with a knife he had grabbed in the store, killing one and injuring six. He told police afterwards it was an Islamic terror attack; however, police had doubts about this as he was psychologically ill. He had earlier been investigated for potential extremist beliefs, but it was concluded that he suffered from a psychological illness and should receive treatment. He never got any (Huggler, 2017).
- A 17-year-old white (non-Muslim) teenager from the small Welsh town of Rhondda Cynon Taff, with no known connection to any extremist organization, changed his Instagram profile picture to the flag of Islamic State and then armed himself with a hammer and a kitchen knife while planning to

carry out a lone attack at a Justin Bieber concert in Cardiff. He had written a martyrdom letter, but was caught by police before he could see through his plan (BBC, November 21, 2017).

- In Stockholm, a failed asylum seeker who expressed sympathies with IS stole a lorry and drove it into members of the public, killing four (Euronews, 2017).
- Darren Osborne, a 47-year-old resident of Cardiff, drove to the Finsbury Park mosque in London (famous as a previous hotbed of radical activity) and thereafter ran over a crowd of worshipers, killing one and injuring 11. He was heard to shout "I want to kill all Muslims!" He had a history of mental illness, and in the weeks prior to the attack he had attempted suicide and asked to be placed within a mental health facility (Ward et al., 2017).
- Republican congressman Steve Scalise was shot along with four others at a baseball event just outside Washington, D.C., by James Hodgkinson, who was killed by police. Hodgkinson had posted anti-Republican and anti-Trump messages on social media (Allen, 2017).
- An Armenian male who wanted to avenge Islamist-linked attacks in Paris attempted to drive his 4x4 vehicle into a crowd of mosque goers in the city, but was thwarted by barriers. (BBC, June 29, 2017)
- A 25-year-old local man, Andrew Schneck, was found and arrested while planting explosives in Houston against a 112-year-old statue of a Confederate officer, Lt. Dick Dowling. Schneck's stated motive was that he "didn't like the guy" (Barned-Smith et al., 2017).
- Ethan Stables, a 19-year-old man, was found in possession of explosives for the purposes of terrorism, and was charged with undertaking reconnaissance on a Gay Pride Evening in a local pub (BBC, December 8, 2017).
- Using two hire vehicles, a Somali asylum seeker ran over and stabbed a police officer in Edmonton, and then mounted a second attack where he drove his vehicle into four members of the public. An IS flag was found in one of the vehicles (Associated Press, 2017).

These are only some of the examples of lone wolf terrorist activity in 2017, but the group act is an excellent indicator of the diversity of locations, actors, and causes involved in this phenomenon across the West. Open-source indications from the authorities involved are that all of these individuals acted alone, with some having documented mental health issues. Their causes range from the extreme right to the extreme left, by way of examples of allegiance to the aims of IS and homophobia.

However, gaining a true picture of lone wolf activity is extremely difficult. Not all of the examples above have been termed terrorist incidents. This results from a failure, particularly on the part of authorities, to accept and move on from significant conceptual problems around *terrorist-inspired* activity. This is perhaps best highlighted in an unusual case from 2016, which is worth considering in detail.

Ali Sonboly—The Identity Terrorist

Ali Sonboly, the son of 1990s Iranian refugees to Germany, and who had undergone two months of inpatient psychiatric treatment in 2015, suffered from depression and was being treated as an outpatient (BBC, July 24, 2016). Sonboly was described as a bullied loner by a classmate. He was 18 when he armed himself with a Glock pistol, obtained via the dark web, and carried out a shooting at a Munich shopping center on July 22, 2016, that left nine dead and 27 injured.

The dead were lured to a McDonald's in the center through a hacked Facebook account post with the promise of a free meal, and appeared to have been targeted for their non-Indigenous German ethnicity. When challenged during the attack by a local resident, who threw a beer bottle and shouted "Fucking Foreigners," Sonboly shouted back at him, "I am German!" Sonboly shot himself prior to capture by the police. He had not been on any intelligence service's database prior to the attack.

Munich chief of police Hubertus Andrae pointed out that the attack occurred on the fifth anniversary of Breivik's far-right-inspired Norwegian lone wolf atrocity, and informed the media of material in Sonboly's possession making the connection between the two incidents to him "obvious" (Shuster, 2016). This is supported further from information provided by his classmates, who stated that Sonboly had changed his WhatsApp messaging service profile picture to that of Breivik.

However, Andrae ruled out the act as one of terrorism, as there was no *political motive* (Nagesh, 2016). It is also interesting to note that in the confusion of the original incident, when it was thought that Sonboly had been shouting "Allahu Akbar" during his shooting spree (it now is almost certain he hadn't been), Andre stated, "Even if he would have said this, it would not automatically indicate anything. Not everyone who uses this saying, which is now famous around the world, is automatically linked to ISIS" (Shuster, 2016).

This was in furtherance of comments made by German interior minister Thomas de Maizière in relation to another attack in Germany during 2016 where an axman on a train attacked fellow passengers shouting "Allahu Akbar," and was later found to have made a suicide video where he pledged allegiance to IS, and vowed to kill nonbelievers. De Maizière saw such an attack as inhabiting a "grey area between a rampage and terrorism" that was an Amoklauf (running amok) as there was no clear political motive (Shuster, 2016).

A further note with respect to Sonboly's antecedents is that during 2015 he visited the site of a 2009 German mass shooting event, taking photographs, and there was a book on mass shootings found in his home.

Speaking after the shooting, the then newly appointed UK foreign secretary (now prime minister) Boris Johnson said, "If, as seems very likely, this is another terrorist incident, then I think it proves once again that we have a global phenomenon and a global sickness that we have to tackle both at the source—in the areas where the cancer is incubated in the Middle East—and also of course around the world. We have to ask ourselves, what is going on? How is the switch being thrown in the minds of these people?" (Wintour, 2016).

When it was ascertained that the attack was not IS inspired, Johnson was castigated for his comments by opposition party members of the UK parliament.

A neighbor of the Sonboly family said after the attack, "I don't think we should go crazy over it. This could happen anywhere" (Schmidt, 2016).

Sonboly's Attack as a Rosetta Stone for the Lone Wolf Issue Faced Today

Let us return briefly to the case of Czolgosz for some historical context. Scholars today widely accept his actions to have been part of the "anarchist wave" that swept the world prior to World War I. And how is his motivation discerned? From his choice of victim, and a crumpled piece of paper referencing a similar action.

We have almost a century of hindsight by which to conceptualize and frame Czolgosz's actions. We do not have this degree of detachment with which to judge Sonboly and his 2017 peer group identified above; however, by deconstructing their actions, we can hopefully go some way to achieving this.

Let us consider the evidence:

- Sonboly chose to carry out his action on the anniversary of Breivik's far-right-inspired attack.
- Sonboly selected a young, ethnically diverse group to send his hacked Facebook post to, and bring into the target area for his attack.
- Sonboly altered his WhatsApp profile image to that of Breivik prior to the attack.
- When challenged about his antecedents, Sonboly shouted, "I am German!"
- Sonboly suffered from mental illness so severe he had been hospitalized, and had ongoing issues with depression.

When mirrored to Czolgosz's accepted "evidence" of anarchist involvement, the similar "evidence" of association to wider motivation on the part of Sonboly looks persuasive, but to what terrorist group is Sonboly aligning himself as a lone wolf? Doesn't his own status as the son of Iranian refugees logically cut him off from alignment to the far right? There are direct parallels to the white non-Muslim IS supporting the 17-year-old from Rhondda Cynon Taff referenced above, who for reasons known only to himself has chosen this very odd alignment. It is in these considerations that we need to work in tandem with Lynch's contention, that is, we need to concentrate on the terrorist, not their chosen "brand" of terrorism or their apparently illogical decisions on alignment.

We are currently experiencing a worldwide alteration of individual and national worldviews. In line with the work of Berntzen and Sandberg (2014), the open-source reporting of these incidences of lone wolf terrorism actions where there may have been reference to wider terrorist groups or ideologies, particularly the prevalence of pledges of allegiance to Islamic State, shows no *collaboration*, in keeping with Becker's definition above. The actors are instead acting independently through their choices, and their actions, based on rhetoric embedded in existing wider social movements they have *chosen* to embrace.

It is the author's contention that both Andrae and De Maizière are wrong in their belief that the chant of "Allaua Akbar" is irrelevant, and that the actions of the ax-wielding assailant are Amoklauf, actors running amok with no political motive. Such actors are expressing the "battle cry" of their chosen vehicle to commit acts of terror and very explicitly stating their allegiance.

Is Islamic State Really a "Religious Terrorism"-Based Organization?

Given the current prevalence of lone wolves displaying allegiance to IS, it seems only proper to give this group, and its adherents, a further degree of consideration. The actions of Islamic State and its removed "lone wolf" adherents are wholly political. The very name of the organization, which contains the term "State," makes its political intentions of nation building clear. It spent its time governing areas of Syria and Iraq attempting, with limited success, to "nation build," even if the nation it was attempting to build bore little resemblance to modern societies we know today. Simply put, the individuals carrying out attacks invoking how great their God is have not been consumed by religious fervor alone.

The main draw is, in fact, an abstract ideal of a caliphate, a utopia they have come to believe they could hold in high regard. This all-too-easy-to-accept fantasy represents the lost golden age when the Middle and Near East were the prominent world powers. The decline and fall of the Ottoman Empire and the brutal regimes that followed held such nostalgia in check through their imposed personality cults, such as those of Sadat, Gaddafi, Saddam Hussein, and the Assad hegemony. As these have ebbed, or been destroyed, by the interventions of the West or the Arab Spring, the natural counter narrative from the history of the caliphate has risen, through its adoption by Islamic State, to be the dominant political agenda at the razor's edge of thought for actors from, or with ties and sympathies toward, those in the region.

The actors we have seen, like the anarchists, likely do not properly understand the geopolitics of their actions, and certainly not the religion they purport to be acting on behalf of. But they do understand they are aligning themselves to a radical movement, atoning (perversely) for past misdeeds, or casting themselves as heroes, a status they would never attain legitimately in the societies where they reside.

We cannot escape the ties to Islam that exist, as there has been no separation between faith and state as occurred hundreds of years ago in the West, but instead see this relationship and narrative as a serious ancillary issue to the main goal sought. Such a focus brings into stark relief the difference between the vast majority of Western Muslims and these extremists. While the overwhelming majority of Muslims in the West simply want to live in the societies they call home while observing their religion, the extremists seek significant *political* change, using their association to religion as a convenient explanation and excuse for their actions. The association to Islam provides a supposed higher purpose, and one who suffers from mental health issues or other extreme self-esteem problems seems to find it all too easy to immerse themselves within it.

If we accept this is the case, then surely it is not a major intellectual hurdle to be overcome in applying the term "caliphites" to these terrorists we face. This seems far more appropriate than "radical Islamists."

Lone Wolf Driving Factors—Individualized Terrorism

The same factors for the "caliphites" apply equally to those on the far right and left as we have identified above. The list of attackers from 2017 does not include well-adjusted, successful individuals who are functioning without difficulty in Western societies. It is a collection of those on the fringes, those who through their own actions, mental health, or situation as a member of the very small number of refugees who cannot adapt find themselves excluded from mainstream society.

Berntzen and Sandberg (2014) reference the myriad of factors that drive independent actors including way of thinking, rationale, motivation, but also psychology, social factors, political opportunities, existential attractions, and plain old excitement. They note with respect to Breivik that "his ideology, world view, and narratives emerged from a large, sometimes radical, and relatively new anti-Islamic social movement. It is thus impossible to understand the Norwegian terrorist attacks without seeing how their rationale was embedded in anti-Islamic rhetoric" (Berntzen & Sandberg, 2014, 772). Lone wolf terrorism had previously been seen as an exception to social movement theory. In common with many recent academic authors, the evidence presented in this chapter tends to suggest this classification as incorrect. Instead, it appears that agreement with Kaplan, Loow, and Makkie is more warranted when they write that "lone wolves, however lonely they seem to be, are much part of a larger community of likeminded actors" (2014, 4). For Kaplan et al., the internet is a key enabler in driving these individuals to develop their ideas into action, through interaction with like-minded individuals they have no direct contact with. Aiken (2016) captures this well in describing the individual's online presences as being bolder, less inhibited, and judgment impaired.

Kaplan and Costa (2015) consider the pull of IS in terms of their notion of New Tribalism, where adherents of terrorist group members have common bonds of kinship or shared history/ideals and aim to establish a lost (or mythical) Golden Age. For Kaplan and Costa, IS are exemplars of this phenomenon, with their drive to reestablish the caliphate. The bonds of kinship here and shared history/ideals do not need to be physical, as Speckhard illustrates with her interviews of jihadists showing a shared fictive kinship in defense of a global population of those ascribing to the Muslim faith (Speckhard, 2012).

What more significant allegiance can a participant in the early twenty-first-century internet age make than altering their profile image to that of the cause to which they subscribe? There is no obvious bitter irony in Sonboly's choice of Breivik as his "face to the world" being expressed through the WhatsApp messenger service. In line with the other evidence above, it seems an all too close, and perhaps far more telling, form of statement of common purpose than Czolgosz's crumpled paper. In writing of Palestinian youths revolting against Israeli settlements, Ehrenreich writes of one activist who has changed his Facebook profile picture to the roadway where two of his friends were shot dead by security forces. He is making a bold statement via the means available to him, social media, of his viewpoint (Ehrenreich, 2016).

It is Naim (2013) who captures, though, that it is not the internet alone that is at work in driving radical behaviors. There are far wider societal changes at work, to which the internet is simply a contributory factor, to a degree a catalyst. The wider changes in society, which he describes as the "More and Mobility" revolutions, have had the effect of "vastly broaden(ing) the cognitive, even emotional impact of more access to resources and the ability to move, learn, connect and communicate more broadly and inexpensively than ever before" (65).

A former al-Qaeda member, Jesse Morton, in considering the attraction of terrorism per se, articulates the motivation of members as not being a reaction to foreign policy but instead "a pre-existing anger and animosity, whether it is to do with child abuse or trauma, a lack of integration and assimilation, or socio-economic grievances. The foreign policy grievance is simply something that allows them to release tensions held deep within them" (Morton, 2016, para 9).

This observation ties in well with identified notions of extreme thrill seeking (Pazzanese, 2015). This is coupled to a form of (perverse) redemption for past-perceived misdeeds, identified among contemporary terrorists (Watts, 2016), and again fits perfectly with Lynch's (2017) contention of analyzing the terrorist rather than their chosen cause.

This is where Boris Johnson, UK foreign secretary, is actually completely right when he described Sonboly's actions as part of a "global phenomenon" and asks the wholly legitimate questions "What is going on? How is the switch being thrown in the minds of these people?"

Naim perhaps captures this brilliantly in his conceptualization of the Mentality revolution, which encompasses the politics of the individual with a grievance. Individuals can now access twisted ideologies that were previously inaccessible, creating on many occasions a bespoke ideology tied to their own particular grievances and foibles. They may not fully understand this ideology, which explains the dichotomy around Sonboly's allegiance and that of 17-year-old from Rhondda Cynon Taff, but can latch onto in ways never possible before. The significant societal changes Naim highlights echo the conditions that Burleigh describes as at work during the anarchist wave, as illustrated above. For increased telegraphy, see the spread of the internet; in turn for successive newspaper cycles, see the spread of live 24-hour news coverage on a plethora of platforms.

The tie to mental health with respect to recent developments cannot be understated. It is estimated that approximately 30% of lone actors have mental health issues (Gardner, 2016). With Sonboly and Osborne (mentioned above, who undertook the Finsbury Park mosque attack), we know from open-source reporting the extent of mental health difficulties experienced by these actors. The problem with properly assessing the scale of this aspect's impact on terrorism is that the vast majority of incidents that would fit a lone wolf definition are not defined or prosecuted as acts of terrorism. Often, although not exclusively (Thomas Mair, the murderer of the British MP Jo Cox in 2016, being a prime example), this is due to attribution to the mental health of the perpetrator.

Spaaij, writing in 2010 at a time when he saw no evidence of the lethality of lone wolf terrorism being on the increase, examined the cases of five lone wolf terrorists at length. He found they all suffered from a variable degree of social ineptitude, with three of the five diagnosed with personality disorders and four of the five experiencing severe depression during their lives. He also noted that lone wolf terrorists create their own ideologies that combine personal frustration and aversion with broader political, social, or religious aims.

In the United Kingdom alone, killings by those deemed to have mental health issues have climbed by 92%, with 423 people killed by mental health patients from 2009 to 2016 (Hudson, 2016). Fiona Petty (2016) describes killings by the mentally ill as an unintended consequence of more liberal mental health treatment regimes. With respect to terrorism and killings by those she describes as "*lonely* wolves," she sees such individuals as not having "slipped through the net," but instead suggests that resources and treatment are so scarce that there is no net to slip through. Such self-evident truths are not, in her view, "popular or comfortable in western civilized society" (Petty, 2016). In engaging with Islamic State and other radical viewpoints online, "the lonely can find solace in internet sites offering self-esteem, a reason for living and above all rewards they can only dream of . . . our values and belief systems cannot understand this rationale but we need to stop bleating about their ideology being so abhorrent and tackle the issue that it has indeed been so successful" (Petty, 2016).

Bhui, Everitt, and Jones (2014) see a spiral at play here. Their groundbreaking study of depression and sympathy for violent protest and terrorism showed a direct correlation between weakened social cohesion, depression, and support for extreme views. It also identified a self-perpetuating pattern, with increased violence and terrorist acts leading to increased breakdown of social capital, depression, and higher sympathy for extreme acts.

In December 2017, the Archbishop of Canterbury, the UK's most senior clergyman, drew stark attention to this weakening social cohesion, stating that "We live in a country where an overarching story, which is the framework for explaining life, has more or less disappeared. We have a world of unguided and competing narratives, where the only common factor is the inviolability of personal choice, which means that. . . . Confidence in any personal sense of ultimate values has vanished."[8]

It is perhaps not surprising, then, that with a seismic shift in values, the most vulnerable in society are finding themselves seeking extreme ways in which to act out the unfettered viewpoints they have reached. Viewpoints that were until recent times the norm have been found to be wholly socially unacceptable.

A good touchstone is perhaps the area of LGBT rights and politics. Felix Ngole, a postgraduate social work student, had placed posts on his personal Facebook account quoting biblical excerpts identifying homosexuality as sinful. He found himself off of his course, and losing a judicial appeal, when it was judged that he could hold these opinions in private but due to his intended profession was not allowed to express them in public (Grierson, 2017). By contract in the UK, state-funded Action for Trans Health, which has provided advice to parliamentary enquiries on transgender issues, has called for the abolition of legal gender, an end to birth certificates, and regarding police participation in a Gay Pride event posted on its website that "the only good 10,000 cops is 10,000 dead cops" (Gilligan, 2017).

Without questioning in any way the efficacy of either point of view (and there are no doubt significant issues around such extreme views being tolerated), it is clear to see that the atmosphere for debate is charged, and that the role of the internet identified by Aiken (2016) is at play. When the mental health of those experiencing these extreme views is precarious, it becomes easier to grasp how they can be easily tipped into "inspired" terrorist action.

This perhaps captures perfectly the situation in Houston, with the attempted statue destruction referenced above. The long-deceased Lt. Dick Dowling had a street in Houston named after him, in addition to his statue. This was recently changed from Dowling to Emancipation Avenue. There is no middle ground in such a move; there is a sharp move from one long-established and apparently largely uncontested norm to a new, currently socially acceptable norm with no transition debate.

Such radical changes (for right or wrong) were arguably at the root of the rioting in Charlottesville in 2017, which saw the far right and Antifa face off, leaving one dead and many injured. It is not difficult to see how Schneck, in carrying out his action in Houston, became aligned to the wider, now FBI terrorist–designated Antifa goals of eradicating the country's perceived glorification of its Confederate past.

In Norway, the head of their national police force, Janne Kristiansen, acknowledged that even the Stasi in the surveillance-heavy days of East Germany could have stopped Breivik (Meyer, 2013); there needs to be an acknowledgment that more needs to be done. In Denmark, there has been a more ready acceptance of the influence of mental health over terrorism-related behavior, seeing the enhancement of an already established legislated police, social services, and psychiatric (PSP) information sharing service (Sestoft, Hansen, & Christensen, 2017). Here a descent into radicalization toward terrorist behavior is seen and accepted as one more potential outcome of mental health difficulties. There is no taboo or bamboo wall separating services, and the mystique of "terrorism," which for many cloaks it in some special status, is removed. Once again, we are looking at the terrorist, not terrorism. There is nothing mysterious or glamorous about those in the 2017 list of lone wolf participants above.

In acknowledging this, and ensuring there is legislated information sharing, the Danes are far ahead of many of their Western counterparts. This is far removed from the tactics of East Germany's infamous Stasi, and far more like the actions of a supportive and sensible twenty-first-century democracy acknowledging a new, reasonably low-level threat it faces. The Danes are working in tandem with the findings of Corner and Gill, whose study of lone wolf terrorists found clearly that "the empirical evidence suggests mental health professionals may have a role in preventing lone actor terrorist attacks" (Corner & Gill, 2015, 10).

The 2017 incidents above were carried out by those acting alone, rather than those who were acting in direct concert with others. An explanation of this can be found in Gardner's noting of the observation from British Secret Service contacts that those suffering from mental health difficulties are likely to be screened out by established terrorist groups (Gardner, 2016). (It has been speculated that similar screening may have been behind Oswald's ejection from the USSR.) The prevalence of those at liberty in Western societies suffering from often extreme mental illness, coupled to their obvious part in the incidents listed above, cannot be dismissed. Mental illness is not a full explanation for the rise in lone wolf cases; however, it has to be acknowledged as a contributory factor. Following Bhui, Everitt, and Jones's (2014) argument of a potential spiral at play, it may become of ever-increasing relevance, particularly seen in the context of the increase in killings as a whole by those suffering mental health difficulties.

This is not to say the influence of groups on individuals is a one-way street. "Death to traitors, freedom for Britain," echoes of the phrases Thomas Mair shouted when appearing in court charged with murdering the British MP Jo Cox, have appeared as taglines on the Google listing for National Action, a (recently proscribed terrorist) organization in the United Kingdom (Gadher, 2016).

This interrelationship between lone wolves and established groups should be seen as symbiotic. Lone wolves carry out acts linked, however indirectly, to a terrorist group's cause and perhaps motivated by it, which the group then claims as its own and appeals for more similar lone actors to come forward. Terrorist groups may not have wanted a lone wolf as a member (should they ever have attempted to join, which many won't have), but they appear only too keen to take kudos from their actions, no matter how indirect their role in inspiring them may have been. IS provides a perfect illustration.

Analogous to this, and a worrying herald of things to come, might just be the apparently senseless acts of an increasing number of youths in Palestine.

"Something new was happening. Fully half of the alleged attackers killed in October (2016) were under twenty years old. All but one was under thirty. . . . Knowing that it would almost certainly mean their deaths, young Palestinians were acting alone or in pairs, striking out at Israeli soldiers with the limited means available to them: kitchen knives, scissors, screwdrivers. Sometimes they tried to hit them with cars. . . . There existed no movement for them to join, armed or unarmed, no viable collective response to a situation . . . even the Israeli intelligence services admitted the attacks were spontaneous and uncoordinated" (Ehrenreich, 2016, 364–365).

One youth, prior to their attack that left two dead, posted on Facebook, "I ask that the political parties do not claim responsibility for my attack. My death was for my nation and not for you" (Ehrenreich, 2016, 365).

The attacks are spontaneous, the attackers self-starters. They are making what they perceive to be rational choices to act based on the (grim) individual worldview they have formed. And they are using social media as their means of proclaiming their driving rationale.

Those on the fringes of our societies are acting, and it appears that those in these fringes are increasing. Significant difficulties with lone wolves may lie ahead, and the FBI's prediction of 2004 might come to be true. In spades.

Conclusions

The neighbor of the Sonboly family said after the attack, "This could happen anywhere."[9] From the examples above they appear to be right. Part of preserving societies in the face of terrorism, though, involves preserving what your core principles are, in defying the actions that are trying to change the function of your society to the extreme viewpoint of the terrorist. Consequently, Janne Kristiansen was right in the aftermath of Breivik's attack to caution against any move toward an Orwellian surveillance society to counter the threat faced, which although alarming is a far way removed from an existential threat to the continued functioning of Western democracies. The lone wolves, despite their media impact, remain small in number. So too do individuals such as Paddock, the Las Vegas shooter. However, while the actions of Paddock are an apparently inexplicable aberration in modern Western society, those acting in a similar vein inspired by terrorism are not. Paddock's actions are not part of a wider cause, contributing to an extreme political outlook's influence and notoriety. The actions of the lone wolves outlined above no doubt are. The fact that we are still referencing the unaligned and generally unconnected anarchists today, a hundred years after the height of their terror, is testament to this.

Acknowledging that society has changed dramatically, and that those on its fringes (particularly those with mental health issues) are having difficulty in accepting new norms and are part of a "blowback," however questionable their understanding of their role, would be a massive step forward. When they see a terrorist cause, and can read of its beliefs and actions, it is not difficult to conceptualize how they can see alignment as in some way beneficial, as a means to escape the marginalization they find themselves within. Their individualized "enrollment" provides them with Kaplan and Costa's "fictive kinship," a membership of elite they could not otherwise obtain. The fact that they will see the actions of other similar lone wolves lionized by groups, as is the current situation, can only enhance this symbiotic relationship.

Denmark, with its PSP approach, seems to have embraced this necessary acknowledgment through legislated interagency cooperations among law enforcement, social work, and psychiatry. This seems a very sensible step.

The low-tech tactics adopted by the lone wolf actors described above illustrate that we cannot "design out" this problem. Kitchen knives are not going to become unavailable. The need is to address the circumstances that are giving rise to extreme action, rather than the extreme action that is being taken. Similarly, the utilization of social media by the lone wolves above, and their use of the internet to gain (some form) of insight to causes they align themselves to, cannot be understated. We live with a variety of individuals who are being inspired to action by terrorism they see occurring, and the causes espoused, whether or not the actor was the intended recipient of the "message" being delivered to inspire.

Authorities need to build some form of assessment around this. If an individual is utilizing the image of a terrorist as their face to the world, as Sonboly did soon after visiting the sight of mass shootings as a tourist, we need to be in a position to react and question such activity. The "how" of this remains to be seen; however, the problem needs to be addressed. If we apply a twentieth-century analogy, if a resident of a Western city last century put a poster of a known terrorist in their front window, there is little doubt the police would have started to ask questions. Is a profile picture on social media today so different?

IS remains the biggest current inspiration for lone wolf actors. The adoption of "caliphites" proposed above may not capture every nuance of the goals of IS-inspired terrorists, but the degree to which they understand their common goals (in tandem with their anarchist predecessors) is questionable. The use of caliphites provides the ability for all to draw a clear distinction between the enemy we face and the peace-loving Muslim populations at large, who simply want to live in their countries as they are, adhere to their religion, and exist in harmony with their neighbors. Our Muslim population face the current threat IS and it's like pose as much as anyone else (as casualties at many incidents show), and it helps no one to continue to fail to draw clear lines of delineation. The caliphites, like the anarchists before them, seek radical *political* change through the establishment of nations. Using this term would assist in identifying those who are aligned to the problem, as opposed to the general population at large.

Recent political changes (Brexit, the election of President Trump, the ascendance of far-right political parties in Austria, France, and the Netherlands) indicate an increase in populism across the Western world. The possibility of a backlash as the newly elected change policy direction and introduce measures at odds with the consensus that has largely existed (for the West) since the end of the Cold War cannot be discounted. The likelihood of such a backlash sits well with Ekblom's (2015) notion of coevolutionary developments in terrorism, counterterrorism, and the politics of the extreme, where significant change in direction by one party is atypically met by a counterreaction, sometimes more violent and impactive than what engendered it, from those in opposition. The LGBT situation outlined in this chapter perhaps captures this perfectly.

Societies change, adapt, and develop. This is how human interactions evolve. However, the more radical the change, the more radical the potential counterreactions the change may engender. Globalization has led to unparalleled change for the modern Western world. We live in an era of unforeseeable individual choice and technological advancement where social media has become incredibly important—particularly, although not exclusively, to the young. If we do not look more closely at those on the fringes, those most reluctant or unable to embrace these changes, we are doomed to see an ever-increasing individualized counterreaction until we do.

Notes

1. For discussion of this debate in detail, see Schmid, A. P. (ed.) (2004), Statistics on terrorism: The challenge of measuring trends in global terrorism. *Forum on Crime and Society*, 4(1–2). https://www.unodc.org/documents/data-and-analysis/Forum/V05-81059_EBOOK.pdf

2. United Nations Security Council, Resolution 1566, 2004, which defines terrorist acts as: "criminal acts, including against civilians, committed with the intent to cause death or serious bodily injury, or taking of hostages, with the purpose to provoke a state of terror in the general public or in a group of persons or particular persons, intimidate a population or compel a government or an international organization to do or to abstain from doing any act, which constitute offences within the scope of and as defined in the international conventions and protocols relating to terrorism, are under no circumstances justifiable by considerations of a political, philosophical, ideological, racial, ethnic, religious or other similar nature." https://www.un.org/ruleoflaw/blog/document/security-council-resolution-1566-2004-on-threats-to-international-peace-and-security-caused-by-terrorist-acts/

3. For an excellent discussion of the difficulties of defining lone wolf terrorism, see Spaaij, R., & Hamm, M. S. (2015), "Key issues and research agendas in lone wolf terrorism." *Studies in Conflict and Terrorism*, 38(3), 167–178. https://doi.org/10.1080/1057610X.2014.986979

4. Burleigh, M. (2008), *Blood and rage: A cultural history of terrorism* (p. 79). London: HarperCollins, 2008.

5. Spaaij, R. (2010). The enigma of lone wolf terrorism: An assessment. *Studies in Conflict and Terrorism*, 33, 854–870. Specifically within this article see discussion of the RAND-MIPT Terrorist Knowledge Base. The database contains information on attacks that have occurred in the United Kingdom, Germany, France,

Spain, Italy, Poland, Netherlands, Denmark, Sweden, Czech Republic, Portugal, Russia, Canada, United States, and Australia.

6. Federal Bureau of Investigation (2004). FBI Strategic Plan 2004–2009 (Washington, DC: Federal Bureau of Investigation). http://www.cfr.org/intelligence/fbi-strategic-plan-2004-2009/p14808

7. Pancevski, B. (2016, October 30). Rise of 'new Reich army' sparks alarm in Germany. *Sunday Times*. http://www.thetimes.co.uk/article/rise-of-new-reich-army-sparks-alarm-in-germany-xmd7jc9b7

8. Rudgard, O. (2017, December 12). Schools "fail to fight extremism." *Sunday Telegraph*.

9. Schmidt, J. (2016, July 24). Munich shooting: Killer was bullied teen loner obsessed with mass murder. *The Guardian*. https://www.theguardian.com/world/2016/jul/23/munich-shooting-loner-facebook-ali-sonboly-bullied-killer

References

Aiken, M. (2016). *The cyber effect*. New York: Penguin Random House.

Allen, N. (2017, July 7). Congressman shot at baseball practice back in hospital. *Daily Telegraph*.

Associated Press. (2016, January 9). 35 years after trying to assassinate Ronald Reagan, John Hinckley Jr. will be released to his mother's home in Virginia. *Los Angeles Times*. https://www.latimes.com/nation/nationnow/la-na-john-hinckley-release-20160901-snap-story.html

Associated Press. (2017, October 2). Edmonton terror attacks: Suspect was known to Canadian security services. *The Guardian*. https://www.theguardian.com/world/2017/oct/01/canadian-police-edmonton-van-knife-attack-terrorism

Baker, A., & Weiser, B. (2017, December 12). "I did it for the Islamic State," bombing suspect told investigators. *New York Times*. https://www.nytimes.com/2017/12/12/nyregion/suicide-bomber-nyc-terrorism-subway.html

Barned-Smith, St. J., Kragie, A., & Blankinger, K. (2017, August 22). Houston man charged with trying to plant bomb at Confederate statue in Hermann Park. *Houston Chronicle*. https://www.chron.com/news/houston-texas/article/HPD-HFD-FBI-on-scene-overnight-at-Rice-11946918.php

BBC. (2016, July 24). Munich shooting: David Sonboly "planned attack for year." *BBC*. https://www.fbcnews.com.fj/world/munich-shooting-david-sonboly-planned-attack-for-year/

BBC. (2016, August 19). Nice attack: What we know about the Bastille Day killings. *BBC*. https://www.bbc.com/news/world-europe-36801671

BBC. (2017, April 7). Westminster attack: What happened. *BBC*. http://www.bbc.co.uk/news/uk-39355108

BBC. (2017, June 29). Paris mosque: Man held after "trying to ram crowd with vehicle." *BBC*. https://www.bbc.com/news/world-europe-40452264

BBC. (2017, November 21). Cardiff terror accused, 17, "hates terrorists." *BBC.* https://www.bbc.com/news/uk-wales-south-east-wales-42071224

BBC. (2017, December 8). Ethan Stables denies gay pride terrorism offence. *BBC.* https://www.bbc.com/news/uk-england-cumbria-42287854

Becker, M. (2014). Explaining lone wolf target selection in the United States. *Studies in Conflict & Terrorism,* 37(11), 959–978.

Bell, D. H. (1987). The origins of modern terrorism. *Terrorism: An International Journal*, 9(3), 307–311. https://doi.org/10.1080/10576108708435634

Berntzen, L. E., & Sandberg, S. (2014). The collective nature of lone wolf terrorism: Anders Behring Breivik and the anti-Islamic social movement. *Terrorism and Political Violence*, 26(5), 759–779. https://doi.org/10.1080/09546553.2013.767245

Bhui, K., Everitt, B., & Jones, E. (2014). Might depression, psychosocial adversity, and limited social assets explain vulnerability to and resistance against violent radicalisation? *PLoS One.* http://doi.org/10.1371/journal.pone.0105918

Burleigh, M. (2008). *Blood and rage: A cultural history of terrorism* (p. 79). London, UK: HarperCollins.

Corner, E., & Gill, P. (2015). A false dichotomy? Mental illness and lone-actor terrorism. *Law and Human Behavior*, 39(1), 23–34. http://doi.org/10.1037/lhb0000102

Ehrenreich, B. (2016). *The way to the spring* (pp. 315, 364–336). London, UK: Granta Books.

Ekblom, P. (2015). Terrorism—lessons from natural and human co-evolutionary arms races. In M. Taylor, J. Roach, & K. Pease (Eds.), *Evolutionary psychology and terrorism* (pp. 83–113). London, UK: Routledge.

Euronews (2017, April 9). Sweden truck attack: Suspect was "wanted for deportation." *Euronews.* https://www.euronews.com/2017/04/09/sweden-attack-police-confirm-suspect-device-found-in-lorry

Federal Bureau of Investigation (FBI). (2014). "FBI Strategic Plan 2004–2009." Washington, DC: Federal Bureau of Investigation. https://www.hsdl.org/?view&did=466149

Gadher, D. (2016, November 27). Neo-Nazis face ban after Cox murder. *Sunday Times.* https://www.thetimes.co.uk/article/neo-nazis-face-ban-after-cox-murder-0hgm3r93q?region=global&ni-statuscode=acsaz-307

Gallagher, M. J. (2017). The 2016 lone wolf tsunami: Is Rapoport's "religious wave" ending? *Journal of Strategic Security*, 10(2). http://doi.org/10.5038/1944-0472.10.2.1584

Gardner, F. (2016, December 12). How MI5's scientists work to identify future terrorists. *BBC.* https://www.bbc.co.uk/news/uk-38252470

Gilligan, A. (2017, December 17). Action for Trans Health activists want free sex-change hormones for children. *Sunday Times.* https://www.thetimes.co.uk/article/action-for-trans-health-activists-want-free-sex-change-hormones-for-children-dhvv5c52v

Grierson, J. (2017, October 27). Christian thrown out of university over anti-gay remarks loses appeal. *The Guardian*. https://www.theguardian.com/uk-news/2017/oct/27/christian-felix-ngole-thrown-out-sheffield-university-anti-gay-remarks-loses-appeal

Harnden, T. (2017, October 29). JFK assassination: Files reveal CIA shied from Moscow link. *Sunday Times*. https://www.thetimes.co.uk/article/jfk-assassination-files-reveal-cia-shied-from-moscow-link-wft30n7mh

Henley, J. (2017, April 21). Paris gunman served more than 12 years in jail for shooting at police. *The Guardian*. https://www.theguardian.com/world/2017/apr/21/paris-shooting-police-search-property-as-isis-claims-responsibility

Hudson, N. (2016, September 15). TV programme spotlights "doubling of killings" by mental health patients since 2009. *Police Professional*. https://www.policeprofessional.com/news/tv-programme-spotlights-doubling-of-killings-by-mental-health-patients-since-2009/

Huggler, J. (2017, July 31). Hamburg knife attacker wanted to be a terrorist. *The Telegraph*. https://www.telegraph.co.uk/news/2017/07/31/hamburg-knife-attacker-had-islamist-motive/

Jensen, R. B. (2009). The international campaign against anarchist terrorism, 1880–1930s. *Terrorism and Political Violence*, 21, 89–109. http://doi.org/10.1080/09546550802544862

Kaplan, J., & Costa, C. P. (2015). The Islamic State and the new tribalism. *Terrorism and Political Violence*, 27(5), 926–969. http://doi.org/10.1080/09546553.2015.1094306

Kaplan, J., Loow, H., & Malkki, L. (2014). Introduction to the special issue on lone wolf and autonomous cell terrorism. *Terrorism and Political Violence*, 26(1), 1–12. http://doi.org/10.1080/09546553.2014.854032

Levenson, E. (2017, October 9). Why does the Las Vegas shooter's motive even matter? *CNN*. http://edition.cnn.com/2017/10/07/us/las-vegas-shooting-motive/index.html

Lynch, O. (2017). Understanding radicalisation: Implications for criminal justice practitioners. *Irish Probation Journal*, 14. http://www.probation.ie/EN/PB/0/BB8E6E5AF58EAF2B802581D00050A0C4/$File/OrlaLynch_IPJ.pdf

Meyer, S. (2013). Impeding lone-wolf attacks: Lessons derived from the 2011 Norway attacks. *Crime Science*, 2(7). http://doi.org/10.1186/2193-7680-2-7

Morton, J. (2016, November 9). "I believed al-Qaeda when they said 9/11 was justified . . . 15 years on, I work for Homeland Security." *Sunday Telegraph*. https://www.telegraph.co.uk/men/thinking-man/i-believed-al-qaeda-when-they-said-911-was-justified-15-years-on/

Nagesh, A. (2016, July 23). Munich attack was not terrorism but "classic shooting rampage." *Metro*. https://metro.co.uk/2016/07/23/munich-attack-was-not-an-act-of-terrorism-6024184/

Naim, M. (2013). *The end of power*. New York, NY: Basic Books.

Pancevski, B. (2016, October 30). Rise of "new Reich army" sparks alarm in Germany. *Sunday Times.* https://www.thetimes.co.uk/article/rise-of-new-reich-army-sparks-alarm-in-germany-xmd7jc9b7

Pazzanese, C. (2015, March 23). How ISIS is wooing converts in the West. *Newsweek.* https://www.newsweek.com/how-isis-wooing-converts-west-315990

Petty, F. (2016, July 27). Lonely wolves and preventing terrorism. *Police Oracle.* https://www.policeoracle.com/news/Lonely-wolves-and-preventing terrorism_92479.html

Rapoport, D. C. (2003). The four waves of rebel terror and September 11. In C. W. Kegley (Ed.), *The new global terrorism: Characteristics, causes, controls.* Englewood Cliffs, NJ: Prentice Hall.

Roberts, R. (2017, December 5). Britain first supporter drove van into curry house with aim of "killing a Muslim." *The Independent.* https://www.independent.co.uk/news/uk/crime/britain-first-supporter-van-attack-curry-house-muslim-kill-latest-a8092136.html

Rudgard, O. (2017, December 12). Schools "fail to fight extremism." *Sunday Telegraph,* https://www.pressreader.com/uk/the-daily-telegraph/20171209/281741269758598

Sageman, M. (2017). *Turning to political violence.* Philadelphia, PA: University of Pennsylvania Press.

Schmidt, J. (2016, July 24). Munich shooting: Killer was bullied teen loner obsessed with mass murder. *The Guardian.* https://www.theguardian.com/world/2016/jul/23/munich-shooting-loner-facebook-ali-sonboly-bullied-killer

Sestoft, D., Hansen S. M., & Christensen, A. B. (2017). The police, social services, and psychiatry (PSP) cooperation as a platform for dealing with concerns of radicalization. *International Review of Psychiatry,* 29(4), 350–354. http://doi.org/10.1080/09540261.2017.1343526

Shuster, S. (2016, July 24). Why Germany—and the world—is arguing over the Munich shooter. *Time.* https://time.com/4420817/munich-attack-terror-motivation/

Spaaij, R. (2010). The enigma of lone wolf terrorism: An assessment. *Studies in Conflict and Terrorism,* 33(9), 854–870. http://doi.org/10.1080/1057610X.2010.501426

Speckhard, A. (2012). *Talking to terrorists: Understanding the psycho-social motivations of militant jihadi terrorists, mass hostage takers, suicide bombers and martyrs.* McLean, VA: Advances Press.

United Nations Security Council Resolution 1566, S/RES/1566. (2004, October 8). https://www.un.org/ruleoflaw/files/n0454282.pdf

Ward, V., Evans, M., & Furness, H. (2017, June 21). Who is Darren Osborne? Everything we know about the Finsbury Park mosque suspect. *The Telegraph.* https://www.telegraph.co.uk/news/0/darren-osborne-everything-know-finsbury-park-mosque-suspect/

Watts, C. (2016, April 4). Why ISIS beats al Qaeda in Europe. *Foreign Affairs.* https://www.foreignaffairs.com/articles/2016-04-04/why-isis-beats-al-qaeda-europe

Wintour, P. (2016, July 24). Boris Johnson rebuked for blaming Munich shooting on terrorists. *The Guardian.* https://www.theguardian.com/politics/2016/jul/24/boris-johnson-foreign-secretary-criticised-munich-shooting-islamist-terrorists

CHAPTER SIX

Relationship of Online Hate, Radicalization, and Terrorism

Elena Dal Santo and Elena D'Angelo

This chapter is intended to examine the circular relation between hate speech and terrorism, to highlight how the two phenomena may influence each other and how preventive and contrasting measures should envisage a holistic approach to these issues. The first part will describe the radicalization process, exploring if and how hate speech can increase the vulnerability of recruitment into terrorism networks. The second part will scrutinize the phenomenon of hate speech on different grounds, its rise after terrorist attacks in Europe, and the main challenges and opportunities related to the online environment. In the conclusion, a set of policy recommendations will be outlined on how to design effective counter-radicalization and anti-hatred measures.

The Radicalization Process

Terrorism has become a hot topic in academia after 9/11. Among all terrorism-related articles published between 1971 and 2002, 54% were dated 2001 or 2002 (Lum, Kennedy, & Sherley, 2006). The proliferation of studies in this subject area has led to the spread of an ad hoc terminology, which requires some explanation and contextualization. Since the Madrid and London bomb attacks, "the term 'radicalization' has become central to terrorism studies and counter-terrorism policy-making" (Kundnani, 2012, 3). Although there is no agreed definition on the meaning of radicalization, it is commonly depicted as a process (Della Porta & LaFree, 2012). Radicalization is linked to the adoption of "an extremist belief system" (Pressman, 2009) with the scope of promoting changes but is not necessarily linked to the use of violence (Schmid, 2013). As a matter of fact, many people hold radical ideas but are not engaging in any terrorist activities (Borum, 2011). Violent radicalization is the "process of adopting an extremist belief system with the intention and justification of using violence to achieve political, religious or social goals" (Pressman, 2016). The term "extremism," often used in connection to radicalization, is a "culturally relative" word in the sense that views are labeled as "extreme within one cultural context or time" (Pressman, 2009). Political ideas/ideologies can be defined as extreme when they "oppose a society's core values and principles" (Neuman, 2010, 12). Similarly to radicalization, extremism is not necessarily linked to violence. "Violent extremism consists in promoting, supporting or committing acts which may lead to terrorism and which are aimed at defending an ideology advocating racial, national, ethnic or religious supremacy or opposing core democratic principles and values" (Council of Europe, 2015). Finally, disengagement and de-radicalization are two widely used terms in counterterrorism literature. The rehabilitation and reintegration of violent extremist inmates often requires disengagement activities aimed at producing a behavioral change, such as, for example, modifying the role played in a group. Disengagement does not necessarily imply "a change in values or ideals, but requires relinquishing the objective of achieving change through violence" (Fink & Hearne, 2008). De-radicalization necessitates "a cognitive shift—i.e., a fundamental change in understanding" (Council of Europe, 2015).

As the phenomenon itself entails a complex and multifaceted nature, the analysis of violent radicalization leading to terrorism has been approached by various disciplines (Bakker, 2015, 76), driven by different research questions and objectives. Notwithstanding that, limited efforts have been devoted to the identification of similarities and linkages between the phenomenon of terrorism and existing theories on political violence as well as on studies on other forms of crime. As a matter of fact, terrorism has just recently become a priority in the criminologist's agenda (Freilich & LaFree, 2015, 2), thus allowing terrorism studies to benefit from the application of criminological expertise, theories, and research methods (Freilich & LaFree, 2015, 6).

The why question has dominated the terrorism studies: Why do people engage in terrorism? What are the root causes of this phenomenon? The answer to this research question remains partially unattended, although various theories and hypotheses have been developed in different disciplinary fields, connecting terrorism to a broader conceptual framework.

Martha Crenshaw, one of the world's most famous terrorist experts, identifies two sets of conducive factors: Crenshaw distinguishes between "preconditions," which are "factors that set the stage for terrorism over the long run," and "precipitants," which are "specific events that immediately precede the occurrence of terrorism" (Crenshaw, 1981, 381). Preconditions can be further divided into "permissive factors," providing the conditions for terrorism to occur, and situational characteristics directly encouraging terrorist acts, such as the grievances of an identifiable subgroup that experiences and/or perceives a sense of injustice, or limited opportunities in terms of political participation (Crenshaw, 1981, 383). Among the permissive factors, Crenshaw identifies modernization and its promotion of interconnected networks of individuals and services, the "social facilitation," namely the fact that terrorism is accepted or even promoted as a viable political custom by a certain society and the institutional unwillingness or inability to prevent terrorism. A clear description of "preconditions" and "precipitants" represents a challenging task. Various authors have examined the permissive factors and the situational motivating elements from specific and diverse perspectives. According to Peter Neumann, for example, three elements play a key role in the radicalization process, namely grievances, ideology and recruitment: "without grievances—real or perceived—radical ideologies will not resonate. Without ideology, grievances may lead to crime and other forms of disorder and delinquency [. . .] and without recruitment, it will be impossible to channel individuals' sense of political frustration into collective action" (Neumann, 2008, 7).

In the last years, terrorism studies have focused in particular on violent radicalization motivated by Islamist ideology, to the point that Olivier Roy theorizes an "Islamization of radicalism" rather than a "radicalization of Islam" (2016). Roy questions the existence of structural causes and explains Islamist radicalization as a generational and nihilistic revolt that "occurs around an imaginary hero, violence and death—not Sharia or utopia" (2016). According to Roy, there is a clear generational factor linked to a psychological dimension: ISIS and al-Qaeda offer to a nihilist generation a way to turn from losers to superheroes by addressing personal grievances, providing a sense of belonging and promoting a sensational narrative (Roy, 2017). This perspective is linked to the anthropological analysis by Atran (2016), according to whom radicalization is the expression of a quest for significance by young people that struggle for an identity in an apathetic and contradictory world negatively affected by globalization. Roy's standpoint echoes Sageman's refusal to identify poverty, lack of education, employment, or social responsibility as radicalization factors (2008). Nevertheless, contrary to Roy, Sageman is more reluctant to use the "youth" lens of analysis, while he sees in networks, namely social and family ties, the mechanism by which people become involved. Bonanate offers a similar view, attributing the origins of terrorism to the self-perpetuating "immobilisme" of a "blocked society" that is strong enough to preserve itself yet resistant to innovation (1979). Crenshaw frames a similar concept stating that "students or young professionals [. . .] are disillusioned with the prospects of changing society [. . .]" (1981, 384).

Alessandro Orsini's theory is linked to Roy's analysis of the psychological frustrations that lead to terrorism. From the analysis of terrorists' biographies, Orsini has developed a model to explain the phases of the radicalization process, known by the acronym DRIA (2011, 67): the first phase is represented by the disintegration of the social identity (D), followed by the reconstruction of the social identity through a radical ideology (R), the integration in a revolutionary sect (I), and the alienation from the surrounding environment (A). Orsini clarifies (2013) that his analysis refers to what he calls "vocational terrorists," namely people that have decided to sacrifice their lives in the name of a spiritual goal, driven by ideological motivations and fearless of death (2012, 678–79). A vocational terrorist is characterized, according to Orsini, by several peculiar characteristics that can be described as: radical catastrophism, waiting for the end, obsession with purity, identification of evil, obsession with purification, exaltation of martyrdom or desire to be persecuted, and purification of the means through the end (Orsini, 2012, 671). These elements lead to the elaboration of a shared narrative on the basis of which vocational terrorists plan their actions in the framework of the "DRIA model": the psychological frustrations, also referred to by Roy, lead to a disintegration of the social identity (D), that is usually followed by the reconstruction of the identity through a radical ideology (R): jihadi ideology is one among other possible ideologies that allows the reconstruction of the identity providing new existential reference points (Orsini & Caillat, 2016, 784).

From a psychopathological perspective, very few studies have been conducted on major clinical illnesses among terrorists, and existing research demonstrates that, generally speaking, terrorists do not suffer from serious psychiatric illnesses or personality disorders (Victoroff, 2005, 12): there is "evidence for lack of abnormality, [. . .] evidence for normality [. . .], and developments in the context of alternative explanations for abnormal (including violent) behavior" (Horgan, 2003, p. 16), which may also be motivated by organizational needs (Horgan, 2003, 6). Notwithstanding that, terrorists "may exhibit identifiable psychological traits or may have been influenced by identifiable social factors" (Victoroff, 2005, 17). First psychological approaches to the study of terrorism, such as the identity theory, the narcissistic rage, and the paranoid theory, draw mainly from the psychoanalytic domain, with a focus on early childhood. The identity theory is particularly efficient when it comes to explaining the radicalization path of young people: according to various scholars, teenagers and young adults turn to violence in search of "a sense of purpose and self-worth" (Victoroff, 2005, 22–23). This explanation recalls the work of Frantz Fanon, who described the violence of the oppressed against the colonial powers as a path to find the self-identity, and is also connected to the politological analysis by Olivier Roy (2017). According to Crayton, narcissism provides an interpretation lens (1983): the so-called narcissistic rage generates an aggressive attempt to eliminate the source of injury. This is partially linked to the identity theory referring to terrorists as "timid, emotionally damaged adolescents [. . .] in search of affiliation and meaning" (Victoroff, 2005, 24) and may also be connected to the novelty-seeking theory, according to which young adults are extremely vulnerable to "ideological and passionate solicitations" as they begin their "lifelong quest for meaning" (Levine, 1999, 342–343). As claimed by Sageman, "[terrorists] believe that they are special, part of a small vanguard trying to build a better world in the name of a cause" (2008, 224). Various authors underline the role played by organizational dynamics in joining terrorist groups and, consequently, the importance of being aware of roles and levels when trying to understand the psychology of terrorists (Schuurman & Horgan, 2016, 57). The search for a role in the group is well depicted by Victoroff (2005, 6) in Figure 6.1.

More recently, it has become evident and generally accepted that the study of terrorism should take into consideration both "psychological predispositions [. . .] and the external environment" (Crenshaw, 2004, 414) because

Sponsor	Leader	Executive Committee	Middle Management	Follower	Lone Wolf
State authority figure	Self-imagined idealist	Political policy maker	Strategist/ technocrat	Foot soldier/ action perpetrator	
Substate group sponsor	Self-imagined messianic	Military policy maker	Recruiter	Technician	
Individual financial contributor	Ethnic or religious animus-driven		Trainer/ dispatcher	Researcher/ surveyor/ errand runner	
	Entrepreneur		Supplier/ armorer	Transporter/ harborer	
				Sympathizer/ fellow traveler	

Figure 6.1 Roles and Types within Terrorist Hierarchies.

Source: Victoroff, 2005.

terrorism is "probably *always* determined by a combination of innate factors, biological factors, early developmental factors, cognitive factors, temperament, environmental influences, and group dynamics" (Victoroff, 2005, 34). In this regard, a major contribution is represented by the work of John Horgan, who abandoned the attempt to explain the root causes of terrorism to focus on the process by which individuals get involved in terrorist groups: "we may never fully crack the code, but we won't make any progress at all by continuing to obsess over the question of Why? [. . .] A better starting point is to answer the How? questions" (Horgan, 2014, 8). Horgan focuses on the features of an environment conducive to involvement in terrorist activities and identifies some "predisposing risk factors": emotional vulnerability; dissatisfaction with current activity; identification with the victims; conceptualization of violence as not immoral; sense of reward arising from the engagement; family/social ties to people sharing similar feelings and experiences (Horgan, 2008, 84–85).

The processual and gradual nature of the phenomenon of radicalization is recognized also by Webber and Kruglanski, who describe the factors that may increase radicalization probability in the three N's model: needs, narratives, and networks (2016). In the N's scheme, radicalization is prompted by the attempt to identify a source of meaning; the identification of the means to achieve the significance (namely violence for the subject under investigation); and the "commitment shift," namely the rise of the identified goal over any other (Kruglanski et al., 2014, 74). The significance quest can be triggered, for instance, by attacks on the identity (Kruglanski et al., 2014, 75). Discrimination toward a group and its values increases the ties within the group and leads to a deep feeling of exclusion toward the outside: these tensions create a conducive environment for terrorism ideology to grow (Kruglanski et al., 2007, 120). Choosing violence as the means to satisfy the need requires a surrounding supporting narrative or ideology (Webber & Kruglanski, 2016), which is usually characterized by the following elements: a sense of grievance and injustice; the identification of a culprit; the elaboration of a morally acceptable method to destroy the injustice (Kruglanski et al., 2007, 77). Finally, as claimed by Sageman, the potential engagement turns into actual involvement through social ties (network) (Sageman, 2004, 130). The role played by family or friends networks is a trigger element in the involvement process, as affirmed by Kleinmann in a study of 83 cases of homegrown Sunni terrorists in the United States: in terms of recruitment, a crucial role is usually played by militants, families and friends, as "internal mechanisms alone are not sufficient for radicalization" (Kleinmann, 2012, 279). In line with a processual and gradual expression of the phenomenon, Moghaddam (2005, 161–169) elaborated the metaphor of the "staircase to terrorism," claiming that the steps become more and more narrow toward the top. At the ground floor the individual suffers from a perceived deprivation; at the first floor they try to identify options to address the injustice and reach the second, displacement of aggression, when previous attempts fail. A moral engagement into the terrorist organization and its narrative brings the individual to the third floor, while the socialization into the tradition, methods, and goals of the group lift them up to the fourth floor. Finally, at the fifth floor the individual is psychologically and morally ready to commit a terrorist act.

The Relationship among Radicalization Processes, Hate Crime, and Hate Speech

Various authors have tried to assess the relationship among terrorism, hate crime, and hate speech as the phenomena share some conceptual characteristics, especially the opposition between the in-group and the out-group. The distinction between "us" and "them" and the subsequent devaluation of the out-group facilitate the discrimination against the "others," which may lead to the extreme consequence of violent episodes. The identification of a scapegoat represents a common feature in various forms of political violence.

In the attempt to identify what connects and what differentiates terrorism and hate crimes, Dunbar, Blanco, & Crèvecoeur-MacPhail (2016) identified some common elements: both phenomena are motivated by hatred or animus with the intent of sharing a broader message by targeting a specific group selected on specific sociocultural criteria. Notwithstanding that, terrorist acts are usually committed by a minority group against a majority, while hate crimes entail the opposite dynamic and are usually less ideologically motivated.

The linkages between these two phenomena may go beyond the characteristics outlined above. As a matter of fact, several authors have tried to assess the existence of a causal and/or temporal relationship between terrorism and hate crimes. Deloughery, King, and Asal (2012) have tested the potential temporal connection between hate crime and terrorism to assess if increasing levels of hate would lead to more violent and extreme terrorist acts. The authors focused on the existence of a progressive relationship between the two concepts, with hate crime representing a preliminary step toward more violent radicalization leading to terrorism. The hypothesis considers the progression to occur among the same actors, supposing that hate crimes would facilitate engagement into terrorist acts over a certain period of time. Through the analysis of data on terrorist attacks and hate crimes that occurred on U.S. soil in a 17-year time frame, no correlation was found to support the idea that hate crimes function as precursors to terrorism. Notwithstanding that, interesting results were identified on the reverse hypothesis, which is that terrorism positively affects hate phenomena: Deloughery et al. (2012) found that hate crimes are often perpetrated in response to terrorist acts.

The hypotheses tested by Deloughery and colleagues (2012) do not address the causal nature of the relationship implied in Kruglanski et al.

theory (2014). According to three N's model, the radicalization process is usually characterized by three phases: the need to identify a source of meaning ("activation of the significance quest"); the identification of the means to achieve the significance (namely violence for the subject under investigation); and the "commitment shift," namely the rise of the identified goal over any other. Hate speech and hate-motivated crimes may have an impact on the first phase of this process by increasing the vulnerability in the significance loss. The attack on the identity, perpetrated through hate speech, can lead to a loss of significance. This is the case, for example, of "Muslim immigrants to Europe who encounter widespread disrespect, if not rabid 'Islamophobia' on the part of native populations in their host countries" (Kruglanski et al., 2014, 75). Discrimination toward a group and its values increases the ties within the group and leads to a deep feeling of exclusion toward the outside: these tensions create a conducive environment for terrorism ideology to grow (Kruglanski et al., 2008, 120) by increasing grievances and frustrations, that are commonly identified as key ingredients in a radicalization process by different disciplines. The findings of Deloughery et al. (2012) have been further expanded by Mills, Freilich, and Chermak (2017), who concluded that "higher levels of various types of bias-motivated or extremist violence are more likely to witness higher levels of other types of bias-motivated or extremist violence" (1214). Further research is thus necessary to further scrutinize this relationship and assess if exposure to hate crimes may lead to engagement into terrorist groups.

Sullaway (2016, 99) recognizes that overlapping between the phenomena may exist, although one phenomenon does not necessarily require the other to occur. The author suggests that the difficulty in further scrutinizing the relationship between the two phenomena is due to the underlying complexity of the two concepts and is also partially linked to the lack of a multidisciplinary approach to the topic (111). In addition, the changing environment in which hate crimes and terrorism take place makes it particularly challenging to evaluate the nature of this relationship. For instance, many authors claimed that terrorism, unlike hate crimes, is characterized by higher levels of "planning and resources" (Mills, Freilich, & Chermak, 2017, 1195). Notwithstanding that, terrorist dynamics have transformed in the last years, and attacks require limited preparation and minor resources. This may be traced back to the evolution brought forward by the Islamic State, which inherited the experience of al-Qaeda but has managed to develop new strategies and tactical approaches as a consequence of globalization (Neumann, 2016). The situation is further complicated by the influence of new technologies, especially the online world.

Therefore, in the next paragraphs, the digital environment will be further analyzed to outline how new technologies entail both challenges and opportunities in the fields of hate speech, freedom of speech, online extremism, and radicalization episodes. As the boundaries can be blurred and religion used as a pretext to manifest different forms of intolerance and violence, an in-depth reflection on hate-motivated violence based on racism and/or religion will be elaborated on to better understand the circular relation between these phenomena in the current international scenario.

The Boundaries between Racist and Religious Hatred

In the previous paragraphs, some initial assumptions were outlined concerning the circular relation among terrorism, hate crime, and hate speech, starting from the idea—common to both phenomena—of the opposition between the in-group and the out-group, also considered as the "others."

The idea of "otherness" is central to different sociological analyses studying how identities of majority and minority groups are constructed. In the effort to define social identity, psychology tends to focus on the characteristics of the individuals, while sociologists mainly work on the concept of social identities (Jenkins, 1996). Social identities reflect the way individuals and groups internalize established social categories within their own societies, including their ethnic, national, cultural, religious, and gender identities. George Herbert Mead (1934) theorizes that social identities are created through our ongoing social interaction with other people and our self-reflection about who we think we are according to these social exchanges. Mead's work also shows that the identity construction is a process, starting from the agreement, then disagreement, and negotiation with other people. For these reasons, the ideas of similarity and difference are both key in the process by which a sense of identity and social belonging is achieved. Zygmunt Bauman (1991) explains that the notion of otherness is central to the way in which societies establish an identity category, arguing that identities are set up as dichotomies. "In dichotomies crucial for the practice and the vision of social order, the differentiating power hides as a rule behind one of the members of the opposition. The second member is but the other of the first, the opposite (degraded, suppressed, exiled) side of the first and its creation. Thus abnormality is the other of the norm [. . .] woman the other of man, stranger the other of the native, enemy the other of friend, 'them' the other of 'us' [. . .]" (Bauman, 1991, 8).

Nowadays, in modern multicultural societies, new exclusion–inclusion lines have been drawn on the grounds of religion and culture. In the aftermath of Islamist-motivated violent episodes or terrorist attacks, haters tend to identify extremists with all Muslims and/or Muslims with the "Arabs," demonstrating serious lacunae at a cultural and religious level. Hate phenomena are deeply connected to the lack of interreligious and intercultural dialogue, and the situation is exacerbated by the so-called "migration crisis." The following paragraphs will thus further analyze the issues of islamophobia and anti-Muslim hatred and its interrelationship with anti-migrant hatred.

A sector where these complex interlinkages have been explored is the legislative arena, which has hosted long discussions about whether or not to couple discrimination and hate-motivated behaviors on the grounds of *race* and *religion* (Noorloos, 2011, 309). Before delving into the thin boundaries between hate crime and hate speech motivated by race and religion, a reflection should follow on "new" forms of racism and discrimination, to better understand the framework of analysis. "Developments in a number of countries worldwide show that the power of racist ideas remains strong, even forging movements and political parties that can result in deadly consequences" (Bajt, 2014). A recent comparative study carried out throughout nine European countries[1] at shows that "[t]here is, as it is easy to imagine, a circular relation between the root causes of hatred and the main bias motives in the different countries. [. . .] racism, xenophobia, discrimination against nationality, ethnicity and religious faith or affiliation are still the main motives behind discrimination practices and hatred incidents. Hostility against particular groups, such as Roma and Sinti, antisemitism and islamophobia are other continuing or emerging phenomena; some countries still manifest historical sentiments—such as sectarianism—while a general anti-refugees and migrants' attitude is affecting almost every country" (RISSC, 2017).

As reiterated by the think tank Runnymede Trust in one of its latest reports on *Islamophobia: A Challenge for Us All* (Conway, 2018), reedited 20 years after its first publication: "Anti-Muslim prejudice has grown further and wider [. . .]. In the intervening 20 years [a number of] particular changes are worth highlighting. [. . .] The first change is that the context [. . .] has transformed fundamentally. After 9/11 and 7/7, Muslims became a greater focus of policymakers and around the world, but framed largely in terms of terrorism or as a civilization threat. This framing of Muslims [. . .] has re-emerged in new and toxic ways" (Conway, 2018). While the terrorist threat is real and its frequency increases public concern and fear, Islamophobia can inflate the fear of terrorism and is, in turn, subject to further diffusion in the wake of terrorist attacks.

Definition of Islamophobia[2]

Islamophobia is any distinction, exclusion or restriction toward, or preference against, Muslims (or those perceived to be Muslims) that has the purpose or effect or nullifying or impairing the recognition, enjoyment or exercise, on an equal footing, of human rights and fundamental freedoms in the political, economic, social, cultural or any other field of public life.

According to Conway (2018), the phenomenon is particularly complex and the reference to "anti-Muslim hate (or even 'anti-Muslim prejudice and discrimination') doesn't fully capture the widespread (or structural) ways racial inequalities persist." It may also get things back to front: prejudicial attitudes about a group develop to justify the economic or political disadvantages experienced by that group. This view can help in understanding why and how different forms of racism contain a "cultural" component: it is generally recognized how the newest forms of racism are more linked to cultural aspects than in the past, when racism was especially based on skin color. Focusing on culture as a key component of current forms of racism is also useful in understanding why racism and its effects persist, even though the so-called biological claims have become more and more unfashionable.

While there is a wide range of diversity among Muslims communities, at the same time all Muslims are potentially exposed and vulnerable to Islamophobia as a form of racism and discrimination.

Although religion is not included in the definition of racial discrimination (in Art. 1 of the International Convention on the Elimination of All Forms of Racial Discrimination), the Committee on the Elimination of Racial Discrimination (ECRI) recognizes, in the light of the principle of intersectionality, that racist hate speech extends to speech "targeting persons belonging to certain ethnic groups who profess or practice a religion different from the majority, including expressions of Islamophobia, anti-Semitism and other similar manifestations of hatred against ethno-religious groups, as well as extreme manifestations of hatred such as incitement to genocide and to terrorism" (ECRI, 2013, par. 6).

Often, religion and culture function as exclusion–inclusion lines in contemporary societies (Noorloos, 2011). Looking at the legal framework concerning hate speech on the grounds of *race* and of *religion*, both the Cybercrime Protocol[3] and the EU Framework Decision on Racism and Xenophobia[4] include religious hate speech if it is used as a pretext for hatred on the ground of race. "This reflects the idea that religious hate speech is of a different kind than racial hate speech—religion involves ideas, practices, ways of life which are [. . .] open to criticism—but that such criticism can easily be used as a pretext for hatred against persons which is actually based on exterior features or descent or which contains the same 'essentialised' thinking. That does, of course, leave unimpeded that it can be very difficult to define when such is the case [. . .]. The CERD Committee[5] deals with religious discrimination only if there is a link with ethnicity—however, this line can be thin" (Noorloos, 2011, 309).

Noorloos's (2011) analysis goes further into details by looking at some specific examples at the country level, highlighting, for instance, that the legislation on hate speech developed in England in 1960 expressly left religion out as, unlike race, it was connected to particular teachings or convictions and thus more open to criticism. Moreover, while in that historical moment there was no clear evidence of hatred incidents motivated by religion, nowadays the situation is profoundly different: religious diversity has greatly increased, and religious identity plays a prominent role in the political debate, on one side, while on the other side Islam has come to the forefront of public debate. The idea of putting race and religion on the same level in the religious hatred law led to several concerns, as many feared that this would pose limits to satire or criticism of religious ideas and traditions. Differently, in the Netherlands, race and religion have always been treated equally in the legislation against hate speech, although different case laws show that the different interpretations of judges play a role in this regard (Noorloos, 2011).

Why is the reflection on the concept of hate speech motivated by race and religion presented above of particular relevance in the assessment of existing relations between hatred and radicalization processes? Focusing on the hate-incidents component, one of the main reasons behind the perpetration of hate against racial, cultural, or religious groups is the lack of knowledge, understanding, and the creation of misconceptions around ethnic or religious groups. While incidents of hate on different grounds should be persecuted, as a deterrent element and to put the protection of human dignity at the forefront, the role of prevention is even more important. In this view, intercultural and interreligious dialogue can play an important role. This aspect will be further explored in the conclusion. Furthermore, in the current international scenario, an additional piece needs to be added to the puzzle—by looking at the increasing phenomenon of anti-migrant hatred, and how this intersects with relevant phenomena such as anti-Muslim hate, the reaction to terrorist attacks, and the rise of extremism.

The International League Against Racism and Anti-Semitism (LICRA) in France recently published a report, within the INACH initiative,[6] on the phenomenon of radicalization of the online debate about refugees and its main causes. LICRA highlighted some of the influencing factors characterizing the current situation in the country. The first element addressed in the report is the tense situation in the coastal city of Calais, where thousands of people are camping there for several years, waiting and hoping for the possibility to get to the United Kingdom.[7] Second, the Front National, the right-wing populist and nationalist political party in France, is having a strong impact on the public discussion about refugees, as the party has adopted a clearly anti-migration and anti-Islam position. Last but not least, the terrorist attacks perpetrated in France[8] by the so-called Islamic State (IS) have had a profound impact on public sentiment and opinion in the whole country: "the attacks sharpened the tone in the discussion of refugees' issues on the Internet. At the same time, next to the well-known narrative of refugees being a burden on the social system, economy and public order, a new narrative found its way in the social media: refugees from Syria and Iraq—a specifically IS active region—are stigmatized and criminalized as IS members and potential terrorists who could pose a danger to life and limb at any time" (Fernanda, Delgado, & Maldini, 2016, 15). Based on the French criminal code, xenophobic expressions or acts against certain groups of people are considered as "incitement to racial hatred" based on a set of criteria, including the person themselves or their background and the context of the statement/action; or the fact that the hate expressed must produce negative feelings such as hostility or rejection toward a group of people based on their actual or supposed ethnic origin, national origin, religion, or belief. However, "hate speech against refugees remains [in most cases] below the limit of being punishable under criminal law in France" (Fernanda, Delgado, & Maldini, 2016, 16).

Examples from other countries, such as Germany, demonstrate how the debate around the "refugees" also functions as a catalyst for right-wing extremist propaganda. The hateful narrative against "foreigners, Muslims or Sinti," made responsible for social grievances, reveal once more the well-known scapegoat mechanism, which is common to various forms of political violence, from hate speech to terrorist acts to genocides and mass atrocities (Staub, 1989, 295). On the basis of this dynamic, Krueger and Malečková (2002, 28) have defined terrorism and hate crimes as "close cousin[s]," given that in both cases the victim is chosen by virtue of their group membership and because both actions have the objective of spreading terror.

These country-based examples already give a preliminary idea of some of the reasons why phenomena such as forms of extremism and radicalization, hate speech and migration, should be looked at through cross-cutting lenses—as they are all linked to each other in different aspects. And, ultimately, they can all lead to an increasing spiral of violence.

The Dutch Meldpunt Discriminatie Internet (MDI)[9] reveals another worrying phenomenon when online hate leads to offline violence and hate crime. In 2015, the institute received 43 reports revealing 125 hateful and discriminatory comments against refugees—against the eight reports received in 2014—where most of the contents where posted on Facebook and Twitter. The hostile feelings and anti-refugee sentiments, fueled by stereotypes and myths, also can fan the flames of the online debates of right-wing populist actors such as the Dutch movement of Patriotic Europeans Against the Islamization of the West (PEGIDA), which is permanently warning against the "Islamization" of the country. There is, according to MDI, a real overlap of the concepts of "refugee," "Muslim," and "migrant," and "these are used nearly inter-changeably when talking about an 'economic migrant' or a 'profiteer'" (Fernanda, Delgado, & Maldini, 2016, 25). Again, this attitude is accompanied by a concern over an "Islamic takeover plot" spread over the Internet, and the fear of terrorists hiding among refugees to reach the Netherlands and commit attacks. While these types of contents disseminated online do not always represent hate speech, they contribute to the normalization of a certain narrative against migrants, refugees, or Muslims—and can even lead to the rise of attacks during specific events. "In December [2016], a debate about plans to build a refugee center took place in the small town of Geldermalsen. Crowds of rioters tried to storm the city hall throwing stones and fireworks; eventually the meeting was closed and the participants had to be escorted by the police" (Fernanda, Delgado, & Maldini, 2016, 26). In view of the debate, the members of a Facebook group were called to action and encouraged to protest and even undertake violent actions.

Online Hate Speech: New Technologies as Threat or Opportunity?

Within this broader and complex framework, what is the role played by the new technologies when looking at hate speech and radicalization phenomena?

On one side, as briefly touched on in the previous paragraphs, terrorist dynamics have transformed in the last years. Attacks require limited preparation and minor resources in line with the evolution brought forward by the Islamic State through the development of new strategies and tactical approaches (Neumann, 2016). The situation is further complicated by the influence of new technologies, especially the role that Internet can play, for instance, in terms of recruitment and radicalization processes. "Exploiting the benefits afforded by the Internet, violent extremists have created and utilized a myriad of online platforms (e.g., websites, forums, blogs, social media) that have abetted and enhanced their recruitment campaign across the world [. . .]. There is a need to understand why their online platforms are so persuasive to certain target audiences" (Khader et al., 2016, 2). Through a study of 100 Facebook pages and 50 Twitter user accounts, Awan has found that ISIS supplies online communication material to spread the group's messages over the main social media sites, such as YouTube, Facebook, and Twitter, and exploits online hate for recruitment purposes (Awan, 2017).

On the other side,

> [t]he Internet is playing a crucial role in the so-called normalization of racism [and intolerance]: racist movements are well aware about the potential of social media in the diffusion of hate speech. They exploit the social media "virality" by cloaking the real source(s) of such messages and promoting sharing of such contents, with the final aim of manipulating people worries and outrage [. . .]. Topics such as anti-social behaviors of the Roma people, the identification of immigration with crime, the danger of certain races, the invitation to sink immigrants' boats—that once a time was a domain (or prerogative) of [some political parties' rhetoric] such as

> the Northern League's in Italy[10] are now spoken publicly . . . and not only by right wing speakers. Hate speech online is therefore a dangerous weapon that potentially everyone, including violent extremists, can use to promote hate and perpetrate hatred behaviors. (Cerase, D'Angelo, & Santoro, 2015)

Furthermore, the distinction between hate speech online and offline is not always clear-cut. On the contrary, the two spheres are often connected in various ways: victims struggle to separate online and offline discrimination and fear the materialization of online threats (Awan & Zempi, 2016).

In light of the vicious circle between online radicalization and hate speech, the Joint Statement of EU Ministers for Justice and Home Affairs following the terrorist attacks in Brussels on March 22, 2016, stated, among other points, that the "Commission will intensify work with IT companies, notably in the EU Internet Forum, to counter terrorist propaganda and to develop [. . .] a code of conduct against hate speech online."[11] The code of conduct was first adopted in May 2016: each of the IT companies that signed this code—Facebook, Twitter, Microsoft, and Instagram—declares its commitment to the fight against illegal hate speech online.

When is Hate Speech Online Illegal?

Illegal hate speech is defined in the EU law—by the Framework Decision on combating certain forms and expressions of racism and xenophobia by means of criminal law—as the public incitement to violence or hatred directed to groups or individuals on the basis of certain characteristics, including race, color, religion, descent, and national or ethnic origin. Even though interpreting the legislation remains the responsibility of national courts in every country, based on the Code of Conduct signed with the EC, the IT companies have to act in line with national laws, in particular those transposing the Framework Decision. "When they receive a valid alert about content allegedly containing illegal hate speech, the IT companies have to assess it, not only against their rules and community guidelines, but, where necessary, against applicable national law (including that implementing EU law), which fully complies with the principle of freedom of expression."

Since the adoption of the Code of Conduct, the Commission already implemented five monitoring exercises concerning its implementation. The latest report on the fifth monitoring exercise (EC, 2020), released on June 22, 2020, highlights that, in the relevant period, IT companies removed 71% of the illegal hate speech notified to them.[12] Compared with the removal rate of

59% in the second monitoring exercise (May 2017) and with the 28% in the first monitoring (2016), the EC is observing a clear and steady increase in the removal of hate speech (EC, 2020). During the latest monitoring, 4,364 notifications have been submitted to the IT companies, covering 23 member states. Facebook received the biggest number of notifications (2,348), followed by Twitter (1,396), and YouTube (464). This is in line with the results presented within the European project eMORE (2016–2018), where according to an online survey involving nine EU countries, "hate speech online happens more often on social networks, by anonymous sources, or sometimes via private messages. Facebook is the first social network indicated in the answers, followed by YouTube and/or Twitter" (RISSC, 2017, 30).

Besides the numbers and the ongoing debate around the efficacy of such measures, which are nowadays the main grounds for reporting hatred in Europe? Among the most commonly reported characteristics of hate speech are xenophobia (including anti-migrant hatred), ethnic origins (15%), anti-Gypsism (9.9%), anti-Muslim hatred (9.4%), national and ethnic origin (8.4%), Afrophobia (4.9%), and race (3.8%), The results, quite in line with the trend already registered back in May 2017, confirm a high predominance of racist hatred against ethnic minorities, migrants and refugees, and Muslims[13] (see Figure 6.2).

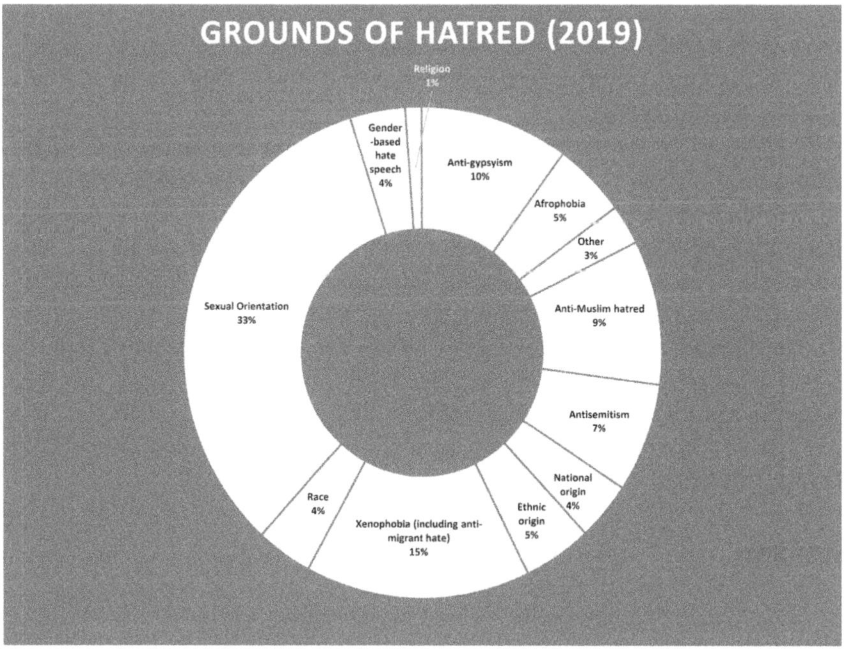

Figure 6.2 Notifications per ground of hate speech (European Commission, 2020, p. 4)

According to Tell Mama (2017), an organization working with Muslim minorities in Britain, "in many of the anti-Muslim incidents reported [. . .] in 2016, perpetrators referred to terrorism, bombs and high-profile international events associated with extremism, terror attacks or crimes in which they attribute blame to Muslims in general. These types of cases, despite taking place in very different circumstances, conform to the popular rhetoric which portray Muslims as an existential threat" (Tell Mama, 2017, 63). This conforms to the "retaliation" and "defensive" typologies for hate crime identified by McDevitt et al. (2002). Based on this model, hate crime perpetrators find their motivation as a reaction to a perceived grievance that they feel themselves or their group have experienced, or to defend their community from "outsiders" that they consider a threat to their own way of life (Lickel et al., 2006, 378).

Several evidences suggest that in the aftermath of terrorist attacks (and the related media coverage), individuals may try to retaliate by abusing people they identify as Muslims—more often through their clothing or ethnicity. This mainly occurs because of intergroup conflict, in this specific case between the "in-group" of people considered as legitimately belonging to a specific group (e.g., the British or the Christians), and the "out-group" of Muslims, who are constructed as "being interchangeable and therefore equally deserving of retaliation for the crimes of a tiny and unrepresentative minority" (Hanes & Machin, 2014, 247–267). Existing literature has highlighted the fact that [British] Muslims have been constructed as a "suspect community" in response to terror attacks (Awan, 2012; Cole, 2014): "potential hate crime perpetrators may pick up on this and act on it, due to their perception that they are 'protecting' British society, by abusing or assaulting Muslims, whom they associate directly with extremism" (Tell Mama, 2017, 64).

Tell Mama reports evidence, based on its experience with victims' support, showing how a casual reference to terrorism directed at Muslims can, on occasion, escalate to more serious, false, and sometimes malicious accusations of extremism, which could have potentially serious repercussions for the individuals they are directed at. "While there have been many cases in which young people needed safeguarding from extremist views, we have received numerous accounts of Muslim individuals being disingenuously reported as 'suspected terrorists' as a form of Islamophobia abuse" (Tell Mama, 2017, 64).

Conclusions

This chapter has attempted to identify the ways and contexts in which hatred phenomena may have an impact on the radicalization process as well as to assess if and how terrorism and terrorist attacks can affect hate crime and hate speech. The theories analyzed in the literature review highlight the existence of various steps, within the radicalization process, where being the victim of hatred can facilitate the recruitment into terrorist groups. This is particularly true for grievances and frustrations arising from the attack, whether real or perceived, on one's identity. The concept of identity is, in turn, crucial also in the study of the hate phenomena: hatred is perpetrated by the "in-group" toward the so-called "out-group," namely a group of people perceived as different, not adhering to the defining values of the "in-group." The boundaries between the "us" and "them" are increasingly linked to religion and culture, to the point that, in the aftermath of Islamist-motivated attacks, haters address their anger toward the entire Muslim society.

Empirical studies to assess the nature of the relationship between hate crimes and terrorism are still very limited; and, although they highlight some forms of connection between the two, at the same time they emphasize the difficulty in scrutinizing the nature of this linkage. The situation is further complicated, in the current international scenario, by the devious role played by the Internet. Although further research is necessary to scientifically analyze the scope of the interplay among hate crime, hate speech, and terrorism, existing studies and countries' lessons learned can be used as a reference point for the elaboration of future policies and lead to claims that preventive and contrasting measures should take a holistic approach to these issues.

First, culture appears to play a central and crucial role in the dynamics examined above. Policies aimed at preventing and combating hate crimes and terrorism should envisage the promotion and the strengthening of intercultural dialogue. Based on the Council of Europe White Paper of May 7, 2008, intercultural dialogue is "a process that comprises an open and respectful exchange of views between individuals, groups with different ethnic, cultural, religious, linguistic backgrounds and heritage on the basis of mutual understanding and respect." If tolerance and understanding of the "other" are two main components of intercultural dialogue, they implicate the development of new forms of creative and expressive communication. In this view, difference becomes a key point for negotiation in dialogue processes: understanding the differences means looking at others' beliefs and cultural principles with new eyes, in an effort to leave behind preconstructed beliefs with the idea that the potential of dialogue practice can be immense. On an institutional level, intercultural dialogue thus becomes an important component of policy documents and a political instrument in managing cultural variation or social inequity.

Among the recommendations developed by the CoE in its white paper, the participation of the civil society should be strongly encouraged, especially for those organizations working with or representing minority groups—including minorities based on religious beliefs. Interfaith dialogue, in fact, can potentially make the difference considering the actual historical moment. As argued by Abu-Nimer et al (2007), "inter-faith dialogue is an underdeveloped but potentially powerful instrument in the peacebuilder's mediation" in the Middle East region.

Engagement with the "other" is the heart of dialogue: it seeks to know the other by listening and attending to the meaning behind the words of the others. Religious symbols or rituals represent forms of discourse through which free expression should be encouraged. The common ground established by intercultural dialogue, including interfaith, is the mutual recognition of human dignity of each individual, regardless of race, ethnicity, religious background, or sexual orientation. It does not mean reducing the differences; on the contrary, it means enriching our own personal experience—by at the same time eradicating the very profound reasons behind hatred and promoting social and cultural inclusion.

A better and more comprehensive understanding of the complex dynamics analyzed in this chapter should also be promoted at the policy level. Assessment should be as comprehensive as possible and also include important factors such as the effect of migration and communication tools on hate phenomena and radicalization processes. While it is generally recognized that no action is sufficient when it comes to online hate against refugees, the effects of hate and discrimination perpetrated through the digital environment are still unclear, and further research should be encouraged—also as a preventive strategy. Countries should elaborate and adopt national and international regulations for the online world, envisaging efficient reporting mechanisms and capacity building for the competent institutions.

A high proportion of perpetrators abuse their victims on the basis of multiple aspects of their identity interchangeably, as Islamophobia, racism, and xenophobic prejudice coalesce. *Intersectionality*, as a concept, is key in identifying how prejudices can compound other types of identity-based discrimination to disadvantage some of the most vulnerable within our society. An in-depth understanding of the peculiarities and specific characteristics of each considered context could represent a useful interpretation for understanding the current challenges and phenomena affecting broader areas and regions. Every political revolution cannot succeed unless it is accompanied by the revolutions of thought—and an in-depth understanding of the different realities, which are part of that revolution, is essential.

Notes

1. The above-mentioned comparative study has been carried out within the project eMORE, cofunded by the European Commission and involving the following EU members: Belgium, Cyprus, Germany, Italy, Malta, Northern Ireland, Portugal, Romania, and Slovenia. For more information, go to https://www.emoreproject.eu.

2. Runnymede Trust developed a working definition of Islamophobia, based on the UN definition of racism. Reprinted with permission from Conway (2018).

3. Additional protocol to the Convention on Cybercrime, concerning the criminalization of acts of a racist and xenophobic nature committed through computer systems—Strasbourg, January 2003, European Treaty Series No. 189.

4. Council Framework Decision 2008/913/JHA of 28 November 2008 on combating certain forms and expressions of racism and xenophobia by means of criminal law.

5. The Committee on the Elimination of Racial Discrimination (CERD) is the body of independent experts that monitors implementation of the Convention on the Elimination of All Forms of Racial Discrimination by its State parties.

6. LICRA is the French member of the international Network Against Cyberhate (INACH). INACH is a foundation under Dutch Law and is seated in Amsterdam, and its main object is to combat discrimination on the internet.

7. For further details on the situation in Calais, see, for instance, the reporting by the BBC at http://www.bbc.com/news/uk-29074736.

8. Main reference is made to the terrorist attacks by ISIS on the French satirical magazine *Charlie Hebdo* and a Jewish supermarket in 2015; the massacre in the Bataclan Theatre and the streets of Paris in November 2015; and the truck rampage in Nice in July 2016.

9. MDI is also a member of INACH and contributed to the report INACH, 2016. Fernanda, R. A., Delgado, P. S., & Maldini, C. A. (2016). *Efecto de la temperatura sobre las limitaciones fotosintéticas de Colobanthus quitensis (Kunth) Bartl.* Concepción, Chile: Universidad de Concepción.

10. The Northern League in Italy, whose complete name is Lega Nord per l'indipendenza della Padania, is a regionalist political party in Italy.

11. http://www.consilium.europa.eu/en/press/press-releases/2016/03/24-statement-on-terrorist-attacks-in-brussels-on-22-march/

12. https://ec.europa.eu/info/sites/info/files/codeofconduct_2020_factsheet_12.pdf

13. Data on grounds of hatred are an indication of trends and may be influenced by the field of activity of the organizations participating in the monitoring. In 2019, organizations working on LGBT rights have been more active in flagging content, as reported in Figure 6.2.

References

Abu-Nimer, M., Khoury, A., & Welty, E. (2007). *Unity in diversity: Interfaith dialogue in the Middle East.* Washington, DC: United States Institute of Peace Press.

Atran, S. (2016). *L'Etat islamique est une révolution.* Paris, France: Les Liens Qui Libèrent Editions.

Awan, I. (2012). "I'm a Muslim not an extremist:" How the prevent strategy has constructed a "suspect" community. *Politics & Policy*, 40(6), 1158–1185.

Awan, I. (2017). Cyber-extremism: Isis and the power of social media. *Society*, 54(2), 138–149.

Awan, I., & Zempi, I. (2016). The affinity between online and offline anti-Muslim hate crime: Dynamics and impacts. *Aggression and Violent Behavior*, 27, 1–8.

Bajt, V. (2014). Contemporary racism across Europe. *Freedom from Fear magazine*—F3, Destabilization, 9, 35–39. http://f3magazine.unicri.it/wp-content/uploads/F3_09.pdf

Bakker, E. (2015). *Terrorism and counterterrorism studies: Comparing theory and practice*. Leiden, Netherlands: Leiden University Press.

Bauman, Z. (1991). *Modernity and ambivalence*. Hoboken, NJ: John Wiley & Sons.

Bonanate, L. (1979). Some unanticipated consequences of terrorism. *Journal of Peace Research*, 16(3), 197–211.

Borum, R. (2011). Radicalization into violent extremism II: A review of conceptual models and empirical research. *Journal of Strategic Security*, 4(4), 37–62.

Cerase, A., D'Angelo, E., & Santoro, C. (2015, September 23). Monitoring racist and xenophobic extremism to counter hate speech online: Ethical dilemmas and methods of a preventive approach. *VOX Pol*. https://www.voxpol.eu/monitoring-racist-and-xenophobic-extremism-to-counter-hate-speech-online-ethical-dilemmas-and-methods-of-a-preventive-approach/

Cole, M. (2014). Austerity/immiseration capitalism and Islamophobia—or twenty-first-century multicultural socialism? *Policy Futures in Education*, 12(1), 79–92.

Conway, G. (2018). *Islamophobia: A challenge for us all: Report of the Runnymede Trust Commission on British Muslims and Islamophobia Runnymede Trust*. London, UK: Runnymede Trust.

Council of Europe (CoE). (2015). Dealing with radicalisation in a prison and probation context. *RAN P&P—Practitioners Working Paper*. https://ec.europa.eu/dgs/home-affairs/what-we-do/networks/radicalisation_awareness_network/ran-news/docs/ran_p_and_p_practitioners_working_paper_en.pdf

Crayton, J. W. (1983). Terrorism and the psychology of the self. In L. Z. Freedman & Y. Alexander (Eds.), *Perspectives on terrorism* (pp. 33–41). Wilmington, DE: Scholarly Resources.

Crenshaw, M. (1981). The causes of terrorism. *Comparative Politics*, 13(4), 379–399.

Crenshaw, M. (2004). The psychology of political terrorism. In J. T. Jost & J. Sidanius (Eds.), *Political psychology: Key readings* (pp. 411–431). New York, NY: Psychology Press.

Della Porta, D., & LaFree, G. (2012). Processes of radicalization and de-radicalization. *International Journal of Conflict and Violence*, 6(1), 4–10.

Deloughery, K., King, R. D., & Asal, V. (2012). Close cousins or distant relatives? The relationship between terrorism and hate crime. *Crime & Delinquency*, 58(5), 663–688.

Dunbar, E., Blanco, A., & Crèvecoeur-MacPhail, D. A. (Eds.) (2016). *The psychology of hate crimes as domestic terrorism*. Santa Barbara, CA: Praeger.

ECRI. (2013, September 26). General Recommendation No. 35 on combating racist hate speech, CERD/C/GC/35, para. 6.

European Commission (EC). (2020). Results of the 5th monitoring exercise.

Fernanda, R. A., Delgado, P. S., & Maldini, C. A. (2016). *Efecto de la temperatura sobre las limitaciones fotosintéticas de Colobanthus quitensis (Kunth) Bartl.* Concepción, Chile: Universidad de Concepción.

Fink, N. C., & Hearne, E. B. (2008, October). Beyond terrorism: Deradicalization and disengagement from violent extremism. International Peace Institute. https://www.ipinst.org/wp-content/uploads/publications/beter.pdf

Freilich, J. D., & LaFree, G. (2015) Criminology theory and terrorism: Introduction to the special issue. *Terrorism and Political Violence*, 27(1), 1–8.

Hanes, E., & Machin, S. (2014). Hate crime in the wake of terror attacks: Evidence from 7/7 and 9/11. *Journal of Contemporary Criminal Justice*, 30(3), 247–267.

Horgan, J. (2003). The search for the terrorist personality. In A. Silke (Ed.), *Terrorists, victims and society* (pp. 3–27). Chichester, UK: Wiley.

Horgan, J. (2008). From profiles to pathways and roots to routes: Perspectives from psychology on radicalization into terrorism. *The Annals of the American Academy of Political and Social Science*, 618(1), 80–94.

Horgan, J. (2014, September 10). Don't ask why people join the Islamic State—ask how. *Vice News*. https://www.vice.com/en/article/wjyygy/dont-ask-why-people-join-the-islamic-state-ask-how

Jenkins, R. (1996). *Social identity*. New York, NY: Routledge.

Khader, M., Neo S., L., Ong, G., Mingyi, E. T., & Chin, J. (2016). Combating violent extremism and radicalization in the digital era. *ProtoView*, 3(28). Ringgold. https://www.igi-global.com/book/combating-violent-extremism-radicalization-digital/142193

Kleinmann, S. M. (2012). Radicalization of homegrown Sunni militants in the United States: Comparing converts and non-converts. *Studies in Conflict & Terrorism*, 35(4), 278–297.

Krueger, A. B., & Malečková, J. (2002). Does poverty cause terrorism? *New Republic*, 226(24), 27–33.

Kruglanski, A. W., Crenshaw, M., Post, J. M., & Victoroff, J. (2007). What should this fight be called? Metaphors of counterterrorism and their implications. *Psychological Science in the Public Interest*, 8(3), 97–133.

Kruglanski, A. W., Gelfand, M. J., Bélanger, A. S., Hetiarachchi, M., & Gunaratna, R. et al. (2014). The psychology of radicalization and deradicalization: How significance quest impacts violent extremism. *Political Psychology*, 35(S1), 69–93.

Kundnani, A. (2012). Radicalisation: The journey of a concept. *Race & Class*, 54(2), 3–25.

Levine, S. (1999). Youth in terroristic groups, gangs, and cults: The allure, the animus, and the alienation. *Psychiatric Annals*, 29(6), 342–349.

Lickel, B., Miller, N., Stenstrom, D., Denson, T., & Schmader, T. (2006). Vicarious retribution: The role of collective blame in intergroup aggression. *Personality and Social Psychology Review*, 10(4), 372–90. https://doi.org/10.1207/s15327957pspr1004_6

Lum, C., Kennedy, L., & Sherley, A. (2006). Are counter-terrorism strategies effective? The results of the Campbell Systematic Review on Counterterrorism Evaluation Research. *Journal of Experimental Criminology*, 2(4), 489–516.

McDevitt, J., Levin, J., & Bennett, S. (2002). Hate crime offenders: An expanded typology. *Journal of Social Issues*, 58(2), 303–317.

Mead, G. H. (1934). *Mind, self, and society from the standpoint of a social behaviorist* (Charles W. Morris, ed.). Chicago, IL: University of Chicago.

Mills, C. E., Freilich, J. D., & Chermak, S. M. (2017). Extreme hatred: Revisiting the hate crime and terrorism relationship to determine whether they are "close cousins" or "distant relatives." *Crime & Delinquency*, 63(10), 1191–1223.

Moghaddam, F. M. (2005). The staircase to terrorism: A psychological exploration. *American Psychologist*, 60(2), 161–169.

Neumann, P. R. (2008). Introduction. *The Adelphi Papers*, 48(399), 5–10.

Neuman, P. R. (2010). Prisons and terrorism radicalisation and de-radicalisation in 15 countries. A policy report published by the International Centre for the Study of Radicalisation and Political Violence (ICSR). https://start.umd.edu/publication/prisons-and-terrorism-radicalisation-and-de-radicalisation-15-countries

Neumann, P. R. (2016). *Radicalized: New jihadists and the threat to the West*. London, UK: IB Tauris.

Noorloos, M. V. (2011). *Hate speech revisited: A comparative and historical perspective on hate speech law in the Netherlands and England & Wales*. Cambridge, UK: Intersentia. https://intersentia.com/en/hate-speech-revisited.html

Orsini, A. (2011). *Anatomy of the Red Brigades: The religious mind-set of modern terrorists*. New York, NY: Cornell University Press.

Orsini, A. (2012). Poverty, ideology and terrorism: The STAM bond. *Studies in Conflict & Terrorism*, 35(10), 665–692.

Orsini, A. (2013). Interview with a terrorist by vocation: A day among the die-hard terrorists, Part II. *Studies in Conflict & Terrorism*, 36(8), 672–684.

Orsini, A., & Caillat, M. (2016). La radicalisation des terroristes de vocation. *Commentaire*, 4, 783–790.

Pressman, D. E. (2009). Risk assessment decisions for violent political extremism. *Her Majesty the Queen in Right of Canada*. https://www.fd.org/docs/training-materials/2016/fjc2016/how-to-prepare-for-a-terrorism-case.pdf

Pressman, D. E. (2016). Risk assessment of radicalization to violence: Application of VERA-2 in Prisons. Council for Penological Co-operation, 11th Working Group Meeting, 11 January. https://rm.coe.int/09000016806f5258

RISSC. (2017). An overview on hate crime and hate speech in 9 EU countries: Towards a common approach to prevent and tackle hatred. eMORE

project. https://www.rissc.it/wp-content/uploads/2020/06/AN_OVERVIEW_ON_HATE_CRIME_AND_HATE_SPEEC.pdf
Roy, O. (2016, January 11). The Islamization of radicalism. http://www.madamasr.com/en/2016/01/11/opinion/u/the-islamization-of-radicalism/
Roy, O. (2017). *Generazione ISIS: Chi sono i giovani che scelgono il califfato e perché combattono l'occidente* (*Le djihad et la mort*, Lonrai: Le Seuil, 2016). Milan, Italy: Feltrinelli.
Sageman, M. (2004). *Understanding terror networks*. Philadelphia, PA: University of Pennsylvania Press.
Sageman, M. (2008). A strategy for fighting international Islamist terrorists. *The Annals of the American Academy of Political and Social Science*, 618(1), 223–231.
Schmid, A. P. (2013, March). Radicalisation, de-radicalisation, counter-radicalisation: A conceptual discussion and literature review. *ICCT Research Paper*. https://www.icct.nl/download/file/ICCT-Schmid-Radicalisation-De-Radicalisation-Counter-Radicalisation-March-2013.pdf
Schuurman, B., & Horgan, J. G. (2016). Rationales for terrorist violence in homegrown jihadist groups: A case study from the Netherlands. *Aggression and Violent Behavior*, 27, 55–63.
Staub, E. (1989). *The roots of evil: The origins of genocide and other group violence*. Cambridge, UK: Cambridge University Press.
Sullaway, M. (2016). Hate crime, violent extremism, domestic terrorism—Distinctions without difference? In E. Dunbar, A. Blanco, & D. A. Crèvecoeur-MacPhail (Eds.), *The psychology of hate crimes as domestic terrorism*. Santa Barbara, CA: Praeger.
Tell Mama. (2017). *Tell MAMA 2016 Annual Report. A Constructed Threat: Identity, Prejudice and the Impact of Anti-Muslim Hatred*. https://tellmamauk.org/wp-content/uploads/2017/11/A-Constructed-Threat-Identity-Intolerance-and-the-Impact-of-Anti-Muslim-Hatred-Web.pdf
Victoroff, J. (2005). The mind of the terrorist: A review and critique of psychological approaches. *Journal of Conflict Resolution*, 49(1), 3–42.
Webber, D., & Kruglanski, A. W. (2016). The psychology of terrorism. In Brad J. Bushman (Ed.), *Aggression and violence: A social psychological perspective* (pp. 290–304). London, UK: Psychology Press.

CHAPTER SEVEN

The Neuroscience of Hate and Bias Ideology: A Brain-Behavior Approach to Bias Aggression

Edward W. Dunbar

Hate: Inherited, Learned, and Habituated

Traditionally, social scientists have viewed out-group bias as a product of the acquisition of social norms that are transmitted to the individual via caregivers, peers, and social institutions. A social learning model would view ascription to out-group bias as a function of formal and informal experiences. These would include conditioning that is reinforced and modeled by members of the individual's in-group. Such an understanding of social bias might treat the acquisition of out-group stereotypes as not significantly different from the acquisition of other learned beliefs and values. A cultural perspective would additionally note that collective learning occurs within a cultural context of the individual's in-group. As has been proposed (Dunbar, 2022), the cultural coherence of social bias would be shared with other in-group members and be expressed via an articulated history of contentious in-group–out-group relationships.

Somewhat differently, though not in opposition to this, a neurobiological understanding of out-group bias would seek to identify specific brain-behavior processes that are repeatedly reinforced and activated. This approach considers how the central nervous system (CNS), moderated by metabolic processes, traumatic experiences, and biochemical agents such as alcohol or drug use, could activate out-group aggression. The neuropsychological study of in-group–out-group perception can help distinguish between the development of normative and aberrant cognitive schema. Developmentally, social bias as such can be considered in terms of the plasticity of the CNS to experience intergroup contact, on the one hand, and the regulation of socially learned stereotypes on the other.

There are a series of relevant questions from a neuropsychological perspective by which to examine hate behavior. These include determining the neurobiological processes related to bias and aggression. Additionally, such a methodology would examine what neuroanatomical regions have been identified in the expression of bias or ideological beliefs. Given that the biological and anatomical processes of the CNS are shaped though experience, it is also important to know more about how developmental events may heighten a brain-behavior predisposition—or *vulnerability*—to hate expression.

There are additional and more complex questions to address in terms of the neuropsychology hate aggression. For example, is there evidence that hate aggression constitutes an epigenetic condition? By this is meant, do environmental factors activate specific neuropsychological pathways. Additionally, does neuroscience research indicate whether different types of hate aggression are expressed via specific brain-behavior processes? These questions will be discussed in what follows.

Hate as a Neural Substrate?

Intergroup hostility has been considered as a distinct neural substrate in the activation of social cognition. A neural substrate refers to a brain-behavior process that elicits specific behavioral responses. Similar cognitive processes have been observed for a range of human and mammalian activities. Research has identified neural substrate for hormone-behavior systems such as empathy (Lamm, Batson, & Decety, 2007), human face processing (Golarai, Liberman, & Grill-Spector, 2017), olfaction and taste (de Araujo et al., 2003; de Araujo et al., 2005), and processing of music (Griffiths et al., 1999).

Mitchell and his colleagues (2006) have considered how the processing of social judgments constitutes neural substrate. As they note, "social cognition may rely on a distinct set of mental processes." These authors consider how using specific methods of examination—employing the fMRI—and observing activation of the medial prefrontal cortex (mPFC) allow inference of the mental state of an individual. What will be considered is both how intergroup experience constitutes normative aspects of such a neural substrate and how pathological brain-behavior activity can result in aberrant hate-based aggression. In what follows, the relationship of human aggression to traumatic CNS injury and neurobiology will be summarized. Thereafter, the role of neuroanatomy and neurotransmission of biochemical agents in the expression of hate as a form of affect dysregulation and ascription to a bias ideology will be reviewed. Finally, the neurobiology of social cognition and social bonding will be examined in terms of the expression of hate aggression.

Brain-Behaviors Processes of Aggression

As has been noted in the behavioral and neurosciences, aggression constitutes a unique brain-behavior event, one that runs the gamut from spontaneous individually expressed hostility to premeditated acts of collective violence. The study of the neurobiological origins of aggression reaches back into the nineteenth century and the incipient days of modern neuropsychology. Walter Cannon's experimental animal studies of aggression in the early twentieth century provide a widely cited example of how CNS injuries can stimulate aggressive responses in mammals. His classic study of aggression in cats observed both physiological arousal—heightened blood sugar, pulse, respiration, and heart rate—and activation in subcortical regions that produced a "sham rage" response in animals (Cannon & Britton, 1925).

A well-documented illustration of behavioral change due to neurological insult is found in the case of Phineas Gage (1823–1860). This case of traumatic brain injury occurred in 1848 when a three-and-a-half-foot iron bar blasted through the skull of Mr. Gage, a well-liked person. Gage, remarkably, survived this workplace accident. Subsequent to this, he evidenced a marked behavioral change, becoming aggressive and hostile in his social interactions. As his physician, Harlow, noted,

> His contractors, who regarded him as the most efficient and capable foreman in their employ previous to his injury, considered the change in his mind so marked that they could not give him his place again. He is fitful, irreverent, indulging at times in the grossest profanity (which was not previously his custom), manifesting but little deference for his fellows, impatient of restraint of advice when it conflicts with his desires, at times pertinaciously obstinate, yet capricious and vacillating, devising many plans of future operation, which are no sooner arranged than they are abandoned in turn for others appearing more feasible. In this regard, his mind was radically changed, so decidedly that his friends and acquaintances said he was "no longer Gage" (https://www.biologycorner.com/anatomy/nervous/phineas.html).

Gage's injury provided a vivid illustration of how damage to the prefrontal cortex (PFC) can result in impulse disturbance, hostility, and profound personality changes while other cognitive and behavioral functions were unaffected. The experience of Gage case has been replicated in less dramatic fashion in the one-and-a-half centuries since his accident. The linkage of traumatic head injury (THI) and subsequent aggression has also been documented with the survivors of warfare, particularly since the end of World War 1 (McKee & Robinson, 2014). This author in his review of convicted crime offenders noted the frequency of prior events of neurological problems (Dunbar, 2003).

Documenting the Neurobiology of Bias and Arousal

Contemporary neuroscience allows for the study of a range of emotional states—such as fear, hostility, and anger. CNS activation has been studied in clinical and experimental conditions via magnetic resonance imaging (MRI), a widely employed method to noninvasively examine brain-behavior activity. This and fMRI—functional magnetic resonance imaging—constitute the technologies of choice to study a range of brain-behavior functions. The MRI is employed in the detection of problems such as aneurysm or abnormal blood vessels. An fMRI measures blood flow in the brain to detect areas of activation. Therefore, whereas an MRI determines the water molecule's hydrogen nuclei and determines differences in tissue type, an fMRI determines the levels of oxygen use in real time found in distinct regions of the CNS.

The employment of fMRI has been extensive during the past decades to examine various neurobiological activity. The role of serotonin or 5-HT has received a great deal of attention in fMRI studies. Meta-analyses of 218 studies revealed that 5-HT had a significant inhibitory effect on aggression (Carrillo, Ricci, & Coppersmith, 2009). The authors found that factors that strengthened this 5HT-aggression relationship included behaviors that were premeditated or predatory, or that occurred over extended periods. Carrillo et al. additionally found *increased-5-HT-facilitated* aggression in animal studies as predicted by social isolation.

Moore, Scarpa, and Raine (2002) have reported that the serotonin metabolite 5-hydroxyindoleacetic acid (5-HIAA) was related to antisocial behavior. In their meta-analysis with 20 studies, they found a significant overall effect size in which lower 5-HIAA was found in antisocial versus non-antisocial groups. This relationship was moderated by the individual's age; individuals under 30 years exhibited larger negative effect sizes than older subjects, with no moderating effects for gender, target of violence, or history of alcoholism. Earlier meta-analytic work on the relationship of antisocial behavior and 5-HIAA was, however, less conclusive (Tuinier, Verhoeven, & Van Praag, 1996). These authors noted that this relationship was only found in younger subjects. As they noted, "taking all the data together, it appears the disturbances in central serotonin neurotransmission, as reflected by lower CSF 5-HIAA levels or blunted prolactin response to a serotonergic challenge compound, may be present in a subgroup of relatively young, male, personality-disordered patients."

The neurobiological agents cortisol (CRT) and testosterone (T) also play an important role in aggression. Specifically, CRT suppresses forms of aggression. Angus and colleagues (2016) considered differences between reactive and instrumental—which they call proactive—aggression and related neurobiological factors. In their review of the literature, they note the importance of both the hypothalamic-gonad-adrenal (HGA) axis—which releases luteinizing hormone (LH) and follicle stimulating hormone (FSH)—and the hypothalamic-pituitary-adrenal (HPA) axis, which is active in the processing of CRT and T in the expression of aggressive behavior. They note that testosterone mediates amygdala activity—resulting in vasopressin genetic expression and approach behaviors. The function of this CNS region and its behavioral correlates is modulated by its interaction with CRT and T.

The amygdala is a subcortical region of the CNS widely implicated in studies on emotion, particularly negative affect, avoidance behaviors, and disgust (Stark et al., 2003). The amygdala is a mass located above the temporal horn of the lateral ventricle and anterior to the tail of the caudate nucleus. This almond-shaped region of the CNS has been implicated in affect regulation, fear response, processing of rewards, and facial recall (Fine & Blair, 2000). The amygdala is an important part of the neuro network regulating emotional processing, learning, and memory. Therefore, the amygdala is critical in the formation of emotion-based memories. Several subnuclei of the amygdala have been studied. The lateral region processes visual, auditory, and somatosensory stimuli; the medial nucleus processes olfactory stimuli, and the central nucleus connects with the brain stem in the regulation of autonomic physiological responses. The amygdala responds to neurotransmission of norepinephrine, dopamine, serotonin, and acetylcholine, all of which mediate excitatory and inhibitory activity.

Recent research has found that the relative balance among neurobiological agents is critical in the expression of aggression. The relationship among testosterone, cortisol, and serotonin has been referred to by van Honk and colleagues as the "triple imbalance hypothesis" of reactive aggression. Cortisol—which stimulates corticotrophin-releasing hormone (CRH) at the amygdala—inhibits T release and increases withdrawal behaviors. These hormones have very different moderating effects on amygdala functioning and in turn on aggressive behavior. The interaction of T and CRT is important in moderating aggressive behavior (van Horn et al., 2010). The testosterone/cortisol ratio (T:CRT) is therefore important in the expression of reactive versus premeditated/instrumental aggression. It is also worth noting that amygdala activation is most pronounced with adolescents. This underscores how the risk for acting on socially acquired bias is particularly significant for an age group characterized by high risk-taking, impulsivity, and high sensation-seeking behaviors.

The relationship among T, CRT, and serotonin modulates the form of subsequent aggressive behavior. The role of serotonin as a moderator agent with CRT and T has been found in several studies (Montoya et al., 2012). These authors note that serotonin has been hypothesized to differentiate between impulsive and instrumental aggression. The work of Dabbs, Jurkovic, & Frady with male offenders (1991) reported that the cortisol–testosterone ratio was related to aggression when the CRT was low. For high CRT levels, the role of testosterone in aggression was not observed. These authors felt this pointed to how lower-CRT-level offenders were predisposed to engage in withdrawal behavior. Additionally, in a study of conduct-disordered girls, Pajer et al. (2006) found similar relationships among T, CRT, and aggressive behavior. They reported that conduct and oppositional–defiant disordered youth were associated with low midmorning CRT levels and that subjects with histories of aggressive conduct disorder produced higher T indexes and lower CRT-to-dehydroepiandrosterone (DHEA) ratios. DHEA is a steroid that regulates mood and attention and typically declines across the lifetime. DHEA levels have been correlated with lower confusion, anxiety, and dysphoric mood (van Niekerk, Huppert, & Herbert, 2001).

Montoya and colleagues also note the importance of the hypothalamus-pituitary-adrenal and the hypothalamus-gonadal-adrenal axes. HGA and HPA in aggression expression indicates "that the adrenal and gonadal systems interact antagonistically, that is the HGA axis inhibits the HPA axis and vice versa." They note that CRT inhibits HPG activity while HPA activity is, in turn, moderated by T levels consistent with that of hypothalamic activity. Therefore, these effects would be expected to vary for men and women, as androgen production (higher in men) would moderate both the HPG and HPA axes. Thus, while HPA and HPG both have an inhibitory effect on aggression for both sexes, the strength of this relationship would be expected to be different for men and women. This is in part due to the contribution of the HPG axis on lower T secretion in females than in males (Montoya et al., 2012).

Neurobiological Characteristics of Hate Expression

While a neurobiological study of hate crime offenders has yet to be undertaken, there are important implications to consider when examining the motivations for perpetrators of hate violence from a brain-behavior perspective. As has been suggested, the commission of hate violence is a function of the offender's affect dysregulation and their bias ideology (Dunbar, 2022).

These two factors may be highly intercorrelated in some cases and largely independent in others. So bias-motivated violence may be a product of either a state of anger or disgust, or an articulated bias ideology. Moreover, the commission of hate violence may be expressed as either premeditated/instrumental or spontaneous/reactive forms of violence. These infractions may also reflect pursuit of intrinsic goals—such as narcissistic aggrandizement or pursuit of in-group status—or extrinsic goals of material reward.

Reward systems in the CNS have been linked to numerous neurobiological and anatomical systems. These include activation of dopaminergic pathways, the limbic system, and subcortical regions. Additionally, the accumbens nucleus or nucleus accumbens (NAc or NAcc) is implicated in both reward pursuit and aversion. Multiple regions of the NAc are related to cognitive and emotional processes. The NAc is related to varying motivational states, which are responsive to the perception of pleasant or emotionally arousing images. Dopamine release in the NAc strengthens stimulus-response conditioning, for example, as when drug use is repeatedly paired with environmental stimuli. The NAc is important for processing fear and avoidant behaviors related to aversion. Activation of D1-type MSNs in the NAc is involved in activation of D2-type medium spiny neurons (MSNs) in the nucleus accumbens, which promotes aversion (Calipari et al., 2016). It is plausible that this association occurs when the offender's in-group peers reinforce the expression of hate-based beliefs or supports the commission of bias-motivated aggression.

A Brain-Behavior Understanding of Hate Arousal

The field of neuroscience can aid in understanding the distinctions between pathologically biased (nonviolent) individuals (Dunbar, 2004) and hate crime offenders. Differences between the expression of bias that is reactive and emotion driven vis-à-vis premediated/planful forms of hate violence—as seen in many acts of domestic terrorism—may be a function of unique brain-behavior processes. Clinical neuroscience may also reveal the pathways in stereotype activation, articulated hate speech, and impulsive/explosive forms of violence. Therefore, hypothetically (at this point), hate violence may be a product of two distinct CNS pathways, one that is manifested during a state of lability and anger and another that is activated for goal-oriented aggression motivated by ideologically stable biases and beliefs.

The heightened expression of hate arousal has been found to be related to reactive (Berkowitz, 1993) aggression (Dunbar, 2016). Hate aggression that is marked by affect dysregulation is moderated by external stimuli—for example, environmental cues—and the individual's neurobiological status. The affect-dysregulated offender may present with co-occurring clinical problems such as attention deficit hyperactive disorder, substance abuse, neurological insult, and the consequences of distal post-traumatic stress. These factors can be expected to moderate the perpetrator's emotional reactance, which in turn may mediate the severity of the hate offense itself. Among clinical disorders, post-traumatic stress disorder and bipolar disorder have been found to be related to risk for reactive aggression (Sullivan & Elbogen, 2013; Vitiello et al., 1990) and the expression of out-group prejudice (Dunbar, 1997; Sullaway & Dunbar, 1996). These factors can moderate the perpetrator's emotional reactance, which in turn may mediate the severity of the perpetrated hate offense. Blair (2001) has argued that reactive forms of aggression are found with patients with "acquired sociopathy" due to orbitofrontal cortex lesions; we will consider this issue in more detail below.

Neuropsychological characteristics of affect-dysregulated offenders have been characterized by arousal of CNS regions regulating affect and motor functions and weak inhibitory systems in the prefrontal cortex. The PFC includes the lateral surface, the medial surface, and the orbital surface. As noted, aggression and impulsivity implicate activation of the amygdala, T: CRT imbalance, and activation of the limbic system. Such an acute state of hate arousal may also be marked by vagal nerve dysregulation, which has been linked to heightened fight–flight behavior (Scott & Weems, 2014). An important example of triggering language and CNS activation is provided by Lee, Chan, and Raine (2008) in studying the response of spousal batterers to angering words. In their experiment with convicted offenders of domestic violence, fMRI differences revealed increased limbic activity and reduced frontal activation for batterers (versus controls) in response to aggressive word prompts. These brain-behavior differences were not found for exposure to neutral linguistic stimulus. This aberrant neurobiological response is only activated when linguistic stimulus is perceived as aversive. This is consistent with the work of Glenberg et al. (2010), in that language can activate a motor-affect response that in the current study was linked to actual violent behavior.

In a particularly relevant study, Zeki and Romaya (2008) found that subjects exposed to images of people they hated produced increased activation of the medial frontal gyrus, right putamen, in the premotor cortex, in the frontal pole, and bilaterally in the medial insula—a region situated within the lateral sulcus between the prefrontal cortex and the parietal lobe. Their subjects reported level of hatred was additionally correlated to activation in right hemisphere areas for the insula (a region activated in states of disgust), premotor cortex, and the fronto-medial gyrus; there was also decreased activation in the right superior frontal gyrus. The intensity of their subject's rated level of hatred (a "hate score") was importantly related to the level of neuroanatomical activation. As the authors noted, these neural networks were distinct from what had been examined with fMRI in identifying states of anger, fear, or aggression. Zeki and Romaya's experimentally observed network revealed activation of brain regions linked to aggressive behavior, motor activation in the putamen (which releases GABA, enkephalin, substance P, and acetylcholine), and—interestingly—regions also activated, as reported by the authors, by feelings of romantic love—the putamen and insula. Interestingly, other studies examining this hate network have noted a decline in activation on resting MRI activity with patients diagnosed with major depression (Tao et al., 2013). A meta-analysis has further noted increased activation of the superior frontal gyrus in response to positive emotional stimuli and decreased activation in response to negative emotional stimuli. This is also found in the insula for decreased basal response to positive and negative emotional stimuli (Fitzgerald et al., 2008).

The role of motor activation—which constitutes part of what Zeki and Romaya have referred to as the "hate circuit"—is also discussed by Page-Gould and Danyluck (2016) in terms of CNS "motor resonance" activation. This resonance condition occurs in situations involving the observation of others—and has been linked experimentally to lower levels of empathy for out-group persons (Gutsell & Inzlicht, 2010). The work of Glenberg and his colleagues (2010) points toward the use of language concerning out-groups as stimulating mirror mechanisms (MMs) and ultimately habituating neuropathways that can—hypothetically—lead to aversive out-group attitudes and, more so, psychophysiological responses of behavioral activation. As with the work of Zeki and Romaya, Glenberg notes that emotionally laden language activates mirror neuro networks for behavior activation, perception, and affect. What he calls simulation theory proposes that specific terms (e.g., "bad hombre") can activate neuro networks that mimic actual behavior. In his work, the notion of speech that activates out-group stereotypes primes the individual to specific affect and behavior states. Socially learned linguistic primes (e.g., hate speech) stimulate activity that is nearly identical to direct experience.

The consequences of these activating processes have been considered in terms of human rights violations. An influential discussion of this relationship has been proposed from a legal perspective by Murrow and Murrow (2015). They proposed that reduced empathy and indifference to pain of dehumanized individuals facilitate the denial of human rights of out-group persons. This reduced attenuation for the pain and suffering of dehumanized social out-groups is automatically reduced because of the reduction in neuropathways for emotional response to out-groups. These authors suggest that this empathy-reduction mechanism can lead to the use of both dehumanizing hate speech and the willingness of the individual to serve as an agent for organizations engaged in amoral actions.

Research on anger further stresses the turning off of cortical areas associated with articulated internal discourse (Damasio, 1999), for example, a silencing of the interior experience of the individual. This is evidenced by insula activation—an area that as we have noted is associated with the processing of emotional and sensory experience. Insula activation has been observed in experiments of verbal problem solving (Aziz-Zedah, Kaplan, & Iacoboni, 2009), whereas in experiments of competition, insula activation and serotonin levels declined (Krämer et al., 2011). Brain imaging research on attitudes concerning devalued out-groups—that is, groups viewed with low warmth and low competence—revealed activation of the insula and amygdala and failure to produce an inhibitory response in the mPFC, a region that as we have discussed mediates social cognition, inclusive of expression of disgust and an absence of empathy (Harris & Fiske, 2006). In two neuroimaging studies, Nam and her colleagues (2018) found that larger bilateral amygdala volume was correlated with support for the existing social order; subjects with larger amygdala volume self-reported a disinclination to engage in social protest. This was observed for both men and women, respectively.

Neurobiological Underpinnings of Bias Ideology

In contrast to hate aggression marked by intense and labile affect, bias ideology constitutes an enduring cognitive schema that the individual subscribes to and (phenomenologically) validates in their daily lives. This belief system is consciously experienced and deviates modestly over time. Ideologically motivated hate aggression is frequently characterized by planning and anticipation (Dunbar, 2003). Behavioral self-regulation often co-occurs in the commission of instrumental forms of aggression. From a brain-behavior perspective, premediated hate violence implicates PFC activation and suppression of affect regions such as the limbic system. Cingulate and amygdala activity increases in the response to conditioned responses of anger and pain. Exaggerated response to anticipated arousal—as reflected by the bias belief system—is also found in thalamic activity.

The perpetration of hate violence under these conditions is goal oriented and consistent with the proscribed tenets of the offender's ideology. The bias-based schema is associated with specific in-group assumptions of the offender's in-group. Emotional stasis and behavioral self-regulation occur during commission of intergroup aggression—for example, the offender is less aroused and more self-regulated in targeting the denigrated out-group person. The core psychological processes include collective defense, revenge, and social dominance (Dunbar, 2017). Psychophysiology of fight–flight activation in such planned forms of violence has been linked to vagal nerve dysregulation, implying a more global mind–body response to experiences of hatred.

The ventromedial prefrontal cortex (vmPFC) is active not only in the expression of reward-driven behaviors and emotional regulation, but also in social group ideology. In a study with individuals with known neuropathology—related to damage to the vmPFC—it was found that authoritarianism and religious fundamentalism were highly endorsed vis-à-vis a control sample of non-neurological subjects, as well as baseline data reported for the employed measures (Asp, Ramchandran, & Tranel, 2012). The authors note that the vmPFC plays a role in maintenance of "normative doubt" and the capacity to think critically of authoritarian arguments.

Another area of the CNS of particular relevance concerns amygdala activation and implicit forms of racial bias. As we have noted, the amygdala is important in the perception of threat in a variety of contexts. In a study concerning recall of the 9/11 terror attack, Hirst et al. (2009) found how flashbulb memories of terrorism as measured with fMRI were characterized by increased amygdala activation. These authors also noted that strong emotional reactions of flashbulb events are more poorly remembered than fact-based or nonemotional features of terror recall—such as where and from whom one learned of the 9/11 attack.

In a study with white and Black subjects, Hart and associates (2000) found increased amygdala activation for both groups. For both groups there was no self-reported change in their emotional state during the study. This suggests that intergroup arousal may be unconscious even when there is activation of neuropathways of threat. Wheeler and Fiske (2005) likewise found that white subjects produced greater amygdala activation in (experimental) situations when presented with faces of Black subjects. Phelps and her colleagues (2000) also reported on the correlation of indirect racial bias on the Implicit Association Test (IAT) with heightened amygdala response for white subjects viewing a Black face.

These studies point to the role of amygdala activation secondary to exposure to a denigrated out-group (e.g., Blacks) for white subjects, illustrating how racism is evidenced as a fear response in neuroimaging studies. Interestingly, however, in her case study with an individual who suffered from bilateral amygdala damage, Phelps found a biased response style on the IAT, implying that racial bias—when using an indirect measure of racism with the IAT—is found in individuals when the amygdala is compromised (Phelps, Cannistraci, & Cunningham, 2003). This indicates that out-group bias can be observed in situations in which the fear response is neurologically compromised.

The relationship of the activation of the amygdala with the PFC is, of course, always important in terms of impulse control. In context of out-group bias, the 25-millisecond-rapid response of the amygdala to sensory stimuli (contact with an ethnic minority) is moderated by a cognitive schema that is regulated by the PFC. What the research indicates is that the conscious response of white subjects to reject racial prejudice—a socially sanctioned rejection of discrimination against minority groups—is accompanied by amygdala activation, which is indicative of aversion and arousal. So, overlearned ethnic/racial stereotypes—leading to amygdala activation—are regulated by PFC functioning in experimental subjects that result in a conscious articulated belief system of racial equity.

The relationship of the PFC and amygdala is also critical to the moderation of aggression. Siever (2008) has noted the failure of what he calls a top-down regulation by the PFC on amygdala activation. The (ineffective) regulatory control of the PFC and an insufficient serotonergic release fail to moderate activation of limbic and insula structures that are stimulated by catecholamine release and imbalance of glutamatergic and gabaminergic systems. The PFC–amygdala process fails to assert behavioral control on the intent to aggress. In a study with pedophilic offenders, Schiltz et al. (2007) noted that pedophiles had decreased volume in the right amygdala, hypothalamus (bilaterally), septal regions, and substantia innominate when compared with healthy controls. Additionally, smaller right amygdala volumes were correlated with the propensity to exclusively engage in pedophilic sexual offenses. The significant modulating relationship of the PFC with amygdala functioning is found in the study of fear-based racial animus on the one hand and in the psychopathology of impulse disturbance and aggression on the other.

In an experimental study, the modulation of amygdala reactivity by two PFC regions (ventral anterior cingulate cortex and ventrolateral PFC), when exposed to angry faces, was influenced by metabolic changes in the CNS—specifically 5-HT (Passamonti et al., 2012). So while 5-HT significantly influences PFC–amygdala circuits that are implicated in aggression, changes in neurotransmission of serotonin or tryptophan are also a critical factor in the expression of violence. The functional dynamics of mPFC are moderated in part by 5-HT and 5-HT2A receptors. Fisher et al. (2009) observed that amygdala reactivity to threat-related facial expressions—as represented by blood oxygen level–dependent functional magnetic resonance imaging—was inversely related to greater mPFC 5-HT2A density, with over 25% of the variability in amygdala reactivity being related to mPFC 5-HT2A density. These researchers also reported a relationship of mPFC 5-HT2A density and the magnitude of right amygdala habituation.

This body of research needs to be considered vis-à-vis the experiences of perpetrators of racial violence. In contrast to the unconscious amygdala activation of racial bias with "civil"—that is noncriminal—individuals to images of out-groups, in research on hate offenders we encounter a conscious *explicit endorsement* of out-group animus. The role of the PFC in hate crime offenders does not provide an effective buffer to suppress the de facto expression of intergroup aggression. For the hate offender this amygdala–PFC connection does not yield a counterresponse to out-group aversion. It can be argued that this neuropathway—which serves to moderate social judgment—for the hate offender may serve to activate racial violence rather than suppress it. What these independent programs of research therefore provide is a strong basis—which at this point is speculative—as to the brain-behavior dynamics likely found in intergroup aggression. An alternative and provocative proposal is that in hate violence the PFC interaction to amygdala signaling of threat is turned on. However, this proposed PFC response is not inhibitory but activating, in that the socially learned presumptions are supportive of out-group stereotypes and denigration. In this proposed scenario, hate violence is not indicative of a top-down failure but rather the amplification of animus from ideation to action. This proposal sees the frontal system as activating out-group aggression rather than inhibiting it.

Therefore, while our experimental studies indicate the amygdala may play a role in responding to a perceived threat cross-racially, we do not yet know what neuropathways are activated when individuals perpetrate hate violence. It is worth considering that in the commission of a hate crime, the expression of animus is consciously and freely expressed.

The Neuroscience of Religious and Political Beliefs

The perpetration of hate violence that is due to relatively stable, strongly held bias implicates a highly problematic form of aggression found in terrorist acts and staged forms of violence (START, 2017). Two relevant forms of ideology—religious and political beliefs—have been studied from a brain-behavior perspective. The study of these belief systems in terms of recent neuroscience research is highly relevant to the examination of ideological violence (Harris et al., 2009).

Across the ages, ideological violence has repeatedly been perpetrated in the name of religious faith; countless millions of lives have been lost because of religious-motivated violence. Religious beliefs, particularly fundamentalism and dogma, often are cited in the manifestos associated with terrorist violence, and are important in recruiting individuals to perpetrate terrorist violence (Rogers et al., 2007). Finding a link between a neurobiological basis of a bias ideology and religious beliefs is complex. Religious belief and faith incorporate not only cognitions but also behavioral intentions and emotions of bonding (Plante & Boccaccini, 1997; Winchester, 2008).

There has been a good deal of attention given to the neurocognition of religious beliefs. In the recent past, there had been discussion of a god spot in the cortex (Beauregard & Paquette, 2006). This notion of a god region in the CNS was at one point of great interest; not, however, without significant skepticism in the scientific community as well (http://www.independent.co.uk/news/science/belief-and-the-brains-god-spot-1641022.html). Therefore, the notion of a region in the CNS where religious thoughts and feelings arise is intriguing if not scientifically established. All the same, the neuroscience of faith has yielded some insight into how ideology is evidenced in the brain. In one study of religious belief conducted with devout Christians, it was found that subjects evidenced activation of the neuropathway from the inferolateral to dorsomedial frontal cortex. Kapogiannis and colleagues (2014) reported that beliefs based upon religious doctrine were characterized by activation of a pathway between Broca's to Wernicke's language areas. Judgments of "true" versus "false" beliefs were associated with greater signal in the ventromedial prefrontal cortex, which, as we have discussed, is related to self-construal, processing of emotional stimuli, and goal-directed behavior. Another study of subjects' endorsement or rejection of religious dogma (Linden et al., 2010) found that both groups revealed vmPFC activation under conditions of statements of agreement for both religious and nonreligious content (which were also more rapidly responded to). When asked to evaluate religious and nonreligious content, it was found for both Christian believers and nonbelievers that fMRI signal was greater in areas throughout the brain when subjects evaluated religious statements compared with nonreligious statements. This study illustrates how thinking about religious orthodoxy is more associated with brain regions that govern emotion, self-representation, and decision-making.

The adherence to religious dogma is important for several reasons. For one, it represents a hardened form of judgment that may indicate mPFC dysfunction; additionally, dogma is consistent with the ascription to authoritarianism, which is relevant to members of ideologically violent groups. One study looked at the ascription to fundamentalist religious beliefs and mPFC damage (Zhong et al., 2017). In this study, adherence to religious fundamentalism was measured on a self-report scale with patients with penetrating traumatic brain injury (pTBI). Endorsed fundamentalist beliefs were related to patients with damage to the vmPFC and dorsolateral prefrontal cortex (dlPFC) lesions. Zhong and colleagues found that dlPFC lesions significantly decreased cognitive flexibility similarly to patients with vmPFC lesions. In their study, vmPFC damage was related to lower scores on openness to experience on the NEO Personality Inventory (the issue of openness is discussed below). These findings indicate that damage to the vmPFC is related to greater religious fundamentalism and restriction of cognitive openness. Another study compared patients with vmPFC damage to neurologically impaired patients with no vmPFC damage and to patients who suffered traumatic non-CNS events (Asp, Ramchandran, & Tranel, 2012). These groups completed self-reported measures of authoritarianism, religious fundamentalism, and endorsement of specific religious beliefs. Patients with damage to the vmPFC had higher scores on authoritarianism and religious fundamentalism than the other patient groups and to normative values; vmPFC patients reported increased specific religious beliefs after brain injury. These studies indicate that cognitive flexibility and openness are necessary for the maintenance of adaptive religious beliefs.

Political attitudes constitute another area in which neuroscience can inform us about the motivation to perpetrate hate violence. There is an active area of research concerning cognitive and social attitudes related to differences between conservative and liberal political beliefs. While some of this research is relevant to understanding the brain-behavior nature of bias ideology, it is important to recall that these studies do not address the issue of the perpetration of political violence. Therefore, much of what we are left to ponder is the inferential relationship of this body of study to commission of hate violence.

Increasingly, political polling is turning to fMRI and related methods of measuring the neurobiological expression of opinion independent of the subjects' expressed political beliefs. As many political scientists now recognize, conventional opinion polling does not measure the implicit subconscious attitudes of voters. Lieberman, Schreiber, and Ochsner (2003) propose that a set of cognitive building blocks moderates political judgment. What they refer to as a reflection-reflexing model includes a set of personally subscribed to goals, primes, expertise arguments, and principles of conflict management. Neurophysiological markers such as brain activity, heart rate, eye movement, changes in facial activity, and measures of physical arousal with electromyography methods can detect response to political primes, much as we have seen in amygdala activation with exposure to faces of racial outgroups. The individual's emotional reaction to political arguments and leaders—as Lieberman and colleagues have noted—is better examined as a natural process of choice that is partly overlearned, habituated, and suppressed when there are concerns of social judgment. As such, political attitudes are influenced by emotions much more than we realize.

An interesting study conducted by Jost et al. (2003) examined self-referenced political conservatism and concerns of personal vulnerability—as found in a meta-analysis with 88 studies. Numerous significant relationships were found between conservative ideology and anxiety about death, social instability, expression of dogmatism, low tolerance for ambiguity, low openness to experience, and need for structure. They argued that political conservatism is evidenced via resistance to change—for example, the 2016 campaign slogan of candidate Trump to "Make America great again"—rationalization of social inequality, and self-interest. Inbar, Pizarro, and Bloom (2008) argued, "Conservatives are more easily disgusted than liberals." What they described as "disgust sensitivity" is related to subject's increasingly conservative political attitudes; they noted this relationship was strongest for issues concerning abortion and gay marriage—what they referred to as "purity-related issues." This study implicates—though does not measure—insula activation for conservatives.

A study conducted with university subjects Kanai and his associates (2011) indicated that self-reported conservatism was correlated to larger amygdala structure. They additionally reported that conservative subjects yielded larger gray volume in the left insula (an area that formed part of the hate neuro-network of Zeki and Romaya) and the right entorhinal region. In this study, anterior cingulate cortex (ACC) volume was larger for the more self-referenced liberal subjects. The ACC is proposed to moderate the processing of ambiguous information. The ACC—which is adjacent to the corpus callosum—is linked to both the limbic system and PFC, suggesting that the ACC plays a role in both affect regulation and more complex cognitive processes (Stevens et al., 2011). Research on the ACC with PET methodology found subjects' response to images of same-race individuals being subjected to painful stimuli was significantly greater than similar images for out-group persons (Xu et al., 1997). This implies that ACC activation significantly decreased when observation of pain was for persons of a racial out-group. This study also found activation of the insula in response to painful images. As Murrow and Murrow (2015) argued, the reduction in CNS mirroring responses is consistent with the violation of the human rights of out-group persons.

The role of neurodiagnostic tools in the surveying of political attitudes can provide a greater understanding of the deeper emotional associations that individuals hold and that exceed the stated beliefs that polling alone cannot reliably address. Polling may remain important for a variety of reasons for social science, but the brain-behavior relationship of political attitudes underscores the gap between reported opinions and indicators found with tools, which examine cortical experiences of political beliefs.

Forms of ideology, inclusive of religious and political attitudes, are both relevant to the examination of hate violence. The further study of the motivators for the perpetration of hate violence may reveal both brain-behavior commonalities as well as differences—expressed via distinct neuropathways. Additionally, an issue that has received some attention in the neurosciences concerns openness to experiences—and what will here be considered as a characteristic of being cognitively closed (e.g., non-open) as a feature of biased judgements and affects.

Openness to Experience and Out-Group Bias

The issue of social bias has been frequently associated with lower levels of general intelligence (Hodson & Busseri, 2012) and in other studies as a poverty of the cognitive capacity for comprehending intergroup and cultural differences (Gutsell & Inzlicht, 2010; Bell & Dunbar, 2012). We might add to this the literature on offenders in general and their level of cognitive functioning, which, similar to the older studies on prejudice and intelligence, suggests that offenders evidence a relative decrement of verbal reasoning in many, though hardly all, instances.

The relationship between diminished intellectual capacity and antisocial behavior has been examined for decades. In a 25-year longitudinal twin study, it was found that lower IQ and reading problems were found with childhood and adolescent antisocial behavior (Simonoff et al., 2004). Other studies have found lower verbal IQ scores versus nonverbal estimates of intelligence (Cornell, 1992; DeWolfe & Ryan, 1984). As with much of the literature on offenders, the examination of the IQ–violence relationship is complicated by social factors of poverty, limited educational opportunities, and childhood forms of deprivation and abuse—issues that are only sometimes considered when the relationship of intelligence to the commission of violence is examined. This reductionist or cognitively closed style found with offender samples is consistent with the ideology found in many hate-orientated groups.

An example of the closed cognitive style is found in many of the right-wing extremist groups' manifestos (Altemeyer, 1988). These groups often espouse a self-referenced patriotic rejection of the rule of law, the role of the federal government—for example, states' rights arguments—and the legitimacy of nontraditional citizen groups, inclusive of immigrants, gays, and lesbians. In essence, these right-wing groups espouse ideological arguments explicitly endorsing prejudice against social out-groups and promote themselves as defenders of their community from unwanted cultural and demographic influences. Common themes of moral adherence, self-defense, and independence from federal oversight are noted (Tenold, 2018). From a psychological perspective, these arguments mirror Adorno's—as well as Altemeyer's—notion of authoritarianism. That is a rule-bound approach to behavior. On closer inspection, and more relevant to our discussion, these rules reflect a closed cognitive framework.

Openness to experience has been long recognized as one of the underlying personality characteristics found in individuals across cultural boundaries. This factor, seen as one of the "Big Five" personality dimesons, has itself been found to correlate with various measures of prejudice and racial bias (Ekehammar & Akrami, 2003). Sutin and colleagues (2009), using resting-state positron-emission tomography (PET) measures, have found that openness to experience correlated with PFC activity for women, anterior cingulate activity for men, and orbitofrontal activity for both men and women. This implicates capacities for cognitive flexibility (women only), monitoring functions (men only), and for men and women reward and emotional processing related to the openness trait.

A related factor in the endorsement of both right-wing extremism and racial bias is the role of social class. Firat et al. (2017) observed how the ventromedial prefrontal cortex (vmPFC) and the amygdala were activated under experimental conditions with patients with the vmPFC or amygdala lesions and healthy adults. They concluded, "Two distinct mechanisms underlie class-based racial evaluations, one engaging the vmPFC for positively identified ingroup class and another recruiting the amygdala for the class groups that are marginalized or perceived as potential threats." They observed how the vmPFC was more responsive to associations with socially valued ingroups (i.e., the middle class) and that the amygdala was more responsive to priming for socially ambivalent and threatening categories (i.e., upper and lower class).

Bonding via Bias Ideology: The Oxytocin Hypothesis

So far, the issues of bias and hatred have been discussed in terms of individual experiences of arousal, impulsivity, aggression, ideology, and social bias. Yet what is perhaps more relevant to many individuals who are affiliated with ideologically based groups is the experience of belonging. In essence, being a member of a bias-oriented group unites the individual with others, specifically others who share similar complaints and concerns about the world in which they live.

Ideological group membership may include the employment of ritual and ceremony, the sense of enhanced collective self-esteem (Ezekiel, 1995) and in situations of aggression, and the experience of deindividuation—in which violence is experienced as a collective rather than as an individually initiated behavior. Stanley Payne's study of European fascism makes the point of the role of ritual and pageant as signifying events of extremist groups in the early twentieth century. As seen in Helene "Leni" Riefenstahl's classic propaganda film *Triumph of the Will*, the role of massive crowds, martial music, and Albert Speer's outsized iconography served as signals of the ritual of Nazi Party membership at the 1934 Nuremberg conference. These experiences bonded individuals together and changed their neuropsychological stasis in the process.

The neuropeptide oxytocin has been closely studied in terms of social group bonding (De Dreu & Kret, 2016), problem-solving (De Dreu, Baas, & Boot, 2016), and in-group favoritism (Balliet, Wu, & De Dreu, 2014). Oxytocin is released via the pituitary gland and interacts with the amygdala and hippocampus as well as the nucleus accumbens. Oxytocin has an impact on the human stress response and recovery from injury. Oxytocin reveals significant binding in the limbic system and has been found to reduce social anxiety (Bale et al., 2001).

Importantly, oxytocin has a significant impact on primate bonding of mother to child (Feldman, Weller, & Zagorry-Sharon, 2007). Attachment has been examined in terms of neurobiological characteristics of peptides, inclusive of not only oxytocin but also vasopressin, opioids, and corticotrophin-releasing hormone (Carter & Keverne, 2002). Animal studies on bonding similarly reveal the synergistic role of arginine vasopressin, oxytocin, and dopamine (Young, Liu, & Wang, 2008). The literature on social bonding in humans frequently has pointed to oxytocin and vasopressin systems in moderating social behavior (Donaldson & Young, 2008).

The neurobiological study of social bonding has been considered in terms of social identity development (Mrazek, Harada, & Chiao, 2015). Social bonding includes the subjective sense of group support and group affiliation. Oxytocin and oxytocin receptor genes have been related to group identity and positive appraisal of other in-group persons (Ten Vender, Daughters, & De Dreu, 2017). Oxytocin and vasopressin also regulate stress responses through the HPA axis (Neumann, 2002). However, the nature of specific emotional associations to in-group membership is far from established (De Dreu & Kret, 2016). This and other studies suggest how membership in ideological antisocial and violent groups may not only enhance a sense of membership but also provide many of the neurobiological needs for an individual. This may be particularly important for individuals who have experienced forms of developmental privation and social isolation, which we will discuss further below. In this regard, oxytocin release when coupled with reported social support buffer the stress response in men, as measured via decreased cortisol secretion (Heinrichs et al., 2003).

Oxytocin has been related to not only social bonding but also punishment behavior. In animal studies, oxytocin triggers protective and nursing behaviors of offspring (Baribeau & Anagnostou, 2015). In an experiment involving dyadic competition, Stallen and colleagues (2018) found that subjects who were given oxytocin engaged in more frequent punishment strategies than other subjects. The authors found that oxytocin played a role in corrective punishments for moderate rule violations (e.g., a "slap on the wrist") to maintain fairness. Interestingly, this study also noted oxytocin upregulates a motivation for the maintenance of fairness: "our results provide evidence for the hypothesis that oxytocin shifts focus from self-interest to overarching, normative, group interests" (2953).

The Stallen study also noted that activation of the ventral striatal region occurred in the punishment of persons who were seen as unfairly competing in a gaming simulation. We should consider that the motivation to punish deviant behavior is a core factor in authoritarianism. The increase in ventral striatal activity (i.e., to punish) was moderated by increased activity in the temporoparietal junction, a region studied in social role-taking and punishment decisions (Carter & Huettel, 2013). While our focus is on more than modest forms of aggression—for example, a "slap on the wrist"—the implications of this study, when brought together with the role of oxytocin in social bonding, is noteworthy.

The implication of oxytocin in the moderation of in-group–out-group bias has been discussed by Shamay-Tsoory and Abu-Akel (2016), which they refer to as the social salience of oxytocin. They note that the moderator role of oxytocin in intergroup relationships is dependent on contextual aspects and individual differences, the latter of which include gender, personality traits, and degree of psychopathology. They note how such social priming can result in out-group antisocial behavior, including aggression and envy. These authors propose that oxytocin plays an overarching role in regulating the salience of social cues through its interaction with the dopaminergic system. Importantly, these authors consider how individual differences—which may also constitute *vulnerabilities*—interact with oxytocin and in turn with social cues in the expression of out-group hostility.

Other Perception and Aggression: The Vasopressin Effect

Another important area of research involves studies on arginine vasopressin (AVP). This neuropeptide is secreted from the hypothalamus and is transported to the posterior pituitary gland. AVP may additionally activate endocrine response and raise arterial blood pressure as part of the fight–flight response.

Arginine vasopressin plays a significant role in punishment behaviors. It has been proposed that while oxytocin moderates the stress response, AVP may facilitate it (Bisagno & Cadet, 2014). As von Dawans (2008) notes, AVP has additionally been found to stimulate amygdala functioning. Measured CSF arginine vasopressin levels are also correlated with a history of aggression with personality-disordered patients (Coccaro et al., 1998).

AVP moderates complex social cognition and regulates in-group and out-group behaviors. AVP and a vasopressin receptor subtype (V1aR) both increase mammal pair bond formation (Winslow, 1993); corrective "altruistic punishment" has been linked to both oxytocin and arginine vasopressin release (von Dawans et al., 2012). Additionally, AVP facilitates aggression under conditions of interpersonal mistrust (von Dawans, 2008) and mediates anxiogenic effects. The element of social bonding and other-mistrust is related to negative intergroup contact (Allport, 1954; Pettigrew & Tropp, 2008) and amygdala activation. This indicates that social perceptions of the target person and the perception of the context are potentially moderated by vasopressin response.

Research reveals how AVP can facilitate judgments concerning intergroup differences and perceived undesirable qualities of the other—mistrust or behaviors that are deemed as aberrant—which may result in aggressive actions. AVP may activate aggression toward out-groups. This is what we will call the vasopressin effect.

It is useful to consider the behavioral manifestations of the vasopressin effect in terms of serving as a precursor to hate violence. As we have discussed, exposure to images of racial out-groups has been found to activate amygdala functioning, which is in turn stimulated by AVP release. In intergroup research, the process of stereotype activation would appear to be a product of this brain-behavior process. As defined by Wheeler and Petty (2001), stereotype activation is "the increased accessibility of the constellation of attributes that are believed to characterize members of a given social category" (797). In situations of intergroup aggression, the role of arginine vasopressin would be expected to activate a fight response—inclusive of psycho-physiological arousal and activation of motor regions in the CNS. A more specific form of hate violence discussed by Green and colleagues (Green, Strolovitch, & Wong, 1998) and others is the defended neighborhood hypothesis, in which detection of out-groups in a neighborhood or social context that is perceived as being the purview of the in-group results in forms of aggression and violence—a fighting-off of out-group members. Again, the AVP response to both amygdala and CNS systems of aggression would characterize these acts of hate aggression. In both instances, AVP would be presumed to prime the stereotypes and the fight–flight network of the CNS in the identification of the provoking target and subsequent violent reaction to their presence.

So the notion of an oxytocin hypothesis and a vasopressin effect in out-group hatred is noteworthy for individuals who desire social bonding and demonstrate a willingness if not per se drive to punish individuals who are seen as violating social norms—a foundation of the notion of authoritarianism. Implicitly, the oxytocin hypothesis suggests how dynamic neurobiological changes can influence brain-behavior activation that results in hate aggression. This in turn leads us to consider whether there is a genetic expression of hostility linked to intergroup differences. We will consider this issue of epigenetic expression below.

Phenotypic Plasticity and Epigenetic Expression of Bias

The study of brain-behavior-mediated violence is evolving rapidly. Ling, Umbach, and Raine (2019) note the growing interest in examination of antisocial behavior in terms of psychophysiological, neuro-anatomical, and genetic processes. While there is significant attention to the gene-behavior interaction with antisocial behavior, the evidence of any specific relationship is elusive. A meta-analysis of the relationship of genetic factors with aggression and nonviolent antisocial behavior was conducted by Vassos, Collier, and Fazel (2014). Their findings failed to find a relationship between identified genetic markers and antisocial behavior, even when examining specific sociodemographic characteristics—such as age or ethnicity—they did not find a consistent relationship.

What has not been considered is whether there is a neurobiological process by which individuals may be uniquely predisposed to hate violence. The issue of phenotypic risk for xenophobia or racism—the epigenesis—itself is an unexplored question. It is most plausible to think that hate violence is expressed where predisposing neurobiological factors are activated by chronic or acute social conditioning factors. The estimate of environmental influences on genetic expression of antisocial behavior, as reported by Gard, Dotterer, and Hyde (2019), is slightly over 30%. As they note, "our review highlights the centrality of environmental moderators of genetic effects" (46). Epigenetic regulation is a change in gene expression, not in the genetic code itself. On a social-psychological level, these epigenetic factors may include warfare, economic deprivation, systematic social exclusion, and segregation, as well as acute events such as experiences of violence.

An even more provocative issue is whether an individual can inherit prior conditioning of one's family or cultural experiences. A well-documented illustration of this is found in the study of the impact of famine almost 200 years ago in a Swedish community, Överkalix. Överkalix is a small town on the Kalix River, in northern Sweden (https://io9.gizmodo.com/how-an-1836-famine-altered-the-genes-of-children-born-d-1200001177). In 1984, Bygren and his associates (2014) examined the histories of 94 individuals born in Överkalix in 1905. Ultimately, the study included subjects born between 1890 and 1920. These results illustrated the interplay of physiological effects of environmental factors on transgenerational epigenetic inheritance. Risk ratios (RR) for mortality for the children and grandchildren of the original sample were determined based on available food supply, as indicated by historical data.

Findings in the Överkalix studies revealed a significant role for food availability in paternal grandmothers' lives, which resulted in an increased risk of cardiovascular mortality in their granddaughters' (adult) lives. As Bygren and colleagues (2014) noted, "We reported earlier that changes in availability of food—from good to poor or from poor to good—during intrauterine development was followed by a double risk of sudden death as an adult, and that mortality rate can be associated with ancestors´ childhood availability of food" (1471). They noted that transgenerational responses (TGR) were predictive of a doubling of cardiovascular risk across three generations. This study has garnered attention as an example of epigenetic inheritance—that is, the inheritance of developmental variations that do not stem from differences in the sequence of DNA.

So by extension of this emerging area of study, an important question for future research concerns what genotypic factors predispose individuals to out-group aggression. Genetic and environmental factors both play a substantial role in the occurrence of aggressive and antisocial behavior. The study of aggression has indicated the role of heritability as found for two distinct factors, general aggression and physical aggression (Yeh, Coccaro, & Jacobson, 2010). Heritability of these factors ranged from .37 to .57 (Coccaro, Berman, & Kavoussi, 1997). This study employed the Life History of

Aggression Questionnaire (Coccaro et al., 1997) in the examination of etiological factors related to these two factors of aggression. Additionally, what is the range of epigenetic possibilities that may be observed based on "genotypic risk"? The prior study points to specific forms of aggression as being observed for both men and women due to heritable and social–environmental factors.

What on one hand seems to be a viable genetic pass-down of metabolic risk, as found in the Överkalix study, would not per se translate into the notion of a genotypic risk for bias on the social group other. However, as much as it is unsupported, it is worth at least considering how distinct social groups may have shared histories over hundreds—and in some cases thousands—of years of shared animus, and in some instances violence, which constitutes a culturally coherent reference of in-group identity. The author is not suggesting this would result in a genotypic condition of, say, Catholics and Protestants or Jews and Muslims hating each other, but it raises the issue all the same.

There has also been an opinion that racism constitutes an evolutionary strategy. Francis Cress Welsing (1974) hypothesized that since Black skin trumps white skin genetically, white people actively engage in forms of genetic genocide, with racism constituting a strategy to ensure white genetic survival. In this sense then, white-perpetrated racial violence against Blacks serves to maintain their genetic presence. Racism, in the view of Welsing, is a conspiracy of genetic hegemony. From this perspective, the denigration of a racial out-group may be a normative process, one that may serve a myriad of evolutionary functions. Furthermore, acquisition of stereotypes might be seen as a form of threat conditioning, or social judgments of group inclusion and exclusion, which may in turn be tied to a host of evolutionary strategies, such as resource sharing or harm avoidance.

This hypothesis of prejudice as a form of genotypic expression—which likely strikes many as a highly controversial topic—may constitute a specific manifestation of a much broader brain-behavior postulate, namely that social cognition constitutes one of the critical aspects of human evolution. As Mitchell and his colleagues (2006) noted, "the fundamental importance of human sociability both to everyday life as well as to cultural achievements of the species prompted some observers to suggest that social cognition may have been one of the primary engines of human evolution. For example, Tomasello (1999) argued convincingly that what sets Homo sapiens apart from other primates is the ability to represent the mind of conspecifics" (78). What the research on nonviolent individuals shows rather powerfully is that humans are prepared to make distinctions about in-group membership based on physical characteristics—as well as other interpersonal factors such as facial expression—in forming social judgments. What might serve as a more viable explanation of the development of aggressive cognitive processes may be attributable to maltreatment and neglect of children. We may not be genetically predisposed to perpetrate intergroup violence as much as we can be conditioned to experience cultural differences into trigger phenomena for retribution and dominance.

Developmental Moderators of Social Neurocognition

The role of early childhood experience has been found to impact phenotypic expression of mood, specifically the ability to identify emotions of anger and sadness (Paus, Keshavan, & Giedd, 2008). Childhood attachment has been found to moderate a range of adult-aged epigenetic expressions of psychiatric disorders, including depression (Murgatroyd & Spengler, 2011). Early parent–child bonding is critical for the development of amygdala, prefrontal cortex, and hippocampal development, which are critical for emotional expression and regulation. The effectiveness of these brain structures is intimately associated with the quality of care received in infancy (Perry, Blair, & Sullivan, 2017). Similarly adverse childhood experience—ACE—is an important construct in developmental status of emotional intelligence (Felitti et al., 1998; see Table 7-1). Higher ACE scores have been related to increased adult maladjustment, including perpetration of domestic violence.

Forms of childhood maltreatment and abuse, as Hoon Oh (2012) and others have noted, impacts amygdala functioning. As Oh reports, chronic exposure to harsh corporal punishment was associated with reduction in gray matter volume in the right mPFC for young adults (18–25 years). There were also possible associations between harsh corporal punishment and reduced gray matter volume in the left dlPFC and the right ACC (Tomoda et al., 2009).

Table 7-1 Adverse Childhood Experiences (ACE)

- Physical abuse
- Sexual abuse
- Emotional abuse
- Physical neglect
- Emotional neglect
- Intimate partner violence
- Mother treated violently
- Substance misuse within household
- Household mental illness
- Parental separation or divorce
- Incarcerated household member

Borderline personality disorder (BPD), a psychiatric diagnosis often observed with survivors of childhood trauma, has been examined in terms of deficits of amygdala-prefrontal cortex interconnectivity. In a positron emission tomography (PET) study (New et al., 2007), it was found that BPD patients had weak correlations between amygdala and the anterior PFC when compared to healthy control subjects. In their study it was noted that the coupling of metabolic activity between right OFC and ventral amygdala found with healthy control subjects was absent with the BPD patients. Additional research has supported this important role of the vmPFC in the suppression of amygdala activity (Foland-Ross et al., 2010).

The roles of childhood abuse and trauma have both been found to result in amygdala hyperactivation in the fear response. Hoon Oh (2012) has noted that traumatic experiences influence amygdala activation. As he notes, "Childhood trauma is associated with increases in amygdala volume, whereas traumatic stress in adulthood is associated with reductions in amygdala volume." Research has shown that chronic witnessing of aggressive behavior moderates accumbal dopamine D2 receptor (D2R) and amygdaloid 5-HT1B receptor (5-HT1BR) densities (Suzuki, Han, & Lucas, 2010). It is worth considering how intergroup childhood trauma—as found in war zones or cultures of apartheid—may condition individuals to enduring forms of neurobiological abnormalities of hatred. Snapshot One, below, provides a brief illustration of this type of offender.

The presence of economic deprivation, trauma, and neurological abnormalities has been documented in the review of the developmental histories of violent hate offenders (Dunbar, 2003). In this review of convicted hate crime offenders, the presence of learning problems, CNS trauma, exposure to childhood violence, and the abuse of drugs and alcohol were frequently observed. Many hate offenders—as with many other career criminals—have higher risk ratings on the ACE criteria. These markers of developmental privation are in turn related to antisocial personality disorder (ASPD). Childhood abuse is an important predictor of ASPD in general and has been found to be frequently reported with bias-motivated homicide offenders (Dunbar, Krop, & Sullaway, 2016). ASPD has been linked to functional polymorphism (5-HTTLPR) in the serotonin transporter gene. 5-HTTLPR has been widely studied as a risk factor for a variety of psychopathologic conditions, including aggressive/violent behavior (Douglas et al., 2011). These authors note that childhood maltreatment increases the risk of antisocial personality disorder, an effect for which there is evidence of moderation by 5-HTTLPR genotype.

Arguably, the more severely traumatized child who as an adult perpetrates hate violence may reveal a more compromised brain-behavior status in terms of their affiliative competence. The neuroscience of attachment also leads us to think about the diversity of experience within hate-oriented offenders. This is found in the perpetrators of hate violence who are isolated from

Table 7-2 Four Status Conditions of Arousal and Ideology in Commission of Hate Violence

	Ideology	
	Low	**High**
	Willing Follower	*Planful Offender*
Pathways	lower hx of CNS impairment	high Pfc mediation of amygdala
Low		
Bio agents	low serotonin/high CRT ratio	A-vasopressin elevation
	high oxytocin response	
Arousal		
	Labile Bigot	*Hate Extremist*
Pathways	low Pfc—amygdala mediation	high Pfc—amygdala mediation
	greater hx of CNS impairment	
High		
Bio agents	low oxytocin response	A-vasopressin elevation
	low serotonin/high T ratio	

bias-oriented cohorts. Frequently referred to as "lone wolf" offenders (Gallagher, 2022), these individuals would arguably experience out-group hostility in a manner that is devoid of the benefits of peer support and the attendant brain-behavior response of oxytocin and other neurobiological reinforcers. Socially isolated individuals who harbor strong out-group animus may furthermore experience bias in a fundamentally different way than the ideology-based group offender. From my clinical experience I have observed how socially isolative individuals with strong out-group bias evidence characteristics of rumination, obsessions, fixed fears, assumptions of malevolence in benign contact situations, and perseverative all-but-paranoid ideation about social out-groups. These hate-based nonjoiners may reveal a very different neurobiological experience of bias than individuals actively aligned with hate networks (see Table 7-2).

Possible Neuropathways in the Expression of Hate Violence

The affect-dysregulated hate offender may reveal some of the brain-behavior processes found in the current research on aggression. Hypothetically, this offender will reveal a neurobiological profile characterized by low

CRT, and high T levels, together with low 5-HT. Additionally, high amygdala activation would reveal low mPFC moderation. Cortically, lower PFC activity would be anticipated. CNS pathways of greater motor activation would also be anticipated.

The neuroscience of aggression and racial prejudice informs us concerning hate expression and bias ideology; this allows us to infer a good deal about the labile/hate-expressive individual. In contrast, the issue of how planful, instrumental forms of hate violence are expressed neurobiologically is less clear. The high-bias ideology offender may evidence some of the same CNS activity found in highly in-group–identified persons, or in the study of religious faith. This would implicate the role of oxytocin neurotransmission, as well as amygdala activity. The expression of a hostile out-group ideology may additionally be a function of activation of the insula. Below are snapshot representations of the brain-behavior issues found in hate crime offender cases. The second case reflects the bonding-follower type we have discussed above.

Labile-Predatory Hate Offender

Male late 20s offender. Periods of homelessness and incarceration. Minimal employment history and failure to finish high school. At time of index offense, offender was living in various homes. He notes being estranged from his family members.

Hate element: Recurrent robbery and assault of gay men in a recognized LGBT community. Discusses retaliatory motives for getting even with "sex offenders." File reports notes highly reactive/labile aggression in commission of hate crimes.

CNS factors: Chronic early childhood sexual abuse, ongoing young adulthood use of meth, history of drug-related loss of consciousness.

Psychiatric status: Distal PTSD, polysubstance history since adolescence, violence since adolescence. Marked dysphoria and flat affect.

While ideologically motivated hate offenders evidence chronic out-group animus, they may also, in some cases, demonstrate significant impulse control. The example of terrorists, who live an embedded lifestyle in countries where they ultimately perpetrate acts of premediated violence, is noteworthy in this regard. These individuals not only engage in extreme forms of violence that are planned for months or even years beforehand, but may live among the very individuals whom they denigrate, even while comporting themselves in a day-to-day fashion as a member of the larger society they target. From a brain-behavior perspective this is intriguing, in that it requires overcoming benign forms of contact with denigrated out-group persons. Their ability to maintain a strong ideological-based animus and still function as a friend or coworker requires the balancing of latent intentions for the commission of violence with the capacity to just get along. Neuropsychologically, this suggests a strong mPFC control over excitatory neural networks. In the forensic sciences, we can argue this is the sign of the clinical psychopath. However, this is probably too easy, and psychopaths, generally, are not ideologues, except in the pursuit of their own needs.

Follower Hate Offender

Male early 20s offender. Member of racialized criminal gang, Prior arrests for nonviolent infractions. Lives with his family; minimal employment history and failure to finish high school.

Hate element: Arrest with fellow gang members in assault on Black neighbor. File report notes likely involvement in turf conflicts inclusive of vandalism and intimidation of Black residents in a Latino-Black community. Minimal expression of motivation other than resentment of Blacks residing in his community. Index offense includes taunting and witnessing violence against victim.

CNS factors: History of family member substance abuse problems. Chronic early adolescence abuse of alcohol and drugs.

Psychiatric status: Conduct and antisocial behavior. Normal to low-normal level of cognitive functioning. No evidence of severe psychopathology.

From a clinical–forensic perspective, hate motivation includes both a strongly help belief system—which in and of itself is comparable to adherence to religious dogma—and the implicit, strongly held animus toward a targeted out-group. A human relations perspective would argue that social cuing and group dynamics would motivate a hate offender to perpetrate acts of violence. By comparison, a neuroscience approach may complicate the hate-arousal and hate-ideology proposal, as put forward here, into more discrete brain-behavior relationships. These could arguably include a neuropathway that activates strongly held attitudes, another that activates a process of premeditation, and potentially another that facilitates openness to engaging in premeditated aggressive behavior.

Labile Bigot Hate Offender

Male late 40s. Offender reports periods of unemployment and homelessness as adult. Prior arrests for vagrancy. No prior violent infractions. The offender has lived in various parts of the country with family members. No reported history of close relationships. Completed high school but has no reported work skills.

Hate element: Arrest for homicide of Latino law enforcement officer. File report notes minimal engagement with the offender when he shot officer at point-blank range. Offender was arrested near crime scene. File report notes the offender's expression of hate motivation for hostility toward non-whites, the government, and immigrants. Argues he killed the officer in self-defense. "White people are targets."

CNS factors: History of violence in family as a child, periods of early childhood physical abuse, absence of parent members as a child. Family member history of alcoholism and (possible) thought disorder. No reported drug/alcohol abuse of offender.

Psychiatric status: Adult history of (nonviolent) antisocial behavior. Evidence of a schizotypal or schizoid personality disorder. Normal to low-normal level of cognitive functioning.

So where does the "hate circuit" identified by Zeki and Romaya (2008) fit into such a proposed system? The role of the insula would appear to be part of the excitatory system with these special-case offenders. As Kanai et al. (2011) observed, insula activation has been related to endorsement of a conservative ideology. As has been noted, aversive emotional and evaluative processes of racial bias are commonly observed in nonviolent subjects. Zeki and Romaya observed that experiences of hate resulted in activation of the putamen and the insula. This in turn reflected heightened aggression and motor activation. Their subjects consisted of a civil sample; it remains important to consider that activation of the hate circuit did not result in violent behavior. This might be anticipated by the role of PFC mediation on the amygdala excitation. Though highly speculative, the perpetration of hate violence may involve both the excitation of the hate network and other moderators such as higher testosterone or lower PFC-amygdala involvement, for example. Replication and extension of these findings bear on a viable neuroscience approach to examining hate violence. To invoke the conventional academic mantra, research is needed on the issue of neurobiological processes of hate offenders.

Contemporary neuroscience research supports the articulation of two brain-behavior processes that are characteristic of hate violence; affect dysregulation and ideologically motivated actions. The affect-dysregulation process would be expected to be characterized by neuroanatomical structures implicating a weak mPFC-amygdala inhibitory response, and activation of the insula and putamen. Amygdala activation would be observed as well. Neurobiological processes of AVP activation, as well as a higher testosterone-to-cortisol ratio, would also be anticipated. There would also be a lower level of serotonin at the synapse. This process would activate reactive forms of hate violence; Snapshot Three provides an example of this offender status. The brain-behavior process of bias ideology would by comparison reveal greater premeditation and planning (Dunbar, 2003). This would implicate mPFC-amygdala activation and suppression of limbic activation. Neurobiological processes of lower AVP levels would be anticipated, as the behavior is absent a reactive/impulsive component. When the perpetrator is part of a hate-oriented network or gang, the influence of oxytocin activation would be expected. Therefore, reactive—labile and impulsive—hate offenses are characterized by low mPFC mediation of stereotype activation and high AVP, serotonin, and testosterone ratios, ideologically, offenses marked by staging and planning are linked to significant prefrontal CNS involvement and higher oxytocin activation. It is also plausible that for these planful offenders there is a greater activation of reward centers in the CNS in the commission of a hate crime. Some of these neuropathways are summarized in Table 7-3 below.

Table 7-3 Proposed Neurobiological Factors of Affect Dysregulation and Bias Identity

	Neuro Pathways	Moderator Variables	Behavioral Manifestation
Affect Dysregulation	Amygdala activation Reduced PFC Temporal activity Limbic system Activation Avassopresin	substance use history of THI poor attachment Impulse disturbance (ADHD, BiPolar DO)	aggression in benign contact retaliatory aggression
Bias Ideology	vmPFC[1] activation Amygdala Activation Oxytocin[2]	social influence: (media and peers) intergroup conflict//duress Powerful other permission-giving	Planned offenses Symbolic acts Domestic terrorism Goal oriented

(Source: Phelps, Cannistraci, & Cunningham (2003)

1. Firat et al. (2017)

2. De Dreu, Baas, & Boot (2016)

In the perpetration of hate violence, the relationship between the offender and the target victim is almost without exception anonymous. In the Zeki and Romaya (2008) study, the target of the animus concerned a specific individual with whom the subject had a prior relationship. Hate offenders target exemplar members of a denigrated out-group, with whom they have no personal experience. From a brain-behavior perspective, it is possible therefore that the neurobiological dynamics are different in terms of the scope of affect processing of the hating subject/perpetrator. The research on hate as affect dysregulation and bias as stereotype activation provides an evidence-based foundation from which the neuropsychological study of hate violence can proceed. The differences, as much as the similarities, of these areas of research can inform us about how to clinically treat and manage perpetrators of hate violence.

Conclusion

Intergroup violence is a chronic problem in human relationships. Violence itself is a defining human experience that may be more enduring than our notion of romantic love. Against the backdrop of a liberal democratic political system and global efforts at promoting a civil society, violence that targets members of specific cultural groups or nation-states pose a lethal threat to the social order. Practitioners actively involved in detection, interdiction, and eradication of the perpetration of violent hate activity need to recognize the power of ideological motivations and the role of impulsive aggression in the commission of these infractions. What is becoming increasingly clear is the need to both understand neurobiological factors in the perpetration of hate violence by individuals and groups and to address the risk of epigenetic expression of out-group violence due to environmental, linguistic, and socially mediated phenomena. The evolving field of neuroscience can both inform and challenge our assumptions about responding to and managing the perpetrators of hate violence.

The brain-behavior basis of hate violence is essentially inferential. Drawing on the evidence from the neurosciences to address this problem is both exciting and challenging. As suggested, it is uncertain whether an offender's hostile ideological beliefs are different from those subscribed to by nonviolent individuals. To date, neuroscience research on social bias provides only a general framework by which to address these issues. We need to remain mindful of the fact that our brain-behavior study of out-group hostility is based on the experiences of nonviolent samples and not violent hate offenders. Furthermore, the notion of an epigenetic basis for intergroup violence needs to consider what forces could lead to gene methylation in the activation of bias expression. Future study on the experiential shaping of genetic potential is one arena in which cultural neuroscience may play an important role in reducing intergroup violence.

We have considered how the role of neuropathways and neurobiological agents may increase the risk for perpetration of intergroup violence. Specific CNS regions that have been implicated by prior research include the amygdala, the PFC, and specific areas of the limbic system—including the insula and putamen. Additionally, the amygdala-PFC pathway has drawn considerable attention in studies concerning aggression and racial bias. Neurotransmitters and other neurobiological agents that may play a role in intergroup violence include serotonin, oxytocin, and arginine vasopressin.

Hate violence requires the interaction of a powerful animus and a willingness to engage in aggressive antisocial behavior. This necessitates the involvement of distinct neuro- networks that are concurrently activated. We have areas of research that constitute a close encounter to such a brain-behavior process, but not to date a program of research that is devoted to the biased judgments and aggression of perpetrators of hate.

References

Allport, G. W. (1954). *The nature of prejudice.* Cambridge, MA: Addison-Wesley.

Altemeyer, B. (1988). *Enemies of freedom: Understanding right-wing authoritarianism.* San Francisco, CA: Jossey-Bass.

Angus, D. J., Schutter, D. J. L. G., Terburg, D., van Honk, J., & Harmon-Jones, E. (2016). A review of social neuroscience research on anger and aggression. In E. Harmon-Jones & M. Inzlicht (Eds.), *Social neuroscience: Biological approaches to social psychology* (pp. 223–246). London, UK: Routledge. https://doi.org/10.4324/9781315628714-12

Asp, E., Ramchandran, K., & Tranel, D. (2012). Authoritarianism, religious fundamentalism, and the human prefrontal cortex. *Neuropsychology*, 26(4), 414–421. https://doi.org/10.1037/a0028526

Aziz-Zadeh, L., Kaplan, J. T., & Iacoboni, M. (2009). "Aha!" The neural correlates of verbal insight solutions. *Human Brain Mapping*, 30(3), 908–916. https://doi.org/10.1002/hbm.20554

Bale, T. L., Davis, A. M., Auger, A. P., Dorsa, D. M., & McCarthy, M. M. (2001). CNS region-specific oxytocin receptor expression: Importance in regulation of anxiety and sex behavior. *Journal of Neuroscience: An Official Journal of the Society for Neuroscience*, 21(7), 2546–2552. https://doi.org/10.1523/JNEUROSCI.21-07-02546.2001

Balliet, D., Wu, J., & De Dreu, C. K. W. (2014). Ingroup favoritism in cooperation: A meta-analysis. *Psychological Bulletin*, 140(6), 1556–1581. https://doi.org/10.1037/a0037737

Baribeau, D. A., & Anagnostou, E. (2015). Oxytocin and vasopressin: Linking pituitary neuropeptides and their receptors to social neurocircuits. *Frontiers in Neuroscience*, 9, 335. https://doi.org/10.3389/fnins.2015.00335

Beauregard, M., & Paquette, V. (2006). Neural correlates of a mystical experience in Carmelite nuns. *Neuroscience Letters*, 405(3), 186–190. https://doi.org/10.1016/j.neulet.2006.06.060

Bell, C. C., & Dunbar, E. (2012). Racism and pathological bias as a co-occurring problem in diagnosis and assessment. In T. A. Widiger (Ed.), *Oxford library of psychology. The Oxford handbook of personality disorders* (pp. 694–709). Oxford, UK: Oxford University Press. https://doi.org/10.1093/oxfordhb/9780199735013.013.0032

Berkowitz, L. (1993). Towards a general theory of anger and emotional aggression: Implications of the cognitive-neoassociationistic perspective for the analysis of anger and other emotions. In R. S. Wyer Jr. & T. K. Srull (Eds.), *Advances in social cognition, 6. Perspectives on anger and emotion* (pp. 1–46). Hillsdale, NJ: Lawrence Erlbaum Associates.

Bisagno, V., & Cadet, J. L. (2014). Stress, sex, and addiction: Potential roles of corticotropin-releasing factor, oxytocin, and arginine-vasopressin. *Behavioural Pharmacology*, 25(5–6), 445–457. https://doi.org/10.1097/FBP.0000000000000049

Blair, R. (2001). Neurocognitive models of aggression, the antisocial personality disorders, and psychopathy. *Journal of Neurology, Neurosurgery, and Psychiatry*, 71(6), 727–731. https://doi.org/10.1136/jnnp.71.6.727

Bygren, L. O., Tinghög, P., Carstensen, J., Edvinsson, S., Kaati, G., Pembrey, M. E., & Sjöström, M. (2014). Change in paternal grandmothers' early food supply influenced cardiovascular mortality of the female grandchildren. *BMC Genetics*, 15(12), 1–6. https://doi.org/10.1186/1471-2156-15-12

Calipari, E. S., Bagot, R. C., Purushothaman, I., Davidson, T. J., Yorgason, J. T., Peña, C. J., & Nestler, E. J. (2016). In vivo imaging identifies temporal signature of D1 and D2 medium spiny neurons in cocaine reward. *Proceedings of the National Academy of Science*, 113(10), 2726–2731. https://doi.org/10.1073/pnas.1521238113

Cannon, W. B, & Britton, S. W. (1925). Pseudoaffective medulliadrenal secretion. *American Journal of Psychology*, 72, 283.

Carrillo, M., Ricci, L. A., & Coppersmith, G. A., & Melloni, R. H. (2009). The effect of increased serotonergic neurotransmission on aggression: A critical meta-analytical review of preclinical studies. *Psychopharmacology*, 205(3), 349–368. https://doi.org/10.1007/s00213-009-1543-2

Carter, C. S., & Keverne, E. B. (2002). The neurobiology of social affiliation and pair bonding. *Hormones, Brain and Behavior*, 1, 299–337. https://doi.org/10.1016/B978-012532104-4/50006-8

Carter, R. M., & Huettel, S. A. (2013). Learning from silver linings. *Frontiers in Neuroscience*, 7, 80. https://doi.org/10.3389/fnins.2013.00080

Coccaro, E. F., Berman, M. E., & Kavoussi, R. J. (1997). Assessment of life history of aggression: Development and psychometric characteristics. *Psychiatry Research*, 73(3), 147–157. https://doi.org/10.1016/S0165-1781(97)00119-4

Coccaro, E. F., Kavoussi, R. J., Hauger, R. L., Cooper, T. B., & Ferris, C. F. (1998). Cerebrospinal fluid vasopressin levels: Correlates with aggression and serotonin function in personality-disordered subjects. *Archives of General Psychiatry*, 55(8), 708–714.

Cornell, D. G. (1992). High intelligence and severe delinquency: Evidence disputing the connection. *Roeper Review*, 14(4), 233–236.

Dabbs, J., Jurkovic, G. J., & Frady, R. L. (1991). Salivary testosterone and cortisol among late adolescent offenders. *Journal of Abnormal Child Psychology*, 19(4), 469–478.

Damasio, A. (1999). *The feeling of what happens: Body and emotion in the making of consciousness*. New York, NY: Harcourt Brace.

De Araujo, I. E., Rolls, E. T., Kringelbach, M. L., McGlone, F., & Phillips, N. (2003). Taste-olfactory convergence, and the representation of the pleasantness of flavour, in the human brain. *European Journal of Neuroscience*, 18(7), 2059–2068. https://doi.org/10.1046/j.1460-9568.2003.02915.x

De Araujo, I. E., Rolls, E. T., Velazco, M. I., Margot, C., & Cayeux, I. (2005). Cognitive modulation of olfactory processing. *Neuron*, 46(4), 671–679.

De Dreu, C. K., & Kret, M. E. (2016). Oxytocin conditions intergroup relations through upregulated in-group empathy, cooperation, conformity, and defense. *Biological Psychiatry*, 79(3), 165–173.

De Dreu, C. K. W., Baas M., & Boot, N. C. (2016). Oxytocin enables novelty seeking and creative performance through upregulated approach: Evidence and avenues for future research. *Wiley Interdisciplinary Reviews. Cognitive Science*, 6(5), 409–417.

DeWolfe, A. S., & Ryan, J. J. (1984). Wechsler performance IQ greater than Verbal IQ index in a forensic sample: A reconsideration. *Journal of Clinical Psychology*, 40(1), 291–294.

Donaldson, Z., & Young, L. J. (2008). Oxytocin, vasopressin, and the neurogenetics of sociality. *Science*, 322(5903), 900–904.

Douglas, K., Chan, G., Gelernter, J., Arias, A. J., Anton, R. F., Poling, J., Farrer, L., & Kranzler, H. R. (2011). 5-HTTLPR as a potential moderator of the effects of adverse childhood experiences on risk of antisocial personality disorder. *Psychiatric Genetics*, 21(5), 240–248.

Dunbar, E. (1997). The Relationship of DSM Diagnostic Criteria and Gough's Prejudice Scale: Exploring the Clinical Manifestations of the Prejudiced Personality. *Cultural Diversity and Mental Health*, 3(4), 247–257.

Dunbar, E. (2003). Symbolic, relational, and ideological signifiers of bias-motivated offenders: Toward a strategy of assessment. *American Journal of Orthopsychiatry*, 73(2), 203–211.

Dunbar, E. (2004). Reconsidering the clinical utility of bias as a mental health problem: Intervention strategies for psychotherapy practice. *Psychotherapy: Theory, Research, Practice, Training*, 41(2), 97–111.

Dunbar, E. (2016). Cultural and psychological characteristics in the evolution of hate crime initiatives. In E. Dunbar, A. Blanco, & D. Crèvecoeur-MacPhail (Eds.), *The psychology of hate crimes as domestic terrorism: U.S. and global issues* (pp. 1–42). Santa Barbara, CA: Praeger.

Dunbar, E. (2018). *Hate unleashed: America's cataclysmic change*. Santa Barbara, CA: Praeger.

Dunbar, E. (2022). Hate, ideology, and intergroup violence: Bias motivation and membership in a multicultural world. In E. W. Dunbar (Ed.), *Indoctrination to hate: Recruitment techniques of hate groups and how to stop them*. Santa Barbara: Praeger.

Dunbar, E., & Blanco, A. (2014). Psychological perspectives on culture, violence, and intergroup animus: Evolving traditions in the bonds that tie and hate. In F. T. L. Leong, L. Comas-Díaz, G. C. Nagayama Hall, V. C. McLoyd, & J. E. Trimble (Eds.), *APA handbook of multicultural psychology, Vol. 2. Applications and training* (pp. 377–399). American Psychological Association. https://doi.org/10.1037/14187-022

Dunbar, E., Krop, H., & Sullaway, M. (2017). Behavioral, psychometric, and diagnostic characteristics of bias-motivated homicide offenders. In E. Dunbar, A. Blanco, D. A. Crèvecoeur-MacPhail, C. Munthe, M. Fingerle, & D. Brax (Eds.), *The psychology of hate crimes as domestic terrorism: U.S. and global issues: Assessment issues with victims and offenders* (pp. 193–225). Santa Barbara, CA: Praeger.

Ekehammar, B., & Akrami, N. (2003). The relation between personality and prejudice: A variable- and a person-centered approach. *European Journal of Personality*, 17(6), 449–464.

Ezekiel, R. (1995). *The racist mind*. London, UK: Penguin Books.

Feldman, R., Weller, A., Zagorry-Sharon, O., & Levine, A. (2007). Evidence for a neuroendocrinological foundation of human affiliation: Plasma oxytocin levels across pregnancy and the postpartum period predict mother–infant bonding. *Psychological Science*, 18(11), 965–970.

Felitti, V. J., Anda, R. F., Nordenberg, D., Williamson, D. F., Spitz, A. M., Edwards, V., Koss, M. P., & Marks, J. S. (1998). Relationship of childhood abuse and household dysfunction to many of the leading causes of death in adults: The Adverse Childhood Experiences (ACE) study. *American Journal of Preventive Medicine*, 14(4), 245–258.

Fine, C., & Blair, R. J. R. (2000). The cognitive and emotional effects of amygdala damage. *Neurocase*, 6(6), 435–450.

Firat, R. B., Hitlin, S., Magnotta, V., & Tranel, D. (2017). Putting race in context: Social class modulates processing of race in the ventromedial prefrontal cortex and amygdala. *Social Cognitive and Affective Neuroscience*, 12(8), 1314–1324.

Fisher, P. M., Meltzer, C. C., Price, J. C., Coleman, R. L., Ziolko, S. K., Becker, C., Moses-Kolko, E. L., Berga, S. L., & Hariri, A. R. (2009). Medial prefrontal cortex 5-ht(2a) density is correlated with amygdala reactivity, response habituation, and functional coupling. *Cerebral Cortex*, 19(11), 2499–2507.

Fitzgerald, P. B., Laird, A. R., Maller, J., & Daskalakis, Z. J. (2008). A meta-analytic study of changes in brain activation in depression. *Human Brain Mapping*, 29, 683–695.

Foland-Ross, L. C., Altshuler, L. L, Bookheimer, S. Y., Lieberman, M. D., Townsend, J., Penfold, C., Moody, T., Ahlf, K., Shen, J. K., Madsen, K.,

Rasser, P. E., Toga, A. W., & Thompson, P. M. (2010). Amygdala reactivity in healthy adults is correlated with prefrontal cortical thickness. *Journal of Neuroscience,* 30(49), 16673–16678.

Gallagher, M. J. (2022). Lone wolf terrorists: Examining motives and methods of stand-alone terrorists. In E. W. Dunbar (Ed.), *Indoctrination to hate: Recruitment techniques of hate groups and how to stop them.* Santa Barbara, CA: Praeger.

Gard, A. M., Dotterer, H. L., & Hyde, L. W. (2019). Genetic influences on antisocial behavior: Recent advances and future directions. *Current Opinion in Psychology*, 27, 46–55.

Glenberg, A. M., Lopez-Mobilia, G., McBeath, M., Toma, M., Sato, M., & Cattaneo, L. (2010). Knowing beans: Human mirror mechanisms revealed through motor adaptation. *Frontiers in Human Neuroscience*, 4, 1–7. https://doi.org/10.3389/fnhum.2010.00206

Golarai, G., Liberman, A., & Grill-Spector, K. (2017). Experience shapes the development of neural substrates of face processing in human ventral temporal cortex. *Cerebral Cortex*, 27(2), 1229–1244.

Green, D. P., Strolovitch, D. Z., & Wong, J. S. (1998). Defended neighborhoods, integration, and racially motivated crime. *American Journal of Sociology,* 104(2), 372–403.

Griffiths, T., Johnsrude, I., Dean, J., & Green, G. (1999). A common neural substrate for the analysis of pitch and duration pattern in segmented sound? *NeuroReport,* 10(18), 3825–3830.

Gutsell, J. N., & Inzlicht, M. (2010). Empathy constrained: Prejudice predicts reduced mental simulation of actions during observation of outgroups. *Journal of Experimental Social Psychology,* 46(5), 841–845.

Harris, L. T., & Fiske, S. T. (2006). Dehumanizing the lowest of the low: Neuroimaging responses to extreme out-groups. *Psychological Science*, 17(10), 847–853.

Harris, S., Kaplan, J. T., Curiel, A., Bookheimer, S. Y., Iacoboni, M., & Cohen, M. S. (2009). The neural correlates of religious and nonreligious belief. *PLoS ONE,* 4(10), e7272. https://doi.org/10.1371/journal.pone.0007272

Hart, A. J., Whalen, P. J., Shine, L. M., McInerney, S. C., Fischer, H., & Rauch, S. L. (2000). Differential response in the human amygdala to racial outgroup vs ingroup face stimuli. *NeuroReport,* 11(11), 2351–2355.

Heinrichs, M., Baumgartner, T., Kirschbaum, C., & Ehlert, U. (2003). Social support and oxytocin interact to suppress cortisol and subjective responses to psychosocial stress. *Biological Psychiatry*, 54(12), 1389–1398.

Hirst, W., Phelps, E. A., Buckner, R. L., Budson, A. E., Cuc, A., Gabrieli, J. D., Johnson, M. K., Lustig, C., Lyle, K. B., Mather, M., Meksin, R., Mitchell, K. J., Ochsner, K. N., Schacter, D. L., Simons, J. S., & Vaidya, C. J. (2009). Long-term memory for the terrorist attack of September 11: Flashbulb memories, event memories, and the factors that influence their retention. *Journal of Experimental Psychology: General*, 138(2), 161–176. https://doi.org/10.1037/a0015527

Hodson, G., & Busseri, M. A. (2012). Bright minds and dark attitudes: Lower cognitive ability predicts greater prejudice through right-wing ideology and low intergroup contact. *Psychological Science*, 23(2), 187–195.

Hoon Oh, D. (2012). *Traumatic experiences disrupt amygdala – prefrontal connectivity*. IntechOpen. https://doi.org/10.5772/48691

Inbar, Y., Pizarro, D., & Bloom, P. (2008). Conservatives are more easily disgusted than liberals. *Cognition and Emotion,* 1(12), 714–752.

Jost, J. T., Glaser, J., Kruglanski, A. W., & Sulloway, F. J. (2003). Political conservatism as motivated social cognition. *Psychological Bulletin*, 129(3), 339–375.

Kanai, R., Feilden, T., Firth, C., & Rees, G. (2011). Political orientations are correlated with brain structure in young adults. *Current Biology,* 21(8), 677–680. https://doi.org/10.1016/j.cub.2011.03.017

Kapogiannis, D., Deshpande, G., Krueger, F., Thornburg, M. P., & Grafman, J. H. (2014). Brain networks shaping religious belief. *Brain Connectivity*, 4(1), 70–79. https://doi.org/10.1089/brain.2013.0172

Krämer, U. M., Riba, J., Richter, S., & Münte, T. F. (2011). An fMRI study on the role of serotonin in reactive aggression. *PLoS ONE,* 6(11), e27668. https://doi.org/10.1371/journal.pone.0027668

Lamm, C. C., Batson, C. D., & Decety, J. (2007). The neural substrate of human empathy: Effects of perspective-taking and cognitive appraisal. *Journal of Cognitive Neuroscience,* 19(1), 42–58.

Lee, T., Chan, S., & Raine, A. (2008). Strong limbic and weak frontal activation to aggressive stimuli in spouse abusers. *Molecular Psychiatry,* 13(7), 655–656. https://doi.org/10.1038/mp.2008.46

Lieberman, M. D., Schreiber, D., & Ochsner, K. N. (2003). Is political cognition like riding a bicycle? How cognitive neuroscience can inform research on political thinking. *Political Psychology*, 24(4), 681–704.

Linden, S. C., Harris, M., Whitaker, C., & Healy, D. (2010). Religion and psychosis: The effects of the Welsh religious revival in 1904–1905. *Psychological Medicine*, 40(8), 1317.

Ling, S., Umbach, R., & Raine, A. (2019). Biological explanations of criminal behavior. *Psychology, Crime & Law*, 25(6), 626–640. https://doi.org/10.1080/1068316X.2019.1572753

McKee, A. C., & Robinson, M. E. (2014). Military-related traumatic brain injury and neurodegeneration. *Alzheimer's & Dementia: The Journal of the Alzheimer's Association*, 10(30), 242–253.

Mitchell, J. P., Mason, M. F., Macrae, C. N., & Banaji, M. R. (2006). Thinking about others: The neural substrates of social cognition. https://sites.fas.harvard.edu/~mrbworks/articles/2006_DUBOIS.pdf

Montoya, E. R., Terburg, D., Bos, P. A., & van Honk, J. (2012). Testosterone, cortisol, and serotonin as key regulators of social aggression: A review and theoretical perspective. *Motivation and Emotions*, 36(1), 65–73.

Moore, M. T., Scarpa, A., & Raine A. (2002). A meta-analysis of serotonin metabolite 5-HIAA and antisocial behavior. *Aggressive Behavior,* 28(4), 299–316.

Mrazek, A. J., Harada, T., & Chiao, J. Y. (2015). Cultural neuroscience of identity development. In K. C. McLean & M. Syed (Eds.), *The Oxford handbook of identity development* (pp. 423–436). Oxford, UK: Oxford University Press.

Murgatroyd, C., & Spengler, D. (2011). Epigenetics of early child development. *Frontiers in Psychiatry*, 14(6), 581–589.

Murrow, G. B., & Murrow, R. (2015). A hypothetical neurological association between dehumanization and human rights abuses. *Journal of Law and Biosciences*, 2(2), 336–364. https://doi.org/10.1093/jlb/lsv015

Nam, H., Jost, J. T., Kaggen, L., Campbell-Meiklejohn, D., & Van Bavel, J. J. (2018). Amygdala structure and the tendency to regard the social system as legitimate and desirable. *Nature Human Behaviour*, 2(2), 133–138.

Neumann, I. D. (2002). Involvement of the brain oxytocin system in stress coping: Interactions with the hypothalamo-pituitary-adrenal axis. *Progressive Brain Research*, 139, 147–162.

New, A. S., Hazlett, E. A., Buchsbaum, M. S., Goodman, M., Mitelman, S. A., Newmark, R., Trisdorfer, R. Haznedar, M. M., Koenigsberg, H. W., Flory, J., & Siever, L. J. (2007). Amygdala-prefrontal disconnection in borderline personality disorder. *Neuropsychopharmacology*, 32(7), 1629–1640.

Page-Gould, E., & Danyluck, D. (2016). Biological perspectives on intergroup relations. In E. Harmon-Jones & M. Inzlicht, *Social neuroscience: Biological approaches to social psychology* (186–198). London, UK: Routledge.

Pajer, K., Tabbah, R., Gardner, W., Rubin, R., Kennethczambel, R., & Wang, Y. (2006). Adrenal androgen and gonadal hormone levels in adolescent girls with conduct disorder. *Psychoneuroendocrinology*, 31(10), 1245–1256.

Passamonti, L., Crockett, M. J, Apergis-Schoute, A., Clark, L., Rowe, J. B., Calder, A. J., & Robbins, T. W. (2012). Effects of acute tryptophan depletion on prefrontal-amygdala connectivity while viewing facial signals of aggression. *Biological Psychiatry*, 71(1), 36–43.

Paus, T., Keshavan, M., & Giedd, J. N. (2008). Why do many psychiatric disorders emerge during adolescence? *Nature Reviews Neuroscience*, 9(12), 947–957.

Perry, R. E., Blair C., & Sullivan, R. S. (2017). Neurobiology of infant attachment: Attachment despite adversity and parental programming of emotionality. *Current Opinion in Psychology*, 17, 1–6.

Pettigrew, T. F., & Tropp, L. R. (2008), How does intergroup contact reduce prejudice? Meta-analytic tests of three mediators. *European Journal of Social Psychology*, 38(6), 922–934.

Phelps, E. A., Cannistraci, C. J., & Cunningham, W. A. (2003). Intact performance on an indirect measure of race bias following amygdala damage. *Neuropsychologia*, 41(2), 203–208.

Phelps, E. A., O'Connor, K. J., Cunningham, W. A., Funayama, E. S., Gatenby, J. C., Gore, J. C., & Banaji, M. R. (2000). Performance on indirect measures of race evaluation predicts amygdala activation. *Journal of Cognitive Neuroscience*, 12(5), 729–738. https://doi.org/10.1162/089892900562552

Plante, T. G., & Boccaccini, M. T. (1997). The Santa Clara strength of religious faith questionnaire. *Pastoral Psychology*, 45(5), 375–387.

Rogers, M. B., Loewenthal, K. M., Lewis, C. A., Amlôt, R., Cinnirella, M., & Ansari, H. (2007). The role of religious fundamentalism in terrorist violence: A social psychological analysis. *International Review of Psychiatry*, 19(3), 253–262.

Schiltz, K., Witzel, J., Northoff, G., Zierhut, K., Gubka, U., Fellmann, H., Kaufmann, J., Tempelmann, C., Wiebking, C., & Bogerts, B. (2007). Brain pathology in pedophilic offenders: Evidence of volume reduction in the right amygdala and related diencephalic structures. *Archives of General Psychiatry*, 64(6), 737–746.

Scott, B. G., & Weems, C. F. (2014). Resting vagal tone and vagal response to stress: Associations with anxiety, aggression, and perceived anxiety control among youth. *Psychophysiology*, 51(8), 718–727. http://doi.org/10.1111/psyp.12218

Shamay-Tsoory, S. G., & Abu-Akel, A. (2016, February 1). The social salience hypothesis of oxytocin. *Biological Psychiatry*, 79(3), 194–202.

Siever, L. J. (2008). Neurobiology of aggression and violence. *American Journal of Psychiatry*, 165(4), 429–442. http://doi.org/10.1176/appi.ajp.2008.07111774

Simonoff, E., Elander, J., Holmshaw, J., Pickles, A., Murray, R., & Rutter, M. (2004). Predictors of antisocial personality: Continuities from childhood to adult life. *British Journal of Psychiatry*, 184(2), 118–127.

Stallen, M., Rossi, F., Heijne, A., Smidts, A., De Dreu, C. K. W., & Sanfey, A. G. (2018). Neurobiological mechanisms of responding to injustice. *Journal of Neuroscience*, 38(12), 2944-2954.

Stark, R., Schienle, A., Walter, B., Kirsch, P., Sammer, G., Ott, U., Blecker, C., & Vaitl, D. (2003). Hemodynamic responses to fear and disgust-inducing pictures: An fMRI study. International *Journal of Psychophysiology*, 50(3), 225–234.

START. (2017). Ideological motivations of terrorism in the United States, 1970–2016. https://start.umd.edu/pubs/START_IdeologicalMotivationsOfTerrorismInUS_Nov2017.pdf

Stevens, F. L., Hurley, R. A., & Taber, K. H. (2011). Anterior cingulate cortex: Unique role in cognition and emotion. *Journal of Neuropsychiatry and Clinical Neurosciences*, 23(2), 121–125.

Sullaway, M., & Dunbar, E. (1996). Clinical manifestations of prejudice in psychotherapy: Toward a strategy of assessment and treatment. *Clinical Psychology: Science and Practice*, 3(4), 296–309. https://doi.org/10.1111/j.1468-2850.1996.tb00084.x

Sullivan, C. P., & Elbogen, E. B. (2013, May 6). PTSD Symptoms and family versus stranger violence in Iraq and Afghanistan veterans. *Law and Human Behavior*, 38(1), 1–9. https://doi.org/10.1037/lhb0000035

Sutin, A., Beason-Held, L., Resnick, S., & Costa, P. (2009). Sex differences in resting-state neural correlates of openness to experience among older

adults, *Cerebral Cortex*, 19(12), 2797–2802. https://doi.org/10.1093/cercor/bhp066
Suzuki, H., Han, S. D., & Lucas, L. R. (2010). Chronic passive exposure to aggression decreases D(2) and 5-HT(1B) receptor densities. *Physiology & Behavior*, 99(5), 562–570.
Tao, H., Guo, S., Ge, T., et al. (2013). Depression uncouples brain hate circuit. *Molecular Psychiatry*, 18(1), 101–111. https://doi.org/10.1038/mp.2011.127
Tenold, V. (2018). *Everything you love will burn: Inside the rebirth of white nationalism in America*. London, UK: Hachette UK.
Ten Vender, F. S., Daughters, K., & De Dreu, C. K. W. (2017). Oxytocin promotes intuitive rather than deliberated cooperation with the in-group. *Hormones and Behavior*, 92, 164–171.
Tomasello, M. (1999). *The cultural origins of human cognition*. Cambridge, MA: Harvard University Press.
Tomoda, A., Suzuki, H., Rabi, K., Sheu, Y. S., Polcari, A., & Teicher, M. H. (2009). Reduced prefrontal cortical gray matter volume in young adults exposed to harsh corporal punishment. *NeuroImage*, 47(Suppl 2), T66–T71. https://doi.org/10.1016/j.neuroimage.2009.03.005
Tuinier, S., Verhoeven, W. M. A., & Van Praag, H. M. (1996). Serotonin and disruptive behaviour: A critical evaluation of the clinical data. *Human Psychopharmacology: Clinical and Experimental*, 11(6), 469–482.
van Honk, J., Harmon-Jones, E., Morgan, B. E., and Schutter, D. J. L. G. (2010). Socially explosive minds: The triple imbalance hypothesis of reactive aggression. *Journal of Personality*, 78(1), 67–94.
van Niekerk, J. K., Huppert, F. A., & Herbert, J. (2001). Salivary cortisol and DHEA: Association with measures of cognition and well-being in normal older men, and effects of three months of DHEA supplementation. *Psychoneuroendocrinology*, 26(6), 591–612. https://doi.org/10.1016/s0306-4530(01)00014-2
Vassos, E., Collier, D. A., & Fazel, S. (2014). Systematic meta-analyses and field synopsis of genetic association studies of violence and aggression. *Molecular Psychiatry*, 19(4), 471–7. https://doi.org/10.1038/mp.2013.31
Vitiello, B., Behar, D., Hunt, J., Stoff, D., & Ricciuti, A. (1990). Subtyping aggression in children and adolescents. *Journal of Neuropsychiatry and Clinical Neurosciences*, 2(2), 189–192. https://doi.org/10.1176/jnp.2.2.189
Von Dawans, B. (2008). *Neuropeptidergic modulation of social behavior in health and social phobia*. Göttingen, Germany: Cuvillier Verlag.
Von Dawans, B., Fischbacher, U., Kirschbaum, C., Fehr, E., & Heinrichs, M. (2012). The social dimension of stress reactivity: Acute stress increases prosocial behavior in humans. *Psychological Science*, 23(6), 651–660.
Welsing, F. C. (1974). The Cress theory of color-confrontation. *Black Scholar*, 5(8), 32–40.
Wheeler, C. S., & Petty, R. E. (2001). The effects of stereotype activation on behavior: A review of possible mechanisms. *Psychological Bulletin*, 127(6), 797–826.

Wheeler, M. E., & Fiske, S. T. (2005). Controlling racial prejudice: Social-cognitive goals affect amygdala and stereotype activation. *Psychological Science*, 16(1), 56–63. https://doi.org/10.1111/j.0956-7976.2005.00780.x

Winchester, D. (2008). Embodying the faith: Religious practice and the making of a Muslim moral habitus. *Social Forces*, 86(4), 1753–1780.

Winslow, J. T., Hastings, N., Carter, C. S., Harbaugh, C. R., & Insel, T. R. (1993). A role for central vasopressin in pair bonding in monogamous prairie voles. *Nature*, 365(6446), 545–548.

Xu, X., Fukuyama, H., Yazawa, S., Mima, T., Hanakawa, T., Magata, Y., Kanda, M., Fujiwara, N., Shindo, K., Nagamine, T., & Shibasaki, H. (1997). Functional localization of pain perception in the human brain studied by PET. *NeuroReport*, 8(2), 555–559.

Yeh, M. T., Coccaro, E. F., & Jacobson, K. C. (2010). Multivariate behavior genetic analyses of aggressive behavior subtypes. *Behavior Genetics*, 40(5), 603–617.

Young, K., Liu, Y., & Wang, Z. (2008). The neurobiology of social attachment: A comparative approach to behavioral, neuroanatomical, and neurochemical studies. *Comparative Biochemistry and Physiology Part C: Toxicology & Pharmacology*, 148(4), 401–410.

Zeki, S., & Romaya, J. P. (2008). Neural correlates of hate. *PLoS One*, 3(10), e3556. https://doi.org/10.1371/journal.pone.0003556

Zhong, W., Cristofori, I., Bulbulia, J., Krueger, F., & Grafman, J. (2017). Biological and cognitive underpinnings of religious fundamentalism. *Neuropsychologia*, 100, 18–25.

CHAPTER EIGHT

Lone Wolves and Wolf Packs: Revenge Porn, Cyber Mobs, and Creepshots

Megan Sullaway

In 2015, in the crowded London tube, I sat next to a young man. He was playing on his phone. In front of us stood a young woman in a knee-length skirt. I noticed he was holding his phone low and parallel to the ground, and suddenly realized he was angling it to take a photograph under the young woman's skirt. The train stopped and she got off. The young man moved toward the door and exited the next stop. It happened quickly; by the time I realized what I was seeing it was over. He was taking an upskirt photo, very possibly to post on any number of sites online.

This was disturbing and infuriating, as well as confusing. Why take a surreptitious image to share? There are ample amounts of pornography on the net, much of it free. What type of person does this, and who consumes it?

In an attempt to answer these questions, I will review the types of internet attacks in which women's personal space and images are shared without consent, and discuss the different forms this may take, as well as attempt to describe and differentiate between types of perpetrators. The chapter is roughly organized based on the relationship (or lack thereof) between perpetrator and victim. For example, as in the situation I witnessed, there are perpetrators who choose victims who are completely unknown to them to photograph and post, inviting comments and critiques. These so-called "creeps hot" photos are posted on various sites. In contrast, in cases of "revenge porn" (also called nonconsensual porn victimization, or relationship retribution), there was, typically, an intimate relationship between perpetrator and victim. The "lone wolf" perpetrator posts intimate photos or video of the victim online. Images posted may or may not have been made with her knowledge. Typically, images are posted to punish the woman post breakup. In doing so, the perpetrator essentially outsources his rage. Consumers of the images spread the images further, comment on the images, and, sometimes, reveal the name, address, employer, and so on of the victim.

"Wolf packs" (in contrast to the "lone wolf" who posts images for revenge against a formerly intimate partner) are groups of perpetrators (essentially, cyber mobs), who attack victims with whom they have had no personal relationship (but may have heard of due to the women's presence in the news or other reason). Such groups are often disorganized. In some cases, the groups can become highly organized and focused in their targeting. In both cases, victims can be terrorized and their careers and lives significantly damaged.

In describing "lone wolf," "wolf pack," and "creepshot" attacks, I hope to offer hypotheses concerning similarities and differences between the various types of perpetrators. For example, how is the lone wolf similar to or different from someone joining a cyber mob against a stranger?

A Note about Gender

Revenge porn, cyber harassment, and aggressive trolling can happen to both men and women. A variety of sources (anecdotal, experimental, self-report surveys, and careful sampling) suggest that while sexualized trolling targets both men and women, young women are overrepresented as victims (Henry & Powell, 2016).

For example, a cleverly designed study of chat room behavior found that simply manipulating the name of a (silent) chat room member dramatically impacted the likelihood of malicious online harassment involving sexually explicit or threatening language. Meyer and Cukier (2006) studied chat room behavior using both humans and bots as silent participants, and assessed responses by real users. Bots with male names received 3.7 malicious private messages/day. Bots given female names received 100 malicious private messages/day. Human players with male names received 27.5; humans with female names received 163 malicious private messages/day: a fairly dramatic demonstration of the gendered nature of unsolicited attacks and the sexualized nature of such.

The 2017 Nationwide Online Study of Nonconsensual Porn (NCP) Victimization and Perpetration (Eaton, Jacobs, & Ruvalcaba, 2017) used a stratified sampling technique to obtain respondents from each state in proportion to the state's population (with respect to the total U.S. population). Eight percent of participants reported being victims of NCP, and women were 1.5 times more likely than men to report having been victims. Disturbingly, 27% of these men and women were under age 18 at the time the image(s) were taken. Women were 2.5 times more likely than men to have been threatened with NCP. Men were twice as likely to report having been perpetrators of NCP than women (7.4% versus 3.4%).

The Pew Research Center published a study of online harassment (2014). Harassment is very common in general: 40% of adult internet users have experienced some form of harassment. Harassment was classified into two categories: 1) embarrassment and name-calling (i.e., "abusive and mean") and 2) "more intense and emotionally damaging including sexual harassment, physical threats, sustained harassment and stalking" (i.e., very sexualized, violent, and off-topic harassment) (12).

> Online harassment is especially pronounced at the intersection of gender and youth: women ages 18–24 are more likely than others to experience some of the more severe forms of harassment. They are particularly likely to report being stalked online (26%) and sexually harassed (25%). In addition, they are also the targets of other forms of severe harassment like physical threats (23%) and sustained harassment (18%) at rates similar to their male peers (26% of whom have been physically threatened and 16% of whom have been the victim of sustained harassment). In essence, young women are uniquely likely to experience stalking and sexual harassment, while also not escaping the high rates of other types of harassment common to young people in general. (14)

Examples of "severe harassment" include "I was told that someone should rape me which was horrific since it's one of the things I fear most," "Online commenters told me I was 'asking to be raped,'" "I was threatened and told that if I stopped communicating with this man he would find me and rape me," "Threatening to harm my pets and myself and my personal property" (34–35).

In 2016, the *Guardian* newspaper "took stock of its vitriolic comments section in 2016 and reported that eight of its most attacked columnists were women, two were men of color, and the most attacked of all was feminist Jessica Valenti" (Gardiner et al., 2016).

Jane Fae, a transgender writer, journalist, and blogger, has a very interesting perspective on cyber abuse received by men and women. "I am in the fairly unique position of having written under both genders. . . . There IS a marked difference. . . . First off, even the nice comments seem, at some level, to be more personal. I won't say I never got strongly dissenting views before I transitioned: but there was usually, mostly, some appeal to the rational argument underlying. Not so much anymore, as many of those critical of what I have to say seem far readier to reach for the personal attack: the implication that I only say what I say because I am a woman . . . an ugly woman" (Lewis, 2011).

Consequently, the majority of anecdotes and research described in this chapter are those in which women were the victims whereas the perpetrators were both men and women.

Basic Definitions

CMC: Computer mediated communication.

Creepshots and Upskirts. From the Urban Dictionary: A picture taken, generally of a woman, without her knowledge or consent. From Reddit (http://metareddit.com/r/CreepShots/): "Creepshots are *CANDID*. If a person is posing for and/or aware that a picture is being taken, then it ceases to be candid and thus is no longer a creepshot. A creepshot captures the natural, raw sexiness of the subject without their vain attempts at putting on a show for the camera. That is the essence of the creepshot, that is what makes a true creepshot worth the effort and that is why this subreddit exists. Use stealth, cunning and deviousness to capture the beauty of your unsuspecting, chosen target."

Cyber Harassment. The National Conference of State Legislatures (2015) define cyber harassment as "threatening or harassing email messages, instant messages, or to blog entries or web sites dedicated solely to tormenting an individual."

Cybermob: Sarkeesian (2012) describes organized group trolling/harassment as a cyber mob. "The usual terms that we use to describe online harassment . . . don't adequately describe a hate campaign of this scale."

Cyberstalking. According to federal cyberstalking statutes, "cyberstalking" includes actions by a perpetrator on the internet that "place the victim in reasonable fear of death or serious bodily injury or causes, attempts to cause, or would be reasonably expected to cause substantial emotional distress to the victim or the victim's immediate family" (18 U.S.C. Section 2261A).

Doxing. A form of cyber harassment that reveals victims' name, address, employment, contact information, social media sites, social security number, and so on, which allows and encourages others to harass the victim and otherwise create havoc. The term comes from the phrase "dropping documents" on someone (Douglas, 2016). Douglas describes three types of doxing: deanonymizing (revealing the identity of an anonymous person), targeted doxing (disclosing personal information), and delegitimizing (offering details to damage credibility).

E-bile. Jane (2014) proposes the term "e-bile," believing that "a new descriptor is required in order to gather under one heading a variety of denunciatory forms that share characteristic, signal features and so demand a broad field of inquiry" . . . (532). It is "broadly defined as text or speech that is technology based and perceived as involving hostility" (533). She notes that such communications are strikingly similar to each other, "involving profanity, ad hominem invective and hyperbolic imagery of graphic—often sexualized—violence" (533).

Incels. "Involuntary celibates" are typically young men on the internet who feel ignored and rejected by women. Incel sites "stoke(s) men's hatred of women who won't date them . . . encourages a hopeless self-hatred that leads many incels to conclude they have little to live for" (Futrelle, May 2, 2018).

Nonconsensual Pornography. This term encompasses revenge porn as well as images stolen from the victims' computer/phone, and images secretly recorded or recorded during a sexual assault. The term "revenge porn," though frequently used, is somewhat misleading. Many perpetrators are not motivated by revenge or by any personal feelings toward the victim. A more accurate term is nonconsensual pornography (NCP), defined as the distribution of sexually graphic images of individuals without their consent (CCRI, 2017).

Revenge Porn. In contrast to nonconsensual pornography generally, this term refers to internet distribution of sexually explicit/nude images/videos by an ex-lover without the former partner's consent, motivated by the perpetrator's desire to harm. Others have used the term "relationship retribution" (Powell & Henry, 2017).

Sextortion. This is a form of cyber extortion in which individuals demand that victims provide them with sexual images, favors, and so on and threaten to post harmful or embarrassing photos or videos of the victim unless the demands are complied with (Clark, 2016).

Trolling. Hardaker (2010) defines trolling thus: "Troller is a CMC user who constructs the identity of sincerely wishing to be part of the group in question, including professing, or conveying, pseudo-sincere intentions, but whose real intention(s) is/are to cause disruption and/or to trigger or exacerbate conflict for the purposes of their own amusement" (237).

In more vivid terms, writer and blogger Lindy West calls internet trolling "gratuitous online cruelty." "Trolling is recreational abuse—usually anonymous—intended to waste the subject's time or get a rise out of them or frustrate or frighten them into silence" (West, February 2, 2015). Courtney Stanton (February 13, 2011) defines it thus: "Troll (n.). 1) One who contributes nothing but noise to a conversation. Often disagrees aggressively and insultingly using personal attacks."

From Phillips (October 15, 2012): "The term has taken on very specific subcultural meaning. Trolling as described by self-identifying trolls is a game, one only the trolls can initiate and only the troll can win . . .

subcultural trolling is predicated on the amassment of lulz, an aggressive form of laughter derived from eliciting strong emotional reactions from the chosen target(s). In order to amass the greatest number of lulz possible, trolls engage in the most outrageous and offensive behaviors possible—all the better to troll you with."

4chan is an image board website, with multiple interest categories. Users can post anonymously. As seen by Beran (2017), "4chan defined itself by being insensitive to suffering in that way only people who have never really suffered can—that is to say, young people, mostly young men, protected by a cloak of anonymity . . . (asserting) their right to do or say anything no matter someone else's feeling . . . posting pornography, swastikas, racial slurs, and content that reveled in harm to other people." It became the primary platform for Gamergate, until those threads were banned.

8chan was created in 2013 when its creator felt 4chan was becoming too restrictive regarding "free speech." More recently it's been linked to alt-right activity and Nazi ideology, including playing a role radicalizing recent shooters at a mosque in Christchurch, New Zealand, and a synagogue in Poway, California. https://www.vox.com/recode/2019/5/3/18527214/8chan-poway-synagogue-shooting-christchurch-john-earnest.

A Typology

One way to conceptualize the types of internet harassment is to organize it based on the relationship (or lack of one) between perpetrator and victim. Similarly, the agency and initiative of the perpetrator differs: it is one thing to upload intimate partner photos, or take photos of strangers and upload them; it is another thing to passively comment on such photos, once posted.

Perpetrator and Victim Knew Each Other Intimately

The widely accepted term "revenge porn" most commonly refers to intimate images and videos that are posted to public sites by angry and vengeful ex-lovers. These "lone wolves" post the photos on sites created for that purpose, typically adding identifying information such as victims' names and addresses. The images and videos may have originally been obtained with the subject's consent (with the understanding they were not to be shared). Alternatively, they may have been taken surreptitiously, or stolen from the subject's phone or computer. In the worst-case scenario, the "lone wolf" poses as the victim (in a Craigslist ad, e.g.), and invites site users to visit the address provided to play out a rape fantasy (Correll, 2010).

The perpetrator essentially outsources his revenge for the breakup or perceived betrayal by the former partner. Once photos are posted, the comments by strangers start, and are typically demeaning and/or threatening.

Victims may be doxed, that is, identified by name, address, occupation; employers and family members may be sent images. Revenge porn as a subset of online harassment more frequently victimizes women for reasons to be explored in this chapter. Langlois and Slane (2017), in an analysis of one revenge porn site, found that 95% of images were of women. One infrequently discussed reason that women are more victimized in revenge porn incidents is simply economic. There is more money to be made in images of women than images of men (Langlois & Slane, 2017).

No prior relationship between perpetrator(s) and victim

"Disorganized wolf packs." Some women are targeted simply because they have come to the attention of (usually) men online. NCP images are not part of the attack, although threats become sexualized as well as violent. One of the more famous cases to be discussed is that of Caroline Criado-Perez, who lobbied the Bank of England to put a woman on a bank note (after the only other woman on a bank note, reformer Elizabeth Fry, was to be removed). The Bank of England chose Jane Austen, announcing the decision on July 24, 2013. The abusive threats started the same day, as many as 50 per hour for about 12 hours. Threats were specific and frightening "I will rape you tomorrow at 9pm." "I've just been released from prison. . . . I'd do a lot worse than rape you." Harassment lacked any reference to the Bank of England decision; Criado-Perez simply came to public attention due to her activism.

While this type of harassment starts in a seemingly unorganized fashion, as will be seen, over time, links may form between perpetrators previously unknown to each other.

"Organized wolf packs." Probably the most famous organized "wolf pack" occurred in "Gamergate," in which anonymous attackers organized through various websites to target particular women who were connected with the gaming world. These attackers were able to use their skills to post their targets' personal information (name and address, schedules, social security numbers, etc.) and to make credible personal threats that lasted months or, in some cases, years.

Creepshots: No prior relationship between perpetrators and victims; victims frequently anonymous

Specialized sites exist for the sole purpose of posting photographs of women taken surreptitiously, including so-called upskirt photos, ostensibly for the purpose of "admiring" the female body, but in reality to sexualize, critique, and mock. One such thread on Reddit was called "Creepshots." Another site, "Auto Admit," was used by law students to post and rate photos of women in law school. One of the threads, "Stupid Bitch to Attend Law

School," included the comment "I think I will sodomize her repeatedly." Another poster noted where his fellow student worked out, noted her gym attire, and commented that he wanted to lick the sweat off her face. As one victim said, "You'd have to be pretty damn steely not to be freaked out by that." As comments were made under pseudonyms, women did not know which of their supposed peers were responsible.

The typology above, based on the relationship (or lack thereof) between perpetrator and victim, doesn't answer the basic question: Who does this, and why? I suspected that members of the proposed typologies differ in their motivations and personal characteristics—that the "lone wolf" has different characteristics and motivations than a member of a loosely organized "wolf pack" or a "creeper." This chapter is an attempt to organize what we do know about perpetrators, to begin to create conceptual models, and to offer hypotheses for future study.

I have directly quoted harassing comments, tweets, and so on. I do not paraphrase what was said, no matter how crude and offensive. Simply describing the nature of the quotes fails to convey their cruelty and terror. Nor do I correct spelling or grammar when quoting. I decided to name only those revenge porn (and related) sites that have been taken down; those that still exist I describe but do not provide the URL, as I do not wish to drive traffic to these sites. Those whose images have been posted, and or who have been attacked, doxed, and so on are referred to as "victims." Those doing the posting, harassing, commenting, and so on are referred to as "perpetrators."

Revenge Porn: Perpetrator and Victim Had Prior Intimate Relationship

Revenge porn is the modern version of the scarlet letter; it is the modern iteration of culturally accepted responses to women's sexual (mis)conduct and/or betrayal. Publicly revealing and condemning a woman for her willing participation in sexual practices has long been a means of ostracizing her (Langlois & Slane, 2017).

Historically, acceptable responses to real or perceived sexual rejection and/or infidelity by a woman can go further than humiliation, and can include murder.

> *It is the cause, it is the cause, my soul,—*
> *Let me not name it to you, you chaste stars!—*
> *It is the cause. Yet I'll not shed her blood;*
> *Nor scar that whiter skin of hers than snow,*
> *And smooth as monumental alabaster.*
> ***Yet she must die, else she'll betray more men.*** [emphasis added]
> *Put out the light, and then put out the light.*
>
> *Othello, William Shakespeare*

The right of a man to kill a woman who sexually betrays him was enshrined in British and American law and precedent for centuries. The "provocation doctrine" allowed for four types of cases in which "a man of honour might overreact and kill when a lesser retaliation would have been appropriate" (Reg. v. Mawgridge, 1707, cited in Regina v. Smith, 2000). Catching a man "in the act of adultery with one's wife" was one of these categories. "For jealousy is the rage of man and adultery is the highest invasion of property" (Reg v. Mawgridge (1707) Keil. 119). Note the use of the term "property." In marriage, a wife gave "herself in this kind unto her husband *which she cannot retract*" (emphasis mine) (Hale, 1847); therefore a wife's infidelity was particularly outrageous.

Late nineteenth-century U.S. courts "held that discovery of a letter revealing complete adultery could sufficiently provoke a defendant, and that learning in other ways of a wife's infidelity sufficed as well" (Taylor, 1985, 1696). As recently as 1956, a court found that "killing to prevent adultery justifies acquittal" (Taylor, 1985, 1697). *Killing to prevent adultery justified acquittal. In 1956!*

In the twenty-first century, some still struggle with the idea of women's autonomy over their sexual behavior, believing it represents a U.S. society that has become matriarchal:

> *Dilbert comic Scott Adams wrote last month that we live in a matriarchy because, "access to sex is strictly controlled by the woman." Meaning that you don't get to have sex with someone unless they want to have sex with you, which if we say it without any gender pronouns sounds completely reasonable. You don't get to share someone's sandwich unless they want to share their sandwich with you, and that's not a form of oppression either. You probably learned that in kindergarten.* (Solnit, 2015)

Adams's quote, above, is weirdly similar to something Elliot Rodger wrote in his "Manifesto": "They (the human female) are the main instigators of sex. They control which men get it and which men don't. . . . Women should not have the right to choose who to mate and breed with." Rodger is the young man who killed and injured people in Santa Barbara, California, as part of his "Day of Retribution."

Less extreme than killing is public humiliation, shame, and ruin. In the opera *La Traviata* (Verdi, 1853), Violetta leaves her lover Alfredo for another man. Alfredo attempts to publicly humiliate her by treating his former lover as if she were no more than a mere prostitute to him:

> **ALFREDO** *You love him, then?*
>
> **VIOLETTA** *Well—I love him, yes.*
>
> **ALFREDO** *(In a blind fury he runs to the door and calls out.) Everyone—come here!*
>
> *(All the guests, bewildered, return to the salon.)*

ALL *You called us? What do you want?*

ALFREDO *(pointing to Violetta, who is leaning against the table in utter humiliation)*

You know this woman?

ALL *Who? Violetta?*

ALFREDO *You don't know what she has done?*

VIOLETTA *Ah, be silent.*

ALL *No.*

ALFREDO *This woman was about to lose all she owns for love of me;*

while I, blinded, vile, wretched, was capable of accepting everything.

But there is still time! I wish to cleanse myself of such a stain.

I have called you here as witnesses that I have paid her all I owe.

(With furious contempt, he throws a purse down at Violetta's feet. Violetta faints in the arms of Flora).

If Violetta and Alfredo lived in the twenty-first century, and if Alfredo had photos, he could have shamed her in an even more public way than he did in the opera. Starting a revenge porn campaign is easy, and in some states legal. An unhappy ex finds an existing revenge porn site. He or she clicks the "submit" button, uploads photos/videos, and completes a form asking for the victim's full name, social network IDs, gender, age, and location, which can include address, employer, school, and so on.

Once the upload is complete, comments by users rapidly follow. A user can search the revenge porn site by geographical location, by victim name, and so on; they can rate the attractiveness or lack thereof of the victim; they can comment on what they'd like to do to the victim, and (commonly) can insult the person who uploaded the photo. Links and photos can be—and are—easily and anonymously sent to employers, family members, and other victim connections.

Hunter Moore, the so called "King of Revenge Porn," created the first such site, "Isanyoneup.com," to show friends photos of a woman he'd slept with. Friends posted their own photos of sex partners, and the site grew in popularity. Angry and rejected ex-lovers started sending the site photos of their exes. Victims commonly learned they'd been posted and doxed when their social media was flooded with sexual solicitations and insults, and/or when they lost their job, as when photos were forwarded to employers. Attempts by victims to get Moore to take photos down met with more ridicule and attack against them. Some victims committed suicide.

Lawsuits against Moore failed. The Communication Decency Act (1996) allows newspapers, books, and so on to be sued for defamatory content, but distributors (such as a newsstand—or a website) can't be sued. Ultimately, the site was purchased by an antibullying site and taken down. Moore was investigated by the FBI for hacking and conspiracy to hack (he stole photos directly from victims' phones and computers) (Hill, 2014). He was indicted on 15 counts, sentenced to 2 ½ years, and was released in March 2017.

"IsAnybodyDown" followed the Hunter Moore model with the added twist of providing "free stuff" to users submitting leads to victims' social media. Victims who paid a fee could (supposedly) have their images taken down—which didn't solve the problem, insofar as the photos may have already spread to other sites. IsAnybodyDown, too, was shut down, but content was simply shifted to another domain.

As of this writing 46 states, D.C., and one territory have revenge porn laws (CCRI, 2017; https://www.cybercivilrights.org/revenge-porn-laws/).

Some revenge porn sites specialize. Facebook has several pages directed toward members of the military. From the "about" section on one of these pages:

> *"Make them famous" CHEATERS, WHORES, BACKSTABBERS, ETC. . . . If you no a MAN or WOMAN who has cheated, been a whore, back stabbed you, or just someone you don't like send me there name & picture and I'll be sure to SHOW THE WORLD & MAKE 'EM FAMOUS!!!!! If you don't like what I post on this page then get over it. This page is to let people know about others. If you have a problem with this page then unlike it. I will post as I please so if anyone has someone they would like to blast let me know.*
>
> *We're back. Soldiers, sailors, airman and marines. You know what to do. If she screwed you over while you were serving, send her in and put her on blast.*

The Psychology of Revenge Porn Perpetrators

We know very little with certainty about revenge porn perpetrators. They are not the easiest population to study, for obvious reasons.

Surveys show that many people who post intimate images without the consent of the victim are acting out of naivete and braggadocio rather than malice. According to the 2017 Online Study of Consensual Porn Victimization and Perpetration, the most commonly chosen reason for perpetration was "just sharing the image(s) with friends and didn't intend to hurt the person" (79%). The Eaton and colleagues study (2017) found that the vast majority of those who shared images would not have done so if they knew it would cause serious consequences (registration as a sex offender, or prison, or was a federal or state felony, etc.). Sixty-four percent said they would not have done it "If I knew how much it would hurt the person," or if they had to reveal their full name with the image (50%). Presumably, then, this group does not have the intent to hurt; they be might reachable through education about penalties and victim impact.

In contrast, revenge porn refers to images posted with deliberate and malevolent intent to hurt, punish, and humiliate. In the 2017 survey described above, 30% perpetrated nonconsensual porn due to feeling "upset" with the victim for cheating, abuse, or conflict (17%), "because it made me feel good" (11%), to obtain internet comments and upvotes (6%), to ruin the victim's life (1%) or to punish a breakup (1%). Langlois and Slane (2017) make the point that revenge porn is also posted "for hacking exploits or entertainment" (p. 3), finding that perpetrators "claim to have been the subject's lover and often express hope to gain some form of social approval and justification for getting revenge" for cheating, promiscuity, lying, and "having done wrong."

Revenge porn is instrumental aggression. It is goal directed and purposeful, and requires planning and forethought. There have been few studies of those who admit to posting revenge porn. The trigger for revenge porn is, typically, a woman's rejection of her partner through a breakup or infidelity, and the partner's desire to punish and retaliate. Perpetrators are aware they are outsourcing their hate: that others will pick up on the images and perpetuate them further, causing more damage. Some clues as to perpetrators' motivations and traits may be derived from literature on physical and emotional aggression in intimate relationships generally speaking, including aggression manifested via the internet.

Pina, Holland, and James theorized that perpetrators of revenge porn have distinct personality profiles (2017). In a sample of men and women, 28.6% expressed the likelihood of committing revenge porn. Of these, the majority endorsed revenge porn enjoyment (87%) and approved of revenge porn (99%). Proclivity to post revenge porn was correlated with the so-called "dark triad" of personality traits.

The dark triad refers to three overlapping personality traits: Machiavellianism, narcissism, and psychopathy. Dark triad traits are associated with infidelity, susceptibility to a partner's infidelity, and the desire for "romantic revenge" in a sample of women (Brewer et al., 2015). These traits along with ambivalent sexism correlated with a tendency to perpetuate revenge porn. Psychopathy alone had independent predictive significance. Narcissism independently predicted revenge porn enjoyment. Some, however, evidence a fourth trait—sadism ("everyday sadism"), described in more detail below, defined as the "dark tetrad." Smoker and March (2017) found an association with "dark tetrad" personality traits and cyberstalking of intimate partners.

Do those who victimize partners via the internet also aggress against them "in real life"? The answer appears to be yes. Cyber victimization in intimate relationships is significantly associated with real-world violence and aggression. "Cyber aggression is the most commonly experienced type of intimate partner violence . . . followed by in-person psychological, physical, and sexual violence victimization" (Marganski & Melander, 2018, 17). Their measure of cyber aggression included items reflective of nonconsensual porn, for example, "Has your partner sent others a private, intimate picture, or video that you shared with him or her without your permission?" Of those who reported in-person intimate partner aggression, most (94.8%) also reported intimate partner cyber aggression.

Similarly, Sargent and colleagues (2016) found that cyber victimization and intimate partner violence (emotional abuse and threatening behavior) were significantly related. Hostile sexism (discussed in more detail below) is associated with men cyberbullying their girlfriends (Martinez-Pecino & Duran, 2016). Cyber aggression has predictive power to in person victimization.

A prospective study found that technology-based sexual coercion (including sharing a sexually suggestive message or picture with a third party) can be predicted by earlier reports of higher levels of rape-supportive beliefs, peer approval of forced sex, number of sexual partners, and exposure to pornography (Thompson & Morrison, 2013). Similarly, nonconsensual sharing of sexts has been weakly, but significantly, related to dating violence (Morelli et al., 2016).

Thus, there appears to be a spectrum of aggressive behaviors against a partner: cyber aggression (including sharing private photos with others), cyberbullying, and intimate partner violence ranging from emotional abuse to threatening behavior. If we extrapolate to revenge porn perpetrators, it seems likely that they, too, are more likely to commit "in real life" violence against their partners (in addition to, or prior to, revenge porn).

Research suggests that common traits of those who commit sexual assault include: endorsement of traditional gender roles, hostility toward women, endorsement of rape myths, and hypermasculinity (Greathouse et al., 2015). They may have distinct attachment styles compared to nonaggressive men, and have lower empathy toward sexual assault victims (17).

These personality traits also characterize those who stalk ex-partners. Stalking is "a set of unwanted, intrusive behaviors, repeatedly directed at a specific individual, that induces fear or distress in the victim" (Spitzberg & Cupach, 2014). Cyberstalkers don't appear to be a different breed than "IRL" (in real life) stalkers: cyberstalking is "simply one more invasive technique available to the stalker" (Sheridan & Grant, 2007, 636). "The Internet has not enabled a new majority stalker type . . . ex-partner stalkers remain the largest group of stalking offenders" (637).

Both stalkers and revenge porn perpetrators remain obsessed with their ex-partner. Both have difficulty moving on. When stalkers are ex-partners, they "are more likely than non-intimate stalkers to behave aggressively, be more persistent and intrusive, engage in a greater diversity of stalking behaviors, and threaten and assault their victims and third parties" (Smoker & March, 2017, 390).

Ex-partner stalkers have been described as evidencing "persistent pursuit" or "obsessive relational intrusion," which can be triggered by rejection by a former partner, unreciprocated desires, and, in intact relationships, a desire to control (Davis, Swan, & Gambone, 2012). It has been hypothesized that this behavior is more likely in individuals with "anxious attachment," that is, an attachment style due to very early childhood experiences that predict concerns in adulthood about abandonment, jealousy, and a controlling style (Davis et al., 2012).

Patton, Nobles, and Fox (2010) found that stalkers/unwanted pursuers scored significantly higher on a scale of insecure–anxious attachment. Tassy and Winstead (2014) and Dutton and Winstead (2006) reported similar findings. Anxious attachment and distress at breakup predicted both pursuit and aggression (Dutton & Winstead, 2006). Need for control and anger/jealousy have also predicted unwanted pursuit behavior (Davis & Frieze, 2000). Men and women both engage in unwanted and persistent pursuit; women, however, are more likely to report fear of their pursuers.

Borderline personality disorder features (a pattern of inadequate interpersonal attachment, limited ability to form and maintain appropriate relationships, emotional lability and instability) are also implicated in stalking (Lewis et al., 2001). Lewis et al. (2001) found that stalking perpetrators were more likely to report borderline personality disorder features relative to a nonstalking group (43% versus 11%). Spitzberg and Cupach (2014) propose a cascade of relationship failure, rumination that intensifies, emotional flooding including jealousy, anger, and shame; all of which bolster relational pursuit and, ultimately, dysregulated behavior (Selby & Joiner, 2009) that may include interpersonal violence and aggression. This model of emotional cascade and poor distress tolerance may very well apply to those who use revenge porn to satisfy their desire to aggress against their former partner. The association between borderline personality traits and obsessive relational intrusion is mediated by distress tolerance (Reilly & Hines, 2017).

Other traits and beliefs characteristic of hostility and aggression toward partners include narcissism, hostile sexism, and vulnerability to sex role threat. Narcissism in men is associated with a greater likelihood of misperceiving women's interest in them; when interest is not reciprocated, men may believe the women are simply being disingenuous and persist, and may meet disinterest with hostility (Wegner & Abbey, 2016). Jones and Paulhus (2010) found that narcissists aggress in response to ego threat provocation, in essence, a personal insult (or, in this case, perceived or real rejection by a woman). In contrast, they found that psychopaths were more likely to aggress in response to physical provocation. Being left by your partner can be an ego threat provocation—narcissists will react aggressively.

Hostile sexism is associated with revenge porn, aggression in intimate relationships, and "rape propensity." Glick and Fiske (1997) described a theory of ambivalent sexism, consisting of hostile sexism ("dominative paternalism, derogatory beliefs, and heterosexual hostility"), and benevolent sexism ("subjectively positive—for the sexist—attitudes toward women in traditional roles: protective paternalism, idealization of women, and desire for intimate relations"). Hostile sexism has been associated with aggression in intimate relationships and with nonconsensual porn.

Hostile sexism has been related to "rape propensity" and an increased likelihood of believing that a woman's resistance to rape is "token" only (Masser et al., 2006). Morelli and colleagues (2016) found that men high in hostile sexism were more likely to share sexts from their partner (who did not consent). Benevolent sexism weakened this relationship.

A partner's perceived commitment may be a mediating variable (Cross et al., 2017). Men higher in hostile sexism were generally more aggressive with their female partner in daily life relative to men lower in hostile sexism, and especially so when the partner was seen as lower in relationship commitment. This is consistent with the notion that men endorsing hostile sexism are more likely to react aggressively if loss is threatened.

Herrera and others (2012) created an experimental computer-based paradigm in which men were assigned a dominant decision-making role and women a subordinate role. Women who did not accept the man's decisions were especially negatively evaluated by men who were high on hostile sexism. These women were viewed as more provoking. Paradoxically, those who complied with the men's decision were described as having more instrumental traits such as "strong" and "bold."

Men who are vulnerable to feelings of sex role threat are more likely to aggress in response to fears of dependence and abandonment. In a study of spouses who killed their partners, Barnard and colleagues (1982) proposed a theory about the motivations of men killing their wives. one that sounds quite familiar to the Cross study cited above: "Men endorsing hostile sexism are theorized to be more fearful of dependence, exploitation and abandonment in a relationship, and are therefore more likely to react aggressively if loss is threatened."

Between 1970 and 1980, researchers studied motivations of male and female offenders who had killed their spouses. Male defendants "identified their relationship problems with their victims as infidelity and desertion" (cited by Taylor, 1985). These men were unable "to accept what they perceived to be a rejection of them or of their role of dominance over their eventual victims" (Barnard et al., 1982, 278). Barnard and colleagues hypothesized that "sex role threat homicides" occurred when men who were not physically threatened killed spouses after real or threatened abandonment. The "key is perpetrators' unspoken sense of dependency on the victim" and real or perceived rejection of them and their dominant role.

Perpetrators of revenge porn don't actually murder their exes, but certainly try to destroy them (their reputations, livelihoods, etc.) in other ways.

The Confluence Model of Sexual Aggression (Malamuth & Hald, 2017), a widely validated model, suggests that sexual aggressors have two pathways to sexual aggression—the hostile-masculinity pathway and the impersonal sex pathway. Hostile masculinity refers to "an insecure, defensive, hypersensitive, and hostile-distrustful orientation, particularly toward women" and gratification obtained by controlling or dominating behaviors toward women. Impersonal sex refers to "noncommittal, game-playing orientation in sexual relations" (Malamuth et al., 1995).

The developmental model theorizes that men who were abused as children and had delinquent peers are susceptible to high levels of hostile masculinity and impersonal sex. Attachment insecurity is related to hostile masculinity (Nguyen & Parkhill, 2014).

As cyber aggression appears to be qualitatively similar to cyber sexual aggression, the application of this model to the study of revenge porn perpetrators would be a fruitful avenue of study.

SUMMARY: Revenge Porn Perpetrators

Few studies exist about perpetrators of revenge porn. Existing research suggests the perpetrators of revenge porn may have previously manifested verbal and physical aggression against their partner. In other words, research studying aggressive partners, especially those triggered by jealousy and/or perceived abandonment, would seem to apply to perpetrators of revenge porn.

A matrix of traits appears to be shared by men who are physically and emotionally aggressive against intimate partners ("in real life" and online) and who are more likely to stalk former partners: these include hostile sexism, sex role threat, difficulty with emotional dependence on their partners, and traits referred to as the "dark triad" or "dark tetrad." Those who perpetrate revenge porn in response to relationships ending and/or perceived or real infidelity may share those traits.

Based on models developed to understand perpetrators of interpersonal violence, stalking, and verbal aggression, a picture emerges of someone who may hold traditional, sexist views of women, is high on hostile sexism, has a desire to be dominant, is uncomfortable with emotional dependence on a woman, and responds to perceived infidelity in particular with outrage.

Such a person may also have elements of attachment issues, particularly anxious attachment.

No Prior Personal Relationship Existed between Perpetrators and Victims: "Wolf Packs"

The prior section focused on those lone wolf perpetrators of revenge porn, who post nonconsensual pornography out of a desire to hurt, punish, and humiliate an ex-partner.

If perps of revenge porn are lone wolves out for revenge against an intimate partner, other perpetrators of internet harassment are like wolf packs, who choose victims seemingly at random, or notice others' cyberattacks and join in for the fun. Women who come to public attention for any reason—for taking an unpopular position or, indeed, any position at all—can be harassed online and doxed with quite frightening results. This type of harassment can be fairly disorganized in nature (i.e., commentators are typically not coordinating with each other in any significant fashion).

Disorganized Wolf Packs: No Personal Relationship Existed between Perpetrator(s) and Victim

"It doesn't much matter what line of argument you take as a woman. If you venture into traditional male territory, the abuse comes anyway. It's not what you say that prompts it—it's the fact that you are saying it" (Mead, 2014).

> *"I want to start very near the beginning of the tradition of Western literature, and its first recorded example of a man telling a woman to 'shut up' . . . At the start of the* Odyssey*. . . . Penelope coming down from her private quarters into the great hall, to find a bard performing to throngs of her suitors; he's singing about the difficulties the Greek heroes are having in reaching home. She isn't amused, and in front of everyone she asks him to choose another, happier number. At which point young Telemachus intervenes: 'Mother,' he says, 'go back up into your quarters, and take up your own work, the loom and the distaff . . . speech will be the business of men, all men, and of me most of all; for mine is the power in this household.' And off she goes, back upstairs."* (Beard, 2014)

The common modern scenario is this: a woman has opinions and expresses them on the internet or television. She starts to receive aggressive messages to, in essence, shut up. Messages contain a "predictable menu of rape, bombing, murder, and so forth" (Mary Beard, quoted by Mead, 2014). "If I'd been trying to keep a tally I would have lost count by now of the number of abusive comments I've received since I first started writing online . . . by abusive I don't mean comments that disagree . . . I'm talking about personal, usually sexualized abuse" (Lewis, 2011).

Recall Jane Fae—the transgender writer, journalist, and blogger—who noted that before she transitioned, "I won't say I never got strongly dissenting views . . . but there was usually, mostly, some appeal to the rational argument underlying," and that after transitioning, "even the nice comments seem, at some level, to be more personal . . . the implication that I only say what I say because I am a woman . . . an ugly woman" (Lewis, 2011).

Typically, the abuse has nothing to do with any substantive issue. Three examples are presented below, and illustrate disorganized wolf pack behavior that nevertheless causes significant fear and damage. In each case, the targets of abuse either took no particularly controversial stand or, in one case, took a stand on a fairly niche issue: Who should go on a 10 pound note? The message of the abuse seems, primarily, to "shut up."

Little research exists on these perpetrators. The anecdotes below suggest these perpetrators seem unthinkingly reactive, uninsightful, and, simply, sad, depressed, and feeling powerless. On occasion, when the victims respond with kindness, some perpetrators apologize. Are the perpetrators described below typical? We do know a little about the nature and pattern of the types of tweets received in one of the incidents described below based on research conducted by McGlashan and Hardaker (2015), and Hardaker (2010).

Dr. Mary Beard

She should be able to analyze Augustus's dictums,
or early A.D. epithets
Without having to scroll through
death, bomb and rape threats
Rhyme sent to Dr. Beard by a fan

In 2010, Mary Beard, Cambridge classicist, appeared on British television in a series of documentaries about Pompeii (*Pompeii: Life and Death in a Roman Town*, 2010) and, in 2012, Rome (*Meet the Romans with Mary Beard*). The documentaries became very popular, as did Dr. Beard, who has a very visible social media presence. Some (male) television critics made very degrading comments about her physical appearance. Simultaneously, Dr. Beard's social media accounts received threatening tweets and emails. These did not debate the finer points of Roman life as presented by Dr. Beard. Rather, they were sexualized, violent, degrading: "You filthy old slut. I bet your vagina is disgusting." Bomb threats were also made.

Beard's reaction to comments and threats was to reach out to some trolls. "The perpetrators are drunk, a bit disinhibited, sad, angry or whatever. When you call them out on it, they often feel dreadful and want to apologize. That's fine by me. We all say and do stupid things . . ." (Dean, 2014). She helped one troll with health-care bureaucracy: "It took two minutes on Google to discover the reciprocal health-care agreement, so I sent it to him," she says. "Now when I have a bit of Internet trouble, I get an e-mail from him saying, 'Mary, are you all right? I was worried about you'" (Mead, 2014).

Caroline Criado-Perez

In 2013, the Bank of England announced it was dropping Elizabeth Fry, the only woman on British currency, from the 5-pound note. She was to be replaced by Winston Churchill. Caroline Criado-Perez lobbied the Bank of England to put another woman on a banknote. Labour Party member Stella Creasy supported her efforts. In July, 2013 the Bank of England announced that Jane Austen would replace Darwin on the 10-pound note.

As Criado-Perez expected, there were some tensions and conflict with those who'd prefer, for example, a Bronte sister to Jane Austen. There were attacks on Austen's looks, on the quote selected for the note, and so on. Criado-Perez did not expect the personal threats she and Creasy received. In the 12-hour period after the Bank of England decision was announced, Criado-Perez received around 50 abusive tweets per hour (Philipson, 2013). Threats described pistol whipping, rape, bombing, and murder. By 2014, some arrests had been made. One perpetrator, Isabella Sorley, sent some of the tweets "off my face on drink." The other, John Nimmo, was described as a "somewhat sad individual" with "some level of learning difficulties" who "is a social recluse . . . he rarely leaves the house" (BBC, 2014). Neither could explain their behavior and didn't appear to care much if at all about the actual issue: a woman on a banknote. In the words of a Slate journalist, those who were ultimately arrested for these threats "can't really have been staunch Charles Darwin defenders or violent Jane Austen haters; they must have been responding more to the idea of a woman saying anything" (Roiphe, 2013).

The extraordinary number of threats was studied by McGlashan and Hardaker (2015) and will be discussed further below.

Lindy West

In 2013, Lindy West, a writer and blogger, started receiving tweets and emails "from" her recently deceased father, with whom she'd been very close. "The person who made the PawWestDonezo account clearly put some time into it. They'd researched my father and my family. They'd found out his name." The PawWestDonezo Twitter bio read "Embarrassed father of an idiot," location "Dirt hole in Seattle" (West, February 2, 2015). "For weeks . . . I was eating 30 rape threats for breakfast at that point" (Lindy West, 2016).

West wrote about the experience for the online site Jezebel. Surprisingly, the perpetrator responded.

> He told me that, at the time, he was about 75 pounds heavier than he wanted to be. He hated his body. He was miserable. And reading about fat people—particularly fat women—accepting and loving themselves as they were infuriated him for reasons he couldn't articulate at the time.
>
> He apologized and tried to explain his behavior: "Hey, Lindy, I don't know why or even when I started trolling you. . . . I think my anger towards you stems from your happiness with your own being. . . . When you talked about being proud of who you are and where you are and where are you're going, that kind of stoked that anger that I had. . . . I'm like, who is this bitch who thinks she knows everything?"

Lindy West's tormentor's rage at fat women who loved themselves as they were (and who, presumably, are having sex) is echoed by the anger at "fat women" expressed in "Incel" (involuntary celibacy) online forums. As observed by Futrelle (2017),

> the guys who hang out on Involuntary Celibacy forums online. . . . spend so much of their time, er, consciousness-raising about the critical issue of *fat women who have sex*. On the Incels subreddit, the regulars return to the topic again and again in innumerable threads decrying the fat girl menace. Their central complaint: *Fat women are able to have sex with pretty much any man they want, while similarly fat men lead lives of not-so-quiet celibacy.* While most incels agree . . . that these fat women are "disgusting"—and one even says that he doesn't "consider them humans"—incels are also furious that these "disgusting," inhuman, sex-having women don't want to have sex with *them*.

The victims noted above were in the public eye; victims of revenge porn may, similarly, be targeted by a disorganized cybermob (commenting and otherwise trolling) despite the absence of any relationship between victim and perpetrator. Researchers are starting to examine users' commenting behavior on revenge porn sites. Themes of shame, disgust, and victim blaming emerge. Users are no longer passive observers, rather, they too become perpetrators of abuse against someone they don't know. Why do they do this?

In a series of fascinating studies, Williams, Gruenfeld, and Guillory (2017) examined individuals with a chronic subjective sense of powerlessness who were given acute (experimentally manipulated) power. Men in that situation showed increased hostility toward a rejecting woman; this did not occur for men who felt chronically higher power. In fact, men in chronic low power were more hostile to an unavailable female work partner (i.e., not overtly rejecting, simply uninterested in dating) when given acute power. In total, the five studies conducted by Williams and her colleagues showed that experimentally manipulated power increased hostility toward women, sexual harassment proclivities, and harassment behavior only among participants with chronically low levels of power.

The authors hypothesize that a chronic sense of being in a low hierarchical position is "degrading, even humiliating. It centers one's attention on the self and on all that one has been unfairly denied . . . acute power . . . may yield sexual harassment and hostility when the object of one's desire is another person" (219). Perhaps the opportunity to comment on and ridicule a woman's body creates the acute power situation described by Williams et al.

Langlois and Slane (2017), in an analysis of comments on a revenge porn site, found comments reflected either "negative disgust" or framing the victim as a porn object. The most frequently used words were "bitch" and "slut"; the most common type of shaming was issuing judgment on specific body parts. "The most common coupling of comments consisted of a physical judgment accompanied by depictions of one-directional sexual or degrading acts" the commenter wished to do to the victim. Victims were "framed as disgusting active female sexual agents, accused of being dirty, diseased, indiscriminate in choosing their sexual partners" (6). Interestingly, comments to the original (usually) male poster were also negative, demeaning, involving sexual shaming and accusations of lying.

Jane (2014) points out the gender stereotypes employed in these comments when directed at women, including "charges of unintelligence, hysteria, and ugliness" (533) plus threats/fantasies of violent sex acts framed as "correctives" to teach a lesson and/or punish. Women are simultaneously sluts who invite attack and unattractive man-haters.

Burns (2015) studied comments on revenge porn sites through the lens of "choice." Three themes emerged around women's choices: 1) You chose to be photographed, 2) The consequences of that choice are your fault and are forever, and 3) It's the viewers' legitimate option/choice to express their views, use the photos to create problems for you, and so on. (And yet, as pointed out by Carrie Goldberg, an attorney representing victims of nonconsensual porn, "Even if you did take a naked picture and send it to somebody, that's not necessarily reckless behavior. That's time-honored behavior! G.I.s going off to war used to have pics of their wife or girlfriend in a pinup pose. It's often part of intimate communication" (Talbot, 2016)).

Who and Why: Hypotheses about Disorganized Trolls

Anecdotally, the perpetrators of the abuse described above do seem rather sad individuals who externalize and displace their misery and have little or no insight into their behavior. When exposed, they are unable to explain why they did it, and they are sometimes apologetic. Their behavior seems entirely reactive, unreflective, and somewhat random in the choice of victim. Yet significant effort is put into the trolling. For example, several of the perpetrators trolling Criado-Perez and West created multiple email and Twitter accounts in order to troll with more impact, and spent a fair amount of time on the project. Research does illuminate psychological, situational, and environmental factors influencing this behavior.

Social Skills. Social skills, internet skills, and verbal aggression interact in interesting ways when it comes to trolling. Savage and colleagues (2017) found that verbal aggression was (unsurprisingly) associated with cyberbullying. However, individuals with high verbal aggression and high internet self-efficacy trolled less as their social skills grew. Kokkinos, Antoniadou, & Markos (2014) found cyberbullies were more callous, impulsive/irresponsible, depressed, high on internet use, and lacking in social skills. These researchers distinguish between "cognitive empathy" and "affective empathy." Cognitive empathy is the ability to identify another person's emotional states. Affective empathy is the ability to emotionally understand and communicate with another person about their emotional state. Kokkinos and colleagues suggest that high cognitive and low affective empathy may characterize antisocial individuals who are impulsive, uninhibited, and "psychopathic-like" (205).

"Everyday Sadism." "Everyday sadism" or subclinical sadism refers to the enjoyment of cruelty and the seeking of opportunities to exercise harm, which is experienced as pleasurable and exciting (Buckels, Jones, & Paulhus, 2013). It predicts bug killing and a willingness to work for opportunities to hurt innocent people. It is associated with violent video game play (Greitmayer, 2015), and higher trait psychopathy and sadism predicted trolling (Sest & March, 2017). Cyber trolls who were high on trait psychopathy who had "cognitive empathy" (ability to predict and recognize victims' emotional distress) were particularly manipulative in their trolling (Sest & March, 2017). Buckels, Trapnell, and Paulhus (2014) found that everyday sadism was the most robustly associated with trolling. Burns (2015) has described sadism in this context as pleasure in attributing guilt and asserting control; that women should be punished and deserve to be outed and punished.

Tweets as a Means to Control Women's Online Discourse. Hardaker and McGlashan (2016) studied 76,275 tweets (912,901 words) directed at and about Criado-Perez collected over three months in order to analyze the language in this social network. Of particular interest were the extreme misogynistic abuse and rape threats, which spread to other women.

"Our approach combines quantitative approaches from the fields of corpus linguistics to detect emerging discourse communities, and then qualitative approaches . . . to analyze how these communities construct their identities" (80) particularly with regard to rape threats. Hardaker and McGlashan interpreted the content of the tweets as a threat and "arguably as a misogynistic weapon utilized to control the discourse of women online. Women were predominantly the target of these threats (both literally and grammatically)." McGlashan and Hardaker (2015) distinguished between "low-risk" tweeters (unpleasant, insulting, misogynistic but not threatening or illegal) and "high-risk" tweeters ("intent to menace," sexual aggression and harassment that violated UK law). "Both the low- and high-risk abusers coalesced not only around the discussion of rape, but also of misogyny, racism, and homophobia." Most frequently used terms by both low- and high-risk tweeters reflect themes of rape (rape, raping), misogyny (cunt, bitch), homophobia (faggot, gay), racism/anti-Semitism (nigger, Jew), and genitalia/anatomy (pussy, penis, fucking, ass, cock).

Despite the rapid and fluid nature of Twitter, McGlashan and Hardaker were able to identify communities or "groups." They also noticed that in the Criado-Perez tweet storm, "risky" users "frequently associated with each other in directed networks" (285); they not only "mention each other (ergo, talking to one another and forming directed networks) but also collectively engage in the use of abusive language." Furthermore, low-risk users could conceivably easily become high-risk users, given the overlap in language used (again typically with discussion of rape, homophobia, and racism).

In other words, even in more or less disorganized wolf packs, patterns and subgroups did begin to emerge and even to coordinate. The nature of this type of attacker is most succinctly described by McGlynn and Rackley (2016) as networks of anonymous men who mobilize to stalk and threaten women to "eliminating and muting women's voices from the internet" (Citron, 2009–2010, 373, 389).

Loneliness. Research conducted in 1985 suggests that lonely men react strongly to rejection, behave aggressively toward a confederate who rejected them, and verbally express hostile attitudes especially toward women (Check, Perlman, & Malamuth, 1985). The stereotypical troll in his mother's basement is, surely, lonely. One wonders if this study were replicated today with a sample of internet trolls would the findings be the same. Furthermore, since the study was conducted, it is likely that lack of social skills is even more problematic than in 1985, when a life conducted predominantly online was not yet possible.

Situational factors influence trolling. Cheng, Bernstein, and colleagues (2017) and Cheng, Danescu-Niculescu-Mizil, and others (2017) similarly found a situational impact on trolling behavior. They conducted an online experiment as well as did large-scale data analysis of over 16 million posts on CNN.com. Trolling behavior was influenced by individual mood (negative mood increasing the probability of trolling in an online news comment section) as well as prior troll posts written by others. Both factors combined doubled baseline rates of trolling behavior. Furthermore, in a discussion, initial posts that were flagged as inappropriate set a precedent for further trolling, and that trolling behavior spreads user to user. Contexts of posts do a good job predicting subsequent individual trolling behavior.

In summary—despite the anecdotes that suggest some trolls readily respond with apologies when caught—existing literature paints a more complex picture. Predictors of trolling behavior include trait psychopathy and sadism, verbal aggression, high internet use, and poorer social skills. Behavior is shaped by other trolls, that is, individual negative mood combined with prior trolling comments by others increases trolling behavior. Disorganized trolling mobs begin to develop some connections with each other (see above). McGlashan and Hardaker (2015) found that "risky" users "frequently associated with each other in directed networks" (285); they not only "mention each other (ergo, talking to one another and forming directed networks) but also collectively engage in the use of abusive language" in the Criado-Perez instance.

No Prior Personal Relationship between Perpetrator(s) and Victims: Attacks Organized and Coordinated

Organized wolf pack attacks are, in essence, cyber mobs or crowdsourced harassment. Threats are frightening and cross over into the "real world." Not surprisingly, harassment that has its origins in the online world of gaming can be quite organized and particularly threatening, as the perpetrators are by definition both comfortable and skilled in the online world.

Gamergate

The person who initiated so-called "Gamergate" was motivated to punish and humiliate an ex-girlfriend. In 2014, Eron Gjoni, a software developer, wrote a highly detailed post about a failed seven-month relationship with Zoe Quinn, a video game developer. He explained, "I dated Zoe Quinn. I thought she was the most amazing, kind hearted person in the world. Turns out she was bullshitting pretty much everything I fell in love with her for, and is actually an unbelievable jerk. . . ." He supported his perspective with evidence: screen caps of texts, photographs, chatlogs, etc. "Here's some stuff she did/does in no particular order or tense [which you can verify using the chatlog images in the footer of Act 1]:" (Gjoni, 2014). He also accused her of getting better reviews by sleeping with a journalist. The ethics in journalism angle led actor Adam Baldwin to coin the term "Gamergate." Julian Assange tweeted about it.

Gjoni explained his intent clearly: "I wrote thezoepost with one main goal and a few side goals. . . . That main goal was to warn people about Zoe Quinn." (This echoes Othello: "Yet she must die, else she'll betray more men.") "After seven months of dating her I learned that she is not the paragon of virtue she pretends to be (I did not even know people could be that self-serving or convincing or cruel before I met her)." When he released his post on August 16, 2014, "he figured the odds of Quinn's being harassed were 80 percent. . . . He ensured it would be seen by posting on two video game sites. From there it was picked up by 4chan. He also published it on a WordPress blog."

Three days after it was published, Quinn was doxed. She learned about the post when the harassment started and blew up. Quinn ultimately was forced to move out and go into hiding. "How could I go back to my home? . . . I have people online bragging about putting dead animals through my mailbox. I've got some asshole in California who I've never talked to hiring a private investigator to stalk me. What am I going to do—go home and just wait until someone makes good on their threats? . . ." (Stuart, 2014, December 3).

Gamergate-related harassment spread to encompass anger against "SJWs" (social justice warriors) who had opinions about the lack of diversity in video games, and spread to women who designed games and/or wrote about gaming. Game developer Brianna Wu retweeted a meme about Gamergate that she found funny on October 9, 2014. She already had a file on her desktop labeled "Just another day at the office" where she saved all the threats and abuse she received before the Gamergate controversy.

By October 10, she, too, was doxed and targeted. "I was literally watching the chat room as the site posted my address and the conversation moved to places that threatened my personal safety." The threats were frightening. One tweet said, "I've got a K-bar and I'm coming to your house so I can shove it up your ugly feminist cunt" (a K-bar is a military combat knife) (Stuart, 2014, October 17).

"I had someone last week that made a video talking about how they're going to murder me," Wu added. "This is not just, 'I'm going to kill Brianna,' this is like a multi-minute rant about why they want to murder me, how. Their face is visible in the video. I have their name and testimony from the people who know them and how unbalanced they are. This person lives 15 minutes from my house" (Merlan, 2015).

Anita Sarkeesian ran a Kickstarter for a video series analyzing gender roles in video games in May 2012. Within months, a "Beat up Anita Sarkeesian" video game was created, in which players could punch her, and see realistic-looking bruises and blood develop on her body. (A writer "outed" the game creator—she, too, was harassed [Lyonnais, 2012; Cheong, 2012].)

The harassment has continued over a period of years. "Ever since I began my Tropes vs Women in Video Games project, two and a half years ago, I've been harassed on a daily basis by irate gamers angry at my critiques of sexism in video games. It can sometimes be difficult to effectively communicate just how bad this sustained intimidation campaign really is. So I've taken the liberty of collecting a week's worth of hateful messages sent to me on Twitter. The following tweets were directed at my @femfreq account between 1/20/15 and 1/26/15." http://internet.gawker.com/criticize-gamergate-as-a-woman-and-your-twitter-mentio-1682121995. The tweets are specific in their violence (the usual themes of explicit rape threats, death wishes, etc.) and can be reviewed here: https://femfreq.tumblr.com/post/109319269825/one-week-of-harassment-on-twitter.

Sarkeesian was scheduled to speak in October 2014 at Utah State University. The school received emailed terrorist threats referencing the 1989 killings at Ecole Polytechnique in Montreal. (Marc Lépine, the Montreal shooter, targeted women only in an engineering class, yelling "I hate feminists" (Csanady, 2014). "I have at my disposal a semi-automatic rifle, multiple pistols, and a collection of pipe bombs," the letter said. "This will be the deadliest school shooting in American history and I'm giving you a chance to stop it." . . . "You have 24 hours to cancel Sarkeesian's talk. . . . Anita Sarkeesian is everything wrong with the feminist woman, and she is going to die screaming like the craven little whore that she is if you let her come to USU. I will write my manifesto in her spilled blood, and you will all bear witness to what feminist lies and poison have done to the men of America" (Hern, 2014). The talk was cancelled as campus police refused to check for weapons—Utah is an open carry state.

In a recent interview, Sarkeesian was asked "'It's getting better, right?' It isn't, and she tells them so" (Duca, 2018). Two panels to discuss harassment in gaming were planned for the 2016 "SXSW Interactive" conference (SXSW is a music festival and conference); SXSW received so many threats of violence regarding the panels that they cancelled them (Kulwin, 2015; Bowles, 2016). After public objections, organizers planned a full-day program on the topic of online harassment, and hired extra security for the purpose (Bowles, 2016).

Research

> *For the world of programmers is not going to change on its own. Many who enter are going to find themselves in the company of sweetly boyish men who bristle at the very idea of anyone unlike them invading their territory, climbing into their treehouse, men who want to humiliate the newcomers, find every error in their work, trap them in a shooting gallery without apologies . . . and then there are the programmers I've met . . . with sparkling, playful minds, for whom I developed an abiding affection.* (Ullman, 2017, 255)

Victims of Gamergate and related harassment believe the cause is simply that women are invading the men's playground. Sarkeesian (2012) uses the gamer analogy of a massively multiplayer online game (MMO) to capture the phenomenon: "In their minds they concocted this grand fiction in which they're the heroic players of a massively multiplayer online game working together to take down an enemy . . . the entire internet (is turned into) a battlefield . . . they also have a home base where they coordinate their raids and work together and communicate . . . on largely unmoderated, largely anonymous message boards and forums. So we have a general structure of a social game. We have players, we have the villain. We have a battlefield. We have this informal rewards system" (of praise and approval of peers for especially brazen and abusive attacks).

Most of the scholarly work to understand perpetrators in this area remains conjectural and theoretical.

Competence at Video Games and Hostility to Women. In a fascinating study of gaming behavior, Kasumovic and Kuznekoff (2015) examined skill at a first-person shooting game, gender, and hostility toward women. "Lower-skilled men were more hostile towards a female-voiced teammate, especially when performing poorly." These same men behaved submissively to a male-voiced player in the same scenario. Higher-skilled men were (relatively) more positive to female players. "The female-voiced manipulations experienced a greater frequency of negative comments, but female-directed negativity decreased as focal-play performance improved" (10) and negativity increased as focal play performance was poorer. In other words, men who were more skilled—that is higher status—were less likely to attack female players.

The authors use an evolutionary psychology perspective, suggesting that when women enter a male-dominated field, low-status males "have the most to lose due to a hierarchical reconfiguration," and female competitors are a threat. This, of course, sounds similar to sex role threat studies previously described linking hostile sexism and anger at women who resist male dominance.

Objectification of Women and Terror Management. Terror management theory (Greenberg et al., 1990) suggests that reminding people of death, activating their fear of death, increases their investment in cultural beliefs and values, and decreases acceptance of "the other" (Greenberg et al., 1990). Goldenberg (2013) linked terror management theory to objectification of women's bodies and disgust at women's physicalness. As previously noted, disgust at the female body is a common theme in comments to posted revenge porn and other images of women. It is interesting to speculate about this theory in light of the fact that video games are often about killing people—clearly a mortality salience situation. Goldenberg cites research that priming mortality increased disgust in response to the body. Landau and colleagues (2006) found that mortality salience decreased men's sexual attraction to a sexualized women (this was not true for women subjects), and that men reminded of corporeal lust after mortality priming "exhibited greater tolerance of aggression toward women" (141).

Creepshots: Perpetrators Select Victims Unknown to Them

I opened the chapter with an anecdote about a creepshot I witnessed on the London Tube. The young man who took the upskirt photo was probably very close in age to the young woman he photographed; both were conventionally physically attractive people. Yet the young man made no attempt to make eye contact or otherwise engage with her as another human being.

I'll be discussing two examples in this section: creepshots on Reddit and the Marines United Scandal.

Creepshots. As described previously, "Creepshots are *CANDID.* If a person is posing for and/or aware that a picture is being taken, then it ceases to be candid and thus is no longer a creepshot. A creepshot captures the natural, raw sexiness of the subject without their vain attempts at putting on a show for the camera. That is the essence of the creepshot, that is what makes a true creepshot worth the effort and that is why this subreddit exists. Use stealth, cunning and deviousness to capture the beauty of your unsuspecting, chosen target."

Violentacrez, "the biggest troll on the web," established/managed subreddits for creepshots, "jailbait" (girls verified to be under 18), and "beating women" (photos of a woman being beaten), and so on. He was "outed" in 2012. In general, defenders of creepshots argue that women lose any right to privacy or permission to be photographed simply by virtue of being in public. Their defense of the behavior ignores or minimizes the fact that victims are very uncomfortable with the behavior.

"What did he (Brutsch) think about those who were on the receiving end of his trolling? It seems he did not think about them at all" (Rosen, 2012). Rosen observed that Brutsch was unable to really explain his behavior. "Brutsch . . . offer(ed) one mild, unilluminating cliché after the other. . . ." In defending his actions: "I got the freedom to talk about my personal life, my personal feelings. People take things too seriously around here." He objected to being "outed," and failed to see the irony in that. Rosen quotes Arendt's essay on Eichmann's war crimes trial:[1] "The only specific characteristic one could detect in his past as well as in his behavior during the trial and the preceding police examination was something entirely negative: It was not stupidity but a curious, quite authentic inability to think."

The Reddit group Creepshots was banned "for violating Reddit rules," but lives on in other forms that "technically" conform to the rules (sort of).

Objectification and Sexual Aggression toward Women. Research suggests that dehumanization of women—specifically, denial of women's human uniqueness—increases scores on men's sexual aggression against women. Creepshots are specifically designed to deny women's humanity (Bevens & Loughnan, 2019).

Marines United. "Marines United" was an invitation-only, military members-only Facebook page with 30,000 members (active & retired Marines, Navy corpsmen, British royal marines). It provided information about a number of topics. In January 2017, a page administrator or user accidentally posted a link to a Google drive with multiple folders of (mostly nude) images of servicewomen. Unlike Creepshots, the women were frequently doxed. Many images had names, ranks, and duty stations listed. Images had been uploaded without the women's consent or knowledge. Many photos were stolen from victims' phones and computers or were photographs/videos taken without the women's knowledge (i.e., while she was showering). Comments were lewd and frequently violent (Brennan, 2017).

Thomas Brennan, a former marine and journalist, and founder of the nonprofit news site War Horse, reported the issue to HQ Marine Corps. Despite actions taken (deleting the google drive), the Facebook page remained active. Photographs were moved elsewhere, and the behavior continued. Brennan and his family started receiving threats, including death threats. Policy changes and legislative action followed and continues.

Various military publications on- and offline have featured stories about this ongoing issue. Comments to articles reveal a split, pro and con. Some view the behavior as beneath Marine tradition and dishonorable ("*This is a dark stain on us all. I served for almost 27yrs in the Army. This disgusts me to no end. I hope those perpetrating this are burned beyond recognition*"). Others are angry at the "snitches" who reported the images and gloat that other sites have replaced the original.

The comments make it evident that many readers don't understand that the women had nothing to do with the photos getting on the net, and may not have even known photos were being taken of them. ("*Stupid is as stupid do. . . . so do not take off your clothes and either allow or take photos and share them.*")

There is a new group of victims, including an unconscious woman who was photographed naked (LaPorta & Laverty, 2017).

Perpetrator Psychology

On a former website, Redditors on the CreepShot subreddit describe themselves as "Immoral, creepy, sinister." "There are a few people who have been upset about the content of CreepShots but it is vital for them to remember this: there is nothing illegal about this subreddit whatsoever. We may be immoral, creepy, sinister (some may even accuse us of being 'disturbed') individuals but there is nothing here that breaks any laws. **When you are in public, you do not have a reasonable expectation of privacy.** We kindly ask women to respect our right to admire your bodies and stop complaining." I have not found any such self-descriptions by organizers of the Marines United.

Scopophilia. Colbeck (2015) links "fetishistic scopophilia" and creepshots. Scopophilia was described by Freud as "pleasure in looking." The essence of the creepshot (or photographs in Marines United) is that the women are not aware they are being photographed; they have no agency in how they are being presented and play no part in the decision to be photographed at all. Colbeck theorizes that creepshots are "actually a method of removing the sexual power of the female and returning her to the passive state dictated to her by the confines of patriarchy" (14). Oliver (2016) goes further in discussing the "valorization" of lack of consent—that the lack of consent is the allure.

Scopophilia has been described as the desire to incorporate the observed and to have an element of sadism (Fenichel, 1937); it has been hypothesized to be linked to fear of object loss early in life (Almansi, 1979).

Common Factors in Lone Wolves/Wolf Packs and Creepshots

Misogyny. Kate Manne's (2018) philosophical analysis of misogyny describes the behavior of all three groups: lone wolf perpetrators of revenge porn, wolf packs, and creepshots. In her analysis, misogyny is not simply hatred of women or simple sexism. Rather, misogyny serves a function: its purpose is punitive in order to shame and silence women who violate social and patriarchal norms. "They put women in their place when they seem to have ideas 'beyond their station'" in ways that are "dynamic, active, and forceful maneuverings" (69).

Thus, women who are publicly visible without the expected "appropriately feminine" appearance (Mary Beard) become a target; Lindy West, unashamed of her weight, becomes a target; Anita Sarkeesian becomes a target for examining or questioning how women are portrayed in video games. A discussion of misogyny also encompasses the idea that women who are "withholding and failing to give . . . being cold, callous, and heartless" (99) "are a blank canvas on which to project a set of grievances borne of unmet felt needs in turn born of a sense of entitlement."

Entitlement and Powerlessness. Kimmel (2013, 2017) draws a through line from some men's anger at perceived loss of themselves as "real men" and anger at those who are to blame for their plight: women in general, feminists in particular, minorities, "SJWs," or "social justice warriors," and others. The common theme is "the feeling of right, or entitlement" (177). It is acceptable to use aggression or violence to defend oneself against the robbery of one's rightful place in society. This implies that men who feel powerless, or whose power is threatened, will be more likely to strike out against those perceived as taking that power.

Low power fosters a desire to acquire products associated with status to compensate for lacking power, as noted by Rucker & Galinsky (2008). "Power is associated with

(a) positive affect, (b) attention to rewards, (c) automatic information processing, and (d) disinhibited behavior. In contrast, reduced power is associated with (a) negative affect; (b) attention to threat, punishment, others' interests, and those features of the self that are relevant to others' goals; (c) controlled information processing; and (d) inhibited social behavior" (Gruenfeld, Keltner, & Anderson, 2003).

This conceptualization echoes that of sex role threat as a trigger to aggression and is consistent with the finding that gamers who were more competent (i.e., higher status) were less likely to strike out against female players (Kasumovic & Kuznekoff, 2015).

Men's Rights Activists (MRA), the "Manosphere," and Incels

MRA groups have organized around themes of men's loss of power, indeed, subordination to women, minorities, and SJWs in general. Subgroups include incels (involuntary celibates) and "Men Going Their Own Way" ("MGTOW"), the latter rejecting any contact or relationship with women.

The Southern Poverty Law Center (n.d.) describes male supremacy as "a hateful ideology advocating for the subjugation of women" who are biologically inferior; necessary for sex and reproduction but not deserving of equality and self-determination. As the shooter Elliot Rodger wrote, "After I picked up the handgun, I brought it back to my room and felt a new sense of power. I was now armed. Who's the alpha male now, bitches? I thought to myself, regarding all of the girls who've looked down on me in the past." This and other forms of male empowerment have been linked to authoritarian political movements. The Southern Poverty Law Center classifies male supremacy movements as a hate ideology, and also notes the overlap between this movement and the alt-right.

Berger (2018) argues that violence that has its origin in the misogyny of the incel movement meets the definition of terrorism: "public violence to advance a political, social or religious cause or ideology." He cites as an example Alek Minassian, a 25-year-old man, who drove a van into pedestrians in Toronto, killing 10. Before doing so, he posted his mission statement: "Private(Recruit) Minassian Infantry 00010, wishing to speak to Sgt. 4 chan please. C23249161. The Incel Rebellion has already begun! We sill overthrow all the Chads and Stacys! All hail the Supreme Gentleman Elliot Rodger."

Berger, an expert on terrorism and extremism, makes the point that this post fits typical extremist belief: an in-group to which the extremist belongs (incels) and an out-group that is targeted (Chads and Stacys, in other words, adults with normal sex lives). Elliot Rodger, is, of course, the "incel extremist ideologue" who raged about "his sexual deprivation and the evils of women" before killing six. Berger makes the very good point that a Facebook post that said "The ISIS Rebellion has already begun! We will overthrow all the kaffir! All hail Abu Bakr al Baghdadi!" before an attack would render the attack unquestionably terrorist in nature.

David Futrelle (2018, May 2), a journalist who has studied the world of the manosphere for almost a decade, ominously comments, "I'm really only surprised there haven't been more Incel mass murders." "On internet forums like Incels.me, incels talk endlessly about violent retribution against the 'Chads' (attractive men) and 'Stacies' (attractive women) they blame for their own misery. . . . They're celebrating Minassian as their newest 'saint.'" Men's rights movements have been called the gateway drug to alt-right radical white supremacy. They share the world view that white men are being victimized by women and minority groups, and deserve to reclaim their power. These groups, by dehumanizing women, increase women's vulnerability to sexualized aggression, including murder as in the case of Elliot Rodger or Alek Minassian. The overlap with alt-right ideology is discussed in more depth below.

Men's rights activists (MRAs) mourn and are angry about the loss of these rights over women. In an article entitled "Women Must Have Their Behavior and Decisions Controlled by Men," Valizadeh (2015) argues that "After a long period in society of women having unlimited personal freedom to pursue life as they wish, they have shown to consistently fail in making the right decisions that prevent their own harm and the harm of others. Systems must now be put in place where a woman's behavior is monitored and her decisions subject to approval of a male relative or guardian who understands what's in her best interests better than she does herself."

Revenge porn in particular has been framed by MRAs as justifiable revenge for being cheated on or dumped. "the belief that you are 'owed' the right to 'revenge' by stalking and humiliating them is rooted in the belief that you own them and their bodies, and what they choose to do with their bodies somehow is a violation of *your* rights" (Marcotte, 2013). In any case, MRAs see revenge porn as yet another example of women escaping consequences of their own bad behavior. From a Reddit thread on The Red Pill (2016): *User iamanarci: So, it is men's fault if revenge porn perpetrated by female. Women's double standards hypocracy at best in victim blaming. Look at the comments by the beta cucks blaming the man.*

User fengpi: But of course. When a man does something illegal, punish the man. When a woman does something illegal, go find a man to punish. Perhaps a random one. Or all men, collectively.

Rinse, lather, repeat.

In an interesting reframing, I found at least one argument (by user JP_Whoregan) that revenge porn was unworthy of a true Alpha:

> *"So the lesson to be learned here, gentlemen, is to* ***ditch your revenge porn fantasies.*** *They are no good for your psyche, and they are no good for the process of unplugging. Here at TRP (The Red Pill), we prefer to deal in truths and realities, not delusions and fantasies.*
>
> *She's gonna get her Beta. Just be glad that now it won't be* ***you.***

> *The* very attempt *of pursuing revenge is a counter-balance against the basis of being an Alpha. An Alpha wouldn't concern himself with her or their past experiences together, so any outright attempt at "rekindling" or readdressing said past would be perceived by her as a "non-Alpha" characteristic.*
> *Not only that, some women will never see you as the Alpha you are."*

Themes of entitlement clearly are expressed by perpetrators of creepshots, and by rage at women's autonomy expressed by members of wolf packs, organized or not.

Facilitating Factors Unique to the Internet

Anonymity on the Net: The Gyges Effect. "Plato wrote the myth of the Ring of Gyges, in which the shepherd, Gyges, discovers a ring that makes him invisible at will. He promptly uses the protection this offers to infiltrate the royal household, seduce the queen, assassinate the king and take the kingdom." Plato goes on: "If now there should be two such rings, and the just man should put on one and the unjust the other, no one could be found, it would seem, of such adamantine temper as to persevere in justice" (Hardaker, 2013).

Moral Disengagement. Page and Pina (2015) reference Bandura's theory of moral disengagement, in which "people are able to convince themselves that moral principles do not apply to them in a particular context . . . creating a version of reality in which detrimental behavior becomes socially and morally acceptable."

Online Disinhibition. Suler (2004) writes extensively about factors unique to online behavior that create disinhibition, including invisibility, dissociative anonymity, and so on.

Diminished Responsibility in Groups. The so-called "bystander effect" suggests that as the number of observers of, for example, bullying, increases, the likelihood that a bystander will help the victim decreases. A recent study found that online "participants tend to help the victims more in incidents with only one or two other bystanders. We also found that, as in the 'offline' realm, bystander effect is not linear: no significant differences were found between incidents with a moderate number (3–10) and a larger number of total bystanders" (Machackova, Dedkova, & Mezulanikova, 2015).

What's Next?

Overlap of Incels with Alt-Right Ideology

Recent research into characteristics of members of the so called "alt-right" suggests two core beliefs: white supremacy and populism. Members of the alt-right share "dark triad" traits, as well as social dominance orientation, authoritarianism, higher aggression, intergroup bias, and dehumanization of others, particularly feminists and minorities. There are overlaps among participants in wolf pack/cyber mobs and alt-right members (Gallagher, 2020). Some Gamergate activists are active in the alt-right. "Weev" (Andrew Auernheimer) is a notorious "provocateur, hacker, and anti-Semite" (Sandoval, 2013) who explicitly said that Gamergate was a major recruiting tool for the alt-right. Weev was jailed in 2013 for releasing email addresses of over 100,000 AT&T customers. He is currently a system administrator for The Daily Stormer. In 2017, he urged readers to find out where the funeral for Heather Heyer was to be held, in order to disrupt it (Heyer was killed at the right-wing rally in Charlottesville in 2017). "What's the location of the fat skank's funeral . . . get on it, e-sleuths."

Weev also doxed "one of the most visible women in tech" with the usual result. His perspective is that "what I do is a comedy act. If you're not laughing, you're probably an authoritarian prick pushing nanny state" (Auernheimer, 2013). Other Gamergate supporters (including Milo Yiannopoulos, Mike Cernovich, and others associated with Breitbart News), and members and supporters of the alt-right (Lees, 2016).

An article entitled "How the Alt-Right's Sexism Lures Men into White Supremacy" (Romano, 2016) suggests that the so-called manosphere (including pickup artist [PUA] culture, "incel" [involuntary celibates] culture, and "men going their own way" [MGTOW]) share a belief that women [and feminists specifically] emasculate and repress men; and that female empowerment disempowers men). The feeling that women are "getting out of hand" is shared by the alt-right. The language of the alt-right shares sexist terms and beliefs with those in the manosphere (cucks, from cuckolds, to describe weak liberals; "soyboys" also refer to liberal, or "beta" men). A post by joe91, quoted in Romano (2016) perfectly captures this merger of the manosphere and the alt-right: "a vote for trump means a rejection of sjws (social justice warriors) and third wave feminism and extreme leftism . . . a vote for Hillary means . . . half the country would be an extremes leftist sjw feminist cuck."

CGI/Deep Fakes

When Hunter Moore started IsAnyoneUp.com, at least one woman was victimized when her head was photoshopped onto an unknown nude body in pornographic poses (Laws, 2013). Computer-generated imagery (CGI) and artificial intelligence (AI) are making it increasingly easy to create extremely realistic "fake media" in which images and voices of people can be used to create forged media (Price, 2017). "There is likely to be significant interest in on-demand pornography produced using these technologies in the years ahead, regardless of whether the subjects of these CGI films give permission."

The Dark Web

As legislation increasingly addresses issues of nonconsensual pornography, it is probable that more sites will simply move to the dark web (or darknet). The dark web is part of the so-called deep web. It is not indexed by or searchable by typical search engines, rather, the dark web is a collection of thousands of websites that use anonymity tools like Tor and I2P to hide their IP address (Greenberg, 2014). It "can be accessed only with specific software, configurations, or authorization, often using non-standard communications protocols and ports. Two typical darknet types are friend-to-friend networks (usually used for file sharing with a peer-to-peer connection) and privacy networks such as Tor" (Darknet, 2021). Tor users believe that those on the Internet should "have private access to an uncensored web . . ." (The Tor Project, Inc., 2021). As such, Tor, it could be argued, is not a promoter of the illegal and immoral activities that occur on the dark web, but it does provide the space for such activities to proliferate.

The Victims

> *"Why do men feel threatened by women?" "I asked a male friend of mine" . . . "I mean", I said, "men are bigger, most of the time, they can run faster, strangle better, and they have on the average a lot more money and power." "They're afraid women will laugh at them," he said. "Undercut their world view." Then I asked some women students in a quickie poetry seminar I was giving. "Why do women feel threatened by men?" "They're afraid of being killed," they said.* (Atwood, 1982, 413)

Gender-based hate and alt-right hate converge in many instances on the net. "Revenge porn victims have reported that their images continued circulating on porn sites years after their original release. . . . The seemingly unstoppable multiplication of these revenge porn images over the years suggests some kind of software-based crawling and reduplication of images available on Google and other search engines and websites, rather than manual, human duplication" (Langlois & Slane, 2017). In general, there is also money to be made by "reputation management" companies to manage search engine results and facilitate content removal.

A more detailed discussion of the impact on victims is beyond the scope of this chapter. Suffice it to say, although women are frequently encouraged to ignore threats made on the net as meaningless and unlikely to be carried out, they would be foolish to do so. In the United States, homicide is one of the leading causes of death for women under 44 years of age. Almost half of these homicides are committed by a current or former male intimate partner (Petrosky et al., 2017).

The Eaton, Jacobs, and Ruvalcaba (2017) study found that victims of nonconsensual porn (NCP) and those threatened with NCP had significantly worse mental health and physiological problems than non-victims. Very much like stalking victims. Sargent and her colleagues found that cyber victimization and intimate partner violence were uniquely contributory to depressive symptoms (2016). Revenge porn in particular resulted in post-traumatic stress disorder, trust issues, anxiety, depression, suicidal thoughts, and other mental health effects in those targeted by revenge porn (Bates, 2017).

> *Women who have been harassed online were more than twice as likely as men to find their most recent experience with online harassment "extremely" or "very" upsetting—38% of harassed women say that their most recent experience falls into this category, compared with 17% of harassed men. On the other hand, 31% of men said that their most recent experience with harassment was "not at all" upsetting, compared with just 12% of women.* (32)

Powerlessness

Objectification. Loughnan et al. (2010) found that objectified women (and men) were denied mind and moral status. "Mind" refers to the degree to which an individual experiences their own mental states (thoughts, intentions, emotions, experiences, etc.). "Moral status" refers to deserving of moral consideration. "Mind" and "moral status" both reflect personhood. Objectified targets were also judged to be less competent and, perhaps, less deserving of moral treatment concerning, for example, pain infliction. Vasquez et al. (2017) found that objectification led to heightened physical aggression toward objectified women in the absence of provocation.

Philosopher Martha Nussbaum (1995) addresses sexual objectification, noting that different types of objectification may or may not be morally objectionable, depending on the nature of the people and relationships involved. However, the one type of objectification that "is always morally problematic" is "the treatment of human beings as tools of the purposes of another." "If it does not take place in a larger context of regard for humanity, it is a central form of the morally objectionable" (289–290).

Authorities don't take seriously this culturally- embedded and chronic social problem. Women are commonly advised to simply stay off the internet in order to avoid gender-aggressive comments. "All the same, you may say . . . why pay it any attention, still less give it publicity?" Several reasons. "First, the misogyny here is truly gob smacking. The whole site is pretty hateful . . . but the whole 'c**t' talk . . . is more than a few steps into sadism. It would be quite enough to put many women off appearing in public, contributing to political debate, especially as all of this comes up on Google" (Baker-Whitelaw, 2013). In addition, as noted previously, although men may fear ridicule, women are wholly justified in their fear of being assaulted or killed by their tormentor. Most individuals who post such hateful, violent, and threatening comments know that they will never act on them, but the target of those comments never knows whether or not they will be victimized. It places the target into a state of near-constant hypervigilance concerning their physical safety.

Another thing to consider are the instances where cyberstalking of former partners and that threats of violence are more likely to occur to women (see United States v. Sayer, 2014; Elonis v. United States, 2014). Again, simply saying to be careful is missing the point. For those who are told to simply stay off-line, this is simply no longer feasible if one has a job, a credit card, or a social life. Much of what previously occurred in real life now transpires online, and to simply tell someone to stay off-line is to ignore how deeply entrenched life online is for most people. To have a "normal" life is to have a life where interactions both in real life and online are safe and free from threats to one's person.

Conclusions

The proposed typology in this chapter is just that, proposed. It offers hypotheses to be tested. Hopefully, there will be further serious work to study and eradicate this emergent problem of a gender-ideology-driven hate. There is a good deal of work to be done by future behavioral scientists. For example, are members of one group (revenge porn perpetrators, disorganized and organized wolf packs, creepshots) different psychologically and motivationally from each other? What characteristics are shared (e.g., hostile attitudes toward women, sadism) and which are not (e.g., attachment style)? Clarifying these issues can help in detection, intervention, and just possible treatment of the perpetrators of these horrifying forms of gendered violence.

Prior to the (current) 5th edition of *The Diagnostic and Statistical Manual of the American Psychiatric Association*, previous editions differentiated between different types of disordered personalities. Cluster A disorders include paranoid, schizoid, and schizotypal personality disorders; "Individuals with these disorders often appear odd or eccentric," may be detached from social relationships; may have "acute discomfort with and reduced capacity for closer relationships." Cluster B disorders include antisocial, borderline, histrionic, and narcissistic personality disorders; individuals with these disorders "often appear dramatic, emotional, or erratic:" may disregard the rights of others; may have very unstable interpersonal relationships; may have an extreme need for admiration and lack of empathy. Cluster C disorders include avoidant, dependent, and obsessive-compulsive personality disorders (not to be confused with obsessive-compulsive disorder); these individuals appear anxious and fearful, and may have difficulty taking responsibility for major areas of their life.

This grouping of personality disorders, while long utilized by mental health professionals, may create a useful basis from which to develop hypotheses. It is also true, however, that this grouping is not clear-cut in reality; personality disorders co-occur and a dimensional model maybe more accurate.

The following hypotheses are proposed:

1. Perpetrators of revenge porn are more similar than not to men who commit domestic violence and stalking. They share hostile sexism, attachment disorders, sensitivity to rejection, poor impulse control, and endorsement of rape myths. If we are to borrow from these DSM classifications, these would seem to be more Cluster B personality types. This encompasses the so-called dark triad or dark tetrad: narcissism, Machiavellism, and sadism.
2. Disorganized packs and, possibly, perpetrators of creepshots are similar to trolls in general, with traits of sadism and indifference to others' pain (doing things for the lulz). Anecdotally, some of those who behave in this manner are "sad, possibly drunk" individuals—perhaps more the Cluster C group. Others share toxic attitudes toward women (Lindy West's tormentor). Still others endorse extremely racist, as well as sexist, beliefs. Perhaps there are two subgroups: one consists of the "sad, possibly drunk" individuals who have a sense of chronic powerlessness, very little insight into their own behavior, and a sense of power from the internet. This trolling behavior is consistent with research suggesting that sense of chronic low power, with an opportunity for acute power, increases bullying in general and sexual harassment/hostility toward women in particular. A second type consists of more sadistically motivated "trolls"—more akin, perhaps, to Cluster A or B personality types.
3. Organized wolf packs. Gamergate is the prototypical example of the organized pack; it has links to the gamer world, to 4 chan, and may overlap with the alt-right and with the manosphere. These seem to verge on hate groups. Women (and other groups) are dehumanized and blamed for the personal failures of the wolf pack members.

   Referring to Gamergate, "we can understand this group as people who have failed at the real world and have checked out of it and into the fantasy worlds of internet forums and video games. These are men without jobs, without prospects, and, by extension (so they declaimed) without girlfriends. Their only recourse, the only place they feel effective, is the safe, perfectly cultivated worlds of the games they enter . . . the distant, abstract concept of women in the flesh makes them feel humiliated and rejected" (Beran, 2017). This description, if accurate, seems to fit the Cluster A personality types: detachment from interpersonal relationships; may seem odd or eccentric.

Multidisciplinary Research Needed: Psychology, Philosophy, Linguistics, Legal

The internet provides an avenue for harassment and aggression. Sometimes it simply provides another avenue for existing problems, such as stalking. Other times it seems as if it has created heretofore unknown avenues of attack—such as those disorganized mobs attacking Mary Beard or Criado-Perez, or the highly organized mobs such as Gamergate. Work must continue to further examine these groups to determine if the proposed typology has merit; and if it does, then appropriate educational programs, interventions, and treatment options must be made available. As was noted earlier in this chapter, many who were confronted with their words replied later that they were upset and were lashing out or that they did not know exactly why they said what they did. These individuals need help learning how to better deal with their emotions, how to develop relationships in real life, and how to work through conflicts without resorting to threats of violence.

Furthermore, as has been shown at other times in history, circumstances can start to turn around, especially if those who belong to the group of the perpetrators come forward and speak up (e.g., the civil rights movement).

Internal self-management (Gamergate). We're the gamers, the dorks. We're the ones who were on our computers during prom. We're the ones that were in the back of the lunchroom who were playing D&D instead of tossing a football around on the quad. We were supposed to be the open, friendly ones, the ones who welcomed all into our wonderful geeky circle. We're not supposed to be a mob that's storming the gates with our pitchforks and torches. Cliff Bleszinski is a game industry veteran, Gear of War designer 3/12/13.

Resources

Protecting Yourself from Online Harassment

Speak Up and Stay Safe(r). A guide to protecting yourself from online harassment. This document includes a wealth of information and how-to for keeping yourself "safe from individuals, loosely organized groups and cyber mobs online." https://onlinesafety.feministfrequency.com/en/

Crash Override "works preventatively and reactively, warning targets and working with them during episodes of harassment to keep them safe and provide them with the means to reduce harm and rebuild, as well as disempower their harassers." http://www.crashoverridenetwork.com/

Electronic Frontier Foundation. Among their numerous activities, "We also develop technologies that can help individuals protect their privacy and security online, which our technologists build and release freely to the public for anyone to use." https://www.eff.org/

Resources for Removing Images from Searches and from the Net

Industry Appendix of Resources on Non-Consensual Distribution of Sexually Intimate Images. https://oag.ca.gov/cyberexploitation/appendix

Google. Google announced that they will honor requests to remove nude or sexually explicit images shared without consent: "Our philosophy has always been that Search should reflect the whole web. But revenge porn images are intensely personal and emotionally damaging, and serve only to degrade the victims—predominantly women. So going forward, we'll honor requests from people to remove nude or sexually explicit images shared without their consent from Google Search results. This is a narrow and limited policy, similar to how we treat removal requests for other highly sensitive personal information, such as bank account numbers and signatures, that may surface in our search results" (Singhal, 2015). More information can be found here: https://support.google.com/websearch/answer/6302812?hl=en, including a link to the request form. Unfortunately, the Google policy page acknowledges that "While we can prevent a page from appearing in our search results, we are not able to remove content from websites that host it, so we recommend reaching out to the webmaster for the site to request removal first."

Microsoft/Bing. "Microsoft will remove links to photos and videos from search results in Bing, and remove access to the content itself when shared on OneDrive or Xbox Live, when we are notified by a victim." The form to request removal is here: https://www.microsoft.com/en-us/concern/bing/. "Please note we can only remove content from Microsoft services. You need to work with other companies, including the owners of any website pages you listed on this form, in order to remove pages from their services. Otherwise, the images will still be accessible on the Internet."

Digital Millennium Copyright Act. For a fee, this site will help take personal content down. "In other words, the fact the content is yours, or in the case of a photo or video the subject is you, can be sufficient enough to request a takedown AND for the content to be taken down." https://www.dmca.com/

Porn hub. "Pornhub takes all content removal requests seriously. Should you be a victim of revenge porn, blackmailing or intimidation because of a video or photo of yourself on our sites that you did not authorize, please complete the form below and we will remove the content expeditiously." https://www.pornhub.com/content-removal

In the State of California. You can find info on industry "best practices," victim resources, law enforcement resources, and so on. Also has info on image removal on several sites, including 4chan, http://www.4chan.org/legal#dmca, Flickr, https://help.yahoo.com/kb/flickr/sln7389.html, and other sites. https://oag.ca.gov/cyberexploitation

Support and Assistance for Victims

Cyber Civil Rights Initiative's (CCRI) mission is "To fight nonconsensual pornography and other forms of online abuse by Providing victims with support and referral services; Advocating for legislation to address such abuse; Collaborating with the tech industry to develop design-based solutions; and Educating the courts, lawmakers, law enforcement, and the general public about the nature and prevalence of online abuse. The URL www.endrevengeporn.org directs to this site. https://www.cybercivilrights.org/

The Cyber Civil Rights Legal Project helps victims of nonconsensual pornography by providing them legal assistance on a pro bono basis. https://www.cyberrightsproject.com/

Without My Consent's mission is "seeking to combat online invasions of privacy. The resources found here are intended to empower individuals to stand up for their privacy rights and inspire meaningful debate about the internet, accountability, free speech, and the serious problem of online invasions of privacy." http://withoutmyconsent.org/

Revenge Porn Helpline. This UK organization offers "practical assistance in reporting and removing content online. . . . We provide coaching and advice on how and when to gather evidence and approach the authorities. . . . We also offer support and legislative advice to law enforcement agencies. . . . our clients are signposted to free, accessible, client-centered legal consultations. . . . We do not have the capacity to provide long term counselling to our clients but do offer non-judgmental, emotional support." https://revengepornhelpline.org.uk/

Note

1. Rosen states, "I by no means intend to make a comparison between the crimes of Eichmann and the trolling of Brutsch. . . . Arendt's observations can be extended far beyond the particular example of Eichmann to many other instances of human action that betray a callous disregard for the lives of others."

References

Almansi, R. J. (1979). Scopophilia and object loss. *Psychoanalytic Quarterly*, 48(4), 601–619.

American Psychiatric Association. (1965). *Diagnostic and statistical manual of mental disorders* (5th ed.). Arlington, VA: American Psychiatric Association.

Arnsdorf, I. (2008). Auto-Admit case moves forward. *Yale Daily News*. https://web.archive.org/web/20080203103848/http://www.yaledailynews.com/articles/view/23231

Atwood, M. (1982, February 9). *Writing the male character*, a Hagey Lecture at the University of Waterloo; reprinted in *Second words: Selected critical prose* (1982). Boston, MA: Beacon Press.

Auernheimer, A. (2013, September 28). Of Sierras and Sandovals. *Pastebin*. https://pastebin.com/DUWEZfTy

The AutoAdmit scandal: The XOXOTH secret forum identities. In *Law Vibe International Law News & Lawyer Lifestyle*. https://web.archive.org/web/20080816182455/http://lawvibe.com/the-autoadmit-scandal-xoxoth/

Baker-Whitelaw, G. (2013, January 30). Hate speech plagues UK professor after debate show appearance. *Daily Dot*. Updated February 24, 2017. https://www.dailydot.com/society/mary-beard-trolls-dont-start-me-off/

Barnard, G. W., Vera, H., Vera, M. I., & Newman, G. (1982). Till death do us part: A study of spouse murder. *Bulletin of the American Academy of Psychiatry and the Law*, 10(4), 271–280.

Bates, S. (2017). Revenge porn and mental health: A qualitative analysis of the mental health effects of revenge porn on female survivors. *Feminist Criminology*, 12(1), 22–42.

BBC. (2014, January 7). Two guilty over abusive tweets to Caroline Criado-Perez." *BBC*. https://www.bbc.com/news/uk-25641941

Beard, M. (2014, March 20). The public voice of women. *London Review of Books*, 36(6), 11–14.

Beran, D. (2017, February 14). 4chan: The skeleton key to the rise of Trump. *Medium*. https://medium.com/@DaleBeran/4chan-the-skeleton-key-to-the-rise-of-trump-624e7cb798cb

Berger, J. M. (2018, April 26). The difference between a killer and a terrorist. *The Atlantic*. https://www.theatlantic.com/politics/archive/2018/04/the-difference-between-killer-and-terrorist/558998/?utm_source=twb

Bernstein, J. (2013, March 14). Gaming doesn't need creeps. *Buzzfeed News*. https://www.buzzfeednews.com/article/josephbernstein/gaming-doesnt-need-creeps

Bernstein, J. (2015, February 23). Gamergate's archvillain is really a trolling sketch comedian. *Buzzfeed News*. https://www.buzzfeed.com/josephbernstein/gamergates-archvillain-is-really-a-trolling-sketch-comedian?utm_term=.ybxlRZ7a7#.akLOMY0e0

Bevens, C. L., & Loughnan, S. (2019). Insights into men's sexual aggression toward women: Dehumanization and objectification. *Sex Roles: A Journal of Research,* 81(11–12), 713–730.

Blackstone, W. (1765). *Blackstone's commentaries*, vol. 1 (pp. 432, 433). Oxford, UK: Clarendon.

Bleszinski, C. (2013, March 12). If video games are going to grow up, then the bullying needs to stop. *Kotaku.* http://kotaku.com/5990184/if-video-games-are-going-to-grow-up-then-the-bullying-needs-to-stop

Bowles, N. (2016, March 12). Internet trolls are "Machiavellian sadists and psychopaths"—expert. *The Guardian.* https://www.theguardian.com/technology/2016/mar/12/sxsw-gamergate-harassment-summit-bullying-panel

Brennan, T. J. (2017, March 4). Hundreds of Marines investigated for sharing photos of naked colleagues. *RevealNews.* https://www.revealnews.org/blog/hundreds-of-marines-investigated-for-sharing-photos-of-naked-colleagues/

Brewer, G., Hunt, D., James, G., & Abell, L. (2015). Dark triad traits, infidelity and romantic revenge. *Personality and Individual Differences*, 83, 122–127.

Buckels, E. E., Jones, D. N., & Paulhus, D. L. (2013). Behavioral confirmation of everyday sadism. *Psychological Science*, 24(11), 2201–2209.

Buckels, E. E., Trapnell, P. D., & Paulhus, D. L. (2014). Trolls just want to have fun. *Personality and Individual Differences*, 67, 97–102.

Burns, A. (2015). In full view: Involuntary porn and the postfeminist rhetoric of choice. In *Twenty-First Century Feminism* (pp. 93–118). London, UK: Palgrave Macmillan.

CCRI. (2017). Cyber Civil Rights Initiative. https://www.cybercivilrights.org/

Check, J. V., Perlman, D., & Malamuth, N. M. (1985). Loneliness and aggressive behaviour. *Journal of Social and Personal Relationships*, 2(3), 243–252.

Cheng, J., Danescu-Niculescu-Mizil, C., Leskovec, J., & Bernstein, M. (2017). Anyone can become a troll. *American Scientist*, 105(3), 152–155.

Cheng, J., Bernstein, M., Danescu-Niculescu-Mizil, C., & Leskovec, J. (2017). Anyone can become a troll: Causes of trolling behavior in online discussions. arXiv preprint arXiv:1702.01119

Cheong, I. M. (2012, July 9). Woman receives death threats for confronting misogynist game designer. *Gameranx.* http://gameranx.com/features/id/7851/article/woman-receives-death-threats-forconfronting-bendilin-spurr-misogynist-game-designer/

Citron, D. K. (2009). Law's expressive value in combating cyber gender harassment. *Michigan Law Review*, 108(3), 373–415.

Clark, J. F. (2016, May). Growing threat: Sextortion. In *United States Attorneys' Bulletin*, pp. 41–45.

Colbeck, Kristen. (2015). Private bodies, public pleasures: Asserting male dominance through internet creepshots. *International Journal of Internet Trolling and Online Participation,* 2(1), 5–25.

Correll, D. (2010, January 11). Former boyfriend used craigslist to arrange women's rape, police say. *Los Angeles Times*. https://www.latimes.com/archives/la-xpm-2010-jan-11-la-na-rape-craigslist11-2010jan11-story.html

Cross, E. J., Overall, N. C., Hammond, M. D., & Fletcher, G. J. O. (2017). When does men's hostile sexism predict relationship aggression? The moderating role of partner commitment. *Social Psychological and Personality Science*, 8(3), 331–340. https://doi.org/10.1177/1948550616672000

Csanady, A. (2014, October 15). Prominent feminist cancels university talk after threats of a "Montreal massacre style attack." *CanadianContent*. https://forums.canadiancontent.net/threads/prominent-feminist-cancels-speech-after-threats-of-a-montreal-massacre-style-attack.128871/

Darknet (n.d.). Wikipedia. https://en.wikipedia.org/wiki/Darknet

Davis, K. E., & Frieze, I. H. (2000). Research on stalking: What do we know and where do we go? *Violence and Victims*, 15(4), 473–487.

Davis, K. E., Swan, S. C., & Gambone, L. J. (2012). Why doesn't he just leave me alone? Persistent pursuit: A critical review of theories and evidence: Issues of gender in stalking research. *Sex Roles*, 66(5–6), 328–339.

Dean, F. (2014). How this woman deals with sexist internet trolls. *Flare*. http://www.flare.com/culture/how-mary-beard-deals-with-sexist-internet-trolls/

Department of Mechanical Engineering. (2006, May 15). Study: Female-name chat users get 25 times more malicious messages. A. James Clark School of Engineering. http://www.enme.umd.edu/news/news_story.php?id=1729

Dickson, A. (2016). "Revenge porn": A victim focused response. *UniSA Student Law Review*, 2.

Douglas, D. M. (2016). Doxing: A conceptual analysis. *Ethics and Information Technology*, 18(3), 199–210.

Duca, L. (2018, May 1). Netizens shows how cyberharassment is trivialized, especially for women. *Teen Vogue: News and Politics*. https://www.teenvogue.com/story/thigh-high-politics-netizens-cyberharassment/amp

Dutton, L. B., & Winstead, B. A. (2006). Predicting unwanted pursuit: Attachment, relationship satisfaction, relationship alternatives, and break-up distress. *Journal of Social and Personal Relationships*, 23(4), 565–586.

Eaton, A. A., Jacobs, H., & Ruvalcaba, Y. (2017, June). 2017 Nationwide online study of nonconsensual porn victimization and perpetration: A summary report. Cyber Civil Rights Initiative, Inc., Florida International University, Department of Psychology.

Editorial Board. (2013, October 13). Fighting back against revenge porn. *New York Times*, 163(56288), 10.

Elonis v. United States, 13-983 730 F.3d 321 (Supreme Court 2015).

The ENOUGH Act of 2017. Ending nonconsensual online user graphic harassment. Sponsors: Harris, Burr, Klobuchar. https://speier.house.gov/sites/speier.house.gov/files/The%20ENOUGH%20Act%20One%20Pager%2011-27-17%20%28002%29.pdf

Fenichel, O. (1937). The scopophilic instinct and identification. *International Journal of Psychoanalysis*, 18, 6–34.

Futrelle, D. (2017, June 12). Fat women who have sex: The ultimate oppressors of men? Creepy incels say "yes." *We Hunted the Mammoth.* http://www.wehuntedthemammoth.com/2017/06/12/fat-women-who-have-sex-the-ultimate-oppressors-of-men-creepy-incels-say-yes/

Futrelle, D. (2018, May 2). The time for "incel" explainers was years ago. *Huffington Post.* https://www.huffingtonpost.com/entry/opinion-futrelle-incels-toronto-terrorism_us_5ae8d130e4b06748dc8d2b95?ncid=engmodushpmg00000004

Gallagher, C. (2020, September 21). Inside politics—The far right in Ireland: Who are they and what are their aims?—with Conor Gallagher. *Irish Times.* https://www.irishtimes.com/news/politics/inside-politics/inside-politics-the-far-right-in-ireland-who-are-they-and-what-are-their-aims-with-conor-gallagher-1.4360557

Gardiner, B., Mansfield, M., Anderson, I., Holder, J., Louter, D., & Ulmanu, M. (2016). *The dark side of Guardian comments.* https://www.theguardian.com/technology/2016/apr/12/the-dark-side-of-guardian-comments

Geek Feminism Wiki. (n.d.). *Geek feminism wiki.* https://geekfeminism.wikia.org/wiki/Timeline_of_incidents

Gjoni, Eron. (2014, September 12). Why does this exist? *The ZoePost.* https://thezoepost.wordpress.com/

Glick, P., & Fiske, S. (1997). Hostile and benevolent sexism: Measuring ambivalent sexist attitudes toward women. *Psychology of Women Quarterly*, 21(1), 119–135.

Goldenberg, J. L. (2013). Immortal objects: The objectification of women as terror management. In S. J. Gervais (Ed.), *Objectification and (de) humanization* (pp. 73–95). New York, NY: Springer.

Greathouse, S. M., Saunders, J. M., Matthews, M., Keller, K. M., Miller, L. L., & Project Air Force (U.S.). (2015). *A review of the literature on sexual assault perpetrator characteristics and behaviors.* Santa Monica, CA: Rand Corporation.

Greenberg, A. (2014). Hacker lexicon: What is the dark web? *Wired.com* https://www.wired.com/2014/11/hacker-lexicon-whats-dark-web/

Greenberg, J., Pyszczynski, T., Solomon, S., Rosenblatt, A., Veeder, M., Kirkland, S., & Lyon, D. (1990). Evidence for terror management theory II: The effects of mortality salience on reactions to those who threaten or bolster the cultural worldview. *Journal of Personality and Social Psychology*, 58(2), 308.

Gruenfeld, D. H., Keltner, D. J., & Anderson, C. (2003). The effects of power on those who possess it: How social structure can affect social cognition. In Galen V. Bodenhausen & Alan J. Lambert (Eds.), *Foundations of Social Cognition* (pp. 245–270). East Sussex, UK: Psychology Press.

Hale, M. (1847). *Historia placitorum coronae: The history of the pleas of the crown,* vol. 1. RH Small.

Hardaker, C. (2010). Trolling in asynchronous computer-mediated communication: From user discussions to academic definitions. *Journal of Politeness Research*, 6, 215–242.

Hardaker, C. (2013). What is turning so many young men into internet trolls? *The Observer*, 3(8), 27.

Hardaker, C., & McGlashan, M. (2016). "Real men don't hate women": Twitter rape threats and group identity. *Journal of Pragmatics*, 91, 80–93.

Henry, N., & Powell, A. (2016). Technology-facilitated sexual violence: A literature review of empirical research. *Trauma, Violence, & Abuse*, 19(2), 195–208. https://doi.org/1524838016650189

Hern, A. (2014). Feminist games critic cancels talk after terror threat. *The Guardian.* https://www.theguardian.com/technology/2014/oct/15/anita-sarkeesian-feminist-games-critic-cancels-talk

Herrera, M. C., Expósito, F., & Moya, M. (2012). Negative reactions of men to the loss of power in gender relations: Lilith vs. Eve. *European Journal of Psychology Applied to Legal Context*, 4(1), 17-42.

Hill, K. (2014, January 1). How revenge porn king Hunter Moore was taken down. *Forbes*. https://www.forbes.com/sites/kashmirhill/2014/01/24/how-revenge-porn-king-hunter-moore-was-taken-down/#fe6759448c09

In re White, 551 B.R. 814 (Bankr. S.D. Ohio 2016).

In re White, No. 15-50031 (Bankr. S.D. Ohio June 23, 2016).

Jane, E. A. (2014). "Your a ugly, whorish, slut." *Feminist Media Studies*, 14(4). http://www.tandfonline.com/doi/abs/10.1080/14680777.2012.741073

"Jill." (2007, March 7). Hi, I'm Jill, and law school sleazebags have gone after me, too. *Feministing*. http://feministing.com/2007/03/07/hi_im_jill_and_scummy_law_scho_1/

Jones, D. N., & Paulhus, D. L. (2010). Different provocations trigger aggression in narcissists and psychopaths. *Social Psychological & Personality Science*, 1(1), 12–18.

Kasumovic, M. M., & Kuznekoff, J. H. (2015). Insights into sexism: Male status and performance moderates female-directed hostile and amicable behaviour. *PloS One*, 10(7), e0131613–e0131613.

Kelly, H. (2013, October 3). New California "revenge porn" law may miss some victims. *CNN*. http://www.cnn.com/2013/10/03/tech/web/revenge-porn-law-california/

Kimmel, M. (2013, 2017). *Angry white men: American masculinity at the end of an era*. New York, NY: Nation Books.

Kokkinos, C. M., Antoniadou, N., & Markos, A. (2014). Cyber-bullying: An investigation of the psychological profile of university student participants. *Journal of Applied Developmental Psychology*, 35(3), 204–214.

Kulwin, N. (2015, October 26). SXSW Interactive cancels two panels on harassment in gaming, citing threats. Vox. https://www.recode.net/2015/10/26/11620048/is-it-really-about-ethics-in-journalism

Landau, M. J., Goldenberg, J. L., Greenberg, J., Gillath, O., Solomon, S., Cox, C., Martens, A., & Pyszczynski, T. (2006). The siren's call: Terror management and the threat of men's sexual attraction to women. *Journal of Personality and Social Psychology*, 90(1), 129–146.

Langlois, G., & Slane, A. (2017). Economies of reputation: The case of revenge porn. *Communication and Critical/Cultural Studies*, 14(2), 1–19.

LaPorta, J., & Laverty, R. (2017). "Marines share photo of nude unconscious woman in new revenge porn leak." Daily Beast. http://www.thedailybeast.com/marines-share-photo-of-nude-unconscious-woman-in-new-revenge-porn-leak

Laws, C. (2013, November 22). One woman's dangerous war against the most hated man on the internet. http://jezebel.com/one-womans-dangerous-war-against-the-most-hated-man-on-1469240835

Lees, M. (2016, December 1). What Gamergate should have taught us about the "alt-right." *The Guardian*. https://www.theguardian.com/technology/2016/dec/01/gamergate-alt-right-hate-trump

Lewis, H. (2011). "You should have your tongue ripped out": The reality of sexist abuse online. *New Statesman*. https://www.newstatesman.com/blogs/helen-lewis-hasteley/2011/11/comments-rape-abuse-women

Loughnan, S., Haslam, N., Murnane, T., Vaes, J., Reynolds, C., & Suitner, C. (2010). Objectification leads to depersonalization: The denial of mind and moral concern to objectified others. *European Journal of Social Psychology*, 40(5), 709–717.

Lyonnais, S. (2012, July 9). Toronto tweeter causes uproar over violent "beat up Anita Sarkeesian" game. *Toronto Standard*. http://www.torontostandard.com/industry/toronto-tweeter-causes-twitter-uproar-over-violent-beat-up-anita-sarkeesian-game/

Machackova, H., Dedkova, L., & Mezulanikova, K. (2015). Brief report: The bystander effect in cyberbullying incidents. *Journal of Adolescence*, 43, 96–99.

Malamuth, N. M., & Hald, G. M. (2016). The confluence mediational model of sexual aggression. In D. P. Boer (Ed.), *The Wiley handbook on the theories, assessment and treatment of sexual offending* (pp. 53–71). Singapore: John Wiley & Sons.

Malamuth, N., Linz, D., Heavey, C., Barnes, G., & Acker, M. (1995). Using the confluence model of sexual aggression to predict men's conflict with women: A 10-year follow-up study. *Journal of Personality and Social Psychology*, 69(2), 353–369.

Manne, K. (2018). *Down girl: The logic of misogyny*. Oxford, UK: Oxford University Press.

Marcotte, A. (2013, December 18). "Men's rights" and "revenge porn" sites seethe with anger over women's autonomy. TruthOut. http://www.truth-out.org/opinion/item/20701-mens-rights-and-revenge-porn-sites-seethe-with-anger-over-womens-autonomy.

Marganski, A., & Melander, L. (2018). Intimate partner violence victimization in the cyber and real world: Examining the extent of cyber aggression experiences and its association with in-person dating violence. *Journal of Interpersonal Violence*, 33(7), 1071–1095.

Martinez-Pecino, R., & Durán, M. (2019). I love you but I cyberbully you: The role of hostile sexism. *Journal of Interpersonal Violence*, 34(4), 812–825.

Masser, B., Viki, G. T., & Power, C. (2006). Hostile sexism and rape proclivity amongst men. *Sex Roles*, 54(7), 565–574.

McGlashan, M., & Hardaker, C. (2015). Twitter rape threats and the discourse of online misogyny (DOOM): From discourses to networks. Corpus Linguistics 2015 Abstract Book. Paper presented at Corpus Linguistics, pp. 154–156.

McGlynn, C., & Rackley, E. (2016, March 9). Not "revenge porn" but abuse: Let's call it image-based sexual abuse. *Everyday Victim Blaming*, 9.

Mead, R. (2014). The troll slayer. http://www.newyorker.com/magazine/2014/09/01/troll-slayer#

Merlan, A. (2015, January 29). The cops don't care about violent online threats. What do we do now? Jezebel. https://jezebel.com/the-cops-dont-care-about-violent-online-threats-what-d-1682577343

Meyer, R., & Cukier, M. (2006, June). Assessing the attack threat due to IRC channels. In *Dependable Systems and Networks, 2006. DSN 2006. International Conference on Dependable Systems and Networks* (pp. 467–472). IEEE.

Moore, H. (2011, November 21). *Anderson Live.*

Morelli, M., Bianchi, D., Baiocco, R., Pezzuti, L., & Chirumbolo, A. (2016). Not-allowed sharing of sexts and dating violence from the perpetrator's perspective: The moderation role of sexism. *Computers in Human Behavior*, 56, 163–169.

Morris, A. (2012, November 13). Hunter Moore: The most hated man on the internet. *Rolling Stone.* http://www.rollingstone.com/culture/news/the-most-hated-man-on-the-internet-20121113

Mueller, M. V. (2016). A not so private matter: Prevalence, attitudes and experiences with "revenge porn." *KSCommons.* http://hdl.handle.net/20.500.12088/7913

National Conference of State Legislatures, State Cyberstalking and Cyberharassment Laws. (2015, January 12). https://www.ncsl.org/research/telecommunications-and-information-technology/cybersecurity-legislation-2015.aspx#2015

Nguyen, D., & Parkhill, M. R. (2014). Integrating attachment and depression in the confluence model of sexual assault perpetration. *Violence Against Women*, 20(8), 994–1011.

Nussbaum, M. C. (1995). Objectification. *Philosophy & Public Affairs*, 24(4), 249–291.

Oliver, K. (2016). Rape as spectator sport and creepshot entertainment: Social media and the valorization of lack of consent. *American Studies Journal*, 61.

Page, T. E., & Pina, A. (2015). Moral disengagement as a self-regulatory process in sexual harassment perpetration at work: A preliminary conceptualization. *Aggression and Violent Behavior*, 21, 73–84.

Patton, C. L., Nobles, M. R., & Fox, K. A. (2010). Look who's stalking: Obsessive pursuit and attachment theory. *Journal of Criminal Justice*, 38(3), 282–290.

Petrosky, E., Blair, J. M., Betz, C. J., Fowler, K. A., Jack, S., & Lyons, B. H. (2017, July 21). Racial and ethnic differences in homicides of adult women and the role of intimate partner violence—United States, 2003–2014. *Morbidity and Mortality Weekly Report*, Centers for Disease Control (CDC). https://www.cdc.gov/mmwr/volumes/66/wr/mm6628a1.htm?s_cid=mm6628a1_w

Pew Research Center. (October 2014). Online harassment. https://www.pewinternet.org/2014/10/22/online-harassment/

Philipson, A. (2013, July 28). Woman who campaigned for Jane Austen bank note receives Twitter death threats. *The Telegraph*. http://www.telegraph.co.uk/technology/10207231/Woman-who-campaigned-for-Jane-Austen-bank-note-receives-Twitter-death-threats.html

Phillips, W. (2012, October 15). What an academic who wrote her dissertation on trolls thinks of violentacrez. *The Atlantic*. https://www.theatlantic.com/technology/archive/2012/10/what-an-academic-who-wrote-her-dissertation-on-trolls-thinks-of-violentacrez/263631/

Pina, A., Holland, J., & James, M. (2017). The malevolent side of revenge porn proclivity: Dark personality traits and sexist ideology. *International Journal of Technoethics (IJT)*, 8(1), 30–43.

Powell, A., & Henry, N. (2017). Towards equal digital citizenship. In *Sexual violence in a digital age* (pp. 237–269). London, UK: Palgrave Macmillan.

Price, R. (2017). AI and CGI will transform information warfare, boost hoaxes, and escalate revenge porn. *Business Insider*. http://www.businessinsider.com/cgi-ai-fake-video-audio-news-hoaxes-information-warfare-revenge-porn-2017-8?IR=T

Reg v. Mawgridge. (1707). Keilways' Reports. 119.

Regina V. Smith (Respondent) (On Appeal from the Court of Appeal (Criminal Division)). ON 27 July 2000. Publications, Parliament UK. http://publications.parliament.uk/pa/ld199900/ldjudgmt/jd000727/smith-2.htm Session 1999–2000. Publications on the Internet. Judgments.

Reilly, M. E., & Hines, D. A. (2017, June 9). Distress tolerance as a mediator of the association between borderline personality symptoms and obsessive relational intrusion: An exploratory analysis. *Journal of Interpersonal Violence*, 35(19–20). https://doi.org/10.1177/0886260517712274

Rodger, E. (uploaded to document cloud May 25, 2014). My twisted world: The story of Elliot Rodger. https://www.documentcloud.org/documents/1173808-elliot-rodger-manifesto.html

Roiphe, K. (2013, August 6). The Bank of England wanted to put Jane Austen on a 10-pound note. Then all hell broke loose. *Slate*. https://slate.com/human-interest/2013/08/the-anger-over-jane-austen-on-a-10-pound-note-proves-people-can-rage-over-anything.html

Romano, A. (2016, April 6). How the alt-right's sexism lures men into white supremacy. Vox. https://www.vox.com/culture/2016/12/14/13576192/alt-right-sexism-recruitment

Rosen, R. (2012, October 16). What was Reddit troll violentacrez thinking? *The Atlantic*. https://www.theatlantic.com/technology/archive/2012/10/what-was-reddit-troll-violentacrez-thinking/263648/

Rucker, D. D., & Galinsky, A. D. (2008). Desire to acquire: Powerlessness and compensatory consumption. *Journal of Consumer Research*, 35(2), 257–267.

Sandoval, G. (2013, September 12). The end of kindness: Weev and the cult of the angry young man. https://www.theverge.com/2013/9/12/4693710/the-end-of-kindness-weev-and-the-cult-of-the-angry-young-man

Sargent, K. S., Krauss, A., Jouriles, E. N., & McDonald, R. (2016). Cyber victimization, psychological intimate partner violence, and problematic mental health outcomes among first-year college students. *Cyberpsychology, Behavior, and Social Networking*, 19(9), 545–550.

Sarkeesian, A. (2012, December 5). TEDxWomen talk about online harassment & cyber mobs. *Feminist Frequency*. https://feministfrequency.com/video/tedxwomen-talk-on-sexist-harassment-cyber-mobs/

Sarkeesian, A. (2015, December 10). Harassment through impersonation: The creation of a cyber mob. *Feminist Frequency*. https://feministfrequency.com/2015/12/10/harassment-through-impersonation-the-creation-of-a-cyber-mob/

Savage, M. W., & Tokunaga, R. S. (2017). Moving toward a theory: Testing an integrated model of cyberbullying perpetration, aggression, social skills, and internet self-efficacy. *Computers in Human Behavior*, 71, 353–361.

Selby, E. A., & Joiner, T. E., Jr. (2009). Cascades of emotion: The emergence of borderline personality disorder from emotional and behavioral dysregulation. *Review of general psychology*, 13(3), 219–229.

Senate Bill S.2162. (2017). 115th Congress, 1st Session. https://www.congress.gov/115/bills/s2162/BILLS-115s2162is.pdf

Sest, N., & March, E. (2017). Constructing the cyber-troll: Psychopathy, sadism, and empathy. *Personality and Individual Differences*, 119, 69–72.

Sheridan, L. P., & Grant, T. (2007). Is cyberstalking different? *Psychology, Crime & Law*, 13(6), 627–640.

Singhal, A. (2015, June 19). Google Search. "Revenge porn" and search. https://publicpolicy.googleblog.com/2015/06/revenge-porn-and-search.html

Smith, H. (2016, September 6). Revenge porn prosecutions number "more than 200" just 18 months after law change. *The Independent*. https://www.independent.co.uk/news/uk/home-news/revenge-porn-prosecutions-number-more-than-200-just-18-months-after-law-change-a7227771.html

Smoker, M., & March, E. (2017). Predicting perpetration of intimate partner cyberstalking: Gender and the dark tetrad. *Computers in Human Behavior*, 72, 390–396.

Solnit, R. (2015, December 15). Men explain Lolita to me. https://lithub.com/men-explain-lolita-to-me/

Southern Poverty Law Center (SPLC). (n.d.). Male supremacy. https://www.splcenter.org/fighting-hate/extremist-files/ideology/male-supremacy

Spitzberg, B. H., & Cupach, W. R. (2014). *The dark side of relationship pursuit: From attraction to obsession and stalking.* New York, NY: Routledge.

Stanton, C. (2011, February 13). A troll case study. *Blogschmog.* http://www.blogschmog.net/2011/02/13/a-troll-case-study/.

Stroud, S. R. (2014). The dark side of the online self: A pragmatist critique of the growing plague of revenge porn. *Journal of Mass Media Ethics,* 29(3), 168–183.

Stroud, S. R., & Henson, J. (2016). Social media, online sharing, and the ethical complexity of consent in revenge porn. In A. C. Scheinbaum, ed., *The Dark Side of Social Media*, vol. 1 (pp. 13–32). London, UK: Routledge.

Stuart, K. (2014, October 17). Brianna Wu and the human cost of Gamergate: "Every woman I know in the industry is scared." https://www.theguardian.com/technology/2014/oct/17/brianna-wu-gamergate-human-cost

Stuart, K. (2014, December 3). Zoe Quinn: "All Gamergate has done is ruin people's lives." https://www.theguardian.com/technology/2014/dec/03/zoe-quinn-gamergate-interview

Suler, J. (2004). The online disinhibition effect. *Cyberpsychology & Behavior,* 7(3), 321–326. https://doi.org/10.1089/1094931041291295

SXSW Schedule. (2016, March 15). SavePoint: A discussion on the gaming community. Austin, TX. https://schedule.sxsw.com/2016/events/event_PP57734

Talbot, M. (2016, December 5). The attorney fighting revenge porn. *The New Yorker.* https://www.newyorker.com/magazine/2016/12/05/the-attorney-fighting-revenge-porn

Tassy, F., & Winstead, B. (2014). Relationship and individual characteristics as predictors of unwanted pursuit. *Journal of Family Violence*, 29(2), 187–195.

Taylor, L. J. (1985). Provoked reason in men and women: Heat-of-passion manslaughter and imperfect self-defense. *UCLA Law Review*, 33, 1679.

Thompson, M. P., & Morrison, D. J. (2013). Prospective predictors of technology-based sexual coercion by college males. *Psychology of Violence*, 3(3), 233–246.

The Tor Project Homepage. (n.d.). Ooni. https://ooni.org/partners/tor-project/

Ullman, E. (2017). *Life in code: A personal history of technology.* New York, NY: Farrar, Straus and Giroux.

United States Attorneys' Bulletin. (2016, May). Cyber misbehavior. U.S. Department of Justice. https://www.justice.gov/usao/file/851856/download

United States Department of Justice, Office for Victims of Crime. https://www.ovc.gov/

United States v. Sayer, 12-2489 (1st Cir. 2014).

User iamanarci. (2016, December 12). So, it is men's fault if revenge porn perpetrated. https://www.reddit.com/r/MensRights/comments/5i071u/so_it_is_mens_fault_if_revenge_porn_perpetrated/

User JP_Whoregan. (2016, November 16). On female consequences and ditching your revenge porn fantasies. https://www.reddit.com/r/TheRedPill/comments/3r94ix/on_female_consequences_and_ditching_your_revenge/

Valenti, J. (2015, August 29). Anita Sarkeesian interview: "The word 'troll' feels too childish. This is abuse." https://www.theguardian.com/technology/2015/aug/29/anita-sarkeesian-gamergate-interview-jessica-valenti

Valizadeh, R. (2015, November 4). Women must have their behavior and decisions controlled by men. Return of Kings. http://www.returnofkings.com/73131/women-must-have-their-behavior-and-decisions-controlled-by-men

Vasiu, I., & Vasiu, L. (2016). Light my fire: A roentgenogram of cyberstalking cases. *American Journal of Trial Advocacy*, 40(1), 41 68.

Vasquez, E., Ball, L., Loughnan, S., & Pina, A. (2017). The object of my aggression: Sexual objectification increases physical aggression toward women. *Aggressive Behavior.* https://doi.org/10.1002/ab.21719

Verdi, G. (1853). *La Traviata.*

Wegner, R., & Abbey, A. (2016). Individual differences in men's misperception of women's sexual intent: Application and extension of the confluence model. *Personality and Individual Differences*, 94, 16–20. https://doi.org/10.1016/j.paid.2015.12.027

West, L. (2015, February 2). What happened when I confronted my cruellest troll. *The Guardian.* https://www.theguardian.com/society/2015/feb/02/what-happened-confronted-cruellest-troll-lindy-west

West, L. (2016, May 13). Shrill: Notes from a loud woman by Lindy West—"I never wanted internet trolls to be my beat." *The Guardian.* https://www.theguardian.com/books/2016/may/13/shrill-notes-from-a-loud-woman-lindy-west-review

Williams, M. J., Gruenfeld, D. H., & Guillory, L. E. (2017). Sexual aggression when power is new: Effects of acute high power on chronically low-power individuals. *Journal of Personality and Social Psychology*, 112(2), 201–223.

Wu, B. (2015, August 21). A moment that changed me—Gamergate. *The Guardian.* https://www.theguardian.com/commentisfree/2015/aug/21/gamergate-sexism-games-industry-women-trolls

CHAPTER NINE

Joining Colombian Illegal Armed Groups and the Role of Ideology

Amanda Davies-Rubio and Lourdes Mirón

According to the Historical Memory Group report (Grupo de Memoria Histórica, GMH, 2013), between 1958 and 2012, approximately 220,000 people have died in Colombia at the hands of the guerrillas, the paramilitary groups, and the armed forces. Each one of these groups is guilty of massacres, assassinations, forced disappearances, torture, sexual violence, kidnappings, pillage, and massive displacements—that is, an endless list of crimes against people, freedom, and property in which the victims have mainly been the civilian population. This is one of the prominent features of the Colombian conflict: out of the total deaths, 81.5% were civilians (mainly peasants) and 18.3% were combatants. As the report points out, peasants and, in general, the civilian population, are used by all armed groups as a source of logistic and financial support, as well as a political and moral alibi for their actions. Furthermore, the support this population is forced to give turns them into a target for the rest of the contenders. In the words of the GMH (2013, 290): "This has been a war without limits in which violence against the civilian population has prevailed more than the actions among combatants."

The excessive violence of the Colombian conflict and its persistence through time are related to very diverse factors. Problems of land issues, its unequal distribution, and the precarious life conditions of peasants that the agrarian reform from the early sixties tried to overcome but never delivered satisfactorily; the historical heritage of a political system in which open confrontation among parties and ideologies is institutionalized and ends up propitiating the creation of armed groups as a source and argument; and narcotrafficking, its expansion, ties to political corruption, and funding of armed groups.

The Colombian conflict is characterized by the existence of three armed groups: guerrilla, paramilitary forces (self-called "self-defense forces"), and the state's national army. The origin of the guerrilla forces, and especially of the Revolutionary Armed Forces of Colombia (Fuerzas Revolucionarias de Colombia, FARC), is found in the mobilizations that the Communist Party and affined peasant groups were involved in during the 1930s. These peasants fought against unequal land distribution and the unjust working conditions to which they were subjected. As the guerrilla groups developed and managed to control large areas in the country (the so-called "red zones"), they started to deviate from their original ideas: they used violence against civilians and resorted to extortions, kidnappings, and stealing in order to get funding and increase their power. As a consequence, during the 1970s, the first armed landowner groups appeared with the intention of fighting against the guerrillas' attacks on their families and property. Similarly to the guerrilla forces, as they gained power and resources, the paramilitary groups got involved in all kinds of abuse against the civilian population that was often even worse than the abuse perpetrated by the guerrillas. The military forces of Colombia, which initially had a common enemy with the paramilitary forces—the guerrillas—worked closely with these groups by offering material and logistic support, but ended up fighting them as well.

The civilian population (mainly peasants) has been the victim of all armed groups. As mentioned, 82% of the total victims were civilians, and the number of displaced individuals as a consequence of attacks or threats has reached 7,246,000 (Internal Displacement Monitoring Centre, IDMC, 2017), making Colombia the country with the largest amount of internal displaced population in the world. When each one of these armed groups took over a territory, it forced the inhabitants to collaborate (those who refused were coerced to leave or killed). This collaboration turned the populace into enemies of the other groups, and therefore, potential victims. Consequently, fleeing was the only way to escape violence.

The ideological background of violence constitutes a central theme in this work. In *The Authoritarian Personality*, Theodor Adorno defines ideology as an "organization of opinions, attitudes, and values—a way of thinking about man and society" that, in spite of being adopted by persons, has "an existence independent of any single individual" (Adorno et al., 1950, 2)—that is, it is one of the group's attributes, although it only materializes through the actions of its members. Luis de la Corte's definition, which is given within the framework of terrorism, could be especially pertinent for our purpose because of the connotation and political objectives that the different actors in the Colombian conflict have had: "we understand ideology as any set of minimally organized beliefs and values that allows members of a group to explain and judge social reality, define political aspirations and orient their actions towards them" (de la Corte, 2005, 164). Martín-Baró (1983), taking Max Weber's concept of social action, would go a step further: ideology would be present in any action. In fact, he defines social psychology as the "scientific study of action as ideology" (17). It is not surprising that one of the components in his psychosocial analysis of violence is precisely its ideological background: every "act of violence is inevitably accompanied by its justification"; it tries to cover the misery that goes with it "with the garments of justification" (Martín-Baró, 2003, 164). Violence, even in its most extreme variant (such as the one that has occurred in Colombia), has its own rationality, that is, it always searches for "a justification to face the reality to which it applies" and tries to legitimate its results: "killing a person ceases to be a crime and turns into a social need" (Martín-Baró, 1983, 375). This means that: a) violence channels social interests, and, b) it tends to hide those interests under the ample garments of justification. Social polarization, the construction of the image of the enemy, and institutionalized lies are a part of the ideological background in Martín-Baró's proposal (see Blanco & de la Corte, 2003, 39–47).

Furthermore, ideology is not immersed in a sociocultural vacuum. Before understanding its microsocial base, we must focus on the macrosocial context in which it develops. Ervin Staub (1996, 2006) developed one of the most relevant theoretical models on the importance of group membership in order to explain progressive intergroup violence (such as is found in Colombia). According to this model, the existence of violent groups is related to a series of historic, cultural, and psychosocial conditions: cultural factors such as a history of devaluation, prejudice, and discrimination against certain collectives (so-called ideologies of antagonism); an emphasis on authoritarianism and obedience; social factors such as unfavorable life conditions (poverty, marginalization); as well as other factors related to socialization contexts such as the existence and witnessing of violence in the neighborhood and home, or the absence of emotional support.

All these factors described by Staub (1996, 2006) are found in the case of Colombia. As proof of the ideologies of antagonism, we find a long history of conflict among clear factions within the country. Developing ideologies that shelter the belief in the guilt of the other—defined as the enemy—allows an explanation of the situation (an understanding of the world), the increase of in-group ties (unity against the guilty party), and the justification of actions that solve the problem (eliminating the cause) by acting against those who act as an obstacle a better future. Martín-Baró (2003) adds sociological and political purposes to the psychological purposes of the enemy: on a sociological plane, the enemy encourages and reinforces repressive actions, it promotes solidarity and group cohesion, it justifies actions and guides behavior; on a political plane, the enemy facilitates the bifurcation of ideal images of what society should be (a "good us" and an "evil them"). In the case of the Colombian conflict, the development of an ideology that identifies an enemy and sets a series of necessary behaviors to face it is especially evident in the paramilitary (self-defense) movement. The actions of the guerrillas toward landowners (kidnappings, extorsions, etc.) led the latter to arm themselves in order to eliminate their enemy (the guerrillas). However, this enemy category grew progressively wider and included more and more people, fundamentally peasants that collaborated (forcibly or willingly) with the guerrillas, and even any other social group that was some source of threat to their power in their zones of action.

The emphasis on authoritarianism and obedience is another one of the factors that Staub (2006) includes as influential in the creation of a context of confrontation and violence. The clearest proof of authoritarianism in Colombia is probably the militarization of society. According to Aranguren Romero (2015), a narrative focused on an internal threat (the guerrilla and communism) appeared during the second half of the twentieth century, which led to a readjustment of the criteria that composed the nation. Since the beginning of the implementation of the National Security Doctrine, a military rationality that the army was the only force capable of integrating the national principles started to impose itself (Costa Pinto, 1969). Thus, the military ended up justifying their occupation of places of power through the rhetoric of national salvation. Aranguren Romero adds that the fact that they called themselves "the builders and protectors of the nation" has allowed military values and their symbols to permeate society. The counterinsurgent manual *Modern Warfare*—which is used by the Colombian National Army—states that since the population is at the center of the conflict and is its most stable element, it must be made a participant in combat (Trinquier, 1964). Furthermore, according to Colombia's law 48/1993, Title II-Chapter I-Article 10, "all Colombian males are obligated to define their military situation starting from the moment in which they become over age, with the exception of high school students, who will define their situation when they obtain their high school diploma." This is in order to obtain what is commonly called the "military booklet" (*libreta militar*), which is the certification of completion of military service and is necessary in order to find a job, Colombian men must go through military training that, of course, includes training in weaponry, as well as fighting in real battles in the context of the Colombian conflict.

During two years,[1] the young recruit is subjected to daily messages from his superiors and fellow soldiers against the enemy (the guerrillas)—which constitute the so-called "counterinsurgent ideology"—and fights (and kills) this enemy.

With regard to poverty, some psychosocial theoretical models are based on the idea that frustration generates an impulse toward violence in the individual (Berkowitz, 1989; Berkowitz & Lepage, 1967; Dollard et al., 1939). Feierabend and Feierabend (1972) outline a model in which they highlight the importance of what they call systemic frustration: the generalized discontent of the population due to the impossibility of reaching the desired goals; a frustration that in their analysis of 84 countries shows itself as one of the correlates of social violence. Authors such as Bandura (1973) and Staub (1996) conclude that situations of poverty and inequality, despite not being the main and direct cause of violence, contribute in creating a context in which it is made more probable. According to the United Nations Program for Development (Programa de las Naciones Unidas para el Desarrollo, PNUD, 2016a), the main threat to progress in Latin America and the Caribbean is poverty. The director of this institution in Colombia, Arnaud Peral, states that the percentage of poverty in the country was 49.7% in 2002 and 27.8% in 2015 (PNUD, 2016b). However optimistic this improvement may be, poverty is, undoubtedly, still one of the country's biggest problems, if not the biggest (Bradshaw-Smith, 2015). Furthermore, it is reinforced by issues that are directly related to conflicts such as displacement and its derived problems in the areas of education, health, housing, employment, and so on. Moreover, these issues are aggravated by serious inequality. According to President Juan Manuel Santos, 1% of the Colombian population owns 40% of the country's wealth. As stated by the World Bank (2015), inequality in Colombia as measured by the Gini Coefficient (in which 0 is total equality and 100 is total inequality) was at 58.7 in 1999 and at 51.1 in 2015, during which year it was positioned as having the third-highest level of inequality in the world.

Inequality and poverty are influential factors in a society's levels of violence. The deadlock of violence in a society ends up producing a culture of violence, in which Colombia is immersed. This culture of violence is characterized by the constant presence of conflict and violent crimes (Waldmann, 2007) that progressively decrease the value placed on the life of others. In this climate, violence permeates all sociocultural structures to the point that it is truly difficult to eliminate (Favre, 2001) because the strategies of damage and coercion become acceptable instruments of conflict resolution as well as social and political goal achievement. One of the most lethal consequences of a prolonged history of violence is its institutionalization, its transformation into a routine in daily life and, by extension, in the different levels of social life. The problem of violence derives not only from the consequences it causes, but from the relational model it establishes: "a model that teaches and reinforces violent response habits in individuals as the most efficient way to solve social and political problems, with the resultant deterioration of social life this entails" (Martín-Baró, 2003, 286).

Method

The study presented in this chapter deals with the sociocultural context in which the beliefs of members of Colombian armed groups have developed, how these beliefs have been a part of their decision to join the group, and the indoctrination process that has taken place after adhering.

The data were gathered through in-depth interviews with 18 demobilized members of the United Self-Defense Forces of Colombia (Autodefensas Unidas de Colombia, AUC) and the guerrillas (FARC and so on) that have participated—directly or indirectly—in violent actions against other people. As Madill (2012) and Polkinghorne (2005) highlight, qualitative methodology, and specifically the in-depth interview, is an ideal method of data collection in order to access information that reflects the subjective experience of individuals because it offers a larger wealth of data than that collected through standardized questionnaires. Moreover, several authors (Altier, Horgan, & Thoroughgood, 2012; Horgan, 2012; Teymur, 2007; Yilmaz, 2009) indicate that this method is especially pertinent in the analysis of the behaviors and experiences of perpetrators of violence.

Participants were contacted through groups of demobilized individuals who had signed up to reintegration programs (n=11) and human rights courses directed to the ones who were imprisoned at the time (n = 7). The access to these samples was possible thanks to the help and support of the Universidad Del Norte in Barranquilla, the Colombian Reintegration Agency (Agencia Colombiana para la Reintegración, ACR), and the National Penitentiary and Prison Institute (Instituto Nacional Penitenciario y Carcelario, INPEC). The goals of the study were explained to the participants, stressing its voluntary and anonymous qualities, as well as the fact that interviews would be recorded. All data were collected through individual interviews. Interviews were recorded and the audio was transcribed. The average number of sessions per person was 1.7 (minimum = 1; maximum = 4). These sessions lasted approximately one hour and 15 minutes each. After each day, the interviews were reviewed in order to detect aspects that needed further clarification. This procedure of combining data collection and its analysis is recommended by different authors when using in-depth interviewing (Burck, 2005; Glaser & Strauss, 1967).

The final sample was comprised of 18 participants, 14 male and 4 female; 11 were reintegrated in society and 7 imprisoned; 13 had been members of paramilitary forces, 2 members of the guerrillas and 3 had belonged to both groups; 15 had been foot soldiers and 3 had held leadership positions (commanders). All of them were adhered to the demobilization program protected by the Law of Justice and Peace of 2005, which was promulgated by the Colombian government and has allowed members of illegal armed groups (mainly paramilitary groups) to demobilize and reintegrate into civilian life. The final sample size is in accordance with the iterative nature of qualitative methodology by which participants are added to the study until information saturation is reached, that is, until it does not seem likely that including new subjects will offer new information about the phenomenon at hand.

The age range of the interviewees was between 22 and 67. Average age was 42. With regard to birth location and upbringing, approximately half of the participants belonged to an urban setting (55.6%) and the rest to a rural one.

The content of the transcriptions of all 18 interviews was analyzed by a group of university professors belonging to the Autonomous University of Madrid (Universidad Autónoma de Madrid, UAM) and the Santiago de Compostela University (USC), in Spain. Each one of the judges carried out an open categorization process (Elliott & Timulak, 2005) by thoroughly reading the interviews in order to detect meaning units and thereby examine, compare, conceptualize, and categorize data until a consensus was reached. Furthermore, as a supplementary tool, the qualitative data analysis software Atlas.ti 7 was used.

Results

The sociocultural context is the container in which the ideology of persons and groups is enclosed. Colombian society presents a series of characteristics that facilitate the appearance of conflict and its actors' ideology: unfavorable life conditions (poverty), socialization context factors (culture of violence), a history of conflict, and emphasis on authority and obedience.

Poverty, perceived injustice, and difficulty in accessing the job market are conditions that are present in the stories of the participants of this study. Eleven out of 18 interviewees explicitly declare that they come from a poor family; that is, 61.1% belong to a population with clear and serious financial problems. In many instances, this family financial situation is aggravated by the death or the separation of the parents as well as by abandoning education, which in turn further limits future possibilities in the job market, thus creating a vicious circle.

> *Cero Uno*[2]*: The financial situation, my father was left without a job, so then my mother sold bollos,*[3] *made arepas (. . .), and with that she supported us while my father found a job. And I wasn't able to continue studying.*

Jairo: Well, I was born into a poor family, very poor (. . .), and in that time I had to do my house chores, to work hard because I wasn't a spoiled child, I had to work. As you know, when you are raised by a poor family you have to work hard (. . .). Financially, my family had ten kids. I worked hard during my adolescence (. . .); I sold avocadoes, yucca, whatever there was, in order to give to my family, to my mother, so that they wouldn't go hungry. I worked until I was 17, until I went to the army.

Participants mention the presence of violence in their surroundings, and they have come to view it as acceptable and justifiable. One of the consequences of the culture of violence in Colombia is that weapons are common in the family home and neighborhood settings. Douglas, among others, alludes to the everyday nature of weapons in his neighborhood and their use in dealing with situations of conflict.

Douglas: Once my cousin shot some people because they were arguing at a party, so he shot them.

Ramón: When I went down to the houses I saw weapons, and as a kid you're very curious, and seeing that, it fascinated me, I wanted to handle weapons.

Moreover, the persistence of the Colombian armed conflict has significant effect on the attitudes of the interviewees. Some of them have been socialized with a specific image of each of the factions, or have even lived under their power.

Ramón: As an example, one of the ideologies of the self-defense forces was that if you lived in their area you had to participate in the ideology they established there.

The group perceptions that are transmitted include group objectives as well as the existence of a relationship between some of these groups and the government. Luis Alfredo, among others, explicitly highlights that the paramilitary forces were an "armed wing" of the Colombian government.

Luis Alfredo: I thought the self-defense forces were like a wing of the government; it seemed to me that they were doing what the state couldn't legally do. That's what I thought when I wasn't part of the self-defense forces.

Many were born in "red zones," areas in which the guerrilla forces have complete power and control. As a consequence, the presence of guerrilla fighters was habitual even in school settings. In these regions, inhabitants live under guerrilla rule and children are raised seeing members of these groups as role models. Furthermore, guerrilla fighters give them gifts, and so they are generally perceived as successful figures that have money, a uniform, and are respected. Our participants, among whom we find Óscar and Sofía, talk about this image they had of the guerrilla fighters during their childhood.

> *Óscar: It was a guerrilla zone. I studied at a public school, I was going at night, and I realized they were recruiting youths.*
>
> *Sofía: (I thought) that they did well because I saw they had money. They had good money and they arrived to the towns and you got a feeling because you want this (money), and you got excited, and people spoke about them.*

Additionally, some of them suffer direct abuse from the armed group. For example, they are forced to displace and lose their land. This is the case for Juan's family: red zone inhabitants dedicated to livestock and agriculture that lived comfortably. However, after refusing to pay extortions to the guerrillas, all of their property was burned down and the family was left in poverty. Other participants, like Ramón (see Davies-Rubio, Blanco, & Mirón, 2016), are also victims of physical violence perpetrated by this group.

> *Juan: We are displaced people, we are displaced. We were a middle-class family and the guerrilla burned down our estate, our properties. I was a kid. The guerrilla asked my father for a vaccine.*[4] *My father started giving it to them but afterwards he rebelled, because they said they were the people's army but that wasn't so. They said they were the people's army and my father said that he didn't see them as any kind of people's army, that what he saw was that they were extorting him. So then they threatened him, he didn't give them the vaccine, and then—it's a good thing he wasn't there when it happened, that he was with us in town—there was a combat there and they burned . . . and we lost it all.*
>
> *Interviewer: What was that like for the family?*
>
> *J: Horrible, it was horrible because when you lose all you have it's very difficult to recuperate it. My father didn't want to go back there for any reason. So then he said: "I would rather we lose it all but we stay alive." It was a memory that was always present. Obviously, it wasn't only us, it was everywhere in the country that there was displacement and death.*
>
> *I: What was said about the guerrilla in your home?*
>
> *J: We had an opinion, a very bad image of the guerrilla. In those days the guerrilla made us feel terror, terror and death.*

The country's history of conflict, and especially having been a victim of it, awakens feelings such as hate and desire for revenge that in some cases act as a motivation to join the illegal armed group. However, intergroup emotions start not only as a result of being a victim but also after fulfilling the military service. During their time in the military, young soldiers end up adopting an image of the adversary (the guerrilla). This is what Fabián, who was a professional soldier in the Colombian army, tells us:

Fabián: I was a person who was completely devoted to the antisubversive cause. What they taught me, what I studied—because that is what you really study in the officer's academy.

When Fabián speaks about ideology, he talks about the "antisubversive cause." This concept is based on the indoctrination that occurs during the military service: being placed as an opponent of subversion. Juan Carlos also talks about ideology, in his case from right-wing and left-wing logic.

I: What opinion did you have of the guerrilla's ideals?

Juan Carlos: That they were opponents of the right.

I: And you considered yourself a rightist?

JC: Yes, of course, I was a rightist.

The issue of ideology starts to appear, albeit in a very simplistic manner, in our participants' stories. Ideology also appears in Pablo's account, the only participant in whom we see a more sophisticated ideology based on leftist ideals related to the guerrillas after being indoctrinated by them.

Pablo: In the countryside it's always the guerrilla, there always has to be an authority, and that maximum authority in the countryside is the guerrilla. In Colombia, the maximum authority in the countryside is the guerrilla. So I started to attend their meetings and they started to brainwash me. At a meeting (they said): "Whoever is capable, raise your hand if you are capable of taking these rules and ideas and spreading them, spreading, and offering the people of the region knowledge." And I raised my hand. I liked it because I was born in poverty, and when I heard those things that I saw, I saw that they were (true). . . . That I had to, I raised my hand, I felt capable and I did it. I took those rules and ideas to many comrades, as you say today, spreading the word. It was, for example, we had to organize six-person cells and continue spreading it so that people knew how we had to act and how we had to attack the government so that the government wouldn't ignore us. My job was to organize cells, organize political cells.

Among our participants, there are only two cases (one of which is Pablo) in whom political ideology is specified as a reason for joining the group,

Table 9-1 Number and Percentage of Interviewees and Their Reasons for Joining the Group

REASONS	N	%
Relatives, friends, or acquaintances within the group	13	72.2
Coming from the army or military service	9	50
Financial problems, employment	7	38.8
Taste for weapons, uniform, and discipline/searching for prestige	5	27.8
Escaping justice or the other group	4	22.2
Living in a group-controlled area, recruited at school or in the neighborhood	3	16.6
Revenge against the opposing group (the guerrillas)	2	11.1
Political ideology	2	11.1

although not exclusively. Therefore, against popular belief but in consonance with other studies focused on collective and political violence (Reinares, 2011; de la Corte, 2006), political ideology does not play a crucial role in joining Colombian illegal armed groups as per our participants' accounts; and when it does appear, it does so in a very unsophisticated manner that is centered around the previous image of the enemy around which all possible negative attributes are gathered. Other reasons for joining are found to be more important among our interviewees, such as financial retribution or the existence of loved ones and acquaintances within the group (see Table 9-1).

However, our interviews show that ideology starts being an important factor *after* joining the group, once the individual is immersed in the group processes. A very important part of group socialization is related to ideological training, which leads to the acceptance of the ideals that lie beneath the group's objectives. This ideology is based almost exclusively on the "us" and "them" distinction, as well as on the adoption of justifications that legitimize the group's actions. Even when at the creation of the groups there was a political–ideological approach (especially so in the case of the guerrillas), the importance of this political ideology decreases as the survival of the group (through drug trafficking, kidnapping, and extortion) becomes the primary motivation for the group's actions. Óscar summarizes this ideological reality in a simple and straightforward manner.

Óscar: The self-defense forces don't manage much ideology, what they are interested in is taking care of the people who give them money.

Notwithstanding that, an ideological indoctrination referring to the learning of objectives, chants, and slogans that govern group life exists on both sides. Thus, the activation and consolidation of divides is produced (Tilly, 2003). These divides are in many cases already known by the members before joining but are now systematized in the process of group identity construction.

Jairo: We were a revolutionary army outside the law that has always tried to fight against the guerrilla, the Colombian guerrilla, so this Colombia does well, for a better Colombia, right? We were an army, like I say, outside the law, but it was for that reason, nothing else. Our enemy then was the guerrilla.

Many of our interviewees clearly identify the objectives for which the self-defense forces trained: this organization is created as a response to the guerrilla forces that are abusing the population and are threatening state sovereignty. However, others summarize this ideology as simply the idea of killing the enemy.

Juan Carlos: As far as I know, the paramilitary ideology was to finish the guerrilla.

Therefore, the main ideology that remains in Colombian armed groups is mere social categorization and the image of the enemy that derives from it. The guerrillas, and especially the paramilitary forces, base their actions on intergroup antagonism in which the in-group is morally superior to the out-group in terms of group exaltation (ethnocentrism) and contempt toward the opponent (Sumner, 1906, 14); thus, group actions are justified based on the definition of the other as an enemy (Blanco, 2008). This intergroup hostility logic is observed time and time again in our participants' accounts in their multiple allusions to "us" and "them." Luis Alfredo offers a clear vision of this social categorization when he talks about the attacks between groups using the analogy of a soccer game in which two teams fight for victory. In his testimony, he states that the actions of the in-group consisted simply of returning received attacks, thus turning the conflict into a game played by good and evil. Luis Alfredo even states that the in-group was on God's side.

Luis Alfredo: We took it like soccer; you went into the field to beat the other team playing. So I took it, in my case, if we're in combat against X front, them against us, but we are the ones on God's side. That's what we had to do. In any case, the war they carried out was that one, and you had to return a same sized bomb, that was common in guerrilla areas. It was them or us, them and us. The same thing they did, we did back to them, the same way.

The reinforcement of these categories is one of the essential elements of the ideological training process. Our participants quickly develop definitions in which there is a clear distinction between partners and enemies. Empathy is felt toward partners, and enemies belong to the world of immorality and strangeness, and therefore, not only do they not awaken empathy, but they are also the object of rejection and even hate.

Pepe: The difference was that hurting a partner, that you had lived with your partner, you saw your partner, you knew that man was on your side. This was not so with the guerrilla fighter. The guerrilla fighter belonged to the opposing side, and we classified them as the enemy, our main enemy. That was the difference I saw.

This difference clearly establishes that "us" is associated with objectives and positive, desirable intentions, while the out-group has evil plans.

Alejandra: Paramilitaries, for example, they kill innocent people, people who have nothing, they kill them.

The construction of group definitions regarding the in-group favoritism and out-group discrimination bias (Tajfel et al., 1971)—which we argue configures practically the complete ideology of the group—is evidenced in the accounts of the three participants who belonged to both groups (guerrilla as well as paramilitary) when they describe their points of view first as a member of the guerrillas and afterward as a member of the paramilitary forces. In each case, it is the others who are wrong and the in-group is the one that carries out the correct behavior. It is worth noting that the fact that there are up to three participants who belonged to both antagonistic groups reaffirms the notion that political ideology is not an important part of joining a Colombian illegal armed group (and not even of its continuing membership).

I: What image did you have of the self-defense forces when you were in the guerrilla?

Óscar: They were quite murderous.

I: So, how did you switch sides?

Ó: I made that change because of the situation I was living at that moment, because I thought—I think—that my life is above all.

This "us versus them" ideology increases the intergroup divide and creates a dichotomic and polarized image. For the guerrillas as well as for the self-defense forces, their actions have the intention of protecting the life and well-being of the Colombian people, which are threatened by the enemy group.

The divide is strengthened to such a degree that the definition of enemy ends up including all of those who do not belong to the in-group. This means that even when both the guerrillas and the paramilitary forces declare themselves the defenders of the civilian population, they end up including any members of this population who do not show loyalty to the group in the category of the enemy.

Juan Carlos: The same with civilians; they either collaborated or they were targeted.

I: The civilians who collaborated with the guerrilla, were they guerrilla fighters?

JC: Yes, ma'am, they were guerrilla fighters.

I: They were given the same treatment as a guerrilla fighter?

JC: Yes, ma'am.

This in-group–out-group differentiation ideology is reinforced by the use of justifications for harmful behaviors. All mechanisms of moral disengagement proposed by Bandura (1999, 2002, 2016) are present in our participants' accounts. This process of moral disengagement is closely related to the ideological training that takes place within these groups; a training that reverts the initial reactions of repudiation and fear toward the act of killing and allows the disengagement of moral regulation that under normal circumstances would block harmful actions against other human beings.

Ramón: We went from innocent to bloodthirsty children; sadly I say it this way, belonging to a criminal group in which we didn't respect anyone. From innocent minds to minds manipulated by ideology or trauma, and I no longer cared who to assassinate or to kill.

Discussion

The shocking Human Rights Watch (HRW) report on child combatants in Colombia points out that, in spite of the different personal stories and reasons, "there are, however, common denominators. In nearly all of the children's accounts, poverty, deprivation, underemployment, a truncated schooling, lack of affection and family support, parental ill-treatment, and insecurity intermingle as 'push' factors" (HRW, 2003, 36). In other words, the ideological factor was absent.

Financial problems are added to conditions of an affective nature. "Pull factors include promises of money (usually broken in the case of the guerrillas), thoughts of an easier life" (HRW, 2003, 36), which contrast with the lack of employment options and job insecurity in Colombian youth. The UNICEF (2004) report points out that in most Colombian rural areas, poorly paid work predominates as the only alternative to joining armed groups. Because of this, in spite of the fact that seven of our participants declare they joined willingly (looking for a job), it may be questioned if this is truly a voluntary membership.

The presence of weapons in their surroundings growing up (home and neighborhood) is a condition that several participants mention. In this regard, it would be advisable to remember the experiments that Berkowitz and Lepage (1967) carried out about the effect of weapons on aggressive behaviors. The presence of and access to a weapon or instrument of violence plays a triggering role in negative emotional states, especially anger derived from frustration. Weapons, Berkowitz says, not only facilitate the exercise of violence, they can also stimulate it: the finger pulls the trigger, but the presence of the trigger can also encourage the finger to pull it. The aforementioned UNICEF (2004) report indicates that 52% of their demobilized minor interviewees expressed fascination toward weapons and army paraphernalia as a motivation for joining the group. It would be sensible to think that they "give the adolescent attributes that, due to his or her developmental stage, he or she is eager to achieve such as recognition, power, feelings of belonging, originality and status that 'promote' him to the condition of an adult" (17). These are characteristics of the culture of violence (Waldmann, 2007), in which there are present patterns, traditions, and rules that lead to the perception of violence as legitimate and as an advisable conflict resolution method. In the culture of violence, violence has an instrumental value. Our participants have lived surrounded by violence and have ended up perceiving it as acceptable and necessary. What is unheard of in countries with a low level of violence becomes commonplace in countries with a culture of violence.

All these conditions (family dysfunctionality, lack of financial resources and a proper job, emotional pressure from family and friends, and daily presence of weapons since childhood, together with society militarization) create the ideal breeding ground for the recruitment of youths into illegal armed organizations.

However, attention is drawn to the scant role that political ideology has played in the decision to join any of these illegal groups. This is not new. In Luis de la Corte's meticulous analysis of the logic of terrorism, he highlights that ideology "is not the only indispensable causal condition for the appearance of terrorism" (de la Corte, 2006, 268). In his work about the Reserve Police Battalion 101, Christopher Browning places a stronger accent on variables that belong to the internal logic of the group (social pressure, obedience to authority, sense of duty, task distribution, etc.) than political ideology: only 25% of the 500 members that made up this battalion were members of the Nazi party, which could be a valid indicator of the existence or not of ideology (Browning, 1992).

In guerrilla groups as well as in paramilitary groups, military training—and not ideological training—was most important of all. In fact, the paramilitary forces had a training academy with instructors in the field of physical education, hand-to-hand combat, weaponry, and military intelligence. Óscar says: *"They train you on how to kill, how to kill someone."* These testimonies do not offer ideological arguments, but they do offer emotional ones: *"as far as I know, the ideology of the paramilitary was to finish the guerrilla"* (Juan Carlos). This approach automatically solves all the intricate complexities of ideology and places group beliefs (Bar-Tal, 1996) in reach for these fighters: a) the essence of the group is to defend its members; b) the limits of the in-group and out-group are marked by a line that divides "us" from "them"; and c) the actions that mark these beliefs are settled on the annihilation of the enemy. It is no longer the simple belief in the in-group's superiority (*"we are the ones who are on God's side,"* Luis Alfredo says), not even contempt toward members of the out-group in the terms in which Sumner (1906) defines ethnocentrism, but the action of taking the pertinent steps toward the enemy's extermination: *"I remember"*, interviewee John says, *"that Carlos Castaño[5] told us we had to finish the guerrilla in cold blood or with fire."* Ramon goes even further: *"All who didn't agree with us had to be eradicated."*

The construction of the image of the enemy culminates the cognitive journey that starts with the categorization process and paves the way to dehumanization in the proposed terms of Bandura (1999). Martín-Baró (2003) studies the image of the enemy in the frame of the social polarization that characterizes the context of war, and lends it a series of diverse and important missions: a) it is a perfect excuse to blame them for all evil, and in an extraordinarily effective game, it allows the justification of actions against them that would otherwise be ethically and politically unacceptable; b) it allows identity reaffirmation; and c) it serves as a pretext for internal control within the group (143).

Two attributes of the enemy acquire special importance. The first one has already been pointed out by Luis de la Corte in his studies on jihadist terrorism: the enemy is a collective agent (de la Corte, 2005, 198). It is a social category to which many different people with just one thing in common belong to: their membership, or in many cases, the perception or claim of that membership (an extraordinarily common process in the Colombian conflict). The second attribute has been highlighted by Aaron Beck: the enemy is perceived as dangerous, evil or cruel, and its image is usually accompanied by feelings of hate and revenge (Beck, 2000). This is the reason why the participants of this study have such ease in morally disengaging, which is just a form of ideology that uses the situation as its main reference and serves as a cognitive mechanism of justification of extremely violent actions perpetrated against the enemy. In the events that took place in Józefów, Browning (2002) says, conformity had special relevance, more so even than authority (320). Ultimately, killing people who belong to the category of "enemies" in cold blood "is part of the set of practical rules of war" (Neitzel & Welzer, 2012, 113).

Notes

1. Recently, a law that reduces the military service to 18 months has been passed.
2. Female participant.
3. A kind of compact bread made from corn, yucca, or plantain that is wrapped in leaves and boiled.
4. Euphemism for extortion.
5. Maximum commander of the AUC.

References

Adorno, T. W., Frenkel-Brunswik, E., Levinson, D. J., & Sanford, R. N. (1950). *The authoritarian personality*. New York, NY: The Norton Library.

Altier, M. B., Horgan, J., & Thoroughgood, C. (2012). In their own words? Methodological considerations in the analysis of terrorist autobiographies. *Journal of Strategic Security*, 5(4), 85–98.

Aranguren Romero, J. P. (2015). Inmunización y militarización del cuerpo social Colombia: El Estado en emergencia permanente. *Athenea Digital*, 15(4), 305–327.

Bandura, A. (1973). *Aggression. A social learning analysis*. London, UK: Prentice-Hall International.

Bandura, A. (1999). Moral disengagement in the perpetration of inhumanities. *Personality and Social Psychology Review*, 3(3), 193–209.

Bandura, A. (2002). Selective moral disengagement in the exercise of moral agency. *Journal of Moral Education*, 31(2), 101–119.

Bandura, A. (2016). *Moral disengagement: How people do harm and live with themselves*. Gordonsville, VA: Worth Publishers.

Bar-Tal, D. (1996). Las creencias grupales como expresión de la identidad social. In J. F. Morales, D. Páez, J. C. Deschamps, & S. Worchel (Eds.), *Identidad social. Aproximaciones psicosociales a los grupos y a las relaciones entre grupos* (pp. 255–285). Valencia, Spain: Promolibro.

Beck, A. T. (2000). *Prisoners of hate: The cognitive basis of anger, hostility, and violence*. New York, NY: Perennial Library.

Berkowitz, L. (1989). Frustration-aggression hypothesis: Examination and reformulation. *Psychological Bulletin*, 106(1), 59–73. https://doi.org/10.1037/0033-2909.106.1.59

Berkowitz, L., & Lepage, A. (1967). Weapons as aggression-eliciting stimuli. *Journal of Personality and Social Psychology*, 7, 202–207.

Blanco, A. (2008). La condición de enemigo: El ocaso de la inocencia. In M. Cancio & L. Pozuelo (Eds.), *Política criminal en vanguardia* (pp. 259–305). Madrid, Spain: Thompson/Civitas.

Blanco, A., & de la Corte, L. (2003). Psicología social de la violencia: Introducción a la perspectiva de Ignacio Martín-Baró. In I. Martín-Baró, *Poder, ideología y violencia* (pp. 9–62). Madrid, Spain: Trotta.

Bradshaw-Smith, A. (2015, March 26). 4.4 million Colombians lifted out of poverty in past 5 years: Santo. *Colombia Reports*. https://colombiareports.com/4-4-million-colombians-lifted-out-of-poverty-in-past-5-years-santos/

Browning, C. R. (1992). *Ordinary men: Reserve Police battalion 101 and the final solution in Poland*. New York, NY: HarperCollins.

Burck, C. (2005). Comparing qualitative research methodologies for systemic research: The use of grounded theory, discourse analysis and narrative analysis. *Journal of Family Therapy*, 27(3), 237–262.

Costa Pinto, L. (1969). *Nacionalismo y militarismo*. México, Mexico City: Siglo XXI Editores.

Davies-Rubio, A., Blanco, A., & Mirón, L. (2016). Hate and revenge in the life of a repented killer. In E. Dunbar, A. Blanco, & D. A. Crèvecoeur-MacPhail (Eds.), *The psychology of hate crimes as domestic terrorism: U.S. and global issues. Volume Two: Assessment issues with victims and offenders* (pp. 263–278). Westport, CT: Praeger.

de la Corte, L. (2005). Sobre Leviatanes, demonios y mártires: Procesos de legitimación del terrorismo islamista. In A. Blanco, R. del Águila, & J. M. Sabucedo (Eds.), *Madrid 11-M. Un análisis del mal y sus consecuencias* (pp. 189–219). Madrid, Spain: Trotta.

de la Corte, L. (2006). *La lógica del terrorismo*. Madrid, Spain: Alianza.

Dollard, J., Miller, N. E., Doob, L. W., Mowrer, O. H., & Sears, R. R. (1939). *Frustration and aggression*. New Haven, CT: Yale University Press. https://doi.org/10.1037/10022-000

Elliott, R., & Timulak, L. (2005). Descriptive and interpretive approaches to qualitative research. In J. Miles & P. Gilbert (Eds.), *A handbook of research methods for clinical and health psychology* (pp. 147–159). Oxford, UK: Oxford University Press.

Favre, H. (2004, June). Daniel Pécaut Guerra contra la sociedad Bogota, Espasa, 2001. In *Annales. Histoire, Sciences Sociales*, 59(3), 686–688. Cambridge, UK: Cambridge University Press.

Feierabend, I. K., & Feierabend, R. L. (1972). Systemic conditions of political aggression: An application of frustration-aggression theory. In I. K. Feierabend, R. L. Feierabend, & T. R. Gurr (Eds.), *Anger, violence, and politics: Theories and research* (pp. 136–83). Englewood Cliffs, NJ: Prentice-Hall.

Glaser, B. G., & Strauss, A. L. (1967). *The discovery of grounded theory: Strategies for qualitative research*. Chicago, IL: Aldine.

Grupo de Memoria Histórica (GMH). (2013). *¡Basta Ya! Colombia: Memorias de guerra y dignidad*. Bogotá, Colombia: Imprenta Nacional.

Horgan, J. (2012). Interviewing the terrorists: Reflections on fieldwork and implications for psychological research. *Behavioral Sciences of Terrorism and Political Aggression,* 4(3), 195–211.

Human Rights Watch (HRW). (2003). *You'll learn not to cry.* New York, NY: Human Rights Watch.

Internal Displacement Monitoring Centre, IDMC. (2017). *Global report on internal displacement.* Oslo, Norway: Norwegian Refugee Council.

Madill, A. (2012). Interviews and interviewing techniques. In H. Cooper (Ed.), *APA handbook of research methods in psychology: Vol. 1. Foundations, planning measures, and psychometrics* (pp. 1–27). Washington, DC: APA.

Martín-Baró, I., (1983). *Acción e ideología: Psicología social desde centroamérica I* (2nd ed.). San Salvador, El Salvador: UCA Editores.

Martín-Baró, I. (2003). *Poder, ideología y violencia.* Madrid, Spain: Trotta.

Neitzel, S., & Welzer, H. (2012). *Soldaten: On fighting, killing and dying.* London, UK: Simon & Schuster.

Polkinghorne, D. E. (2005). Language and meaning: Data collection in qualitative research. *Journal of Counseling Psychology,* 52(2), 137–145.

Programa de las Naciones Unidas para el Desarrollo. (2016a). *Informe sobre desarrollo humano 2016.* New York, NY: United Nations.

Programa de las Naciones Unidas para el Desarrollo. (2016b, July 1). Colombia en el Informe de desarrollo humano. https://www.co.undp.org/content/colombia/es/home/presscenter/articles/2016/07/01/colombia-en-el-informe-de-desarrollo-humano-progreso-multidimensional-bienestar-m-s-all-del-ingreso-.html

Reinares, F. (2011). *Patriotas de la muerte.* Barcelona, Spain: Taurus.

Sánchez Pedraza, M. A. (2014, December 17). Santos ordena a Planeación Nacional destapar la riqueza de los más adinerados. https://www.larepublica.co/economia/santos-ordena-a-planeacion-nacional-destapar-la-riqueza-de-los-mas-adinerados-2203711

Staub, E. (1996). Cultural-societal roots of violence. The examples of genocidal violence and of contemporary youth violence in the United States. *American Psychologist,* 51(2), 117–132.

Staub, E. (2006). Reconciliation after genocide, mass killing, or intractable conflict: Understanding the roots of violence, psychological recovery, and steps toward a general theory. *Political Psychology,* 27(6), 867–894. http://www.jstor.org/stable/20447006

Sumner, W. (1906). *Folkways: A study of sociological importance of usages, manners, customs, mores and morals.* Boston: Atheneaum Press.

Tajfel, H., Billig, M., Bundy, R., & Flament, C. (1971). Social categorization and intergroup behaviour. *European Journal of Social Psychology,* 1(2), 149–178.

Teymur, S. (2007). *A conceptual map for understanding the terrorist recruitment process: Observation and analysis of DHKP/C, PKK and Turkish Hezbollah terrorist organizations.* Denton, TX: University of North Texas.

Tilly, C. (2003). *The politics of collective violence.* Cambridge, UK: Cambridge University Press.

Trinquier, R. (1964). *Modern warfare: A French view of counterinsurgency*. New York, NY: Praeger.

United Nations Children's Emergency Fund (UNICEF). (2004). Boletín 8. La niñez en el conflicto armado colombiano (1st ed., p. 43). Bogotá: UNICEF. Recuperado de. https://www.unicef.org/colombia/pdf/boletin-8.pdf

Waldmann, P. (2007). Is there a culture of violence in Colombia? *Terrorism and Political Violence*, 19(4), 593–609.

World Bank. (2015). Índice de Gini. https://datos.bancomundial.org/indicador/SI.POV.GINI?locations=CO

Yilmaz, I. (2009). *Patterns of differential involvement in terrorist activities: Evidence from DHKP/C and Turkish Hezbollah*. Richmond, VA: Virginia Commonwealth University.

CHAPTER TEN

Group Indoctrination: Techniques of Depersonalization and Domination of Individual Consciousness

Milton J. Bennett

Fake news and fake allegations of fake news are just the currently popular forms of deception. In fact, we are surrounded by deception. Birds do it (cuckoos), bees do it (with orchids), and primates certainly do it. So, it is not surprising that we humans have an extremely well-developed technology for manipulating misinformation. And as we have developed more self-reflexive perception that is capable of deconstructing deception, it is equally unsurprising that techniques for suppressing that kind of critical thought have also proliferated.

This chapter will explore one particularly disturbing form of human deception: the group manipulation of trust for the purpose of domination. When this effort is successful, individuals are discouraged from exercising critical thought about the culture of the group and encouraged to unquestioningly acquiesce to authority. Of course, all cultural groups, by definition, demand conformity, but the focus of this chapter will be on those groups that intentionally use techniques of depersonalization and domination of individual consciousness to ensure acquiescence to authority. And while all communication is to some extent persuasive and goal oriented, here the focus is on communication that is intentionally coercive toward the goal of control.

My professional background is in cognitive linguistics and intercultural communication, and my PhD research was on constructivist theories of consciousness (summarized in Castiglioni & Bennett, 2018). This somewhat unusual combination led me to be particularly interested in the relationship of culture and consciousness. One of the foundational principles of intercultural communication is that culture operates as a kind of group consciousness—a tacit agreement among people on how they should coordinate meaning and action in the group (Hall, 1959). Within this definition my research has focused on how people become aware of their own cultural contexts and how they can consequently develop the ability to shift among different forms of group consciousness (Bennett, 2013). I believe this development of cultural meta-consciousness (*intercultural consciousness*) is the underlying competence of intercultural communication. Specifically, my work has suggested a developmental path from *ethnocentrism*, the unconscious experience of one's culture as the only reality, to *ethnorelativism*, the ability to consciously experience the world in multiple ways (Bennett, 2017).

Loss of Consciousness

Through this lens of intercultural consciousness, I was struck by what appeared to be an extreme ethnocentrism generated by groups I called "culting organizations." While I was concerned with the reports of psychological abuse by former members ("brainwashing," using the controversial term coined by Lifton, 1969), I was more intrigued with the strategies being used by group leaders to create such extreme social environments. That intrigue turned to severe concern after the tragedy of Jonestown in 1978, where over 900 people were murdered and committed suicide at the behest of their leader, Jim Jones. During the 1980s, initially in partnership with Bill Casey, I organized my observations into a model of cult indoctrination that formed the basis of some university courses and educational programs. In 1984, I found myself the local (Portland, Oregon) media expert on the unfortunate descent into culting by the very creative and interesting Rajneeshpuram community. The 1993 travesty of the Branch Davidians in Waco, Texas, where David Koresh and various U.S. government agencies created a standoff in which four officers were shot to death and 83 members of the group were burned to death, finally brought some attention to the unique qualities of dealing with culting organizations. As part of an educational effort undertaken by the FBI, I compiled my observations into an article, "Communicating with Cults," which attempted to differentiate the worldview of an errant culting organization from that of more normal groups of criminals or hostages (Bennett, 1997; Van Zandt, 1997).

As implied by the title of this chapter, my concern is with group dynamics rather than individual pathology. This level of analysis is important in addressing much of the criticism of Singer (1995) and others who assumed that the coercive conversion techniques of "cults" could generate individual pathology. That view, which became the core of an anti-cult movement, was eventually criticized by many mainstream psychologists who questioned both the appropriateness and the rigor of the movement's psychopathology explanations. According to Melton (1999), most psychologists came to agree with the position exemplified by Galanter (1982), who suggested that the noncritical behavior of people in cults (or, as he preferred to call them, "new religions") was simply adaptation to particular social environments. I will maintain that frame of social adaptation rather than individual pathology, but the implications of group indoctrination are really no less troubling than those of individual pathology.

Apparently, people can rather easily adapt to social conditions that demand uncritical acquiescence to authority (e.g., Asch, 1952; Milgram, 1974; Zimbardo & Andersen, 1993). This would be consistent with the suggestion of Julian Jaynes (1976) that self-reflexive, or critical, consciousness is a relatively new phenomenon in human experience. Jaynes argues that consciousness in the sense of critical self-awareness (or authorship) is not necessary to the basic coordinating function of culture, as evidenced by the aforementioned birds and bees or even ants being able to coordinate group action quite effectively without (assumedly) individual consciousness. The fact that human language is more complex than birdcalls or insect dances allows humans to coordinate more sophisticated action in larger groups, but it does not automatically imbue them with self-awareness. According to Jaynes, self-awareness is the consequence of a particular self-referential application of language that defines a "self" through the objectified metaphor of "me" and its causal analogue, "I." In this assumption he parallels Mead (1934), whose seminal work in social constructionism also posited the construction of "me" as a metaphorical social object. However, Jaynes speculates that this form of individual consciousness was originally an adaptation to dealing with a rapid increase in cross-cultural contact that occurred in many parts of the world about 3,000 years ago. This view is consistent with the basic assumption of adaptation that underlies current evolutionary psychology (e.g., Dawkins, 1989; Dennett, 1991).

If self-reflexive consciousness is a relatively new human capability, it is likely to be inconsistent and unstable; consciousness may be adaptive to differing degrees in different or shifting contexts. For instance, people who need to manage higher levels of cross-cultural contact may be impelled to develop more skill in contextual awareness, an observation consistent with most treatments of intercultural communication (Bennett, 2017). Or, as is commonly observed in liberal arts education, higher levels of critical thinking correlate with exposure to multiple disciplinary perspectives (Scheuer, 2015). By contrast, the restriction of access to multiple perspectives typical of doctrinal parochial education, cults, or new religions is likely to inhibit the development of self-reflexive consciousness and critical thinking. If it is true, as claimed by Jaynes, that the preconscious human world was ruled by gods and god-kings whose authority was conveyed by hallucinatory voices, then most of human existence has been lived in an unquestionable condition of acquiescence to authority—of obeying the voices of the gods. So, a return to that condition is not pathological, as the term "brainwashing" might imply, but rather a diminution of a particular adaptive behavior.

In a recent related publication, I argued that the instability of critical consciousness could explain the apparent ease with which people retreat from tolerance to systematic hatred toward groups of others (Bennett, 2016). Here I will further suggest that group leaders can intentionally, systematically, and relatively easily create the conditions for suppression of self-reflexive consciousness. Like building a fire that exercises a mysterious draw on people around it, they are building a structure that evokes a kind of species memory. As Jaynes (1976) states it,

> The mind is still haunted with its old unconscious ways; it broods on lost authorities; and the yearning, the deep and hollowing yearning for divine volition and service is with us still. (314)

Culting Techniques

There are three techniques that appear in nearly every description of culting groups: *control, coercion,* and *conversion*. In the following paragraphs I will explicate each technique, and then in the subsequent section I will describe the sequential process of applying the techniques that allows groups to recruit and maintain obedient members. For reasons of possible legal liability, I will sometimes avoid mentioning the names of groups. I leave it to the readers to determine if my descriptions of the general pattern fit their personal experience or knowledge of such groups.

Control. Culting groups often have a charismatic leader who consistently exercises authority—notoriously, Jim Jones of Peoples Temple, or Reverend Sun Myung Moon of the Unification Church. While these and a few other leaders of large groups are well known for their authoritarianism, such leadership is more common in smaller groups that operate like "personality cults." In larger groups, the founder of the group may have abdicated or died, yet the group maintains control nevertheless. This is because authority is institutionalized in what Robert Lifton (1991) calls "milieu control:"

> Milieu control is maintained and expressed by intense group process, continuous psychological pressure, and isolation by geographical distance, unavailability of transportation, or even physical restraint. Often the group creates an increasingly intense sequence of events such as seminars, lectures and encounters which makes leaving extremely difficult, both physically and psychologically. (1–2)

In his seminal work *Thought Reform and the Psychology of Totalism* (1969), Lifton noted that for "brainwashing" to be effective, the victim must be restricted from leaving the context (e.g., imprisoned). In his later work (e.g., Lifton, 1991), he affirms that the restriction might not just be a physical restraint; it could be a self-imposed reluctance to leave the context. For instance, the lure of graduating to a higher spiritual level could impel one to voluntarily accept degrading treatment or choose to turn over large sums of money. While from the outside, those actions might seem imposed, they could well be experienced both at the time and later as free choices. The line between freely buying the product and being conned is not so clear. In the scholarly treatment of her own culting experience, Lalich (2004) calls this a "bounded choice"—yes, a choice, but one that is heavily influenced by the boundaries of a desired context.

A new form of "bounded choice" may be our reliance on social media and other internet groups. For instance, in a study of exchange students, Castiglioni (2011) found that voluntary participation in social media dramatically reduced students' willingness to engage a new cultural environment. This and similar observations (e.g., Turkle, 2011) point to a new form of self-imposed control—addictive participation in virtual groups that exercise milieu control at a distance. On the surface, addiction to social media seems to be destructive of actual social relations. But a deeper implication of these studies may be that in accepting a high level of milieu control, people are making themselves susceptible to culting manipulations. Stories of individuals radicalized by the Islamic State (ISIS) seem to be examples of this phenomenon. In an exploration of the culting aspects of ISIS, Wood (2015) suggests that its rise to power is like "the realization of a dystopian alternate reality in which David Koresh or Jim Jones survived to wield absolute power over not just a few hundred people, but some 8 million." In an investigation of ISIS's recruiting, Graham (2017) points to the sophisticated internet materials that make up the bulk of ISIS's communication with outsiders:

> ISIS recruiting pitches on the Internet are warm and welcoming, with stirring imagery and professionally produced videos. Most are reasonable in tone and content. They are expertly targeted to address real or imagined ambitions and grievances, to appeal to a potential recruit's sense of adventure, and to offer an attractive cause worth fighting for. The pitches are designed to produce and support a virtual community of ISIS fans, an echo chamber reinforcing the description of ISIS as a social movement devoted to protecting Muslims and to fighting an unfair global system. (3)

Graham uses the popular term "echo chamber," which here and in other situations such as the 2016 U.S. American presidential race refers to the idea that people voluntarily wall themselves into a network of contacts and information that is extremely susceptible to manipulation. For example, alt-right groups introduce explicitly racist, sexist, and fascist material into the echo chambers with an overlay of irony and cynicism, allowing people who actually agree with the material to disavow (perhaps even to themselves) that agreement (Romano, 2017). The groups exercise virtual control by discouraging participants from venturing outside the network, much as the Unification Church (Moonies) once insisted on members cutting ties to their families and avoiding contact with nonbelievers (Underwood & Underwood, 1979).

The alt-right redefinition of "trolling" is one way that culting groups do not just control the environment—they control the meaning that is attached to all behavior inside and outside the boundary of the group. So, for instance, once having bought the idea that a spaceship will extract chosen people from the impending apocalypse, it is relatively easy for the group to transform "abusive behavior" into something like "the redemptive punishment for past sins that must be endured to enable the transition." The control of meaning is intertwined with the control of behavior. This, of course, is the point notably made by Orwell (1949); in *Nineteen Eighty-Four,* thought control is supported by a Ministry of Truth, whose function is to rewrite history and translate it into "newspeak." In my own research on communication with cults, I repeatedly encountered cases where group members were instructed in secret new meanings for common terms. In the many groups that define "levels" of enlightenment, learning the new meanings was part of the initiation into higher levels. Failure to use words in the newly defined ways was cause for correction of group insiders and for ridicule or condemnation of outsiders (Bennett, 1997)

Coercion. Classical rhetoric distinguishes among *information, persuasion,* and *coercion* (Howell, 1973). Information increases choices by generating more viable alternatives, persuasion argues for making one viable choice over another, while coercion restricts choice by making all but one choice unviable. For instance, providing information about different religious beliefs increases the number of choices available for spiritual experience, allowing for a persuasive argument that spiritual experience A is superior to spiritual experience B. The persuasion shades into coercion when experience B is labeled as an evil that damns one to eternal perdition, while A is presented as the only path to salvation. Of course, the ultimate coercion is "do this or I will kill you."

Schein (1961) uses the term "coercive persuasion" to convey the idea that brainwashing is not so much a violent imposition as a form of manipulation. Under the controlled conditions described above, aggressive persuasion takes on the character of coercion by making agreement with the argued choice the only viable way to remain a member of the beloved group. Culting organizations coercively limit information in several ways: (a) the living environment of members may be specified; (b) contact with outsiders is prohibited; (c) news and other information originating outside the group is considered suspect, if not intentionally misleading (fake news!). Through these and other techniques, the culting group limits alternatives to only two: the absolute verity of the group's philosophy or the abysmal perversion of any other position. The penalty for choosing falsehood over truth is unequivocal damnation or its equivalent, eternal separation from the group. In some cases that I personally investigated, former members believed that if they deviated in thought or deed from the group dogma, they would die. In this condition, attempts by outsiders to exert persuasion or counter-coercion will usually fail. If group members are already in the ultimate state of coercion—they must believe or die—no other argument or threat is meaningful.

Conversion. Unlike other groups that may use control and coercion, culting organizations have the specific agenda of conversion. While this may seem a small distinction, it restricts our discussion to groups that are attempting to control both beliefs and behavior. For instance, while evangelical religious groups focus on conversion, they may or may not use control and coercion as part of their effort. If they do not, then they are engaging in ordinary missionary efforts—activity that should not be conflated with culting. Similarly, activities such as military training may use control and coercion, but they are not usually aimed at conversion, and thus they also should not be seen as culting. The restriction of "culting" to the combination of all three elements addresses some of the criticism of earlier treatments of cults, which was that too many new religious or political groups were being unfairly labeled with the term (Melton & Moore, 1982).

Culting organizations do usually define themselves as contrarian, like many new religious or political groups. However, they particularly want to maneuver recruits into a position where previous beliefs can be "disintegrated" and supplanted by the new beliefs touted by the group. As noted by Hoffer (1951) in his definition of a *true believer*, there is nothing more powerful than a newly acquired belief, and culting organizations seek that level of commitment from their members. For instance, ISIS does not just want to reinforce Islam, it wants to convert Muslims into its particular fundamentalist belief system (Wood, 2015). The resulting true believerism supports the extreme behavior of the group and generates a strong desire to convert others to the new belief. In nearly all culting groups that I encountered in my research, a doctrine like "heavenly deception" encouraged those conversion efforts to be duplicitous. (See Underwood & Underwood, 1979, for a long description of heavenly deception.) The benign appearance of ISIS recruitment efforts or the cynical mask of alt-right racism extends duplicitous conversion efforts into virtual space.

The Culting Process

To further restrict the definition of culting groups to those that are intentionally using duplicitous and coercive methods to convert people, it has been useful to identify a sequential process commonly used by such groups. I have named four "stages" of that process 1) seduction, 2) disorientation, 3) snapping, and 4) maintenance (Bennett, 1997). It is possible to observe other kinds of groups using some of the techniques described below, but, by definition, only culting organizations exhibit all four of the stages in this order. Further, the techniques as they operate in the culting process appear to be orchestrated—almost as if there exists a manual on how to do it. In fact, one culting group (EST) that spawned several imitators is well known for providing such directions (Rhinehart, 1976). In the current internet environment, finding directions for doing just about anything is taken for granted, and it apparently is not difficult to hire an expert in data manipulation. But for the most part, the culting process is so prevalent because it works—a fact that is discovered repeatedly by aspiring leaders.

Seduction

Recruitment into culting organizations is usually deceptive. Seduction is *the effort to attract new members to a group whose hidden purpose is conversion*. In some cases, the term is literally descriptive; recruits are tempted by offers of sex. But more often, recruits are figuratively seduced by appeals to various other needs. In my earlier study of culting groups I concluded that these appeals are so sophisticated and so varied that anyone, no matter how mentally stable, is potentially susceptible to one of them.

Recruitment is a central activity for culting organizations. In some cases, the motivation for recruitment is clear—fundraising. New recruits may be encouraged to contribute their entire savings and sign over their homes to the group. The recent documentary on the Rajneeshees, *Wild Wild West* (2018), notes that many people contributed their entire worth to Rajneeshpuram in Antelope, Oregon, as a sign of their devotion. That was just part of a sophisticated fundraising effort conducted by the group from its beginning in India (Zaitz, 1985)—an effort that depended on fresh supplies of devotees to fund the group's activities (including maintaining a fleet of Rolls Royce automobiles for the Bagwan Rajneesh).

A less obvious, but perhaps more important, reason for ongoing recruitment is to maintain the "salvation" mission of the group. While the Rajneeshees were apparently not motivated by traditional salvation, most culting organizations portray themselves as purveyors of some truth that will save members from an ignoble end, frequently one that is imminent. The apocalyptic vision may be the traditional biblical one, or it may predict various forms of social, economic, or galactic collapse. A surprising number of long-lived groups were originally founded around immediate end-of-the-world scenarios, which then needed to be downplayed as deadlines passed. Still, the apocalyptic vision may continue to be accepted by members as the motivation for recruiting and saving as many (deserving) people as possible (Festinger, Riecken, & Schacter, 1956).

The seductive specializations of culting groups can be roughly categorized by Maslow's (1968) Hierarchy of Needs:

Physiological needs. Survivalist groups do this best, providing members with woodsman skills, freeze-dried food, and weapons training to protect their stocks from others with less foresight. These groups are nearly always driven by an apocalyptic theme, and the seduction is simple physical survival. Like all culting groups, there is also the seduction of elitism: we, and only we, have the foresight to prepare for this cataclysm, and so we will be the most deserving of survival. Following a military model, many of these groups use control techniques extensively.

Security Needs. The "prosperity cults" specialize at this level, usually taking the form of weekend seminars or pyramid marketing schemes. Recruits are seduced by the assurance of riches, frequently attainable without much effort or training via special imaging techniques taught in subsequent (expensive) sessions. This seduction is often driven by testimonials from people who have ostensibly used the system successfully. While certainly oriented toward conversion, generally these groups are not heavily controlling or coercive.

A more enduring type of group that addresses security needs is the "therapy cult"—organizations that offer salvation from alcohol, other drugs, or debilitating mental conditions. The seduction is getting straight or becoming centered, but the route to that stability is pure culting process. Testimonials are employed extensively in the seduction, along with reminders of the sorry state in which recruits have arrived. With the rationale that addicts respond only to this treatment, culting therapy groups depend heavily on control and coercion to achieve conversion. As a result, these groups have a higher probability of becoming virulent; for instance, Jim Jones's People's Temple began as a therapy cult.

Social Needs. All culting organizations, like most other voluntary associations, stress the social benefits of belonging to the group. In a culting organization, however, the benefits are often exaggerated in deceptive ways. For example, one group is known for "love bombing" prospective recruits. This procedure is defined by a former member as "persistent psychological effort to disarm a skeptical recruit by excessive attention in order to get him or her into the cult" (Underwood & Underwood, 1979, 300). Prospective recruits may be overwhelmed by the ostensible acceptance they experience and thus be drawn further into the culting process (Appel, 1983).

Status and Self-Esteem Needs. Most groups also play on these needs as part of their seduction, but some groups are particularly effective at this level. Elitism may be fed by the promise of attaining secret knowledge, meeting the new avatar, hanging out with celebrities, or acquiring special cosmic skills such as astral travel, reading auras, or levitation. Groups at this level may be less coercive than some others, and control is exercised through a kind of "keeping up with the Joneses" conformity. An exception to this generalization is when self-esteem is being offered as a remedy for people who have been disadvantaged by discrimination, poverty, or addiction. Despite being couched in self-esteem terms, these groups look and act like "therapy cults," and they have more potential for becoming seriously coercive.

Self-Actualization Needs. Many culting groups operate seductions at this level, including both those that label themselves as secular and those that claim to be religious. Completing a "personality test" and receiving information on how to clear your life of obstacles certainly appeals to this need for psychological growth. Other appeals are to altruism, unconditional love, self-knowledge (including knowledge of past lives), and the attainment of happiness. In self-actualization groups, the exercise of control and coercion is mixed. At the entry levels of many of these groups, there is more persuasion than coercion, and control follows the conformity model of the self-esteem groups. However, the advanced training conducted by the weekend groups and the "development" courses offered by other groups involve increasing amounts of control and, by some accounts, extreme coercion against advanced participants who leave or criticize the group (Conway & Siegelman, 1979).

Transcendent Needs. Most of the Western and Eastern religion-based culting groups appeal predominantly to these needs. The seduction is "oneness" with a supernatural order or being—a condition that can only be attained through the special procedures taught by the group. Neo-Christian groups generally appeal to dissatisfaction with mainstream churches and propose radical alternatives that claim previously hidden truths. These groups additionally offer a disciplined morality and salvation from ambiguity. Non-Western groups in the United States are often based on small sects of Hindu, Buddhist, or Islamic traditions that have been fanned into new life by emigrant charismatic leaders. They offer trendy meditation practices and a new vocabulary for discussing consciousness. Previously, New Age groups succeeded in addressing self-esteem, self-actualization, and transcendent needs with custom-designed beliefs drawn from traditional religions, ancient wisdom, magic, psychic phenomena, psychology, and capitalism. In the current polarized political climate of the United States and many other nations, political culting groups also are appealing to transcendent needs in this way. Of course, national socialism under Hitler was a classic example of the mix of quasi-religious symbolism, psychic phenomena, and industrialism. As noted by many (e.g., Berlet & Lyons, 2000; Riemen, 2018), populist movements are brewing a similar mix of ingredients, now potentiated by manipulative and coercive uses of the internet.

Because their philosophies are all encompassing, quasi-religious culting groups are more likely to be pervasive in their influence on members. Traditionally, control has been exercised through required communal living, group rituals, nonstop proselytizing, and fundraising activities. With the development of internet connectivity, control also can be exercised in the echo chambers of social media. Leaders of these groups are more likely to fit the "charismatic" model, and the potential for virulence is high.

The purpose of the seduction is usually to move a potential recruit into a controlled environment where the next stage of culting can occur. A controlled environment is one where, for physical or psychological reasons, exiting is difficult. The place might be a somewhat isolated camp, a large room with "guards" at the doors, or any other place where social pressure can be applied to discourage leaving. Most writers such as Lifton (1991), referenced earlier, suggest that the pressure applied at this stage is rarely, if ever, physical; people are not forcefully restrained. But the calculated use of psychological and social pressure is so effective that leaving is either unthinkable or extremely difficult.

Disorientation

Once in a controlled environment, recruits are subjected to intentional disorientation. For these purposes we can consider disorientation to be *over-stimulation or under-stimulation for the purpose of decreasing reasoning abilities and increasing suggestibility.* This idea is similar, of course, to Robert Lifton's notion of brainwashing discussed in the classic book on this subject, *Thought Reform and the Psychology of Totalism* (1969). But here the term is used in a less politicized way. Disorientation can be used at varying levels of intensity, by any person or group, for any purpose. For instance, therapists sometimes use disorientation techniques with their clients, discount grocery stores employ low levels of disorientation to encourage buying, and all sorts of bands, shows, and other forms of entertainment use some of these techniques to enhance their performances. At the other extreme, disorientation can be used for torture. In a recent discussion of that topic, Leach (2016) suggested that when people are in environments "marked by more intense stimuli and a real or perceived lack of control," they may experience psychological disorientation (isolation, sensory deprivation, sensory overload, sleep deprivation, temporal disorientation), psychophysiological disorientation (thermal, stress positions), and psychosocial disorientation (cultural humiliation, sexual degradation). According to Leach, these stimulus conditions can be coordinated to undermine the will or resistance of people in controlled situations.

In the case of culting groups under consideration here, techniques of disorientation are used to alter normal states of consciousness—normal perceptual functioning that is tuned to a particular kind and level of stimulus is disrupted, creating an altered state of consciousness. In a controlled environment, the natural tendency to return to a normal state of consciousness is blocked by continued disorientation, so the altered state becomes fixed. New perceptual connections are sought to restabilize the worldview in the altered state, and thus the conditions for conversion are established. Further, in culting groups these techniques are employed as part of a carefully orchestrated effort that began with Seduction and will continue into snapping and maintenance.

Psychological and psychophysiological disorientation is a common part of the culting process. For instance, many culting groups immediately require recruits to fast or in other ways radically change their diets, and nearly all deprive them of sleep. Overstimulation may occur through excessive exercise, marathon lecturing, loud music or noise, frenetic activity, and instigation of anger, fear, or other high-intensity emotional states. Under-stimulation techniques include silence, low lighting, confinement, long meditation or prayer, and breathing exercises. In some cases, drugs may also be used to induce disorientation.

Psychosocial disorientation occurs when normal patterns of human interaction are disrupted. For instance, many former members report that as recruits they were accompanied by members at all times, even when using the toilet. Other disorienting events that have been reported are personal confessions, self-abrogation, restriction of privacy, intimate questioning and the reliving of traumatic experience, restriction of normal feedback in communication, and public attacks. Public attacks are disorienting not only to the immediate target, but also to those who witness them. Any dramatic breaking of social norms has this disorienting effect, and masters of the culting process use that fact with extreme effectiveness. (See Zimbardo & Andersen, 1993, for more examples of this kind of disorientation.)

In addition to the categories of disorientation suggested by Leach (2016), I would add the category of *cognitive disorientation*. Severe attacks on peoples' beliefs in controlled circumstances can lead to an ambiguity and uncertainty of thought. In uncontrolled situations people might argue with the attacker, or, if the attacker seemed closed to dialogue, they might just leave. In a controlled culting environment, leaving is not a viable option. Some former "trainers" reported to me that they welcomed argument; it gave them a chance to ridicule and humiliate the intrepid participant, thus adding social disruption to the overall cognitive disorientation. Recruits sometimes feel that leaders or trainers can "read their thoughts," so uncannily accurate is their rendering of the predictable attempts recruits make to protect their beliefs. One by one, these beliefs are deconstructed, dismantled, and destroyed, leaving a void waiting to be filled with new meaning.

The orchestration stimuli in disorientation yields massive amounts of ambiguity. Everything is uncertain—how you feel, who you are, and what you believe. At just the right moment, a resolution of the ambiguity is offered, setting up the next stage of snapping.

Snapping

This term is borrowed from the title of Conway and Siegelman's 1979 book. The book was an early (before Jonestown) look at the proliferation of culting groups in the seventies. The authors noted the growing incidence of "sudden personality change" that seemed to accompany membership in some groups, a phenomenon they labeled "snapping." The definition of snapping I use here is *a radical and sudden shift in belief system*. It is the adaptation to an abrupt shift in worldview that generates the appearance of personality change, probably not a change in the basic structure of personality. Rather than being pathological in those terms, snapping is more like a prolonged case of culture shock.

When enough ambiguity has been generated by disorientation, recruits are offered a completely new belief system that mitigates the uncertainty. It really doesn't matter what the new beliefs are, nor is it even important that they are internally consistent. The crucial factor seems to be that the beliefs are proffered at the correct time, and that they are presented as comprehensive and absolute. When these conditions are met, the recruit "snaps" into the new beliefs.

Accompanying the sudden shift is a whole host of physiological and emotional symptoms. It does not matter what beliefs are abandoned or what beliefs are newly embraced—the same symptoms occur. Vision takes on a new clarity. Smells become almost unbearably intense. One's body feels strong and light, muscles taut. Relationships seem bottomless in their depth and limitless in their intensity. People are suffused with a feeling of certainty, of knowing, as if the universe had suddenly opened to their view. The new belief is attached to these experiences. When a person such as a charismatic leader or guru is the focus of the snap, recruits are encouraged to attribute their feelings to the overwhelming love of the leader for them. If the focus of the group is a philosophy, the snapping is attributed to the inherent truth and power of the ideas. In all cases, the recruit is presented with what seems to be a simple empirical proof: "You would not be feeling this way if this idea (or person) were not uniquely powerful."

New culting groups create an ever-expanding list of words to describe snapping, each new term implying its uniqueness from all the other snapping experiences: getting visions, new clarity, ecstasy, complete realization, theophany, eureka, born again, getting it, enlightenment, blissing out, finding it, getting clear, epiphany, letting go and letting god, seeing the light, coming over, arriving, getting there, ah-ha, getting elegant, celestialized, finding your diamond, waked . . . and more. Clearly the experience is a powerful one, and this discussion is not meant to trivialize its importance. But when the experience is embedded in the culting process, the experience of snapping is turned from exploration to exploitation, from commitment to conversion. Many of the world's great religions teach us to accept the self and seek transcendence. In contrast, the culting process leads us to reject the self and develop dependence.

At this point, leaders of culting organizations face a choice. They can consider their job of conversion accomplished and send the recruits home, where they will encourage their friends and partners to enroll in the next seminar ("I can't tell you any more about it—you just have to experience it yourself"). Or the organization can decide that it is a community that should have a separate identity. It is the latter decision that sets up the final stage of culting.

Maintenance

New belief systems instilled during snapping are not very resilient in the everyday world. They quickly fall prey to the prevalent worldview of family and society unless they are reinforced and nurtured in a like-minded community. So, culting organizations set up maintenance: *the use of group cohesion techniques to reinforce commitment to new beliefs and new community.* This attempt to maintain and intensify the conversion often seems to have a life of its own, leading groups to become more and more isolated and fearful.

The first phase of group maintenance does not look dissimilar from other support groups. A minimal degree of cohesion creates an *us/them group.* With this relatively mild distinction, people recognize one another as "members" without exaggerating their separation from society at large. If members live together in the same house, the arrangement tends to be a casual one with people moving in and out of the environment. More often, groups in this phase simply have meetings together where they share testimonials and affirm their commitment to the group philosophy. If the preceding culting stages have not been particularly strong, groups may stay in this phase. However, maintenance at this level seems to be the exception rather than the rule for culting groups.

The second phase of maintenance is a *superiority group.* Here, the we/they distinction is hardened, generating fairly clear boundaries between group insiders and outsiders. Commitment to the group does not just distinguish the members from others; it makes them better. In most cases, the superiority group simply provides its members with an exaggerated sense of importance at the expense of others who unfortunately or foolishly missed the teaching. Occasionally, such groups denigrate outsiders, a tendency that is intensified in the next level.

The third phase is the *restricted contact group.* At this point, outsiders are at least inferior to group members, and they may be evil. In the latter case, outsiders have the capacity to taint the purity of members simply through contact. These groups nearly always live in communal situations. Certain trusted members of the group whose belief is strong enough to withstand the contamination of the outside world are chosen as spokespersons and recruiters. If relations with families and friends on the outside are maintained at all, they become stilted and instrumental, tending mostly toward rationalizing beliefs or soliciting money.

The structure of maintenance groups begins to change at this level. Once contact with the environment is restricted, the social mechanisms that normally contribute to group stability and adaptability are lost. These mechanisms need to be replaced with something, or the group becomes increasingly disorganized and chaotic. That something is nearly always *authority.* The more isolated the group, the more authoritarian it becomes. Usually, the authority manifests as a rigid hierarchy composed of many well-defined layers of control, replete with "lieutenants" who have special access to the leader and thus rule in their name. More lowly members of the group do not complain about the harsh treatment because they believe people higher in authority are also more enlightened. The acceptance of authority may become so extreme that sexual predation, beatings, and even murder can be countenanced as divine right.

The last stage of maintenance is the *paranoid group*. Outsiders are now not only evil—they are conspiring to destroy the group. Isolation is intensified, and even recruitment may be suspended. Weapons may be acquired and elaborate defense plans fabricated. The organization severs most of the ties that anchored it within a wider social context, and, like other organisms cut off from their environment, it begins to die. To compensate for the ensuing entropy and instability, greater authority is brought into play. Structures and procedures that were authoritarian at the last level become draconian in the paranoid group. Unchecked by any normal process within or outside the group, leaders and their lieutenants may pursue insane courses of action, including preemptive strikes on the alleged enemy.

Paranoid groups cannot last long. In my observation, these groups disintegrate in one of three ways: (1) many members become fed up with the escalating authoritarianism and leave the group, often with sorrow at the "change" in the group; (2) one faction leads a rebellion against another faction, bifurcating the group and creating two, more benign organizations; or (3) the group literally self-destructs, either through suicide or through such provocation of outside authorities that they are killed.

Regaining Consciousness

In the early days of the anti-cult movement, some success was reported in using counter-conversion strategies to break down the effects of the culting process. People such as Ted Patrick (Patrick, 1976) claimed that they could reverse the effects of conversion by "deprogramming" group members, which sometimes involved the use of deception, dualistic argument, and even physical restraint. Aside from the ethical question of means and ends that this procedure calls forth, there were obvious legal difficulties associated with it (Melton & Moore, 1982). Other counter-conversion efforts under the name "exit counseling" were more educational and consensual, although, like the culting process itself, they are carefully orchestrated (Clark et al., 1993; Langone, 1993; Singer, 1995).

I tend to agree with the critics mentioned in the introduction that have resisted pathologizing indoctrination techniques, and I also am critical of using the same techniques to "cure" former members of those groups. To reiterate the introductory point, succumbing to group indoctrination is not an individual pathology—it is a retreat from self-reflexive consciousness. Particularly under the stress of rapid change, our species history inclines us to seek solace in submission to authority. An aspiring authoritarian leader does not have to be particularly clever to evoke that history, and the formula for success is clear. First, exaggerate the danger of every change and nurture the naturally stressful human reactions; second, present oneself and/or one's beliefs as an antidote to change; and third, initially request and then demand that people turn over their decision-making to you. The more mercantile of these aspiring leaders will suggest that people also turn over their money, and the more narcissistic of them will demand that they receive only compliments for their benevolence.

Culting organizations are like little temporal anomalies (i.e., black holes) that open into our preconscious past. On a small scale, they may seem quaint, curious, or even romantic. Aside from the occasional clash with the realities of current time, we could relax and let them be. However, on a larger scale, the very same processes of group indoctrination and suppression of consciousness underlie fascism and other forms of totalitarianism. The culting techniques of control, coercion, and conversion and the culting process of seduction, disorientation, snapping, and maintenance are clearly exhibited in recent history (including, but not exclusive to, the development of Nazism, Stalinism, and Maoism), and current developments in the period since 2016 bear some disturbing parallels. Some of my sociologist and political scientist colleagues rightly point out that one cannot justifiably make comparisons such as, "Donald Trump is like Adolf Hitler." And certainly, that must be true beyond the fact that Hitler apparently did not have *Mein Kampf* ghostwritten. So, if we cannot learn from the large-scale past, maybe we can learn something from the small-scale temporal anomalies. Here are a few lessons I have drawn from my research.

Lesson One. Everyone is susceptible to culting appeals of one sort or another. Claiming invulnerability to authoritarian appeals on the basis of education, or wealth, or enlightenment is not only elitist, it is dangerous. In assuming that susceptibility is some kind of character flaw or weakness, we inappropriately conflate social processes and personal traits. This confusion of level of analysis inclines us to unrealistically hold individuals responsible for resisting social conformity and to underestimate the power of group indoctrination. Just recently, *all* of us were obeying the voices of the gods. And "we have a deep and hollowing yearning. . . ."

Lesson Two. Traditional education is insufficient to counteract culting appeals. As a professional educator, it is difficult for me to say this. I wish it were the case that education equipped one with the kind of critical thinking that could identify the fake news, deconstruct the phony appeals, and pull back the curtain on Oz. But there is not a lot of evidence that critical thinking improves at all over four years of university education (Roksa & Arum, 2011). If education instead yields a greater store of knowledge, isn't that still a good thing? Maybe, but not apparently as a hedge against culting. The problem seems to be that knowledge is necessarily contextual and only critical thinking is good at identifying patterns across contexts. Culting organizations (including the large-scale incidences) are really good at defining themselves as unique—they explicitly disavow being part of a pattern of authoritarianism. Given our predilection toward authority in the first place, and then our inability to see through the claim of uniqueness, we think that this time, this group, this charismatic leader, is the real thing. (For some, it will be meaningful to remember Charlie Brown and the football.)

Lesson Three. With humility born of the first two lessons, we can nevertheless work on preserving and improving our recent heritage of self-reflexive consciousness. To do so, we need to expand the way we've been thinking about critical thinking. Too much effort has been going into the deconstruction of context and not enough into recognizing the construction of context in the first place. We have been teaching *awareness* with the vague and vain hope that it will turn into *consciousness*. But the root of consciousness is not awareness of context—it is recognizing that we ourselves are the creators of context, including the contexts of our observation. As Maturana (1988) states in the ending quote, our collective reality is constantly being modified by the explanations we make of it. We need to understand this process to be able to manage it intentionally. We haven't always needed self-reflexive consciousness to live, but in a world where consciousness has allowed our collective and individual thoughts to be intertwined, and in that same world where consciousness allows some people to deny consciousness to others, we do need it to stay alive.

> The praxis of living, the experience of the observer as such, just happens. . . . Because of this, explanations are essentially superfluous; we as observers do not need them to happen; but when it happens to us that we explain, it turns out that between language and bodyhood the praxis of living of the observer changes as he or she generates explanations of his or her praxis of living. This is why everything that we say or think has consequences in the way we live. We can be aware of this now. (27)

References

Appel, W. (1983). *Cults in America: Programmed for paradise.* New York, NY: Henry Holt.

Asch, S. E. (1952). Effects of group pressure on the modification and distortion of judgements. In G. E. Swanson, T. M. Newcomb, & E. L. Hartley (Eds.), *Readings in social psychology* (2nd ed., pp. 2–11). New York, NY: Holt.

Bennett, M. (1997). Communicating with cults. In R. G. Rogan, M. R. Hammer, & C. R. Van Zandt (Eds.), *Dynamic processes of crisis negotiation: Theory, research, and practice.* Westport, CT: Praeger.
Bennett, M. (2013). *Basic concepts of intercultural communication: Paradigms, principles, & practices.* Boston, MA: Intercultural Press.
Bennett, M. (2016). A constructivist epistemology of hate. In E. Dunbar (Ed.), *The psychology of hate crimes as domestic terrorism: US and global issues.* Westport, CT: Praeger
Bennett, M. (2017). Developmental model of intercultural sensitivity. In Y. Kim (Ed.), *Encyclopedia of intercultural communication.* Hoboken, NJ: John Wiley & Sons.
Berlet, C., & Lyons, M. (2000). *Right-wing populism in America.* New York, NY: Guilford Press.
Castiglioni, I. (2011, September). Chronophagy in our embodied intercultural experience: A case of student exchange and virtual social networking. Presentation for Society of Intercultural Education, Training, and Research Europa, Krakow, Poland.
Castiglioni, I., & Bennett, M. (2018). Building capacity for intercultural citizenship. *Open Journal of Social Sciences,* 6(3), 229–241. https://doi.org/10.4236/jss.2018.63016
Clark, D., Giambalvo, C., Giambalvo, N., Garvey, K., & Langone, M. (1993). In M. Langone (Ed.). *Recovery from cults: Help for victims of psychological and spiritual abuse* (pp. 155–180). New York, NY: Norton.
Conway, F., & Siegelman, J. (1979). *Snapping: America's epidemic of sudden personality change.* New York, NY: Dell/Delta.
Dawkins, R. (1989). *The selfish gene* (2nd ed.). Oxford: Oxford University Press.
Dennett, D. (1991). *Consciousness explained.* Boston, MA: Little Brown.
Duplass, M., Duplass, Nishimura, L. (Producers), Way, M., Way, C. (Directors). (2018). *Wild wild country.* https://www.netflix.com/
Festinger, L., Riecken, H., & Schacter, S. (1956). *When prophecy fails: A social and psychological study of a modern group that predicted the destruction of the world.* Minneapolis, MN: University of Minnesota Press.
Galanter, M. (1982). Charismatic religious sects and psychiatry: An overview. *American Journal of Psychiatry,* 139(12), 1539–1548.
Graham, J. (2017, December 6). Who joins ISIS and why? *Huffington Post.* https://www.huffingtonpost.com/john-graham/who-joins-isis-and-why_b_8881810.html
Hall, E. (1959). *The silent language.* Garden City, NJ: Anchor.
Hoffer, E. (1951). *The true believer: Thoughts on the nature of mass movements.* New York, NY: Harper & Row.
Howell, W. (1973). Rhetoric and persuasion. University of Minnesota, Minneapolis Graduate Course.
Jaynes, J. (1976). *The origin of consciousness in the breakdown of the bicameral mind.* Boston, MA: Houghton Mifflin.

Lalich, J. (2004). *Bounded choice: True believers and charismatic cults.* Berkeley, CA: University of California Press.

Langone, M. (1993). Introduction. In M. Langone (Ed.). *Recovery from cults: Help for victims of psychological and spiritual abuse* (pp. 1–22). New York, NY: Norton.

Leach, J. (2016). Psychological factors in exceptional, extreme, and torturous environments. *Extreme Physiology and Medicine,* 5(1), 1–15. https://doi.org/10.1186/s13728-016-0048-y

Lifton, R. (1969). *Thought reform and the psychology of totalism: A study of brainwashing in China.* New York, NY: Norton.

Lifton, R. (1991). Cult formation. *Harvard Mental Health Letter,* 7(8), 5–6.

Maslow, A. (1968). *Toward a psychology of being.* New York, NY: Van Nostrand.

Maturana, H. (1988). Reality: The search for objectivity or the quest for a compelling argument. *Irish Journal of Psychology,* 9(1), 25–82.

Mead, G. (1934). *Mind, self, and society.* In C. W. Morris (Ed.). Chicago, IL: University of Chicago Press.

Melton, J. (1999, December 10). Brainwashing and the cults: The rise and fall of a theory. Center for Studies on New Religions. https://www.cesnur.org/testi/melton.htm

Melton, J., & Moore, R. (1982). *The cult experience: Responding to the new religious pluralism.* New York, NY: Pilgrim Press.

Milgram, S. (1974). *Obedience to authority: An experimental view.* New York, NY: Harper & Row.

Orwell, G. (1949). *Nineteen eighty-four.* New York, NY: Harcourt Brace.

Patrick, T. (1976). *Let our children go!* New York, NY: Ballantine.

Rhinehart, L. (1976). *The book of est.* New York, NY: Holt, Reinhart, & Winston.

Riemen, R. (2018). *To fight against this age: On fascism and humanism.* New York, NY: Norton.

Roksa, J., & Arum, R. (2011). *Academically adrift: Limited learning on college campuses.* Chicago, IL: University of Chicago Press.

Romano, A. (2017, January 11). How the alt-right uses internet trolling to confuse you into dismissing its ideology. VOX. https://www.vox.com/2016/11/23/13659634/alt-right-trolling

Schein, E. (1960). Brainwashing. Center for International Studies, MIT, Cambridge. http://dspace.mit.edu/bitstream/handle/1721.1/83028/14769178.pdf

Schein, E. (1961). *Coercive persuasion: A socio-psychological analysis of the "brainwashing" of American civilian prisoners by the Chinese Communists.* New York, NY: Norton.

Scheuer, J. (2015, November-December). Critical thinking and the liberal arts. *Academe, American Association of University Professors,* 101(6). https://www.aaup.org/article/critical-thinking-and-liberal-arts#.YPScK0ApBPY

Singer, M. (1995). *Cults in our midst: The hidden menace in our everyday lives.* San Francisco, CA: Jossey-Bass.

Turkle, S. (2011). *Alone together: Why we expect more from technology and less from each other.* New York, NY: Basic Books.
Underwood, B., & Underwood, B. (1979). *Hostage to heaven: Four years in the Unification Church.* New York, NY: Clarkson N. Potter.
Ungerleider, J., & Wellisch, D. (1979). Coercive Persuasion (brainwashing), religious cults, and deprogramming. *American Journal of Psychiatry*, 136(3), 279–282.
Van Zandt, C. (1997). Negotiating with cults: A practitioner's perspective. In R. G. Rogan, M. R. Hammer, & C. R. Van Zandt (Eds.), *Dynamic processes of crisis negotiation: Theory, research, and practice.* Westport, CT: Praeger.
Wood, G. (2015, March). What ISIS really wants. *The Atlantic.* https://www.theatlantic.com/magazine/archive/2015/03/what-isis-really-wants/384980/
Zaitz, L. (1985, July 18). Rajneeshees in Oregon: An untold story, part 17: Methods of extracting donations vary. *The Oregonian.* Portland, Oregon.
Zimbardo, P., & Andersen, S. (1993). Understanding mind control: Exotic and mundane mental manipulations. In M. Langone (Ed.), *Recovery from cults* (pp. 104–125). New York, NY: Norton.

CHAPTER ELEVEN

Disengagement and Societal Reintegration after Violent Extremism

Edward W. Dunbar

All things truly wicked start from innocence.

—Hemingway

Problem Statement: Challenges in Hate Offender Desistance

No one is born a hate crime offender. There are, however, numerous pathways that lead to the perpetration of hate crimes. Conversely, there is but one way out—desistance from hate violence. The pathways to perpetrate hate violence can result in lone wolf offenders (Gallagher, 2022), or involvement in cultlike hate-oriented groups (Bennett, 2022). Collective group violence (Blanco, Blanco, & de la Corte, 2022) emphasized the role of interpersonal bonds to establish group and ideological identities. Ituarte (2022) found that many of the hate offenders she interacted with struggled with important life tasks and frequently had poor familial supports. Many hate crime offenders evidence significant criminal histories that have no clear relationship to a bias ideology (Dunbar, 2003). Importantly, desistance from hate violence is realized via personal and collective change. The process of desistance will be examined in terms of strategies to effect personal and collective change.

Pursuing change involves finding a pathway for individual desistance from future hate violence. This includes changing of social norms politically and culturally to support the eradication of intergroup violence. It is best to consider these issues as being both distinct and inherently interlinked. The most critical factor in rehabilitating hate offenders is that the society in which the infraction occurs views the behavior as problematic. If the standing government however, is indifferent to, or covertly supports, hate violence, the probability of desistance declines dramatically.

Asking the Right Questions: Effecting Change

A common question that this writer is asked about hate crimes is "what makes someone do this?" This is a perfectly understandable question, one that is responded to (by me) with a somewhat more detailed and less than sound-bite comprehendible answer. Frequently, this is not the critical issue. As Carl Bell once said, it is important to ask the right question (Norris, 2019). When it comes to the issue of reducing hate violence, the better question is "what has to happen to make someone stop?"

Warning, Caveats, and Best Intentions: Making Matters Worse

A lot of hardworking, dedicated, and "good" people have spent years trying to reduce the risk for hate violence of individuals and to eradicate outgroup hostility. In too many cases, their efforts have had minimal success. Sometimes we even get it wrong, which make things worse. Below are some of the caveats in rehabilitating hate crime offenders.

Incarceration. "Locking the offender up" is generally a problematic strategy to reduce future hate violence. As Copp (2020) notes, the benefits of incarceration are modest or negative—that is, "slightly criminogenic." We would add to this the harmful socialization experiences of incarcerated hate crimes offenders. Prison life is de facto a racialized experience (Thistlethwaite, 2017) resulting in greater in-group bonding and greater out-group animus. Additionally, an inmate identified as a perpetrator of hate violence will be protected by their hate-oriented peers. The consequence most typically is one of an increased in-group identity reinforced by the experience of imprisonment. Furthermore, the incarcerated hate offender is often given special status by other in-group inmates; this enhances the individual group identity.

Ignoring Non-Hate Recidivism Risk. As with many offender groups, hate crime perpetrators evidence a range of recidivism risk factors. It is critical to recognize that a bias ideology for many offenders is peripheral to other barriers to desistance. For these offenders, co-occurring problems include substance use, psychopathy, limited work skills, and a paucity of social supports outside of criminal networks. It is problematic to focus on the hate element of an offender's lifestyle and ignore these other high-risk determinants of criminal behavior. In many cases, the non-hate factors pose a greater threat for recidivism than the bias of the offender.

Recidivism risk is significant for many of these individuals. In the review of the criminal and developmental histories of 204 adult (an average age of about 33 years) hate offenders Dunbar, Quinones, and Crevecoeur (2005) found that nearly half of the offenders had prior criminal infractions. Forty-five percent had previous misdemeanor convictions, and 36 percent had one or more prior felony convictions. Of these offenders, only 16 percent were clearly identified as being members of hate-oriented criminal gangs or groups. This underscores the presence of many career criminals in hate offender groups.

A significant case for seeing the victimizer-as-victim can be made from research on the developmental histories of bias homicide offenders. In a study with 54 convicted homicide offenders, Dunbar, Krop, and Sullaway (2016) found in record review the presence of very severe distal sexual and physical trauma, which was greater than found in other studies on convicted violent offenders. This points toward an association between severe childhood victimization and subsequent violence, in this case involving bias against a targeted out-group. In several instances, violence was perpetrated against opposition-gender targets as a self-referenced form of retributional aggression. Davies-Rubio and Mirón (2022) implicitly raise the issue of long-term effects of trauma, as well, in their work with members of death squads in Colombia who perpetrated hundreds of homicides in many cases.

Mandated Diversity Education. Requiring convicted hate offenders to participate in educational trainings on cultural differences—referred to as "diversity education"—has been a source of debate for some time now. Bell, Connerley, and Cocchiara (2009) has noted the questionable benefit of requiring diversity and sensitivity training for hate crime parolees. There is evidence that for highly prejudiced civil subjects, diversity education frequently increases the level of bias as a function of enhancements.

There can be a variety of unintended consequences related to mandatory diversity interventions with hate offenders. This writer has treated hate offenders who "passed" as not being mandated for diversity treatment in community programs—this increased their perception of being able to deceive and control "the normies." It is also problematic when mandated participants denigrate these programs in their interaction with other offenders.

Additionally, establishing a content-valid strategy to engage hate offenders about cultural attitudes that is distinctly different from that which is employed in work and educational settings is needed. As such, the propriety and viability of mandating diversity education with offenders need to be considered with real caution.

Tearing Down the Racist Character. Some of the work with violent hate offenders and domestic terrorists has sought to reorient not just their attitudes but also their self-concept. Yochelson and Samnow (1986) have detailed their efforts to reconstitute career criminals—akin to a tearing down of the criminal identity. In one often-cited study, an intensive immersion program with offenders was found to be beneficial in reducing recidivism for non-psychopathic participants. Conversely, offenders who scored highly on the Hare Psychopathy Checklist-Revised were significantly more likely to re-offend when having participated in this whole-change treatment strategy (Harris, Rice, & Cormier, 1991). In this writer's study of the histories of hate offenders (Dunbar, 2003; Dunbar, Krop, & Sullaway, 2016), a significant number of these individuals met the criteria for psychopathy. It is important to consider what constitutes effective change with a hate offender. We will argue that desistance of aggression targeting social out-groups is the singular goal. As such, the emphasis needs to be on behavior change, not personality change. Our interventions should be focused accordingly to this end.

Homogeneity of Hate Perpetrators. Legally, hate offenders are indeed indistinguishable from one another in that they have all met the legal standard of committing a crime due to their bias toward a cultural out-group. The psychological reality is, of course, more complex. Individual hate offenders, as with most offenders, have distinctly different histories and problems with their rehabilitation. As noted previously, there are diverse motivational factors that lead to hate crime perpetration; the diversity of these motives also points to the need for diverse strategies in the management and rehabilitation of this special class of offender.

In Table 11-1, these points are summarized. If you are a probation officer, put this up on your bulletin board.

Table 11-1 What Does Not Work to Attain Individual Desistance

	Problem	Solution
Incarceration	socializing/reinforcing hate identity	use of alternate sentencing guidelines and diversion options
Ignoring non-hate Risk factors	poor intervention plan; increased recidivism	tailored change goals and use of risk-reduction treatments
Mandated diversity Training	poor match of content to hate problems; risk of heightened bias	tailor intervention to realities of hate violence; clearer selection criteria
Tearing down racist character	adverse impact of heighted bias or violence risk	detailed clinical assessment tailor intervention to realities of offender psychopathology
Homogeneity of hate offenders	indiscriminant management and intervention plan	tailor to the personal and contextual situation

Hate as an Identity Development Problem

An important issue for offender intervention concerns moderating their identity status (Thompson & Carter, 2013). There are two aspects of identity that impact offender rehabilitation: the identity of the collective self (Luhtanen & Crocker, 1992) and the ascription to violence as a solution to intergroup problems. From a cultural and rehabilitative perspective, both of these problem areas need to be actively engaged.

Awareness of intergroup differences—the identification of a cultural self and a cultural other—is first observed in early childhood. Racial awareness in children is typically established between ages four and seven, with white children in the United States being able to identify their racial identity between ages four and six (Fishbein, 2002). As Van Ausdale and Feagin (2001) note, children employ race in establishing social dominance, and young children appropriate language about race to enforce social exclusion (Connolly, 2002). Consistent with Connolly, Monteiro and colleagues (2008) found that six- to seven-year-old white children discriminated against the Black children. This research suggests that racial awareness and even racial discrimination are a normative part of the developmental experience. What needs to be considered is how these normative processes lead some individuals to adopt a violent out-group animus; this experience can furthermore become a critical aspect of one's collective self-identity and self-construal in terms of race and ethnic identity.

The study of racial identity provides a conceptual model to understand the role of hate as an organizing experience for the individual (Helms, 1990, 1995). The developmental approach employed in the model illustrates the fluid nature of attitudes about race and one's self-ascription to race. This model has been related to well-being as well as out-group racial mistrust and stereotype adherence (Kohatsu et al., 2000). Research on white racial identity (Carter & Helms, 1990) has been related to anti-Black racism in a civil sample (Pope-Davis & Ottavi, 1994). The stage of white racial identity related to the abandonment of racism, reintegration, emphasizes pro-white/anti-Black racial attitudes. This identity stage of heightened in-group identity and aversive out-group attitudes is characteristic of many racial hate offenders.

The role of identity and hate violence has been a critical issue in the work of Karen Franklin (2004) in examining young men's motivation to perpetrate violence targeting sexual minorities. As she noted, these forms of violence are intertwined with the offender's gender identity expression. She found that the targeting of sexual minorities served as a form of enacting masculinity. As discussed in her clinical research, anti-LGBT violence establishes a young man's heterosexist dominance and enhances their status among their peers. Franklin also suggested that many perpetrators of LGBT violence might not perceive themselves as culturally deviant but rather engaging in aggression that is sanctioned by the larger society. This writer would emphasize that this assumption is particularly true when the community or the standing government broadly condemns the rights of sexual minorities.

This writer has proposed that a hate identity can be viewed as culturally deviant in a liberal democracy (see Chapter 2 in this book). Desistance from a hate lifestyle, as implied by racial identity theory, suggests the individual may become more culturally adaptive and flexible. For the ideologically motivated violent offender, the process of desistance may involve feelings of guilt, loss, alienation, and confusion. For this writer, many ex-hate offenders present a poorly articulated narrative of their evolution "out" of the movement; these individuals can strike one as being like the proverbial dry drunk of Alcoholics Anonymous. Desistance is attained, but meaning is elusive. Akin to this, Simi and colleagues (2017) discussed the lingering impact of a hate identity for individuals who have abandoned this lifestyle. Self-described former white supremacists, examined via structured interviews, characterized their feelings about their hate identity as being not unlike an addiction. Simi et. al. (2017) note how some individuals viewed their basic self-construal as being rooted in out-group hatred; likewise the loss of this identity and group removal were considered in terms of the neuropsychological consequences of the extermination of neural pathways that increase dopamine—and implicitly, as this writer has suggested, the loss of the oxytocin response found for willing followers. These individuals, as with alcoholics, may relapse and return briefly or permanently to a hate-based lifestyle.

A second critical issue with hate offenders concerns their identity attitudes that influence the personal decision to perpetrate violence. If we view violence as a choice—as a volitional action—that can be stimulated in situ or that is a function of cognition and planning, then this process must say something about the individual's identity. The role of in-group deprivation, connectedness to mainstream society (friendships and psychological closeness to majority individuals), and in-group identity factors—that is, strength of in-group identity and perceived in-group superiority—all contribute to the endorsement of violence.

Hamelin and colleagues (2010) identified factors triggering potential attitude change favoring terrorism. Their model was based on survey research in Morocco on the openness to perpetrating terrorist activity. Community-based trigger factors that influence the support for perpetration of violence included lack of faith in social equality and support of the individual's social network. The endorsement of violence to effect political change was based on concerns about endemic corruption and an absence of social justice.

A triggering factor in Hamelin et. al.'s research on the choice for intergroup hostility was the influence of friends and social networks, leading actors to perpetrate hate violence. Soriano (2017) addressed the issue of choosing to perpetrate domestic violence. Her subjects stated their violence was based on learned behavior witnessed in their family of origin.

To summarize, the management and rehabilitation of hate offenders is hindered by the presence of common criminological problems as well as the ideological and cultural alienation of these individuals. Further, the level of psychological conflict and psychopathology may both heighten the barriers to hate ideology desistance. Recent work on the issue of white supremacists and mental health suggests that problems of anger, paranoia, and social alienation are common conditions for members of hate groups (Bubolz & Simi, 2019).

Intervention Strategies Focusing on the Individual

How do we rehabilitate hate offenders? To effectively reintegrate ex-hate offenders into society requires ameliorating a range of cognitive, emotional, and social deficits. As noted, these individuals pose distinct recidivism risks due to their out-group animus. Their post-incarceration social reintegration is uniquely compromised for individuals immersed in a hate-based lifestyle. Hate offenders have described to this writer their feelings of being ostracized from society after their institutional release. Post-incarceration status leaves these individuals in a community at best indifferent but often hostile toward them. As discussed by gang specialists or in Bennett's (2022) observation about cults, the ex-hate offender loses their social network and place of coherence if they remove themselves from contact with friends and family members who hold hate-based beliefs. Again, given that hate violence is inherently political, the policies and practices of the standing government may range from endorsement to denigration of the ex-offender's actions. How these individuals are monitored and prosecuted underscores the attitudes of stakeholders with whom they interact. In one Eastern European country, for example, a police officer said skinheads were frequently admired for keeping ethnic minorities—for example, Roma—off the streets.

Interventions and the Two-Factor Model of Bias Aggression. As proposed in (Dunbar, 2022), hate violence is a product of the emotional state and the capacity for aggression in interaction with out-groups. The level of emotional lability and out-group hostility for each individual varies; therefore, the tasks of risk assessment and intervention need to vary, contingent on the relative severity of these two problems. In other words, if some individuals perpetrate hate crimes due to their impulse disturbance, whereas others execute premeditated and planned forms of violence, it would be expected that their risk for bias aggression is driven by divergent factors. For example, a perpetrator high in both hate arousal and bias ideology would pose a greater management challenge than an offender low in both of these motivators. Making evidence-based distinctions in risk assessment is important in determining an offender's intervention goals.

As a general framework, then, risk assessment with labile hate offenders would need to focus on characteristics such as substance use, stabilization of mood, and treatment of hyperarousal. The distinction drawn for ideological and affect-dysregulated hate is relevant in terms of the process of desistance from a hate-based lifestyle. This ideology and affect-disturbance distinction may prove useful in conceptualizing both issues of entry-to-membership status as well in developing strategies for rehabilitation.

It is critical to consider the inherently fluid nature of in-group identity and identification with a hate-based worldview. Equally, the largely intractable nature of neurologically mediated impulsivity, aggressiveness, and rage needs to be recognized. Therefore, while hate group followers may benefit from psychoeducational interventions, the highly labile offender may only be treated via biochemical intervention.

Planned and ideologically motivated offenders may instead pose issues of risk for future violence as a function of ideological rigidity, problems of cognitive concreteness and stereotype adherence, and a paucity of critical thinking skills. This latter issue also raises the question of the age of the offender, as there is some evidence that desistance from an antisocial lifestyle may be a function of developing critical thinking and stress-tolerance skills in young at-risk offenders. Some of the specific interventions to treat these offenders are provided below.

Intervention with at-Risk Youth: MST. Multisystemic therapy (MST) is an intensive family- and community-based treatment for serious juvenile offenders with possible substance abuse issues and their families (Henggeler et al., 2009). The primary goals of MST are to decrease youth criminal behavior and out-of-home placements. Multiple studies demonstrate that this wraparound mental health and social services model serves to respond to individual and familial forms of distress (Henggeler, 1999). Integrating therapeutic and psychoeducational methods, MST has been found to significantly reduce antisocial behavior of targeted at-risk individuals (Borduin et al., 1995). MST targets many of the individuals found to perpetrate hate violence—young distressed and oppositional males. MST provides an effective intervention model to reduce of non-bias-related risk factors of hate offenders.

Stand-Alone Domestic Terror Diversion. The "Life after Hate" diversion program was sponsored by the U.S. Department of Homeland Security under the Obama administration. This program sought to provide a comprehensive program to counter violent extremism, and to help individuals leave neo-Nazi and white supremacy groups. An early action of the Trump administration was to cut these programs. This effectively stopped the federal effort to intercede in the desistance of right-wing violence (Beinart, 2018).

Naturalistic Contact. Benign intergroup experience may constitute an anxiolytic effect on out-group hostility and aversion. Contact as a specific form of intergroup experience has been extensively studied (Pettigrew & Tropp, 2008). The contact hypothesis was presented in Allport's seminal work *On the Nature of Prejudice* (1954). Allport proposed that positive effects of intergroup contact were contingent on in-group-out-group interactions moderated by the conditions of equal status, intergroup cooperation, shared goals of both parties, and support by social powerful others. It is viable that when these conditions are present, desensitization to (intergroup) anxiety might occur for the cooperants. A good deal of the neuroscience on in-group-out-group perceptions would readily fit into such a model of contact as a form of smoothing of hostile and anxious brain-behavior mechanisms. If the social context can trigger a neurobiological pathway of out-group fear or hostility, it is also true that interpersonal experience can ameliorate overlearned associations of hostility, as well.

Pharmacological Treatments of Hate Violence. As neuroscience research suggests (Dunbar, 2022a), the potential exists for using psychotropic medications to treat perpetrators of hate aggression. Currently, none of the neuropsychological studies on aggression has been applied in the intervention with hate offenders. However, Terbeck (2006) has proposed that our current armament of psychiatric medications may also influence pro-social and antisocial behaviors; as such, psychopharmacology needs to be viewed in terms of clinical research on social cognition. She notes, "Psychopharmacology, amongst other methods, might deliver a novel methodological approach to determine the involvement of neurotransmitter functions in racial biases" (29). In a subsequent study, Terbeck and colleagues (2012) reported promising results experimentally for propranolol to reduce implicit racial bias on the Implicit Association Test (IAT). In this study with a white civil sample, propranolol reduced heart rate and implicit racial bias, without affecting the measure of explicit racial prejudice. This is consistent with the argument that out-group bias is moderated by psychophysiological symptoms of anxiety in nonviolent individuals (Bell & Dunbar, 2012). Speculatively, the role of psychophysiological hyperarousal—as considered in terms of the labile component of hate violence—may be treated via pharmacologically based noradrenergic interventions. Reduction of hyperarousal may reduce the risk for the perpetration of reactive aggression and ameliorate the impaired emotional intelligence of offenders in intergroup contact situations. This being said, the author has treated ruminative and premeditated hate offenders and seen how the use of serotonin-acting medications may make them less worried—however, if they were in treatment, this is usually a function of their involvement with the criminal justice system. Consistent with Trebeck et al., this pharmacological treatment seemingly made little impact on their underlying biased beliefs.

There is, however, reason to consider the potential contribution of psychotropic medications. While there is no evidence-based medication strategy to reduce aggressive-bias behavior, there are many opportunities to use medication to reduce recidivism risk. Broadly, three classes of pharmacotherapy might assist in reducing recidivism: (1) mood stabilizers—selective serotonin reuptake inhibitor (SSRI) and anticonvulsant class drugs; (2) antidepressant medications (including SSRIs); and (3) antipsychotic-class medications. If we employ the arousal-planning typology, we can consider some of the opportunities to address different levels of recidivism risk. To characterize the relative opportunity to use medication, the most frequent group, the willing follower, does not clearly fit an intervention profile. The low-arousal and low-identity offenders are a relatively heterogeneous and non-pathological group and the most common type of hate offender. The labile bigot, as a class of offender, can be expected to respond favorably to mood-stabilizing medications—for example, SSRI and anticonvulsant-class medications to reduce hypermania and arousal. The planful offenders and hate extremists may include persons with more obsessional and bizarre ideation and may respond favorably to antipsychotics.

Economic Sanctions. Fees and fines are employed in various criminal settings. Offender restitution can be managed as part of a sentencing decree. There is some evidence that this strategy increases recidivism. Piquero and Jennings (2017) found in a two-year follow-up that monetary penalties were related to an increase in recidivism. Therefore, their results suggest this might not work: this in in contrast to the clinical wisdom arguing that more premeditated and/or emotionally controlled offenders may be only responsive to material penalties. In this regard, the planful hate offenders would be most likely to be the target with financial penalties. These material punishments can be a source of real frustration for the convicted hate offender. As one young hate offender stated, "No one will hire me because of the hate crime."

Elements of a General Model of Offender Rehabilitation

So what are the core objectives of an intervention to eradicate individual risk for hate violence? In our review of the limited evidence we have, the following areas of change are proposed for intervention with individual offenders: (1) specialized justice initiatives, (2) life skills development, (3) psychosocial integration, and (4) impulse risk regulation. These are discussed briefly below.

Specialized Justice Initiatives. The initial step of engaging the issue of offender desistance is the process of prosecution and sentencing. This process allows for sentencing options inclusive of diversionary and treatment programs as well as therapeutic jurisprudence vis-à-vis incarceration and punishment. Justice-treatment initiatives for hate offenders are still novel ideas; these are more established in other arenas of criminal justice—such as offenders of sex crimes and gender violence (Hausmann & Wanke, 2016) and substance abuse cases (Crèvecoeur-MacPhail, 2016). Determining the best option of case disposition involves (a) comprehensive assessment of the offender's risk for reoffending, (b) establishing a hierarchy of intervention targets, and (c) referring the individual to appropriate psychoeducational and diversionary programs.

Life Skills Development. Many young adult hate crime offenders have a minimal stake in the larger society. Moreover, many of these individuals are occupationally and economically marginalized. As Ezekiel (1995) suggested, for some highly entrenched hate group members, an economic pathway out of the group was critical in establishing a viable independence from these recidivistic influences. Frequently for members of racialized criminal gangs, economic privation literally forces the members to adhere to a biased lifestyle as a form of economic and social survival. Basic skills training and assistance with job placement, as well as viable educational opportunities, may be critical for the long-term removal from a lifestyle of violence and hate.

Psychosocial Integration. As has been noted, for a meaningful number of hate offenders, participation in a criminalized gang is an important part of their identity. Desistance from a bias-oriented lifestyle requires challenging peer relationships and breaking down the groupthink of these groups. The goal of psychosocial interventions also needs to create a viable bond to more prosocial groups, a point raised by Ituarte (2020). This may be the most important intervention target for the less violent and culturally ambivalent willing followers. Addressing other forms of recidivism risk—most notably, substance and alcohol dependence—is highly relevant to the stabilizing of the ex-offender's lifestyle. The role of religious beliefs and 12-step models of sobriety in recovery are often critical to the offender outcome.

Psychosocial integration, in comparison to punishment, seeks to ameliorate the individual's recidivism risk to potentially destabilizing social contexts. An integrative/therapeutic approach might include individual or group psychotherapy, psychiatric monitoring and pharmacotherapy, and in some instances therapeutic judicial oversight and guidance.

Impulse Risk Regulation. For a minority of these offenders, the primary goal is behavioral self-regulation. To use the proposed offender typology, the impulse-disturbed and (in some cases) the hate extremist offenders will most clearly require care to decrease risk for future violence. A core task is the management of impulsivity and behavioral dysregulation. Monitoring and psychological interventions are needed to address the status of the erratic and disturbed offender. This may include psychiatric treatment and social services work. For some but not all hate offenders, psychoeducational interventions can help to develop problem-solving and critical thinking skills.

Developing critical thinking skills to reduce recidivistic behavior is critical to offender rehabilitation for this offender (Friendship et al., 2003). The development of an alternative ideology—as Raphael Ezekiel (1996) discussed in his work with young men of hate groups—was part of the challenge to countering their biased worldview. This centers on love and work, in which finding paid employment or creating a romantic attachment outside of the world of the hate group becomes the path out. Individually, it requires a great deal of energy to think critically, to make decisions based on logic and culturally prescribed assumptions rather than emotions and the dictum of a group that bonds around hate and aggression. Table 11-2 summarizes the desistance goals for the four offender types below.

Structural Change and Reduction of Hate Violence Risk

The process of desistance from hate violence ultimately revolves around individual and societal change. The individual's capacity to desist from hate violence is often moderated by small group and organizational sanctions (Blanco, Blanco, & de la Corte, 2022). As Davies-Rubio and Mirón (2022) noted, in some paramilitary settings, the ability to end hate-based violence is held hostage by the group to which the individual belongs. The World War II German soldiers of Unit 101 were "ordinary men" who slaughtered Polish Jews during World War II, as Christopher Browning (1998) detailed, and this would not end until the regime of Nazism was toppled. Milgram (1963) taught us this more than half a century ago, if leadership promotes harm, we, the followers will comply, in far too many cases. Hate crimes are implicitly a social problem and therefore must be addressed at a group and a societal level.

Political and economic influence on societal change may shift intergroup relationships rapidly, often in a matter of years (Dunbar, 2018). In many contexts, intergroup violence is a function of deeply rooted intercultural conflicts that may span a millennium. Violence in the Middle East from the Islamic–Jewish conflict today and the Saracen–Christian conflict of the crusades of the Middle Ages are two such examples. The chronic tit-for-tat violence in African tribal warfare or Irish–UK retributional violence provides other well-recognized examples. The interplay of societal forces on the individual's choice to perpetrate hate crimes is numerous. Below we summarize briefly some of these societal factors that moderate hate violence.

Reduction in Civic Engagement. An issue of concern to social scientists is the harmful effects on society when there is a reduction in social engagement of diverse social groups, and for our purposes particularly when there is a diminishment in the interaction of diverse cultural groups. Across numerous indices, a decline of social participation and congregant experiences has been a source of concern since the age of Tacitus, who discussed the decline

Table 11-2 Intervention Strategies based on Offender Characteristics

	Sentencing Options	Assessment Issues	Psychosocial Integration	Risk Management
Willing Follower (49%)	diversion/drug court options; therapeutic jurisprudence	job assistance; naturalistic contact	social skills training; psycho-educational treatment	general population
Labile Bigot (34%)	diversion/drug court options; therapeutic jurisprudence	assess for severe psychopathology	AA/12 step groups; mental health svcs.	specialized probation; pharmacotherapy
Planful Offender (8%)	financial sanctions; incarceration	assess for psychopathy & severe psychopathology	mental health svcs.	specialized probation
Hate Extremist (9%)	incarceration; financial sanctions	assess for psychopathy	job assistance; mental health svcs.	specialized probation; pharmacotherapy

Note: percentages are from a sample used in the analysis of 555 hate offenders.

of ancient Rome as a function of the breakdown in society (Mason, 1965). More currently, the issue of social alienation has been framed as "the tragedy of the commons." This failure of affirming contact experiences is a consequence of the diminishment of collective material goals due to enhancement of individual opportunity for resource consumption. The social context is normalized to view personal need as superordinate to common good (Hardin, 1968). From a social learning model, the concern for persons who are socially distal will diminish more than intimates or members of social in-groups. This diminishment of investment results in a decline in moral commitment to equal protection under the law or viewing culturally diverse individuals as holding an equity position in resource competition. These inherently conservative political arguments are consistent with our understanding of the tolerance for hate violence by bystanders. Attitudes about victims of violence become less supportive as cultural divisions are more pronounced (Johnson & Byers, 2003). This larger social intolerance is sometimes referenced by violent hate crime offenders, in which the offender feels that police and average citizens have no concern for victims who are immigrants or sexual minorities, for example.

Localizing Violence from External Threats. As the United States has witnessed, geopolitical conflict has resulted in a rise in violence against in-country ethnic groups. The experiences of the harassment of Asians under the COVID pandemic and the violence against perceived Middle Easterners after the 9/11 terror attacks (see Chapter 1) are two relatively recent examples of how a social context is vulnerable to in-country violence that is secondary to international conflicts. This is commonsensically viewed in terms of concurrent forms of violence; however, it is also clear that in-group violence within a political sphere may continue for years after the occurrence of international conflict. Once again, the holding of collective grievances may lead to perpetration of hate violence by the few and tolerance of such actions by the many. Many historians, for example, note how frustration with the economic sanctions enacted in the Treaty of Versailles at the end of the First World War paved the way for the ascension of national socialism a mere decade later (Wilde, 2020).

The holding over time to deep cultural resentments reveals a glacial change of intergroup relationships. This writer has noted the relationship between Black lynching activity in the United States and its relationship to lower reportage of hate violence by law enforcement, on the one hand (Dunbar, 2022b), and the likelihood of supporting candidate Trump in the 2016 U.S. presidential election (Dunbar, 2018), make this point. Likewise, the pattern of enactment of Jim Crow laws in the Confederate states 30 years after the end of the Civil War is another case of using legislation to foment racial divides and support intergroup aggression; this will be discussed further below.

Charismatic Political Leadership. An important intersect between psychological science and history is found in the scholarship of authoritarian and charismatic leadership. The concept of charismatic authority was proposed by Max Weber (Joosse, 2014). An important example was found in the work of Fiol, Harris, and House (1999) in their examination of U.S. presidents. In analysis of the speeches of the presidents, they noted how the charismatic leaders utilized a communication tactic to effect social change. The recent study of this process in U.S. presidents found that charismatic leaders influence their followers' values to promote social change via challenging norms, identifying with their follower, and then providing an alternative ideology that the follower is beholden to (Seyranian & Bligh, 2008). The use of rhetoric to negate was significant in proscribing behaviors to change and identification with the follower in the process of shifting to a new model of adherence. As research by Schuh, Zhang, & Tian (2013) on this relationship found, charismatic leadership can be a "mixed blessing," one that can promote either collaboration or greater intergroup divisiveness. As Kiazad and colleagues (2010) noted, follower perceptions of authoritarian leadership in organizations "fully mediated the relationship" between asocial Machiavellianism and forms of abusive power. In other words, the influence of authoritarianism on the perceptions of the follower can obfuscate issues of impropriety or immorality. Influential charismatic leadership can motivate antisocial or asocial attitudes by minimizing the darker side of the consequence of obedience. This is well recognized by forensic psychologists and gang experts, in their efforts to reduce small-risk-taking by identifying and containing highly influential group members who advocate heightened violence and aggression.

Important to hate offender assessment is the unexamined issue of the relationship of charismatic leaders and psychopathy. The common themes of verbal persuasiveness, motivation to challenge norms, and encouragement of nonconventional ideas are shared by both of these constructs. Again, such an asocial leadership style may be employed to seek a greater good as well as to promote violence against noncombatant fellow citizens.

Policies of Inclusion/Exclusion. An important approach to reducing intergroup violence is to create a civil society. This is accomplished through legislation, policy, and pronouncements of politician leadership. Government-driven initiatives to promote inclusion and equity can serve to socialize the population away from hostility as a means of addressing cultural differences and cultural change.

An important example of this is found in the work of Levy and Levy (2017). They addressed the issue of whether public policies on gay and lesbian rights had an impact on the incidence of hate crimes targeting sexual motivation. They considered how legal inequalities increase hate crimes based on sexual orientation as a function of "discursive opportunities" for bias, discrimination, and violence in their examination of reported hate crimes from 2000 to 2012. They found that laws promoting hate crime reporting and workplace nondiscrimination reduced the frequency of hate crime incidence. They note how institutional heterosexism is related to the commission of hate crimes against sexual minorities. Their work argues that legal equality serves as a tool to mitigate against violence targeting sexual minorities.

A final and yet very critical structural intervention concerns the regulation and use of social media to influence help-seeking networks for hate crime victims and, importantly, establish a level of intergroup cooperation that can serve to minimize hate violence. Anti-hate interventions, for example, could foster a sense of common goals—the promotion of a commons-type political collective—or seek to reduce a perception of government corruption. These strategies would be relayed to diverse communities via effective social media engagement. Hence, the government may choose to act in this direction by curbing the perceived sense of impunity in the case of corruption or tolerance of intergroup violence. A government modeling itself on a liberal democratic tradition would need to establish a tone that discourages violence against minority populations. Conversely, a regressive autocratic form of government power may well give permission to hate-based aggression or minimally communicate an intolerance of social equity. This later posture can result in a level of intergroup violence that unleashes deeper cultural assumptions of privilege and power, even over a numerical majority membership of a community or country.

Conclusion: The Narrative Needs a Rewrite

Interventions with hate crime offenders need to lead to desistance from future bias-motivated aggression. Eradicating violent behavior is the target of change and not per se of underlying social attitudes. Our hard interventions—incarceration and economic sanctions, a plausible intervention for planful offenders—may harden the potentially fluid hate identity of many hate perpetrators. Worsening an ex-offender's economic status, for example, is a potentially dangerous form of intervention. Mandated diversity training—which may be fruitful with younger offenders or the classic follower member of a hate group—runs the risk of engendering resentment in the rehabilitation of the more bias-committed—hate-extremist—participant.

Individual risk factors for recurring criminal behavior, such as the paucity of critical-thinking skills or the holding of a bias ideology, are important targets for intervention. Ultimately, the minority of hate crime offenders who hold a deeply entrenched bias ideology face a personal crisis of confidence about their identity as a non-hate person. Stakeholders need to find supports and practices to help the at-risk individual to make such a transition.

Structural implications for desistance of hate violence involve social media that influences political leadership and the rule of law. The promulgation of policies of the standing government significantly influences the societal response to intergroup violence. Increasingly, social media can moderate the formation of hate ideology and the mobilization of deep cultural change in the perpetration of intergroup aggression.

It has now been nearly 30 years since the passage of our federal hate crime laws. There is a notable plot hole in the narrative of this country and in our response to these societally wounding acts of violence. The storyline on how states and the central government have responded to intergroup violence is marked by an inconsistency to identify a clear pathway out for the perpetrator and their communities. Currently there is no evidence-based approach to individual or group desistance from hate violence. Our deep cultural norms of personal independence extends to attitudes about wearing personal protective equipment during the COVID-19 pandemic as well as finding a way to end hate aggression. If violence is a choice, it appears to be a painfully individual one, with little in the way of guidance or support to "fill the hole" of hate with a more viable identity, one that makes sense in a multicultural society. The loose ends in the narrative of ending hate in the United States remain unresolved. For this writer, the issue is one of great importance, one that is only passingly addressed here. More needs to be done, documented, and shared.

References

Allport, G. W. (1954). *The nature of prejudice*. Cambridge, MA: Addison-Wesley.

Beinart, P. (2018, October 29). Trump shut programs to counter violent extremism. *The Atlantic*. https://www.theatlantic.com/ideas/archive/2018/10/trump-shut-countering-violent-extremism-program/574237/

Bell, C., & Dunbar, E. (2012). Racism and pathological bias as a co-occurring problem in diagnosis and assessment. In T. A. Widiger (Ed.), *The Oxford handbook of personality disorders* (pp. 697–708). New York, NY: Oxford.

Bell, M., Connerley, M., & Cocchiara, F. (2009). The case for mandatory diversity education. *Academy of Management Learning & Education*, 8(4), 597–609. https://www.jstor.org/stable/27759197

Bennett, M. (2022). Group indoctrination: Techniques of depersonalization and domination of individual consciousness. In E. W. Dunbar (Ed.), *Indoctrination to hate: Recruitment techniques of hate groups and how to stop them.* Santa Barbara, CA: Praeger.

Bergena, D. V., Feddesb, A. F., Doosjeb, B., & Pelsc, T. V. (2015). Collective identity factors and the attitude toward violence in defense of ethnicity or religion among Muslim youth of Turkish and Moroccan Descent. *International Journal of Intercultural Relations,* 47, 89–100.

Blanco A., Blanco, R., & de la Corte, L. (2022). Motivations for hate group membership. In E. W. Dunbar (Ed.), *Indoctrination to hate: Recruitment techniques of hate groups and how to stop them.* Santa Barbara, CA: Praeger.

Borduin, C. M., Mann, B. J., Cone, L. T., Henggeler, S. W., Fucci, B. R., Blaske, D. M., & Williams, R. A. (1995). Multisystemic treatment of serious juvenile offenders: Long-term prevention of criminality and violence? *Journal of Consulting and Clinical Psychology,* 63, pp. 569–578.

Browning, Christopher R. (1998). *Ordinary men: Reserve Police Battalion 101 and the Final Solution in Poland.* New York, NY: Harper Perennial.

Bubolz, B. F., & Simi, P. (2019). The problem of overgeneralization: The case of mental health problems and U.S. violent white supremacists. *American Behavioral Scientist,* 1–17. https://doi.org/10.1177/0002764219831746

Carter, R. T., & Helms, J. E. (1990). White racial identity attitudes and cultural values: Black and white racial identity. *Theory, Research, and Practice,* 105–118.

Connolly, P. (2002). *Racism, gender identities and young children: Social relations in a multi-ethnic, inner-city primary school.* London, UK: Routledge.

Copp, J. E. (2020). The impact of incarceration on the risk of violent recidivism. *Marquette Law Review,* 103(3), 775–792. https://scholarship.law.marquette.edu/mulr/vol103/iss3/5

Crèvecoeur-MacPhail, D. A. (2016). Innovative approaches to hate crime prosecution: The role of therapeutic jurisprudence and specialty court programs. In E. Dunbar, A. Blanco, & D. A. Crèvecoeur-MacPhail (Eds.), *The psychology of hate crimes and domestic terrorism.* Santa Barbara, CA: Praeger.

Davies-Rubio, A., & Mirón, L. (2022). Joining Colombian illegal armed groups and the role of ideology. In E. W. Dunbar (Ed.), *Indoctrination to hate: Recruitment techniques of hate groups and how to stop them.* Santa Barbara, CA: Praeger.

Densho. (2016, December 6). What Pearl Harbor Meant for Japanese Americans. Densho Blog. https://densho.org/remembering-pearl-harbor/

Dunbar, E. (2003). Symbolic, relational, and ideological signifiers of bias-motivated offenders: Toward a strategy of assessment. *American Journal of Orthopsychiatry,* 73(2), 203–211.

Dunbar, E. (2018). *Hate unleashed: America's cataclysmic change.* Santa Barbara, CA: Praeger.

Dunbar, E. (2022a). The neuroscience of hate and bias ideology: A brain-behavior approach to bias aggression. In E. Dunbar (Ed.), *Indoctrination to hate: Recruitment techniques of hate groups and how to stop them.* Santa Barbara, CA: Praeger.

Dunbar, E. (2022b). Hate, Ideology, and Intergroup Violence: Bias Motivation and Membership in a Multicultural World. In E. W. Dunbar (Ed.), *Indoctrination to hate: Recruitment techniques of hate groups and how to stop them.* Santa Barbara, CA: Praeger.

Dunbar, E., Quinones, J., & Crevecoeur, A. (2005). Assessment of hate crime offenders: The role of bias intent in examining violence risk. *Journal of Forensic Psychology Practice*, 5(1), 1–19.

Dunbar, E., Krop, H., & Sullaway, M. E. (2016). Behavioral, psychometric, and diagnostic characteristics of bias-motivated homicide offenders. In E. Dunbar, A. Blanco, & D. A. Crèvecoeur-MacPhail (Eds.), *The psychology of hate crimes and domestic terrorism*. Santa Barbara, CA: Praeger.

Ezekiel, R. S. (1996). *The racist mind: Portraits of American neo-Nazis and Klansmen*. New York, NY: Penguin.

Fiol, C. M., Harris, D., & House, R. (1999). Charismatic leadership: Strategies for effecting social change. *Leadership Quarterly*, 10(3), 449–482. https://doi.org/10.1016/S1048-9843(99)00021-1

Fishbein, H. (2002). *Peer prejudice and discrimination: The origins of prejudice*. Mahwah, NJ: Lawrence Erlbaum Associates.

Franklin, K. (2000). Antigay behaviors by young adults: Prevalence, patterns and motivators in a noncriminal population. *Journal of Interpersonal Violence*, 15(4), 339–362.

Franklin, K. (2004). Enacting masculinity: Antigay violence and group rape as participatory theater. *Sexuality Research & Social Policy*, 1(2), 25–40.

Friendship, C., Blud, L., Erikson, M., Travers, R., & Thornton, D. (2003). Cognitive-behavioural treatment for imprisoned offenders: An evaluation of HM Prison Service's cognitive skills programmes. *Legal and Criminological Psychology*, 8(1), 103–114.

Gallagher, M. (2022). Lone wolf terrorists: Examining motives and methods of stand-alone terrorists. In E. W. Dunbar (Ed.), *Indoctrination to hate: Recruitment techniques of hate groups and how to stop them*. Santa Barbara, CA: Praeger.

Hamelin, N., Houda, A., Monette, C., & Kalpakian, J. (2010). Trigger factors of terrorism: Social marketing analysis as a tool for security studies—a Moroccan case study. *International Journal of Euro-Mediterranean Studies*, 3(2), 223–250.

Hardin, G. (1968). The tragedy of the commons. *Science*, 162(3859), 1243–1248.

Harris, G. T., Marnie E. Rice, & Cormier, C. A. (1991). Psychopathy and violent recidivism. *Law and Human Behavior*, 15(6), 625–637.

Hausmann, B., & Wanke, P. (2016). Forensic practice and management of violent offenders targeting women: Clinical and conceptual issues. In E. Dunbar, A. Blanco, & D. A. Crèvecoeur-MacPhail (Eds.), *The psychology of hate crimes and domestic terrorism*. Santa Barbara, CA: Praeger.

Helms, J. E. (1995). An update of Helm's white and people of color racial identity models. In J. G. Ponterotto, J. M. Casas, L. A. Suzuki, & C. M. Alexander (Eds.), *Handbook of multicultural counseling* (pp. 181–198). Thousand Oaks, CA: Sage.

Helms, J. E. (Ed.). (1990). *Black and white racial identity: Theory, research, and practice*. Westport, CT: Greenwood Press.

Henggeler, S. (1999). Multisystemic therapy: An overview of clinical procedures, outcomes, and policy implications. *Child Psychology and Psychiatry Review*, 4(1), 2–10. https://doi.org/10.1017/S1360641798001786

Henggeler, S. W., Schoenwald, S. K., Borduin, C. M., Rowland, M. D., & Cunningham, P. B. (2009). *Multisystemic therapy for antisocial behavior in children and adolescents* (2nd ed.). New York, NY: Guilford Press.

Johnson, S. D., & Byers, B. D. (2003). Attitudes toward hate crime laws. *Journal of Criminal Justice*, 31(3), 227–235.

Joosse, Paul. 2014. Becoming a god: Max Weber and the social construction of charisma. *Journal of Classical Sociology*, 14(3), 266–283.

Kiazad, K., Restubog, S-L, D., Zagenczyk, S. T., Kiewitz, C., & Tang, R. L. (2010). In pursuit of power: The role of authoritarian leadership in the relationship between supervisors' Machiavellianism and subordinates' perceptions of abusive supervisory behavior. *Journal of Research in Personality*, 44(4), 512–519.

Kohatsu, E. L., Dulay, M., Lam, C., Concepcion, W., Perez, P., Lopez, C., & Euler, J. (2000). Using racial identity theory to explore racial mistrust and interracial contact among Asian Americans. *Journal of Counseling & Development*, 78(3), 334–342. https://doi.org/10.1002/j.1556-6676.2000.tb01915.x

Levy, B. L., & Levy, D. L. (2017). When love meets hate: The relationship between state policies on gay and lesbian rights and hate crime incidence. *Social Science Research*, 61, 142–159. https://doi.org/10.1016/j.ssresearch.2016.06.008

Luhtanen, R., & Crocker, J. (1992). A collective self-esteem scale: Self-evaluation of one's social identity. *Personality and Social Psychology Bulletin*, 18(3), 302–318.

Mason, H. (1965). The sincerity of Augustus. *Harvard Studies in Classical Philology*, 69, 139–162.

Milgram, S. (1963). Behavioral study of obedience. *Journal of Abnormal and Social Psychology*, 67(4), 371–378.

Monteiro, M. B., Xavier de França, D., & Rodrigues, R. (2008). The development of intergroup bias in childhood: How social norms can shape children's racial behaviours. *International Journal of Psychology*, 44(1), 29–39. https://doi.org/10.1080/00207590802057910

Morella, M. (2012). How America changed after Pearl Harbor. The December of 1941 radically altered America and its global role. *U.S. News & World Report*. https://www.usnews.com/opinion/articles/2012/01/06/how-america-changed-after-pearl-harbor

Norris, L. (2019, August 9). Dr. Carl Bell always asked the hard questions. https://www.mdedge.com/psychiatry/article/205943/dr-carl-bell-always-asked-hard-questions?

Pettigrew, T. F., & Tropp, L. R. (2008). How does intergroup contact reduce prejudice? Meta-analytic tests of three mediators. *European Journal of Social Psychology*, 38(6), 922–934.

Piquero, A. R., & Jennings, W. G. (2017). Research note: Justice system–imposed financial penalties increase the likelihood of recidivism in a sample of adolescent offenders. *Youth Violence and Juvenile Justice*, 15(3), 325–340. https://doi.org/10.1177/1541204016669213

Pope-Davis, D. B., & Ottavi, T. M. (1994). The relationship between racism and racial identity among white Americans: A replication and extension. *Journal of Counseling & Development,* 72, 293–297. https://doi.org/10.1002/j.1556-6676.1994.tb00937.x

Schuh, S. C., Zhang, X., & Tian, P. (2013). For the good or the bad? Interactive effects of transformational leadership with moral and authoritarian leadership behaviors. *Journal of Business Ethics,* 116(3), 629–640. https://doi.org/10.1007/s10551-012-1486-0

Seyranian, V., & Bligh, M. C. (2008). Presidential charismatic leadership: Exploring the rhetoric of social change. *Leadership Quarterly,* 19(1), 54–76.

Shirley, C. (2013). *December 1941: 31 days that changed America and saved the world.* Nashville, TN: Thomas Nelson.

Simi, P., Blee, K., DeMichele, M., & Windisch, S. (2017). Addicted to hate: Identity residual among former white supremacists. *American Sociological Review,* 82(6), 1167–1187. https://doi.org/10.1177/0003122417728719

Soriano, L. M. (2017). *Male perpetrators' perspectives on reasons for domestic violence in heterosexual relationships, and the support services and coping mechanisms.* Master's thesis, California State University, San Bernardino.

Terbeck, S. (2016). The neuroscience of prejudice. In *The social neuroscience of intergroup relations* (pp. 29–49). New York, NY: Springer International Publishing.

Terbeck, S., Kahane, G., McTavish, S., Savulescu, J., Cowen, P. J., & Hewstone, M. (2012). Propranolol reduces implicit negative racial bias. *Psychopharmacology,* 222(3), 419–424.

Thistlethwaite, A. B. (2017). Racial conflict in prison. In K. R. Kerley (Ed.), *The encyclopedia of corrections,* 1–5. https://doi.org/10.1002/9781118845387.wbeoc008

Thompson, C. E., & Carter, R. T. (2013). *Racial identity theory: Applications to individual, group, and organizational interventions.* London, UK: Routledge.

Van Ausdale, D., & Feagin, J. R. (2001). *The first R: How children learn race and racism.* Lanham, MD: Rowman and Littlefield.

Wilde, R. (2020). How the Treaty of Versailles contributed to Hitler's rise. ThoughtCo. https://www.thoughtco.com/treaty-of-versailles-hitlers-rise-power-1221351

Yochelson, S., & Samnow, S. (1986). *The criminal personality.* Lanham, MD: Jason Aronson.

About the Editor and Contributors

Editor

Edward W. Dunbar, PhD, is a practicing psychologist in metropolitan Los Angeles. He has served as coordinator of the Los Angeles Regional White House Program on Hate Crimes; development coordinator for the L.A. County District Attorney's Office Hate Victim Mental Health Panel; and coordinator of the Conference on Hate Crimes Research, Policy, and Action for the California Psychological Association. Dunbar is the author of *Hate Unleashed: America's Cataclysmic Change* and coeditor of *The Psychology of Hate Crimes as Domestic Terrorism: U.S. and Global Issues*.

Contributors

Milton J. Bennett founded and directs the Intercultural Development Research Institute located in Hillsboro, Oregon, USA, and Milano, Italy (http://www.idrinstitute.org). Dr. Bennett is also an adjunct professor of intercultural communication at the University of Milano Bicocca and a consultant on the topic to corporations, universities, and exchange organizations in Europe, Asia, and the United States. Dr. Bennett studied physics and cognitive psychology as part of his BA degree from Stanford University, has an MA in psycholinguistics from San Francisco State University, and holds one of the first PhD's in intercultural communication (University of Minnesota). A completely revised version of his textbook *Basic Concepts of Intercultural Communication* was published with the subtitle *Paradigms, Principles, and Practices* (2013; in Italian, 2015). The same book was first published in Chinese with the title *Constructing Intercultural Communication* (2012).

Amalio Blanco, PhD, is a social and group psychologist professor at the University Autónoma of Madrid. He is also a guest professor at several Latin American universities in the fields of social psychology and community intervention. His current research focus is on intergroup bias as a source of collective violence, on the psychosocial consequences (psychosocial trauma), and on intervention programs to deal with the interpersonal, intergroup, and community after-effects of collective violence, mostly in Colombia and El Salvador. He is the coeditor of *The Psychology of Hate Crimes as Domestic Terrorism*.

Rubén Blanco is a nurse who currently works in the Hospital Universitario Ramón y Cajal in Madrid. He has a master's degree in healthcare research, is an expert in sports nursing, and is finishing his PhD. His current line of research focuses on violence against health-care workers, especially horizontal violence.

Elena D'Angelo is currently research associate at UNU-ViE SCYCLE. Since she joined the SCYCLE team in 2016, she has been mainly involved in the coordination and research activities of EU-funded projects dealing with transnational waste crimes, as well as in research activities dealing with mercury waste and circular economy. She works as research coordinator and senior researcher at the Research Center on Security and Crime (RiSSC) and she is a consultant for UNICRI, where she worked for the past eight years. Her work is mainly focused on applied research and training for law enforcement and legal professionals. Ms. D'Angelo is the author and co-author of several publications on the following topics: transnational organized crime, environmental crimes, ICT and e-wastes, counterfeiting, and anti-discrimination, including hate speech. Before joining UNICRI, Ms. D'Angelo worked with multiple international organizations and NGOs, both at the institutional level and in the field, dealing with development and gender-related issues.

Elena Dal Santo graduated in international relations and diplomatic sciences at the University of Trieste with a thesis on "The Practice of extraordinary Renditions with Reference to National, European, and International Law: The Case of Abu Omar" and holds a joint European master degree in human rights and genocide studies with a final dissertation focused on the impact of terrorism on European migration policies. Since 2015, she has been a PhD candidate in political science at the University of Genoa, and her research project focuses on the analysis of the radicalization process in Italy. Since 2012, Elena has also undertaken several collaborations with local NGOs and international organizations, including ICCT—The Hague and UNICRI—Turin, working on security-related projects.

Amanda Davies-Rubio, PhD, holds a doctorate in social psychology and a master's degree in methodology from the Autonomous University of Madrid (Spain). Her research focuses on the roots of collective violence through the study of perpetrators.

Luis de la Corte holds a PD in psychology. He is director of strategic studies and intelligence in the Institute of Forensic and Security Sciences and full professor in the Department of Social Psychology and Methodology of the Autonomous University of Madrid (Spain). His main research topics are terrorism, political violence, organized crime, security and strategic studies, and intelligence. He is author of numerous scientific papers and chapters and several books on those topics.

Martin J. Gallagher, PhD, superintendent, Police Scotland, is currently deployed to the force's Criminal Justice Division. He has recently completed a successful three-year ICT project and was previously the area commander for Paisley. He is a former reserve army officer, having served with the Argyll and Sutherland Highlanders. He holds a BA (Hons) in philosophy (Stirling), master's degrees in criminal justice studies (Portsmouth) and terrorism studies (St. Andrews), and a PhD in criminology (Lancaster). Martin's policing background is mainly in intelligence and the investigation of serious crime. He has also worked directly with executive staff in a number of roles including national crisis events, the London Olympics, and the closure of the Association of Chief Police Officers in Scotland. He was extensively involved in establishing local authority CONTEST (Counter Terrorism) structures, supporting this through founding and chairing the "Grey Space" Community Tension monitoring group. The membership was broad, including the Catholic Church; the Church of Scotland; local mosques; the Buddhist community; the Guru Ravidas Community; West of Scotland Racial Equality Council; Renfrewshire Effort to Empower Minorities; LGBT+; the Polish community; West College Scotland; University of West of Scotland (including corporate/student body and academic research staff); the "I Am Me" disability awareness charity; NHS; and the local authorities. Martin has been awarded three commendations for bravery during his police service.

Martin writes on terrorism, organized crime, police leadership, and police technology. His work has been covered by the BBC, the Sunday Times, and Jane's Intelligence Review. He has lectured on policing for over 15 years, and is an established conference panel member.

Dr. Silvina Ituarte is a professor of criminal justice at California State University East Bay after having completed her academic training in social ecology at the University of California at Irvine and in criminal justice at Rutgers University. She has presented both nationally and internationally, and her teaching and research interests primarily focus on issues related to youth empowerment, bias crimes (hate crime), community-based programs, and restorative justice.

Lourdes Mirón, PhD, is associate professor of social psychology, and director of the master's program in psychology at the University of Santiago de Compostela (Spain). She is also a member of the research group Social Problems: Analysis, Evaluation and Intervention; her research interests focus on group delinquency and aggression, and aggression and gender.

Megan Sullaway, PhD, is a partner with Pacific Psychological Associates and a clinical professor in the Department of Psychology at the University of California, Los Angeles. She has published on a variety of topics, including extreme prejudice as a clinical issue and domestic terrorism. She currently is interested in the psychology of cyber harassment and revenge porn. Dr. Sullaway is in practice in the Los Angeles area.

Index

Note: Figure pages are in *italics*, and tables are **bold**.

www.ingramcontent.com/pod-product-compliance
Ingram Content Group UK Ltd.
Pitfield, Milton Keynes, MK11 3LW, UK
UKHW020845290926
15470UKWH00004B/1569

9 781440 857003